ADDITIONAL PRAISE FOR
THE BOGLEHEADS' GUIDE TO RETIREMENT PLANNING

"If you're interested in funding your own retirement rather than some Wall Streeter's retirement, this is the book for you. Read it cover to cover and you'll end up knowing more than 90 percent of financial professionals. Hats off to the Bogleheads for the great service they have done for consumers with this book."

Allan S. Roth, CFP®, CPA, MBA,
Author of *How a Second Grader Beats Wall Street*

"To find true financial joy, you need to integrate sound financial principles into your life. Retirement is an opportunity to live the life you always dreamed of—but only for the prepared. That's where the Bogleheads shine. You can always count on them for straight talk, thoughtful commonsense commentaries, and a willingness to help others. We can all learn from their grassroots, solid approach to retirement planning that is consistently supplemented with the powerful, rich conversations that take place every day at www.bogleheads.org."

Sue Stevens, President,
Stevens Wealth Management LLC and
Financial Happiness LLC

The Bogleheads'
Guide to
Retirement Planning

The Bogleheads'

Guide to
Retirement Planning

Taylor Larimore
Mel Lindauer
Richard A. Ferri
Laura F. Dogu

Foreword by John C. Bogle

WILEY

John Wiley & Sons, Inc.

Published by John Wiley & Sons, Inc., Hoboken, New Jersey.
Published simultaneously in Canada.

For general information on our other products and services or for technical support, please contact our Customer Care Department within the United States at (800) 762-2974, outside the United States at (317) 572-3993 or fax (317) 572-4002.

Wiley also publishes its books in a variety of electronic formats. Some content that appears in print may not be available in electronic books. For more information about Wiley products, visit our web site at www.wiley.com.

Library of Congress Cataloging-in-Publishing Data

The Boglehead's guide to retirement planning/Taylor Larimore . . . [et al.]; foreword by John C. Bogle.
   p. cm
Includes index.
ISBN 978-0-470-45557-9 (cloth); ISBN 978-0-470-91901-9 (paper)
   1. Retirement income—Planning. 2. Finance, Personal. I. Larimore, Taylor, 1924-
HG179.B5688 2009
332.024'014—dc22
                                                   2009021676

Printed in the United States of America

10 9 8 7 6 5 4 3 2 1

This book is dedicated to John C. Bogle.
For his wisdom, kindness, and unselfish devotion to helping individuals achieve their dreams.

All royalties from the sale of this book are being donated to:
The National Constitution Center
Philadelphia, PA

Contents

FOREWORD BY JOHN C. BOGLE   XIII
PREFACE   xix
ACKNOWLEDGMENTS   xxix

PART I
THE BASICS

CHAPTER 1
THE RETIREMENT PLANNING PROCESS BY
THOMAS L. ROMENS   3

CHAPTER 2
UNDERSTANDING TAXES BY NORMAN S. JANOFF   21

PART II
SAVINGS ACCOUNTS AND RETIREMENT PLANS

CHAPTER 3
INDIVIDUAL TAXABLE SAVINGS ACCOUNTS BY DAN KOHN   35

CHAPTER 4
INDIVIDUAL RETIREMENT ARRANGEMENTS BY JIM DAHLE   47

CHAPTER 5
DEFINED BENEFIT EMPLOYER RETIREMENT ACCOUNT
BY THE FINANCE BUFF   61

CHAPTER 6
   DEFINED CONTRIBUTION PLANS BY DAN KOHN   77

CHAPTER 7
   SINGLE-PREMIUM IMMEDIATE ANNUITIES
      BY DAN SMITH   91

                        PART III
           MANAGING YOUR RETIREMENT ACCOUNTS

CHAPTER 8
   BASIC INVESTING PRINCIPLES BY BOB DAVIS   119

CHAPTER 9
   INVESTING FOR RETIREMENT BY
      DAVID GRABINER AND ALEX FRAKT   135

CHAPTER 10
   FUNDING YOUR RETIREMENT ACCOUNTS BY
      DAVID GRABINER AND IAN FORSYTHE   151

                        PART IV
                THE RETIREMENT PAYOFF

CHAPTER 11
   UNDERSTANDING SOCIAL SECURITY BY
      DICK SCHREITMUELLER   169

CHAPTER 12
   WITHDRAWAL STRATEGIES BY CAROL TOMKOVICH   187

CHAPTER 13
   EARLY RETIREMENT BY JEFF McCOMAS   201

PART V
PROTECTING YOUR ASSETS

CHAPTER 14
INCOME REPLACEMENT BY LEE E. MARSHALL   221

CHAPTER 15
HEALTH INSURANCE BY LEE E. MARSHALL   239

CHAPTER 16
ESSENTIALS OF ESTATE PLANNING BY
ROBERT A. STERMER   255

CHAPTER 17
ESTATE AND GIFT TAXES BY
ROBERT A. STERMER   273

PART VI
FINDING GOOD ADVICE WHEN YOU NEED IT

CHAPTER 18
SEEKING HELP FROM PROFESSIONALS BY
DALE C. MALEY AND LAUREN VIGNEC   285

CHAPTER 19
DIVORCE AND OTHER FINANCIAL DISASTERS BY
DAVID RANKINE   303

CHAPTER 20
MEET THE BOGLEHEADS BY
TAYLOR LARIMORE AND MEL LINDAUER   315

APPENDIX I: PEARLS OF WISDOM   327

APPENDIX II: RECOMMENDED READING   333
GLOSSARY   337
ABOUT THE EDITORS   351
INDEX   355

Foreword

It's hard to imagine a more fortuitous time to write a guide to retirement planning. The global financial crisis and the recession and bear market it has brought in its wake have exposed the tenuous condition of the retirement savings of millions of Americans, who would undoubtedly benefit from the sort of advice the Bogleheads dispense in this book.

On the other hand, it's also hard to imagine a time when investors might be more reluctant to read *anything* that has to do with investing. Their nest eggs often depleted and sometimes shattered, and dreams of retirement delayed if not deferred—largely due to the recklessness of a select group of Wall Street experts who seemed unable to measure the risks on the balance sheets of the firms they ran—one could hardly blame an investor who says "the heck with it all," writing off the financial markets as a rigged game, one in which their capital is used, first and foremost, to enrich the insiders.

But the fact that such a reaction is understandable doesn't make it correct. For better or worse, most Americans today who want to enhance the modest retirement income distributed through our Social Security system have been given the responsibility of funding and managing their own retirement accounts, charged with investing their way to a secure financial future. The current economic crisis will not absolve us of that responsibility, even as it makes it more difficult. Invest we must.

But that by no means implies that investors should continue blithely along the path they'd been on. As the current bear market has made plain, too many Americans were ill-prepared to shoulder the responsibility that had been placed upon them. Even worse, our mutual fund industry was equally incapable of providing the assistance our nation of amateur investors needed. The conflicts of interest mutual fund managers face—seeking to maximize their own earnings, which reduce, dollar for dollar, the returns earned by their mutual fund investors—proved too great a temptation for them to resolve in favor of their fund investors.

So what is an investor to do? First and foremost, seek wisdom. "Wisdom excelleth folly as far as light excelleth darkness." I used those words from Ecclesiastes some 15 years ago, in the epilogue of my first book, *Bogle on Mutual Funds,* as a way of introducing my Twelve Pillars of Wisdom, which I described as "lamps to guide you on your search for a sensible, productive investment program."

Reviewing them recently, I was struck by how well they have stood the test of time. I'll let you judge for yourself:

1. *Investing is not nearly as difficult as it looks.* Successful investing involves doing just a few things right and avoiding serious mistakes.
2. *When all else fails, fall back on simplicity.* There may be a handful of alternatives that prove to be better than simply buying and holding a portfolio balanced equally between a total stock market index fund and a total bond market index fund over the long term, but the number of alternatives that will prove to be worse is infinite.
3. *Time marches on.* The majesty of compounding returns is remarkable. Over 25 years, an 8 percent annual return grows a $10,000 investment by $58,500. But the tyranny of compounding costs is remarkably destructive. Annual costs of 2.5 percent would reduce that return to 5.5 percent and slice your portfolio's long-term growth by more than half, to $28,100.*
4. *Nothing ventured, nothing gained.* Yes, the stock market is volatile. Yes, its future returns are unknown. But eschewing the stock market incurs its own risks. Our recognition of that and our faith in the resiliency of American capitalism compel the majority of American investors to allocate at least some portion of their nest egg to stocks in an effort to reach their long-term goals.
5. *Diversify, diversify, diversify.* While it's impossible to eliminate all of the risk associated with investing, risk can be greatly reduced by diversifying broadly within each asset class (ideally, using a low-cost total market index fund) and then constructing a well-balanced portfolio that owns an appropriate mix of stocks and bonds.
6. *The eternal triangle.* Risk, return, and cost are the three sides of the eternal triangle of investing, inextricably linked to the long-term growth of your portfolio.

---

*Over an investment lifetime of, say, 50 years, the final values are, respectively, $459,000 and $135,400, a reduction of fully 70 percent.

7. *The powerful magnetism of the mean.* Investment superstars come and go, the vast majority proving to be comets who briefly illuminate the firmament with spectacular performance, only to see their returns deteriorate, returning to, and then lagging, the average returns of their peers and the market.

8. *Don't overestimate your ability to pick superior equity mutual funds, nor underestimate your ability to pick superior bond and money market funds.* In equity funds, past returns tell us nothing about what the future holds. Performance comes and goes, and yesterday's leaders are likely to be tomorrow's laggards. The top-performing bond and money market funds, on the other hand, are typically populated by the lowest-cost alternatives. In these areas, investors can choose the low-cost leaders with a reasonable amount of confidence in their favorable prospects for continued success.

9. *You may have a stable principal value or a stable income stream, but you may not have both.* Intelligent investing involves choices, compromises, and trade-offs, perfectly illustrated by the choice between a 90-day Treasury bill's fixed value and volatile income stream, on one hand, and a long-term Treasury bond fund's volatile market value and relatively stable income stream on the other.

10. *Beware of fighting the last war.* Too many investors—individuals and institutions alike—become infatuated with the recent past and find themselves eternally (and futilely) reacting to what has happened in the financial markets instead of building a portfolio that can withstand whatever the future holds, recognizing that particular cycles and trends never last forever.

11. *You rarely, if ever, know something the market does not.* The financial markets reflect the hopes, the fears, even the greed of all investors everywhere. It is nearly always unwise to act on insights you think are your own but are in fact shared by millions of others.

12. *Think long term.* The daily volatility of the market is often "a tale told by an idiot, full of sound and fury, signifying nothing." The wise investor tunes out this noise and patiently focuses on the long term while staying the course.

Of course, these 12 pillars are more than just an epilogue to a 15-year-old book. They represent the foundation on which I built The Vanguard Group. From its inception in 1974, I strove to make Vanguard a firm that emphasized the simple over the complex, the enduring over the ephemeral, and the low-cost over the costly, represented most clearly by the broad market index fund, which guarantees its investors nothing more (and nothing less) than their fair share of whatever returns our financial markets provide.

And as pleased as I am that, 35 years later, history has shown the merit in such an approach to investing, I'm even more pleased with how broadly it's been embraced by millions of investors, none more so than the group that calls themselves the Bogleheads.

I met my first Boglehead on February 3, 1999. I had flown to Miami to deliver a speech, and Taylor Larimore, the group's unofficial leader, invited me to join a group of his compatriots for dinner at his home that evening. Taylor and his friends proved to be as wonderful a group of people as I had ever met—intelligent, thoughtful, trustworthy, and eager to help others—in short, good human beings. We all had so much fun that our gathering quickly became an annual event. We've held our reunions in cities all over the country, and each one has been larger than its predecessor. Bogleheads 8 is scheduled for Dallas, Texas, in September 2009.

This group of like-minded investors represents the promise of our electronic age, which combines a seemingly endless amount of information with an unprecedented ease of communication. Harnessing both, the Bogleheads band together to help and encourage all comers to sort through the noise in the pursuit of their financial goals. Collectively, the group provides a vast gold mine of wisdom and experience waiting to be explored.

The Bogleheads' Guide to Retirement Planning is a true gem from that gold mine, a book whose advice is firmly built upon those Twelve Pillars of Wisdom. Truly a group effort (no fewer than 40 Bogleheads contributed to it in some capacity), this book provides the reader with a first-rate primer on saving and investing for retirement, covering everything from opening and funding a retirement account, to investing it wisely, to drawing down your account, to estate planning—not quite cradle-to-grave coverage, but pretty close.

Importantly, these investors/writers/believers do so in a way that even the most novice investor will be able to follow. I'm admittedly not the most impartial judge of their work—heck, I'm probably the *least* impartial person you could find for that task—but I'm certain that our nation of investors would be far better served if more of them acted on the advice the Bogleheads dispense in this book.

I'm often asked what it's like to have a group of people name themselves after you. It is, I readily admit, more than a little surreal, at least in the abstract. But getting to know the Bogleheads over the past 10 years or so—both in person and by following their online community—has been one of the more rewarding experiences of my long career, not because of the undeniable boost they provide my ego (though that never hurts!) but because the Bogleheads represent the fulfillment of what I have dedicated my career to building.

When I founded Vanguard all those years ago, I did so in the face of enormous skepticism. It was a brand-new organization—one operating with a then-as-now unique structure—whose success depended not on a vast marketing budget or an army of sales representatives but on faith—a faith that individual investors, one by one, would come to recognize that this then-tiny firm, doing things differently, would serve their own economic interests, and a faith that that would be sufficient to ensure our enterprise's success.

When I chat with the Bogleheads, they almost invariably thank me for starting Vanguard. But in reality, it is I who should be thanking them. It is investors like these fine human souls who validated my leap of faith and who allowed the Vanguard experiment to flourish. And that success, such as it were, has provided me with far more acclaim than any one person deserves. It is hardly an overstatement to say that whatever success I may have enjoyed in my long career is due entirely to the fact that my faith in investors like the Bogleheads has been so well placed.

And so it is with immense pleasure that I commend *The Bogleheads' Guide to Retirement Planning* to you. After reading this book, I'm confident that you'll agree with me that the Bogleheads, this diverse collection of caring individual investors, are a remarkable group. Even better, when you learn from their collective wisdom, you'll join the ranks of investors who are well on their way to realizing their investment goals.

JOHN C. BOGLE

Valley Forge, PA

Preface

We live in a country facing many challenges. No one can deny the importance of a strong national defense and an aggressive response to the terrorist threats that we face. No one can turn away from the importance of assuring a sound physical infrastructure when we see pictures in our newspapers of major interstate highway bridges collapsing under the load of rush hour traffic. We all agree that our secondary schools and colleges seed the future of America and they must offer a top-notch education. And we all know that without health, we cannot have wealth. Affordable health care is paramount to the long-term well-being of our citizens and an important driver of worker productivity in a competitive global marketplace.

There are many worthwhile claims on our time and money, but there is one that has major long-term economic implications if not addressed wisely and with resolve. A growing portion of America's population will reach retirement age over the next 25 years. If we do not seriously address how those retirement income streams will be funded, we run the risk of allowing the greatest single threat to American prosperity to overtake us because of procrastination. The American people, including the younger members of our society, need clear and comprehensive guidance to deal with the challenges we all face on the issue of preparing to meet a burgeoning retirement challenge in the years ahead.

The *Bogleheads' Guide to Retirement Planning* is a grassroots call to action. It encourages a broad, individual response to prepare for retirement.

The individual chapter authors are not professional writers. They are people just like you: skilled laborers, white-collar workers, teachers, entrepreneurs, small-business owners, and the like. The authors have no incentive in this not-for-profit endeavor except to make a difference—to help people who want to be helped by providing valuable information on a range of retirement planning topics. What has been written in these chapters has been learned through self-education, primarily by reading books, articles, and research and by participating on the Bogleheads.org forum. Most important, it is information gathered by the life experiences of many people. These authors are a part of a remarkable group of people who call themselves *Bogleheads.*

THE BOGLEHEADS

Boglehead is the name adopted by individuals who follow the business and investing beliefs of an extraordinary man, John C. Bogle, founder and former CEO of the Vanguard Group of mutual funds. Jack, as he likes to be called, is credited with being the father of index mutual funds.

In 1975, under Jack's leadership, the newly formed Vanguard Group launched the very first publicly available index fund, the Vanguard First Investors Trust. The fund tracked the popular S&P 500 Index of mostly large U.S. common stocks. The fund was later renamed the Vanguard 500 Index Fund and eventually grew to become the largest mutual fund in history. The very low mutual fund expenses and sensible investment strategies of the Vanguard Group have allowed millions of individual investors to save billions of dollars in costs over the years, and that money saved is money earned.

But Vanguard is not the whole story behind Jack Bogle. He is also a model of business integrity. He stands like a pillar of ethics in a world seemingly gone mad with Ponzi schemes and multimillion-dollar golden parachutes paid to failed CEOs. Jack is a reformer. He relentlessly offers a host of practical business advice through his writings and speeches in an attempt to restore integrity in corporate America and to protect small investors' interests. For his efforts, John C. Bogle has been granted many honors, including inclusion in *Time* magazine's "world's 100 most powerful and influential people" and *Fortune* magazine's "four Giants of the 20th Century" in the investment community.

Jack Bogle has tens of thousands of followers, and many of them communicate with each other regularly. The main communication network for the Bogleheads is over the Internet on a dedicated web site, www .Bogleheads.org. Members of this free online community discuss topics ranging from mutual funds to complex investment strategies to who is the most famous guitarist of all time. On any given day, the forum hosts thousands of participants and visitors. Any person visiting Bogleheads.org may read the conversations, but you must register to participate in the discussions. That involves selecting a screen name and agreeing to follow certain ethical guidelines. Registration is free.

Bogleheads.org evolved from the Morningstar Vanguard Diehards forum established in March 1998. Taylor Larimore posted the first of his more than 24,000 forum contributions on the Morningstar site in

Conversation #1. Mel Lindauer was another pioneer whose investment and business experience soon made him a forum leader. As the Morningstar forum expanded over the years, it became necessary to create a stand-alone web site that had added functionality and oversight. Thus, Bogleheads.org was born. The web site is now the largest not-for-profit investment site on the Internet.

A relatively new and exciting part of the Boglehead.org online community is the Bogleheads Wiki. It was a pioneering project by Barry Barnitz and a small group of forum members. The Wiki is an online encyclopedia of sorts that is a collection of content and Web page links designed to educate investors. The group quickly realized the valuable contribution they could make to both the forum and the greater investing community at large by creating the Bogleheads Wiki site.

Off-line, the Bogleheads have expanded to include regular local chapter gatherings and a national reunion. There are now 38 local chapters throughout the United States and Europe. Local chapter members meet periodically to discuss investing topics of interest with other members from their area. Each year, a local chapter volunteers to host the Bogleheads reunion, which Jack Bogle traditionally attends. The 2009 conference visits the Lone Star state with a meeting in Dallas/Fort Worth. Information on all these activities can be found on the web site.

Our family of Bogleheads is vast and growing, but you do not need to register to consider yourself a follower. Being a Boglehead is a state a mind, not a web site. Anyone who believes in Jack Bogle's philosophy on good business ethics and low-cost investing principles is already a member. Chapter 20 is dedicated to the hard work and countless hours all Bogleheads have volunteered to promote this message.

THE COMING RETIREMENT BOOM OR BUST

This book addresses the enormous issue of retirement in America. Each year for the next 25 years, more people will reach retirement age but will find fewer resources for them to draw from. The senior population has grown by 50 percent since 1980, from 25 million to nearly 40 million in 2009. Retirees are living longer and are healthier. In 1985, more than a quarter of the 85-plus population lived in nursing homes. By 2008, that proportion had fallen to only 13 percent of people this age because of advances in health care and better fitness.

With so many people entering retirement over the next couple of decades and retirees living longer, where are the resources going to come from? In 1980, many people retired with a defined benefit pension paid by their employers. Today, traditional pensions paid by employers are disappearing, and personal savings and employee-funded retirement plans must make up the difference. But are we saving enough? How much is enough? This book teaches people how to come up with those answers.

Changes Coming in the Social Network

Some people still believe that Social Security and Medicare will provide adequate income and health benefits after age 65. Unless you are already well into your retirement years, it is probably a good idea to make other plans. Our social services networks are woefully underfunded and cannot deliver the level of economic welfare that many people expect.

Some prognosticators suggest that all we have to do is rearrange our economic activities to spur greater economic growth to address the shortfall in Social Security and Medicare. The reality is that economic growth becomes stifled with growing government entitlements and a smaller workforce to draw from. Unless we change the work behavior patterns of the adult population, our demographic structure will mean that labor force growth rates will drop to near zero in the 2010s. Even if we can achieve higher levels of productivity, much of this expected productivity improvement is already committed to support the higher need for services related to our aging population. Increasing costs of health services worsen the situation.

These facts cannot be dismissed, nor can a future retiree ignore the inevitable changes in benefits that are coming. It is likely that eligibility ages under Social Security and Medicare will have to be raised again. Raising the retirement age will give workers a longer time to contribute to their retirement plans and reduce the rate at which they have to contribute. In turn, it will simultaneously reduce the number of years a person is in retirement and the amount of resources needed to sustain a lifestyle that is acceptable after the work career has ended. Simply put, most people should plan to work longer.

The Saving Status of Americans

Just two or three decades ago, saving for retirement in the United States was based heavily on employer-provided defined benefit plans. Benefits after retirement were typically received through monthly or biweekly payments from lifetime income annuities. Now personal tax-advantaged accounts such as the 401(k), 403(b), IRA, and Roth IRA plans have become the primary form of saving for retirement. These private retirement accounts hold assets that are currently about four times the size of defined benefit programs.

Self-funded retirement accounts place the responsibility for preparing for retirement squarely on the shoulders of the individual. Workers must have the discipline to save significant sums consistently for many years. And workers in many defined contribution plans must also wrestle with investing their funds. That is not an easy task, and some workers don't want to do it. Consequently, many participants put their money in low-yielding money market accounts that have no probability of growing faster than inflation over time. In addition, at the time of retirement, the participant has sole control of the rollover assets and must determine what to invest in and when and how to withdraw assets from those accounts. These are not easy decisions for most people. Fortunately, all of these issues are discussed by the authors of this book.

We could not write a retirement planning book without addressing risk. There is investment risk any time an investor attempts to achieve returns higher than Treasury bills. During 2008, major U.S. equity indexes were sharply negative, with the S&P 500 Index losing 37 percent for the year. As the market moved lower, it translated into corresponding losses in 401(k) plans. The nonpartisan Employee Benefit Research Institute (EBRI) published an analysis of the impact of the recent financial crisis on 401(k) retirement account balances in 2008. The EBRI analysis, published in the February 2009 *EBRI Issue Brief,* used a database of more than 21 million participants to estimate the impact of market activity on 401(k) account balances.

Not surprisingly, how the recent financial market losses affect individual 401(k) account balances is strongly affected by the size of a participant's account balance. Those with low account balances relative to contributions experienced minimal investment losses that were typically more than made up by new contributions. Those with less than $10,000 in account balances had an average growth of 40 percent during 2008, because contributions had a bigger impact than investment losses. However, those who had balances of $200,000 or more had an average loss of more than 25 percent because contributions made up a significantly lower portion of the account balance.

The loss in retirement savings has a profound impact on future retirement trends. It is likely to take several years before the balances of some workers reach their prerecession highs, and that includes new contributions made during the next few years. But that does not mean people should abandon their efforts; far from it. Some belt tightening may be needed, but the plan must continue. As our mentor, Jack Bogle is fond of saying, *stay the course!*

ABOUT THIS BOOK

There is a bull market in uncertainty in America and around the globe. So wide and deep are the issues that it is difficult to grasp all that has changed and will change in the months and years ahead. But one thing has not changed: your need to prepare. You must continue to strive for a viable retirement plan by evaluating the best ways to save, the best accounts to save in, the right amount to save, a reasonable estimate of the role government entitlements will play, how you will insure against setbacks, and how you handle a financial crisis.

This book was written for all people who are planning to retire at some time in life. We certainly encourage young people to read this book. However, we understand that most young people who enter the workforce for the first time may *save* for retirement but tend not to *plan* for retirement. Planning for retirement tends to begin around midlife, when the bones get a little creaky and the cage upstairs starts to shed a few neurons. When retirement thoughts start popping up at any age, don't ignore them. Move those thoughts to the forefront of your thinking because you're ready to start planning. So what should you do? How do you start? How much do you need? And who should you trust for answers?

The *Bogleheads' Guide to Retirement Planning* is a great place to start building a long-term viable plan. The book covers most of the basics. However, it does not provide definitive answers to all questions. More research on your part is needed. Appendix II has a great book list compiled by Boglehead Taylor Larimore. Although Bogleheads tend to be do-it-yourself people, some issues do require the help of a professional. Trying to cut corners by doing complicated tasks yourself is not always the best course of action.

CHAPTER REVIEWS
Part I: The Basics

Chapter 1, "The Retirement Planning Process," by Thomas L. Romens provides a great overview of things to come in the rest of the book. Tom takes you through the highlights and distinguishes the difference between saving for retirement and actually planning for it.

Chapter 2, "Understanding Taxes" by Norman S. Janoff is an important introduction to all types of taxes that can affect your retirement plan. Minimizing the impact of taxes while in retirement is critical because it maximizes your discretionary income from pensions, Social Security, and your portfolio.

Part II: Savings Accounts and Retirement Plans

Chapter 3, "Individual Taxable Savings Accounts," by Dan Kohn explains why a taxable savings account is the most straightforward way of holding investments, though seldom the best way because you will be taxed on the income and capital gains each year.

Chapter 4, "Individual Retirement Arrangements," by Jim Dahle shows why an individual retirement arrangement (IRA) is one of the best ways an investor can save for retirement. The advantage is that the assets in an IRA grow without being taxed each year, leaving more money to compound for your future benefit.

Chapter 5, "Defined Benefit Employer Retirement Account," by The Finance Buff (an alias, of course). The focus of this chapter is on defined benefit plans. Funded by employers, an employee's income benefit at retirement depends on salary and years with the employer.

Chapter 6, "Defined Contribution Plans," by Dan Kohn covers an assortment of retirement plans, including the popular 401(k) and 403(b) plans, as well as profit-sharing arrangements and ESOPs. Dan explains the benefits and disadvantages of each plan.

Chapter 7, "Single-Premium Immediate Annuities," by Dan Smith tackles the subject of guaranteed income streams in retirement. This interesting chapter covers all types of immediate payout annuities and includes a guide for getting the best deal.

Part III: Managing Your Retirement Accounts

Chapter 8, "Basic Investing Principles," by Bob Davis covers exactly what the title says. The chapter includes good Boglehead principles, such as diversifying your investments to reduce the risk of a large loss, maximizing your return by minimizing expenses, and sticking with your plan.

Chapter 9, "Investing for Retirement," by David Grabiner and Alex Frakt discusses the details of a good investment strategy while saving for retirement. This chapter focuses on creating the road map to a solid investment plan.

Chapter 10, "Funding Your Retirement Accounts," by David Grabiner and Ian Forsythe provides an order to funding your retirement. It is devoted to helping you make an informed decision from among the various types of accounts available to you.

Part IV: The Retirement Payoff

Chapter 11, "Understanding Social Security," by Dick Schreitmueller is a critical chapter for everyone to read. Social Security is a primary source of income for many retirees, yet few people know as much as they should about this vast program.

Chapter 12, "Withdrawal Strategies," by Carol Tomkovich explains that the end result of your retirement plan is to provide stable income that is high enough to maintain the lifestyle you wish to live. But how do you efficiently take money out of your various accounts? This chapter helps answer these important questions.

Chapter 13, "Early Retirement," by Jeff McComas may sound impossible in today's economic environment, but it is not. This chapter describes strategies to bridge the income gap between your last day of full employment and your first Social Security check.

Part V: Protecting Your Assets

Chapter 14, "Income Replacement," by Lee E. Marshall is a critical chapter. The focus of this chapter is on life and disability insurance programs. With life's uncertainties, protecting your future earnings from premature death or disability is a necessity.

Chapter 15, "Health Insurance," by Lee E. Marshall is another issue that cannot be ignored in a good retirement plan. Planning for medical care provides a solid foundation for retirement.

Chapter 16, "Essentials of Estate Planning," by Robert A. Stermer provides an overview of how you can control decisions made on your behalf when you are not able to do so. It includes life preservation directives during a critical medical problem and how your worldly possessions will be distributed after you are gone.

Chapter 17, "Estate and Gift Taxes," by Robert A. Stermer provides insight into the complex and often changing world of distributing wealth without taxation. Planning today for sharing your wealth can save your heirs thousands of dollars in the future.

Part VI: Finding Good Advice When You Need It

Chapter 18, "Seeking Help from Professionals," by Dale C. Maley and Lauren Vignec offers guidance on whom to trust in the finance industry. This chapter will help you understand different types of financial advisers, how they work, how they are paid, and how to choose one for the need you have.

Chapter 19, "Divorce and Other Financial Disasters," by David Rankine is required reading. The world is not perfect; people lose jobs, good health turns bad, and more than half of marriages end in divorce. David's enlightening chapter will assist you to find the help you need to protect your retirement plan when life's ugly side turns your way.

Chapter 20, "Meet the Bogleheads," by Taylor Larimore and Mel Lindauer is a special chapter about how this group helps thousands of individuals. You'll learn a bit of the history of how the Bogleheads came to be, what happens on the Bogleheads.org forum, and how the Bogleheads organization has flourished.

Appendix I, "Pearls of Wisdom," is a collection of thoughts and sayings that are near and dear to the hearts (and wallets) of people who participate on the Bogleheads.org forum. Some of the pearls are originals, and others are oldies but goodies.

Appendix II, "Recommended Reading," is a selection from Taylor Larimore's popular "Investment Gems" on the web site. Taylor has read hundreds of investment and financial planning books. These are some of his favorites.

Acknowledgments

There were many people who generously contributed their time and effort to this ambitious project. First, we thank John C. Bogle for his vision and guidance and for agreeing to write the foreword. Second, we thank Bill Falloon of John Wiley & Sons for enthusiastically supporting this book. This would not have materialized without Bill's strong backing. Finally, we wish to thank all the Bogleheads who participated in this bold experiment. They are listed alphabatically within categories:

Boglehead Book Committee

Laura F. Dogu

Richard A. Ferri

Taylor Larimore

Mel Lindauer

Chapter Authors

Jim Dahle

Bob Davis

The Finance Buff

Ian Forsythe

Alex Frakt

David Grabiner

Norman S. Janoff

Dan Kohn

Dale C. Maley

Lee E. Marshall

Thomas L. Romens

Dick Schreitmueller

Dan Smith

Robert A. Stermer

Carol Tomkovich

Lauren Vignec

Fact Checkers and Go-To People

Ned Benz

Arleigh Clemens

Jason Good

Zack Hiwiller

Moira Keane

Paul Krafter

Shawn Larsen

Pat Marshall

Josh Meyer

Jeff McComas

David Rankine

The MN Bogleheads

Marlene Perrin

Amy Shao

Wendy Swanson

Other Contributors

Adem A. Dogu

Derin B. Dogu

Daria A. Ferri

PART I

THE BASICS

CHAPTER ONE

The Retirement Planning Process

Thomas L. Romens

INTRODUCTION

Retirement! You'll be ready, but will you have the money to do it? Retirement planning is an exploration of alternatives that link present decisions to future implications. The objective of a retirement plan is to identify strategies that you can use to realize your financial goals—goals that will support your plan for living your postretirement years. Failure to link your retirement financing to your life plan in retirement might result in planning for the wrong future or failing to provide financially for the future you planned.

Saving for retirement and planning for it are two different topics. Young people who enter the workforce for the first time are encouraged to save for retirement, but they are not *planning* for retirement—at least not yet. But you are ready to plan. What should you do? How do you start? How much do you need?

The Bogleheads' Guide to Retirement Planning explores the planning process itself, emphasizing the linkage between saving for retirement and actually planning for it. We'll introduce some basic financial planning concepts and provide suggestions regarding how much to save for retirement and how to budget for those savings. Lifestyle choices today directly impact the ability to save for the future. As the poet Robert Burns wrote, "The best laid plans of mice and men often go awry," it is necessary to create a dynamic plan to address the uncertain nature of everyone's health and financial and personal future.

LIFE IN RETIREMENT AND YOUR RETIREMENT WELL-BEING

Retirement as we know it did not exist until the twentieth century. People worked until they could not physically work anymore. There were no pensions, no Social Security, and no Medicare. You were on your own. Most people retired to their children's home or another relative's home, where they lived out the rest of their days.

A new concept of retirement evolved in the 1900s. It focused on a life of rest and leisure paid for by a pension from many years of hard work in an industrial world and modest government subsidies from government-paid Social Security and Medicare. At first, retirement was expected to last only a few years. The retirement age was 65 years when Social Security was created in 1935. That was life expectancy at the time. Accordingly, many people were not expected to live long enough to collect.

Times have changed since the early 1900s; people are living longer, private pensions are diminishing, Social Security benefits are likely to be reduced in the years ahead, and Medicare coverage is becoming very costly. These changes have dramatic implications for future retirees. Baby boomers and beyond must plan retirement differently than their parents or grandparents. Perhaps retirement should be viewed as a third phase in life, potentially equal in duration to the earlier development and full-time work phases of life.

Imagine yourself in retirement for potentially 30-plus years. Where will your income come from? How will you structure this time? Undoubtedly, you will see yourself as a healthy, active person. Following good health practices today, such as watching your weight, cholesterol, and blood pressure and getting regular exercise, can increase your chances of a longer, healthier life span. Unlike earlier phases of your life, you see retirement as unburdened by the pressure to pursue an education and a career. You will want to pursue all the leisure, social, or perhaps political activities that you had no time for while working full-time. A 2004 AARP survey on baby boomers' expectations of life in retirement found that 70 percent of the baby-boom generation expects to spend more time on a hobby or interest, 68 percent will have more time for recreation, and 51 percent expect to be involved in community service or volunteering.

Those goals are all commendable. But how do you generate the income for your living needs, given diminishing pensions and the cloudy outlook for Social Security? The big change in retirement is that you will probably not be fully retired from gainful employment. Numerous surveys have found that more than 70 percent of retirees expect to work in some capacity, and for some of them, the primary reason will be social fulfillment. Retirement certainly has the potential to be a multifaceted phase of your life.

Money is undoubtedly important, and a steady source of income is critical to a happy retirement. However, money cannot buy happiness. In her book, *You Don't Have to Be Rich: Comfort, Happiness, and Financial Security on Your Own Terms*, Jean Chatzky reports that at the $50,000 income level, increases in happiness level off. Statistically, people who earn around $50,000 a year are just as happy as those earning more than $100,000 per year. Your lifestyle is your choice; simply be aware that studies show that a more expensive lifestyle does not necessarily correlate with additional happiness.

Retirement is about what you are retiring to, not what you are retiring from. In addition to your financial goals, your retirement goals should include the elements of health, social interaction, intellectual stimulation, and happiness. In their book *What Color Is Your Parachute? In Retirement*, Richard N. Bolles and John E. Nelson present some of the findings of Charles Morris, who attempted to define a "good life." His characterization of "ways of life" is a purposeful synopsis of what you might aspire to retire to. Some ways of life described are (a) improvement, working for realistic solutions to specific problems; (b) service, devoting yourself to the greater good and to others; (c) enjoyment, pursuing pleasures and festivities; (d) contemplation, introspection to achieve a more rewarding inner life; and (e) action, using physical energy to accomplish things.

If you are retiring as a couple, it is very important that you agree on a common vision for the future and the strategies that are needed to reach your financial goal. Without consensus, there is the chance that you may be at cross-purposes, a potential recipe for conflict. Planning for the future involves trade-offs; you should agree on what you are willing to give up today in return for your shared vision of life tomorrow.

WHEN TO BEGIN THE RETIREMENT PLANNING PROCESS

Financial planning to support yourself in retirement should begin early in life, although planning *how* you will live your future life in retirement may not take place until well after you reach your mid-50s. Accumulating assets for retirement can and should begin as soon as you earn steady income, and even before. Parents who have children with earned income can set up a custodial Roth IRA and fund the account up to the extent of the child's earnings, or the maximum allowable by law, whichever is less.

Early retirement planning should begin when you have your first full-time job. Planning at this stage involves having a savings plan so that 40 years later you will have *something* put away for retirement. You may not know how much to save or how long you will need to save, but saving is the beginning.

Many employers have a 401(k), 403(b), or other self-funding defined contribution retirement plan. Study the defined contribution plan options offered by your employer. Choose a broad-based low-expense mutual fund, and contribute at least enough to capture your employer's match. Contribute more if you can—10 to 15 percent of gross income is a good target—but especially take advantage of any raises you earn to increase your contributions. If your employer does not offer a plan, or if the only investment choices are high-expense funds with no employer match, you may be better off establishing a Roth IRA at an investment firm that offers low-cost plans and a low minimum investment amount. All of these concepts are discussed in other chapters throughout this book.

Choosing the right mix of assets at the beginning of your career is not as important as getting started on retirement early and establishing good financial habits. At the beginning, it is the amount that you put into a plan that counts, rather than the return of the investment in the plan.

It is not difficult to budget for retirement savings at an early age because your spending habits have not been developed. One core strategy that works is living below your means; this strategy entails distinguishing between wants and needs and deferring gratification (minimal use of credit and avoiding revolving credit altogether). There are also psychological benefits to getting started early. Money deferred from your paycheck has an out of sight, out of mind quality, and the quarterly statements that report your fund's growth typically offer positive reinforcement for the decisions you have made.

THE TIME VALUE OF MONEY AND OTHER IMPORTANT CONCEPTS

Letting your money work for you is a key component of saving for retirement. Compound interest, dollar cost averaging, tax-deferred savings, and diversification help lower your risk and boost your return on investment over time.

Compound Interest

Compound interest is the interest on your principal plus interest on the interest you earned previously. For example, a single investment of $10,000 at 5 percent compounded annually earns $10,789 in interest over 15 years for a net amount of $20,789. Straight interest would accrue at the rate of $500 per year, $7,500 in total interest, for a net amount of $17,500. When interest is reinvested and compounds at 5 percent, it adds another $3,298 to the value. That is the magic of compound interest. To calculate compound interest, use one of the many compound interest calculators available on the Internet.

Rule of 72

The rule of 72 offers another interesting perspective on compound interest. Divide the interest rate that an investment is earning into 72, and the quotient is the approximate number of years it will take for that investment to double. For example, an investment with a 7 percent total return will double in about 10 years and a 10 percent return will double in about 7 years.

Starting Early

To illustrate the connection between compound interest and the importance of starting early, here is an example using a scenario from the *Bogleheads' Guide to Investing*. Eric Early starts investing at age 25 and invests $4,000 each year in a Roth IRA until age 35 and then invests nothing. At 8 percent interest his $40,000 grows to more than $629,000 by age 65. Larry Lately begins at age 35 and invests $4,000 for the next 30 years. Assuming the same 8 percent rate of return on his $120,000 investment, Larry's Roth account balance at age 65 is $489,000. It's the power of compound interest over long periods of time that gives Eric the advantage.

Dollar Cost Averaging

Dollar cost averaging is another math-based approach to investing that can boost returns over time. Dollar cost averaging is periodically investing a fixed dollar amount to purchase shares (usually a mutual fund). For example, if you set aside $100 each month and buy shares in the same mutual fund every month with that contribution, you are dollar cost averaging. It works to your benefit by buying more shares when the price is down and fewer shares when the price is up. Over a period of time, it lowers the average cost of the shares purchased. If you contribute to a retirement account each year, then by default you are dollar cost averaging.

Tax-Advantaged Savings

Taxes erode retirement savings more than any other expense. You can grow your retirement account faster by using a tax-deferred savings account such as a 401(k), 403(b), 457, SIMPLE or SEP account, traditional IRA, or tax-tree Roth IRA. Assume you save $500 per month for 30 years at 5 percent interest in a tax-deferred or tax-free account. The account grows to a total of $417,863. If you save the same amount for 30 years in a taxable account, the result is $364,201 at a 15 percent tax rate or $324,290 at a 28 percent rate. You will learn more about tax-advantaged strategies in other chapters throughout this book.

Risk Tolerance

All investors should assess their risk tolerance when getting started in investing. Your risk tolerance is an assessment of how you will react psychologically when the stock market and your investments go up and down.

Investors who buy riskier mutual funds could use one or more of the Internet-based risk tolerance assessment tools to help them determine what percentage of their investments they wish to have in stocks and what percentage they wish to have in less volatile investments like bonds and certificates of deposit (CDs). A high risk tolerance indicates an investor who is less likely to sell shares when the market is down, a key attribute needed if you hope to match or beat overall market performance. Do be aware that you probably can't really appreciate your risk tolerance until you pass the sleep test during a major market downturn such as those experienced in the early 1970s, 1987, early 2000s, and in 2008. Down markets of 20 percent or more happen more frequently than people think.

Diversification (Asset Allocation)

Overall portfolio risk is controlled through diversification. In financial planning, diversification of a portfolio is usually referred to as asset allocation. In its simplest form, asset allocation is a recommended percentage of assets that should be in equities (stocks or stock mutual funds) or in fixed income (bonds, money markets, or certificates of deposit).

Rebalancing is the process whereby you periodically adjust the current allocation of your portfolio to stay close to your desired asset allocation, thus controlling your portfolio risk. For example, when the equity percentage is too high because your stocks went up in value, sell some equities and buy more bonds. This sell high and buy low transaction can be an effective strategy to keep you on track to meet your goals. No matter what your risk tolerance is, your asset allocation should become more conservative as you approach retirement age or as you realize your planning goal—regardless of age. Later chapters cover rebalancing in more detail.

CALCULATING YOUR NUMBER

Most couples planning for retirement want a savings number that will tell them when they can retire. In his book *The Number*, Lee Eisenberg refers to it as "how much [you] need to walk away on [your] own terms, never to look back." Coming up with an accurate savings or net worth number is difficult because you have to weigh numerous factors that affect your decision about when to voluntarily retire: health, age, savings, and lifestyle.

The rule of thumb many financial planners use to determine how much income you will need to maintain your current lifestyle in retirement is 70 to 80 percent of your income while working. Unfortunately, the 70 to 80 percent guide can be an erroneous amount because it is based on earnings, not spending. Many people live on much less than they earn, and others with the same income struggle from paycheck to paycheck. The 70 to 80 percent guide also oversimplifies the issue since it fails to take into account your age at retirement, pension from an employer, eligibility for Social Security benefits and Medicare, postretirement health insurance costs covered by your employer, your health, and even your lifestyle. A better approach is to do a financial plan that includes a detailed retirement budget, as Eisenberg suggests.

LIFESTYLE IMPACT ON SETTING A RETIREMENT DATE

Although many of the elements that comprise our lifestyle do not necessarily bring us more happiness or meaning, we should also consider the trade-offs that lifestyle choices represent. The basic needs of families in the twenty-first century are food, clothing, shelter, and health care. Beyond these needs, most items fall into the wants category, wants being an indicator of your lifestyle and a variable that you can control. A frugal lifestyle would allow you to retire much earlier than a lifestyle designed to keep up with the Joneses. How big a house do you need? How often do you buy a new car? How important is dining out and entertaining? How important are designer labels and fashion? Think about your value system and what provides meaning and happiness in your life.

Adam Smith, the father of modern economics, made this comment about lifestyles in *The Wealth of Nations* in 1776: "The desire for food is limited in every man by the narrow capacity of the human stomach; but the desire of the conveniences and ornaments of buildings, dress, equipage, and household furniture, seems to have no limit or certain boundary."

LIFESTYLE CONSIDERATION: THE COST OF TRANSPORTATION

The cost of owning an automobile is a significant expense over a lifetime. When buying an automobile, consider not only the purchase price of the vehicle itself but also the opportunity cost (investment return on money not spent). For example, compare two similar highly rated cars, one with the standard nameplate and the other in the luxury line. Buying the standard version for $10,000 less every five years results in an out-of-pocket saving of $80,000 over 40 years. The opportunity rate on those savings in a Roth IRA at 5 percent compound interest for 40 years is $279,038.

HOW TO CALCULATE YOUR NUMBER

You are now ready to calculate your number, the principal indicator of your ability to support your life plan in retirement. There are many ways to do this calculation; some are simple, and others are very complex. Here is a three-step simple method to *estimate* your number without getting too detailed:

1. Examine your current spending after taxes as a basis for your desired annual income in retirement. Don't include items such as a child's college cost because that will be over by the time you retire.
2. Estimate your future sources of retirement income before investment income. If you are in your mid-50s or older, you can get a fairly accurate picture of your future Social Security benefits from the annual statements provided by the Social Security Administration.
3. Subtract your annual spending before taxes from your future Social Security income and any pension income to find the amount of investment income needed in retirement. The only thing missing is income taxes, which are typically low for a retiree because you are no longer earning high income and you are not paying into Social Security or Medicare. A small adjustment for income taxes may be needed, but don't overestimate that expense.

This calculation may result in a projected annual income shortfall. That difference will have to be made up by taking a distribution from your savings. The question is how to calculate the lump sum you will need based on the annual shortfall.

There are two ways to determine the amount you need at retirement. Financial planners consider a safe withdrawal amount from a retirement portfolio to be about 4 percent of the value per year. That is the industry standard amount that planners believe you can withdraw for the rest of your life and not worry about running out of money. Based on this standard, to find the lump sum amount you need, divide your shortfall by 4 percent (0.04) to calculate your savings goal. For example, if your annual spending, minus projected Social Security and pension benefits, is a $40,000 shortfall, then you would need investment assets of $1 million: ($40,000/0.04 = $1,000,000). Another method to find your lump sum number is to multiply the shortfall by 25 years: ($40,000 × 25 = $1,000,000). The 25-year number is derived by dividing 100 percent by 4 percent.

From the $1 million, subtract your current savings to determine how much you need to accumulate. You can estimate that part of your accumulation will come from growth of your current investments. If you subtract that potential growth, you will arrive at the additional savings you need. For example, if you have already saved $600,000 and you expect those savings to grow to $765,000 prior to retirement, the savings target becomes $235,000: your savings goal during your remaining working years. Note: If you are planning to retire before you receive Social Security or a pension, you will have to plan for additional outlays from savings in your initial retirement years and adjust the numbers accordingly.

A WARNING ABOUT USING SCIENCE IN FINANCIAL PLANNING

Scientific formulas are fine for physics, where there are rigid laws of nature. But they can give you false information in the subjective world of financial planning. The simple method for calculating your number has many assumptions built into the formula, some of which may not be realistic. For example, a 4 percent income level from investments assumes that you desire to have your heirs inherit every dime you ever saved after inflation. If leaving every penny to heirs is not part of your estate plan, or you do not care what anyone gets after you are gone, then you could take out more money without worry. Perhaps you could take out 5 percent per year rather than 4 percent. In that case, you would multiply your income shortfall by 20 rather than 25 to find the number.

Also, the idea that someone is going to spend the same amount of money at age 65 as they do at age 85 is simply not realistic. Department of Labor surveys show that spending goes down with age, particularly when people get into their 80s. At that point, people start to downsize by selling the second car and selling the second home; they do not travel as much or go out to eat as much. Adjustments can and should be made to the number to approximate these decreasing spending habits. Perhaps a realistic number is closer to 17 or 18 times annual income shortfall rather than the rule of thumb of 25 times.

To assure that your retirement assets provide for 30 to 40 years of retirement, you need to do a new calculation each year and adjust for inflation accordingly. These readjustments to your goal account for market fluctuations and other factors that affect your ability to save for retirement. Downsizing and/or relocating to a less costly area are additional means of reducing the difference between total annual income in retirement and the amount indicated as a safe withdrawal from your savings.

Even if you spend considerable time and effort calculating a savings number that will produce a safe, sustainable withdrawal rate in retirement, it is prudent to note an important caveat: Applying rigid scientific formulas to finance are helpful in that they are conceptual, but those formulas cannot account for the unknowns.

Compound interest calculators and savings calculators can project average returns over time, but they cannot project the impact of a major market downturn in the years just before retirement. Nor can they project the loss of a job or a severe decline in real estate values for someone hoping to relocate.

Many financial planners use complex Monte Carlo simulation analysis to predict the probability of successful withdrawal rates, taking into account past inflation and market performance. But those formulas are built around strict scientific laws that do not apply to future economic events. Monte Carlo simulation cannot forecast changes in the tax code, the bankruptcy of a pension plan, or an inheritance.

BUDGETING FOR RETIREMENT

How do you budget for the seemingly staggering amounts needed for retirement? If you are a young investor just starting out, make early, regular contributions to your employer's deferred compensation plan, and establish a savings pattern and lifestyle that never take into account that portion of your income. As an older investor, you have to consider retirement savings a necessary expenditure, not a discretionary one. You will also have the challenge of applying more strategies to meet your goal.

The Young Investor

When starting a new job with an employer who offers a salary deferral or defined contribution plan, how much should you defer? Based on the Social Security tax of 12.4 percent of wages and the fact that Social Security retirement benefits pay out about 40 percent of earnings at age 67, your strategy should ultimately be to save 15 to 20 percent of gross income—more if you plan to retire early. You don't have to start at that level if part of your strategy is to dedicate some or all of your future salary increases to savings until you reach that level. If you are barely making enough to get by, set up a budget and track your spending habits over a few months. Distinguish between wants and needs.

Controlling out-of-pocket expenses can help fund a retirement plan. A partial list of expense items to consider includes credit card debt, clothing purchases, personal care expenses (cosmetics, haircuts, hair dying, manicures, pedicures, spa treatments, etc.), cell phone plans, eating out (both lunch and dinner), expensive entertainment, daily lattes and happy hours, lottery tickets, grocery bills (prepared foods and deli items are expensive; many store brands are indistinguishable from national brands), DVDs, iPods, and music downloads.

Also consider some less frequent expenses, such as insurance deductibles and the big hitters—transportation and housing costs. No one expects you to be a hermit, but there are many small purchases made each week that do not significantly impact happiness, social interactivity, or well-being. Jean Chatzky characterizes some of this spending as "unconscious consumption"; if unchecked, such spending undermines your savings goals.

The Older Investor

At this point in your life, your well-established spending habits have provided you with a good idea of how much annual income you will need in retirement. The Social Security and pension income numbers you provided when calculating the savings needed to support your future lifestyle are fairly solid. The gap remaining will need to be filled by future savings and the income from your investments. Returning to the example of a $1 million goal with $600,000 saved, if you are 5 years (60 months) from retirement and you expect your investments to return a conservative 5 percent, the calculation is as follows: the $600,000 current savings earn 5 percent per year over 5 years to grow to about $765,000, leaving a gap of $235,000 for which you have to budget. Using a compound interest calculator with length of savings equal to months to retirement, you would have an approximate savings goal of about $3,500 per month. (This assumes that half of the savings go into tax-deferred accounts.)

If you know how much you can afford to save and how much you need to save, you can also use the same formula to solve for the number of months you must continue to work until you can afford to retire. Choose from a number of online interest calculators at www.analyzenow.com, www.choosetosave.org, www.AARP.org, or www.MSNMoney.com.

If you are approaching retirement, you may need a strategy of savings and cost reductions that go beyond the daily expense controls employed by the younger investor. Think of the process as a lifetime spending plan where you can adjust either your lifestyle today or your time line for tomorrow to achieve your goal. In the example, the $3,500 per month needed for five years is reduced by $1,000 per month if you delay retirement by two years.

If you have a hard retirement date, here are some expense reduction and savings strategies: If you have credit card debt, pay it off by using funds you may have in taxable low-yield savings, suspending Roth IRA contributions, taking out a home equity loan if you have a lot of equity (over 50 percent) in your home, or refinancing your mortgage if interest rates are favorable for doing so *and* if refinancing does not greatly extend the length of term of your mortgage. If you own more house than you need, consider downsizing. If you are making car payments or are leasing a car, try to reduce your transportation outlay by selling it and buying a dependable used car for cash. You could also reduce your support of children in college if they are eligible for educational loans since they can borrow for college, particularly if they are old enough to be in a graduate program.

Another cost-saving strategy is adjusting your insurance. Consider raising the insurance deductibles on your home and the collision deductible on your car—or drop the collision deductible altogether if the value of the car is less than $5,000. If you are paying for a portion of your health care and are in good health, look for a cheaper plan and/or raise your annual deductible. If you are taking prescription medicines, ask for a generic equivalent. Live a healthy lifestyle by not smoking, not drinking in excess, and getting regular exercise. Last, if no one is dependent on your income, drop your life insurance, and if you have a dependent, buy term life insurance.

ADDITIONAL STRATEGIES TO CLOSE AN ANNUAL INCOME GAP

You may be able to reduce some, if not all, of any projected annual income shortfall by selling your home and moving to a less expensive location. If you are a retired couple, ask yourself if you regularly use all the space you have and if you want the furnishings, maintenance, and taxes that go with it. Downsizing from a four-bedroom to a smaller three-bedroom home (net 500 square feet reduction) has the potential of freeing up $100,000 in cash and reducing ongoing costs for taxes, insurance, and utilities by 5 percent or more per year. Moving to another town may also reduce costs. For example, moving from Chicago to Champaign-Urbana, Illinois, will reduce your living costs by more than 10 percent. Retiring to Mexico or another location south of the border can reduce your living costs by a considerable amount. If you do move out of the country, rent for the first year or so to ensure that the lifestyle suits you.

CHECKING ON YOUR PROGRESS AND MAKING ADJUSTMENTS

A key strategy to keep your plan on track is an annual portfolio checkup as suggested later. Rebalance your asset allocation if the situation warrants. A semiannual review is recommended for individuals in their 50s. The closer you are to your retirement age, the less time you have to recover from adverse events.

ANNUAL AFFORDABLE SPENDING CALCULATIONS

Check your spending and saving habits at least annually, and make adjustments to your retirement savings when necessary. Has the contribution limit for tax-deferred savings increased? Can you save more or redirect savings from a taxable account to a tax-deferred account? Did you get a raise? Did you reduce ongoing expenses, and how did you redirect the money? Have health-care expenses changed? These adjustments do not require a detailed tracking of expenditures, only a big picture approach. Situations change over time, and we all need to be flexible enough to adjust.

CHECKING STRATEGIES AND TRACKING PROGRESS

In the decade before retirement, an annual review should include looking at all the major items that affect your ability to draw down assets at your desired rate in retirement. This includes reviewing your annual Social Security statement and its income projections, employer pensions, employer-sponsored plans (such as 401(k), 403(b), 457, SIMPLE, and SEP), traditional and Roth IRAs, savings in taxable accounts, other sources of income, and any amount that might be freed up from downsizing. On the expense side of the ledger, subtract your savings for the year and your Social Security taxes from your gross income to get a rough estimate of your cost of living. Make adjustments for changes in housing costs, transportation costs, health-insurance premiums, and changes in tax laws that affect both wage earners and retirees. Use an online retirement savings calculator to see if your current level of savings will allow you to reach your retirement goal.

As you get close to retirement, you can examine the percent withdrawal rate that might be right for you. Based on your current savings and projected postretirement income, how much do you really need to withdraw annually to live comfortably? If you have been a consistent saver and live well below your means, you may find that a 3 percent withdrawal rate allows you ample resources and additional peace of mind.

LIFE'S UNKNOWNS AND THEIR IMPACT ON RETIREMENT PLANNING

According to a 2008 AARP survey, 51 percent of workers reported retiring earlier than anticipated. Of those who cited one or more negative reasons:

* 54 percent reported leaving due to health or disability
* 33 percent reported leaving due to downsizing or layoffs
* 25 percent left to care for a spouse or other family member

While we can plan for our future and work to create a future of our choosing, we cannot guarantee results. Life happens. We can only anticipate some of the potential threats and prepare contingency plans. The death of a family member, serious illness, and natural disasters are phenomena most dreaded by all of us. Events such as these may alter our lives, our goals, and our futures. Conservative planning, insurance, and emergency savings can cushion some of these blows, but they will still be felt.

Divorce is often a monumental financial setback for both parties. It can be very costly, financially and emotionally, and leave both parties to fend for themselves, rather than pooling their assets and talents. Many divorces result in individuals starting over again with their financial savings. Even living a frugal lifestyle and saving aggressively may not provide enough savings to allow retirement at the desired age.

Loss of employment, family-owned business bankruptcies, and frozen or bankrupt pension plans may also be devastating events. If these setbacks happen to couples as they approach retirement, there is little time to recover, and the only solutions are to continue working past the planned retirement age, or accept a retirement that potentially provides less opportunity to pursue postretirement goals.

The condition of the financial markets has a huge impact on individuals approaching retirement, as well as those who have just entered retirement.

These investors are the most vulnerable to market downswings because they are at a point in their lives when their net worth is at its highest. Higher returns come only with higher risk. If you have reached your financial goal in advance of your desired retirement age, there is good reason to take a more conservative approach to investing.

The effect of a market downturn can be seen in the Employee Benefit Research Institute (EBRI) Survey in Table 1.1. In the 2008 data, note the 15 percent drop in retirees' confidence that they would have enough money to live comfortably in their retirement years. This survey was

TABLE 1.1 RETIREE CONFIDENCE IN HAVING ENOUGH MONEY TO LIVE COMFORTABLY THROUGHOUT THEIR RETIREMENT YEARS

	VERY CONFIDENT	SOMEWHAT CONFIDENT	NOT TOO CONFIDENT	NOT AT ALL CONFIDENT
2008	29	35	17	17
2007	41	38	10	11
2006	40	33	12	13
2005	40	40	12	7
2004	42	27	16	13
2003	39	35	12	11
2002	40	32	16	11
2001	37	37	10	11
2000	34	41	14	11
1999	31	39	20	8
1998	19	28	24	24
1997	33	34	18	11
1996	26	42	20	8

Source: Employee Benefit Research Institute and Mathew Greenwald & Associates, Inc., 1996–2008 Retirement Confidence Surveys®

conducted in January 2008, nine months prior to the financial crisis in October 2008.

Housing downturns also put your plan at risk. As evidenced by the 2008 housing downturn and credit crisis, even the family home can be at risk. Traditional thinking on housing was to buy the biggest house you can afford because it will always go up in value. That may no longer be accurate. The foresight not to put more money into housing than is needed to meet your needs may help you stay on track for retirement.

Changes in the law or the tax code are also unpredictable events that could affect disposable income needed in retirement. Changes that have been proposed in the past, such as increasing income taxes or capital gains taxes or reducing the cost of living adjustment for Social Security benefits would also have an impact on a retiree's standard of living. People approaching retirement and those already retired should be flexible in their planning *and living* to adjust to changes as they occur. Tax law changes may mean a few years of no inflationary increase in annual withdrawals from retirement funds and/or reductions in some discretionary expenses.

Health-care costs in retirement represent both the greatest known additional expense for retirees and the greatest potentially unknown cost. Be mindful that cost of coverage is likely to continue to increase in the years ahead and that the benefits from government programs are apt to decrease. It is prudent for retirees to overestimate health-care costs and underestimate benefits from government health insurance programs.

Although computer models can provide a withdrawal strategy based on inputs, they cannot anticipate scenarios where future investment returns and rates of inflation are vastly different from those of the past or tell you what the cost of health care will be when you really need it. The only way to protect against these unknowns is to rework your plan annually to reflect the new realities.

ADDITIONAL RESOURCES

General Planning for Retirement

- Richard N. Bolles and John E. Nelson, *What Color Is Your Parachute? In Retirement.* Berkeley, CA: Ten Speed Press, 2007. The most introspective book in terms of planning what to do in retirement.
- Jean Chatzky, *You Don't Have to Be Rich: Comfort, Happiness, and Financial Security on Your Own Terms.* New York: Portfolio, Penguin Group USA, 2003. This book is a more balanced mix of the two topics.

- Lee Eisenberg, *The Number: A Completely Different Way to Think about the Rest of Your Life.* New York: Free Press, 2006. An autobiographical style with interesting profiles and case studies.

Financial Planning for Retirement

- Taylor Larimore, Mel Lindauer, and Michael LeBoeuf, *The Bogleheads' Guide to Investing.* Hoboken, NJ: John Wiley & Sons, 2006. A complete guide to investing principles.
- Henry Hebler, *Getting Started in a Financially Secure Retirement.* Hoboken, NJ: John Wiley & Sons, 2007. A well-rounded guide to financial planning and investing for retirement.
- Ed Slott, *Your Complete Retirement Planning Road Map.* New York: Ballantine Books, 2007. More of a reference book than a narrative, with many useful forms and checklists covering a variety of retirement planning situations.

CHAPTER SUMMARY

Saving for retirement should start at an early age, as soon as a person has steady income from employment. Planning for retirement is done later in life, once a person has lived a good many years and is comfortable with present living standards. Everyone over the age of 50 should have a written plan that lays out goals for retirement living and the financing that will support them. Younger planners, too, should have a written plan. Their plan should focus more on examining their personal and financial values, committing to a plan with their partner, establishing some long-range financial goals, and indicating the strategies they will use to achieve them.

If you are within a decade of retirement, your planning should add detail about what you expect to do during your postretirement years. Your annual financial plan adjustments should reflect changes in your life and explore additional strategies for achieving your financial goals if it appears you will fall short. Creating a clear vision of your future life provides the positive affirmation you need to choose the most meaningful course of action today, without a feeling of regret or denial. Above all, stay on track as best you can through good and bad economic times. Focus on what brings happiness to your life, and consider your financial resources as a means to that end.

CHAPTER TWO

Understanding Taxes

Norman S. Janoff A.K.A. Azrunner

INTRODUCTION

Benjamin Franklin is credited with the saying "Nothing is certain except death and taxes." Uncle Sam is our partner in everything we do, and that means paying him part of our income. Why are we taxed? The grander purpose of paying income tax was articulated by IRS Tax Commissioner Mark W. Everson in IRS Publication 17: "Paying taxes is a unifying experience fundamental to democracy and the rule of law. Each year, almost two hundred million taxpayers carry out this vital obligation by filing their return." In the United States and in all great democracies, people are resigned to paying income taxes. In performing their duty to their country, citizens complete their tax forms and send in checks when necessary. However, we also have an obligation to ourselves not to overpay; rather, we should strive to pay only the minimum amount of tax legally attributed to us.

Understanding how different types of income and capital gains are taxed is the starting point for managing your tax obligation. This chapter helps you understand the key aspects of income tax as they pertain to retirement planning. Minimizing the impact of taxes while in retirement is critical because it maximizes your discretionary income from pensions, Social Security, and your portfolio.

WHY AMERICANS SHOULD UNDERSTAND U.S. TAX LAW

Our tax law is long, complex, and intimidating. Nevertheless, you should make an effort to understand how taxes work because that will save you money. This chapter focuses on understanding the relevant parts of the federal and state income tax laws pertaining to your savings. By knowing the law, you can avoid the unpleasant surprise of an unexpectedly high tax bill. The good news is that most people planning for retirement need to be concerned with only a small subset of the tax law.

Some people say they do not need to know any tax information. They say, "Well, that is why I hire a tax professional." Hiring a professional tax preparer is fine, but like most aspects of life, it is best to have some knowledge of the information yourself so that you can either prepare your taxes yourself or engage in a useful dialogue with your tax professional. The more you know about taxes, the better off you will be.

One of the best places to gain tax knowledge is directly from the tax collectors. The Internal Revenue Service (IRS) has a library of tax documents at our disposal. It is easy to access IRS forms and publications online at www.irs.gov. At a minimum, you should obtain a copy of *Your Federal Income Tax for Individuals*, Publication 17. It is your first reference for tax questions. States that collect state income tax offer similar publications.

Invest the time necessary to understand the tax code that relates to your specific situation. From that solid foundation, paying attention to tax-changes that take place from time to time is relatively painless and will keep you up-to-date and informed concerning your own taxes. One caveat: the tax code is the product of a political process and typically has many exceptions for each rule. It is therefore important to investigate each case where you do not exactly fit the standard rule. References at the end of this chapter will provide the tools you need to fully explore your specific situation.

FEDERAL INCOME TAXES

Most income tax paid by individuals is paid to the federal government. A fundamental aspect of our federal income tax system is that it is progressive; that is, the tax rate increases as the taxable amount increases. In other words, people with higher taxable incomes pay a higher tax rate on their income than people who earn less. Table 2.1 illustrates the 2009 tax brackets for married taxpayers filing jointly and for single filers.

The IRS tax tables show marginal tax rates, the rate at which your next dollar of income would be taxed. For example, assume married taxpayers file a joint return showing taxable income of $68,000. Any money earned between $67,800 and $137,050 is taxed at 25 percent, the marginal tax rate.

How your next dollar of income is taxed may have an impact on how you invest. It is an important concept because how that next dollar is treated may affect your decision to invest in taxable bonds, tax-free bonds, or another investment. Understanding your marginal tax rate will make these investment decisions easier.

TYPES OF INCOME FOR TAX PURPOSES

With the concepts of a graduated income tax and your marginal tax rate in hand, next it is important to understand that different types of income may be taxed at different rates. The rest of this section on federal income taxes will explore in detail the different types of income and how they are taxed. If you have a copy of your latest Form 1040 tax return handy, pull it out, and you can follow along as the various types of income are discussed.

Earned Income and Other Types

On the 1040, the first type of income listed is "wages, salaries, tips, etc." As Form 1040 says, "Attach Form(s) W-2." This form is supplied by your employer to you (and to the IRS). All income reported on a W-2 is taxed as ordinary income, as shown in Table 2.1. If you received a raise during the year, those additional dollars are taxed at your marginal tax rate.

Other income that is taxed as ordinary income includes taxable interest, ordinary dividends, taxable refunds, alimony received, business income (or loss), IRA distributions, pensions and annuities, rental real estate, royalties, partnerships, trusts, and unemployment compensation.

TABLE 2.1   2009 FEDERAL INCOME TAX RATES

2009 TAX RATE	MARRIED FILING JOINTLY	SINGLE FILERS
10%	Not over $16,700	Not over $8,350
15%	16,700–67,900	8,350–33,950
25%	67,900–137,050	33,950–82,250
28%	137,050–208,850	82,250–171,550
33%	208,850–372,950	171,550–372,950
35%	Over 372,950	Over 372,950

Source: U.S. Internal Revenue Service

Interest Income

Interest from bank accounts, certificate of deposits (CDs), taxable money market instruments, and taxable bonds are taxed at ordinary income tax rates. Investors receive a Form 1099-INT at the end of the tax year from the issuer documenting the amount of interest earned from that specific investment. Stock and bond mutual funds refer to their income as dividends, which is reported on Form 1099-DIV. You should refer to these Form 1099s and other tax documents when completing your tax returns.

Interest from most municipal bonds and municipal bond money market funds is tax-exempt, meaning that the interest is free from federal income tax. The exceptions are private purpose bonds issued to finance such projects as a sports stadium. These bonds are subject to the Alternate Minimum Tax (AMT). Your mutual fund will notify you if it holds any of these private purpose bonds.

Dividends

Dividends are payments by corporations on their outstanding stock. They are also the portion of payment from mutual funds that is reported to the IRS as a dividend rather than as interest. The present tax code applies lower tax rates for certain corporate dividends and mutual fund dividends. They are called qualified corporate dividends. The tax rate on qualified dividends is between 5 percent and 15 percent, depending on your marginal tax rate.

For dividends to be qualified, the investor *must have held the stock for more than 60 days during the 121-day period that begins 60 days before the ex-dividend date,* per IRS Publication 550. There is a caveat. If you have a stock mutual fund that pays dividends, both you and the fund must satisfy the holding period requirement for the dividend to be qualified. Form 1099-DIV will list both ordinary dividends and qualified dividends from mutual funds.

Avoid Buying the Dividend

When it comes to mutual funds, capital gains and dividend distributions are paid to you or credited to your account and are reported in box 2a of the Form 1099-DIV that you receive. The key point on these reported capital gain distributions is that you report them as long-term capital gains, regardless of how long you owned your shares in the mutual fund. Thus, before buying a mutual fund, you should inquire as to the date of the fund's capital gain and dividend distribution and the estimated distribution to avoid "buying the distribution." This is easily done by making your purchase after the distribution date rather than just before it. Buying the dividend is not a concern in a tax-advantaged account.

Capital Gains

Capital gains occur when you sell an investment at a gain. The amount you pay in capital gains tax depends on how long you held the investment and what the investment is. Short-term capital gains are taxed as ordinary income, but long-term capital gains are taxed at a different scale than marginal rates, although it is a progressive scale. Long-term capital gains from stocks, bonds, and mutual funds are taxed at a lower rate than gains from selling certain property, gold, jewelry, art, and other collectibles.

To fully understand how your long-term capital gains are taxed, use the Schedule D worksheet that is part of your tax preparation booklet. The worksheet shows what amounts are taxed at the various rates and how capital gains interact with your ordinary income tax rate.

When you sell any asset, you realize a capital gain or loss. Each transaction will be classified as either short-term or long-term, and sometimes a combination of both. Short-term gains and losses are taxed based on ordinary income tax rates. *Short-term* is defined as a holding period of one year or less. *Long-term* is defined as a holding period of more than one year. For stocks and bonds, the tax rate is 5 percent or 15 percent (if your marginal tax bracket is 25 percent or higher). Thus, long-term capital gains on financial assets are taxed at more favorable rates than ordinary income tax rates. However, certain long-term capital gains are taxed at the 28 percent rate, such as the sale of coins, jewelry, and metals.

A capital loss may be deductible from capital gains if an investment was sold below its basis. Fundamental to realizing a capital gain or loss is the concept of basis. The basis of property is its cost. For stocks and bonds, the basis is generally the purchase price plus any costs of purchase such as commissions. If you buy the same stock or mutual fund at various times and then sell the entire lot, your basis will be your average cost. If you only sell a portion of an investment, then you may want to assign a basis to each tax lot. There are a number of ways to calculate your basis. These are covered in the IRS Publication 550 (see Stocks and Bonds under Basis of Investment Property).

Be aware that you cannot deduct losses from sales or trades of stock or securities if you create a wash sale. A wash sale occurs when you sell or trade stock or securities at a loss and, within 30 days before or after the sale, you buy substantially identical stock or securities. If your loss is disallowed because of the wash sale rule, add the disallowed loss to the cost of the new stock or security. This adjusts the basis in the new stock or security.

To compute your taxes with respect to capital gains and losses, you first combine all short-term capital gains and losses to figure your net short-term capital gain or loss. You then combine your long-term capital gains and losses to figure your net long-term capital gain or loss. You then combine your net short-term gain or loss with your net long-term capital gain or loss to determine if you can claim a capital loss deduction or if you will have a net capital gain that is taxed at a lower rate than other income. For a net capital loss, the IRS limits the amount of the loss for any one taxable year to a maximum of $3,000 ($1,500 if you are married and file a separate return). You can use your total net loss to reduce your income dollar for dollar, up to the $3,000 limit.

Capital Loss Carryover

If your total net loss is more than $3,000, you can carry over the unused portion to the next year. The loss can be used to offset gains in the future or to offset $3,000 in ordinary income. Losses carry forward until the entire capital loss is completely used or the taxpayer dies. Only a surviving spouse can use capital loss carryover. It cannot be inherited by anyone else.

Selling Your Home

Taxes may be owed when you sell a home. This section discusses the tax implications of selling your primary residence, which is the main home you live in for more than two years.

The gain or loss on the sale of your main home is the selling price less the adjusted basis. Determine the adjusted basis by adding the price you paid for the home plus any capital improvements on the home. The adjusted basis is increased by additions and other improvements that have a useful life of more than one year, special assessments for local improvements, and amounts you spent after a casualty to restore damaged property. See IRS Publication 523 for details. Part of your cost basis is certain settlement or closing costs but not fees and costs for getting a mortgage loan. Chapter 13 of IRS Publication 17 has a list of settlement fees and closing costs that you can include in the cost basis of property.

There is a significant tax advantage with the sale of your main home. You may exclude up to $250,000 of the gain on the sale of your main home ($500,000 if you are married and file a joint return) if you meet the ownership test and the use test and if during the two-year period ending on the date of the sale, you did not exclude the gain from the sale of another home. This tax advantage pertains only to your main home. It does not pertain to vacation homes or rental property.

Ending on the date of the sale, you must have owned the home for at least two years and lived in the home as your main home for at least two years out of the last five years (or up to fifteen years for those in the military). If you do not meet the ownership and use rules, you may still claim a reduced maximum exclusion by reviewing all the details of your situation against the relevant tax code. IRS Publication 17 has a summary of these exceptions.

Capital Gains on Collectibles

Long-term capital gains on financial assets such as stocks and bonds (or mutual funds holding stocks and bonds) are eligible for the preferred maximum tax rate of 15 percent. However, the sale of such items as collectibles (art, coins, stamps, bullion, etc.) held more than one year is taxed at a maximum rate of 28 percent.

Some mutual funds invest in gold and other alternative assets. How those funds are taxed depend on what is actually held in the fund. If the fund holds hard assets such as gold bullion, you will pay 28 percent capital gain taxes when you sell the fund or when assets in the fund are sold to meet redemptions. If the fund invests in derivatives such as future and swap contracts, a portion of the gain will be taxed as ordinary income and a portion will be taxed as long-term capital gains. See your 1099-DIV for a breakdown.

FEDERAL TAXES ON SOCIAL SECURITY INCOME

An entire chapter is devoted to understanding Social Security, and you should refer to that chapter for details. The focus in this chapter is on how these benefits are taxed. Social Security benefits are superprogressive.

Not only does the tax on Social Security income increase as your income increases but also the percentage of the payment that is taxed goes up. It is a double whammy by Uncle Sam. For example, if you receive very little taxable income in addition to Social Security, then you are in a low tax bracket, and none of your Social Security is taxable. However, if you have substantial income beyond Social Security, then 85 percent of your benefit is taxable at a high marginal tax rate.

ALTERNATIVE MINIMUM TAX (AMT)

The alternative minimum tax (AMT) is an extra tax some people have to pay on top of their regular income tax. AMT rates start at 26 percent and move to 28 percent at higher income levels. By comparison, the regular tax rates start at 10 percent and then move through a series of steps to a high of 35 percent. You calculate the tax by completing Form 6251 provided by the IRS.

The original idea behind AMT was to prevent people with very high incomes from using special tax benefits to pay little or no tax. The AMT has increased its reach, however, and now applies to some people who don't have very high income or who don't claim lots of special tax benefits. Proposals to repeal or reform the AMT have languished in Congress for years. Until Congress acts, almost anyone is a potential target for this tax.

The name comes from the way the tax works. The AMT provides an alternative set of rules for calculating your income tax. In theory, these rules determine the minimum amount of tax that someone with your income should be required to pay. If you're already paying at least that much because of the regular income tax, you don't have to pay an AMT. But if your regular tax falls below this minimum, you have to make up the difference by paying an alternative minimum tax.

The AMT also eliminates itemized deductions, such as investment expenses, employee business expenses, and some medical and dental expenses. It also counts as income the interest from private-activity bonds, a type of tax-exempt bond issued by governments, usually to finance sports stadiums and the like. Finally, AMT rules force you to pay taxes on the spread between the market price and the exercise price of incentive stock options granted by your employer.

STATE TAXES

There are separate tax codes covering each of the 50 states, the District of Columbia, Puerto Rico, the Virgin Islands, and Guam. For the purpose of this book, all of these are classified as state taxes.

States have various means of collecting taxes from its residents. They include but are not limited to income tax, sales tax, real estate tax, and property tax. If you are considering relocating to another state, one of the factors to consider is the overall tax burden you will face for your particular situation. The Retirement Living Information Center has a summary of taxes for each state at www.retirementliving.com. Another useful site is from the Tax Foundation at www.taxfoundation.org. One of the tools compares each state's tax rate across the years to the U.S. average state tax rate.

Income Tax Rates

Tax rates run from a low of 0.36 percent in Iowa to a high of 11 percent in Hawaii. Most states have a progressive tax system similar to federal tax rates. All states have a minimum income below which no income tax is imposed. Then the rate goes up based on income. For example, Maryland has seven brackets ranging from $1,000 to $500,000.

Seven states have a flat tax, which means one tax bracket after certain deductions and exemptions. Those states are Colorado, Illinois, Indiana, Massachusetts, Michigan, Pennsylvania, and Utah. All taxpayers pay the same rate after meeting the minimum income threshold.

Seven states, Alaska, Florida, Nevada, South Dakota, Texas, Washington, and Wyoming, have no income tax. New Hampshire and Tennessee only tax interest and dividend income.

Personal Exemptions

Like federal income tax calculations, most states allow a deduction for your personal exemptions (yourself, your spouse, and your children). And like federal taxes, those exemptions can phase out at higher incomes. Colorado and Pennsylvania remain true to their flat tax philosophy and offer no personal exemption deduction.

Federal Tax Deduction

Your federal income tax allows you to deduct your state income taxes on your federal return. However, only a few states (Alabama, Iowa, and Louisiana) allow the full federal income tax to be deducted on the state income tax return. A few others (Missouri, Montana, and Oregon) provide a deduction but limit the amount that can be deducted.

Sales Tax

State sales taxes became increasingly popular after Congress changed the federal tax code to allow taxpayers to deduct state sales taxes. Sales taxes range from a low of 2.9 percent in Colorado to a high of 7.01 percent in Tennessee. States also vary on whether food or drugs are taxed and at what rates. Local municipalities often add their own sales tax to these state sales tax rates. (California and Virginia have a statewide 1 percent local sales tax.) Five states (Alaska, Delaware, Montana, New Hampshire, and Oregon) impose no sales tax.

Adjustments to Gross Income

States do not tax interest earned on U.S. Treasury securities, including savings bonds. Almost every state does not tax interest on its own state bonds, with the exception of most bonds issued in Illinois. A few states do not tax the interest on other state bonds, although that is rare. In addition, some states offer tax breaks for donations made for certain nonprofit activities.

Personal Property Taxes

Some states impose a tax on your property (such as a tax on your car that is charged annually when you renew your vehicle registration). This tax is calibrated to the market value of your vehicle and is deductible on your federal income tax. Personal property taxes are popular with city, county, and other local governments.

LOCAL TAXES

Although many communities extract local taxes, generally your largest local tax is your real estate tax. Real estate taxes are usually collected by counties, and the revenue is split between county use and public schools. The tax rates can be quite different from region to region. Real estate taxes are typically high when a state has low or no state income tax and low or no sales tax. Real estate taxes are deductible on your federal income taxes, along with sales taxes and state income taxes.

ADDITIONAL RESOURCES

- Your local library is a great resource for learning more about taxes. There are many fine books and articles. Make sure you read current information because the tax code can change quickly.
- The Internal Revenue Service prints Publication 17, *Your Federal Income Tax for Individuals* each year. This free document covers most

of the information needed to prepare your return. For an online version, go to the IRS web site at www.irs.gov.

* To learn more about how different states compare across the entire range of state taxes, take a look at the following web sites:
  * Retirement Living Information Center, www.retirementliving.com
  * Tax Foundation, www.taxfoundation.org

CHAPTER SUMMARY

Taxes are complicated, confusing, frustrating, and a necessary evil. This chapter highlights that portion of the tax code that is particularly significant to the retiree. The amount you pay in taxes has a direct impact on your standard of living. Only by understanding taxes and their implications for your particular situation can you plan properly to minimize the amount you pay.

Several web sites can help you estimate your total tax liability based on where you live and how much income you have. There are many tools available on those web sites for doing an annual tax analysis. Time spent studying how taxes affect you will lead to better retirement planning decisions.

PART II

SAVINGS ACCOUNTS AND RETIREMENT PLANS

CHAPTER THREE

Individual Taxable Savings Accounts

Dan Kohn

INTRODUCTION

A taxable account is funded with after-tax savings. You are taxed on the income and capital gains from taxable accounts when you submit your personal tax returns in April. Investors open taxable accounts for different purposes: from saving for a house down payment to saving for retirement.

A taxable savings account is the most straightforward way of holding investments, though often not the best way because of tax considerations. As a general rule for retirement investing, taxable accounts should be your last resort if you are in a high income tax bracket. Tax-advantaged accounts help lower the amount of your money that you will pay in income taxes each year, and those tax savings compound in your account. Less tax today earns more for your retirement even after you withdraw the funds and pay income taxes on those withdrawals. Consult your tax advisor for your best savings account option.

TYPES OF TAXABLE ACCOUNTS

The main types of taxable accounts are personal, joint, and trust. When you set up a new account, the first question is whether you want to set up a retirement account, an account for general investing, or an account to save for college and children. General investing refers to a taxable account. The next question is whether you want a personal, joint, or trust account.

A personal account is an account for a single person. There is one name and one Social Security number on the account, and one person makes all the investment decisions. A personal account is the simplest account you can set up.

Joint accounts are for investors with a spouse, domestic partner, or significant others. Joint account registration designates that two or more individuals share ownership of the funds equally. The most common joint account is a joint tenancy with right of survivorship. Upon the death of an owner in this kind of account, the shares pass to the remaining owner.

The advantage of a joint account is that when one of the joint holders dies, the surviving account holder automatically inherits the assets. There is no probate or legal proceeding required to transfer the assets to the surviving account holder. Probate, the legal process of distributing a deceased person's property, can be expensive and time consuming. Joint accounts are a great option for ensuring that assets are immediately available to a surviving spouse, child, or partner.

Of course, there are also special reasons why a married couple might not want to have a joint account. Perhaps one or both are in a second marriage. In that case, trust accounts may be more appropriate. Trust accounts are designed for more complex situations. Generally, their purpose is to reduce estate taxes, to provide more control over how assets are transferred to survivors, or both.

An example of a trust is an AB Disclaimer trust. It provides a way to reduce your estate taxes when you have more assets than the federal estate tax exemption ($3.5 million in 2009). Before setting up a trust account with your mutual fund company, bank, or brokerage firm, you'll need to first set up the trust. This means you will need to visit an estate-planning attorney who understands trust law and can word the document correctly. Trusts can be tricky business. Don't try to write one on your own.

There are many different types of trust accounts, and they are discussed in more detail in Chapter 16.

TAX LOSS HARVESTING

An advantage of taxable accounts is the ability to use the losses that inevitably occur in some years to lower your tax bill. This is called tax loss harvesting. There are three benefits. First, tax losses represent an interest-free loan that defers capital gains taxes you would otherwise owe into the distant future and can even eliminate them entirely when you die. Second, you can use remaining tax losses to deduct $3,000 from your regular income taxes each year, which can mean an extra $750 or more in your pocket if you are in the 25 percent federal tax bracket. Third, any remaining losses are carried over into the subsequent years, so each year until your losses are used up, you can defer your capital gains and apply up to $3,000 against your income.

Suppose that you had invested $10,000 into a mutual fund in a taxable account and that with the steep decline in 2008, your holdings are now worth only $6,000. Since you plan to continue holding that fund, you might be inclined to ignore the losses and wait for the fund to eventually recover. Instead, using tax loss harvesting, you'd sell the fund and then buy it back 31 days later. In the meantime, you can either hold the cash in a money market fund or invest it in a similar, but not identical fund. This has the effect of booking a $4,000 capital loss, while returning you to your original position 31 days later.

The capital loss is valuable in several ways. Before you pay any capital gains taxes each year, you use your capital losses to offset any capital gains, and you pay taxes only if you have more gains than losses. If you have more losses than gains, you can apply up to $3,000 of your remaining capital losses against your regular income. And whatever capital losses are still left over (in this case, $1,000, which is the $4,000 in losses minus the $3,000 deduction) can be carried forward indefinitely into future years. Each year, you get to first apply the carried-forward losses against capital gains and then use any remainder (up to $3,000) to reduce your ordinary income.

Using tax loss harvesting to offset capital gains doesn't actually eliminate the capital gains taxes you would have paid. Instead, it defers those taxes into the future. (In our example, you will owe more capital gains taxes in the future because you bought back the fund at a cost basis that is $4,000 lower.) However, because future money is worth less than money today, there's a saying in public finance that a tax deferred is a tax avoided. Using tax loss harvesting to defer capital gains taxes is like receiving an interest-free loan from the IRS. Also, if you (and your spouse) are still holding the shares when you die, your heirs will receive a stepped-up basis, and you will have gotten the up-front benefit from tax loss harvesting while avoiding the taxes on the back end entirely. Finally, the extra capital gains you owe in the (possibly distant) future will be at the (lower) capital gains rate, while the benefit you receive today of the $3,000 deduction is at your (higher) marginal income tax rate.

Avoiding Wash Sales

If you buy the same security that you sold at a loss within 31 days, the IRS considers it to be a wash sale, and you will not be able to claim the tax loss. Even if you buy a security that is, according to tax law, substantially identical within 31 days, the IRS considers that to be a tax wash. For example, if you buy options on a stock to replicate the action of a stock you sold, the IRS sees this as a synthetic security that is substantially identical to the stock, and the loss will be disallowed. The IRS also counts wash sales across accounts, so you cannot sell a fund from your IRA and buy the identical fund in your joint taxable account.

The IRS has not defined *substantially identical* very well, but there are some reasonable guidelines to follow. The stock of one issuer isn't substantially identical to stock of a different issuer, even if they are in the same industry. For example, Dell Computer (Ticker: DELL) isn't substantially identical to Hewlett-Packard (Ticker: HPQ). If you have a loss on one of these companies, you can buy the other one without having a wash sale. However, an index fund that tracks the S&P 500 Index may be found to be substantially identical to another index fund that tracks the S&P 500 even though different fund companies manage the two funds.

It is probably fine to move between funds that track different indexes, such as Vanguard Total Stock Market and Vanguard Large Cap Index. These funds track different indexes, but the returns are similar, so they are good alternatives for domestic holdings. Vanguard Total International Stock Market and Vanguard FTSE All-World ex-US also have similar performance while tracking different indexes.

If you hold ETFs, iShares Dow Jones U.S. Index (Ticker: IYY) is a good substitute for Vanguard Total Stock Market ETF (Ticker: VTI), and SPDR MSCI ACWI ex-US (Ticker: CWI) is a good substitute for Vanguard FTSE All-World ex-US ETF (Ticker: VEU). These non-Vanguard ETFs have higher expense ratios and track different indexes than Vanguard ETFs, but their performance should be nearly identical to their Vanguard equivalents.

There has been ample opportunity to tax swap over the past several years. Even in an up year, there are occasional down months when you could decide to sell the specific shares that have losses (generally, the newest shares that you purchased) to book the loss.

An alternative to swapping into a similar fund is to hold cash. Simply place the sale proceeds in a money market fund for 31 days and then buy back the original holding. The downside to this approach is that you could be out of the stock market during a month when there is a large rally.

Other Important Points When Tax Loss Harvesting

* If you hold shares for less than 61 days, the dividends you receive will not be qualified, and you'll pay a higher tax rate on them, even though your fund company may tell you that they are qualified.

* If you set your dividends or capital gains to automatically reinvest and then want to sell the fund less than 31 days later, you will trigger a wash sale for the amount of the reinvestment. In taxable accounts, it is generally easier to have dividends and capital gains paid into a money market and then manually reinvest a few times a year, which makes it easier to track tax lots and to avoid accidental wash sales.

* To avoid frequent trading, some fund companies, such as Vanguard, require you to wait 60 days before buying back a fund that you have sold. However, this restriction generally applies to online and phone transactions. Instead, you can often sell a fund online and then send a letter by mail to buy it back 31 days later.

* Buying and selling an ETF incurs commissions and bid/ask spreads on each transaction. Harvest tax losses only when the tax savings outweigh these expenses.

* If you want the ability to tax loss harvest a portion of a security rather than your entire holding, you will need to use the specific identification of shares method of tracking your cost basis by lot. Vanguard requires you to send a secure e-mail through their web site or to send the request by mail. More information is at www.bogleheads.org on the Wiki site.

* If you exchange from your preferred holding to a near-equivalent, and then prices go up and stay up, you will probably want to hold the new fund for more than a year. At that point, you can exchange back to your preferred holding and pay only the lower long-term capital gains tax on your profits. If, at any time during that year, prices drop below where you bought the new holding, you can sell immediately, take this new tax loss, and move back to your preferred holdings, provided you've held the shares for at least 31 days.

MINIMIZING TAXES

To maximize the return of your taxable account, you want to minimize the taxes you pay. That means using tax-efficient mutual funds and exchange-traded funds.

Stock Funds

There are several advantages to holding tax-efficient equity mutual funds in your taxable account. First, when you eventually begin to sell these funds in retirement, you will pay the lower capital gains tax rate on funds you hold in your taxable account. If you held those same funds in a tax-deferred account such as an IRA, you would pay ordinary income taxes at a potentially higher marginal tax rate. Second, your heirs will receive a stepped-up cost basis on your taxable holdings after your death. That means neither you nor your heirs will owe taxes on the appreciation that occurred in the securities. There is no stepped-up basis for funds in a tax-deferred account.

Avoid using stock mutual funds that have a high portfolio turnover of securities unless it is in an exchange-traded fund, which has a different tax structure. Funds that have a high turnover of stocks generally distribute the most capital gains each year. You can identify funds that have high turnover by reading that turnover ratio listed in the fund prospectus. The lower the turnover ratio in the fund, the less churning of securities and the more tax efficient it is.

Perhaps the most tax-efficient domestic stock holding for taxable accounts is a total stock market index fund. This fund holds essentially all U.S. publicly traded companies. This means that the fund is not churning between different holdings, so capital gains are rarely generated.

International Stock Funds

Holding international equity funds in a taxable account also has added advantages. There are three benefits to holding international equity funds in taxable accounts:

1. The foreign tax credit is a refund you can claim on your tax return for foreign taxes paid by your international holdings. The amount of the credit is generally only 0.1 to 0.2 percent of the fund, but there is no downside to claiming it. The credit is available only if you hold your international stocks in a taxable account.
2. The international funds in many 401(k) and 403(b) accounts are egregiously expensive. Vanguard offers a great deal on all of their funds, but on a relative basis, their international funds may be the biggest value, as their expenses are often just one-tenth of the expense ratio of an actively traded international fund.
3. International funds can be volatile, which increases the opportunity for tax loss harvesting.

Vanguard's FTSE All-World ex-US (Ticker: VFWIX) and Vanguard's Total International Stock Market (Ticker: VGTSX) funds are two of the best options if you're going to hold an international stock fund in your taxable account. Both funds hold individual stocks, which qualifies them for the foreign tax credit. The FTSE All-World ex-US includes Canada, while Total International and Vanguard Tax-Managed International do not. More information is available at www.bogleheads.org/wiki.

Taxable and Municipal Bond Funds

Investors in higher tax brackets should avoid holding taxable bonds and bond funds in a taxable account. The interest those bonds pay is taxable at your marginal tax rate. Consider holding municipal bond funds in a taxable account if you are in a high marginal tax rate. For investors in lower tax brackets, the after-tax return may be higher by using a taxable bond fund and paying the tax each year. You can determine whether regular taxable bonds or municipal bonds are a better choice for your taxable account by using Vanguard's Tax Equivalent Yield Calculator at www.Vanguard.com.

Target Retirement Funds

Low-cost target retirement funds such as those from Vanguard are an excellent way to create an extremely simple portfolio that is well diversified and low cost and that automatically becomes more conservative over time. But if some of your retirement savings are in a tax-advantaged account and some in a taxable account, then target retirement funds may not be the best choice for the taxable account. That's because all target retirement funds hold bonds, and holding bonds in a taxable account can create an unnecessary tax bill.

Generally, you should hold target retirement funds in a taxable account only if you are in one of the lower tax brackets or are spending (rather than reinvesting) all dividends. Other balanced funds that hold a combination of stocks and bonds have the same problem.

Putting It All Together

Saving more money than will fit in your tax-advantaged accounts is a classic good problem in that it is a sign that you are serious about saving. Many investors hold all of their retirement savings in tax-advantaged accounts. These investors can often hold the same target retirement fund in different IRAs and 401(k)s, thus putting their investing decisions on autopilot.

If you also have retirement savings in a taxable account, you may need to hold a slightly more complex portfolio than the appropriate target retirement fund. When your retirement savings will be mixed between taxable and tax-advantaged accounts, it is generally best to keep your bonds in your tax-advantaged accounts and your tax-efficient equities in your taxable account. If you can fit all of your bonds and some of your equities in your tax-advantaged accounts, put your international equity funds in your taxable account. If you don't have enough room in your tax-advantaged accounts for your desired bond allocation, you should first fill your tax-advantaged accounts with as many bonds as will fit. Unless you are in a very low tax bracket, you would then want to hold municipal bonds in your taxable account to fill out your bond allocation.

NONRETIREMENT TAXABLE ACCOUNTS

In the first part of this chapter, we've discussed taxable retirement accounts. But even if all of your retirement savings are in tax-advantaged accounts like 401(k)s and IRAs, you will probably still want to have at least one taxable account for holding your emergency fund and for transferring money into and out of your retirement accounts.

When Do You Need the Money?

If you intend to access your money in less than two years, it is important to invest it only in safe investments where the principal is not at risk, such as high-interest savings accounts, money markets, and certificates of deposit. If you have a two- to five-year time horizon for this money, short-term bond funds might also be suitable, but you may experience small fluctuations in principal. For money needed in five to ten years, investing in intermediate-term bonds should work. Only for longer term investments should you consider holding equities. And the sooner you need the money, the larger the percentage of cash and bonds you should hold.

It's essential that all investors have access to an emergency fund for dealing with issues like layoffs, a car breakdown, or the need for sudden travel. The main issues to consider when selecting where to keep your emergency fund is safety, liquidity (how easily you can get your money), taxation, and return. Because you may need access at any time, it could be a mistake to hold anything other than cash-equivalent securities as an emergency fund.

Banks and Money Markets

The safest place to keep your money is an FDIC-insured bank, as long as you don't exceed the maximum FDIC-insured amount. These funds are insured by the full faith and credit of the U.S. government. When a bank fails, the FDIC has consistently made funds available the next business day. Unfortunately, most FDIC-insured banks do not pay overly generous interest rates.

Since inflation averages around 3 percent a year, a checking account that pays a lower interest rate loses spending power over time. However, checking and saving accounts are safe and liquid. Although you owe taxes on any interest earned, the returns are relatively low and the tax is normally not very much.

An alternative to the lower rates offered by your local bank is using the Web to find an FDIC-insured bank that is offering higher rates on savings or checking accounts. Many of these accounts can be set up entirely online. The best site for finding these deals is bankdeals.blogspot .com. Unfortunately, most of these offers last for only six months or so and then revert to an uncompetitive rate. Internet savings accounts may make sense only if you are willing to repeatedly move your money around to chase the highest rates.

The second safest place to save your money is a money market fund that invests in high-quality securities. Money market funds invest in high-quality, short-term securities and are designed to provide a higher return than a bank account, while never losing principal. Unfortunately, a major retail money market fund lost money in 2008, which tarnished this fund class for some people.

Vanguard money market funds have never lost money and are managed much more conservatively than the fund that did lose money. Vanguard runs some of the largest money market funds in the industry and is able to take advantage of its economies of scale to offer the lowest expense ratios available to individual investors. This also means that they don't need to chase yield by taking on riskier investments to compensate for their expense ratio. A money market fund from Vanguard provides safety, although it is not insured by the FDIC. It has excellent liquidity (you can get your money immediately) and has historically offered the highest return for a generally safe asset. You can choose whether to use taxable or tax-exempt funds, based on your situation.

Many Bogleheads use Vanguard money markets to hold their emergency fund. If you are in the 25 percent or lower tax bracket, the Vanguard Prime Money Market is generally the best choice. For those in higher tax brackets, a state-specific fund such Vanguard New York Tax Exempt Money Market or the national tax-exempt fund may provide higher after-tax returns. Given your tax rate, you can figure out which is the better choice by using Vanguard's Tax Equivalent calculator at www.vanguard .com. If the yield of the Prime Money Market is higher than your tax-equivalent yield for the appropriate tax-exempt money market, you are better off using prime. Otherwise, use a tax-exempt fund.

Certificates of Deposit

Certificates of deposit (CDs) provide a higher return in exchange for losing access to your money for a set period. CD rates are higher than a checking account, and CDs often offer a higher return than Vanguard money markets, particularly for longer terms. As long as you have less than the maximum amount insured by the FDIC in each bank, CDs are perfectly safe.

Most CDs are not suitable for an emergency fund because you do not have immediate access to the money. An exception could be made for some CDs that allow you to get your money back early for a small fee, such as forgoing three months of interest. If you're certain that you will not need access to this money for a year or more, a CD can be a good option.

If you need to save more than the FDIC insurance limit in CDs, be careful to hold the CDs in different banks to avoid exceeding the FDIC insurance limit. There are a number of ways that you can title multiple accounts to increase your FDIC coverage, including payable on death (POD) designations. For example, a husband and wife with two children could set up nine differently titled accounts to increase their FDIC insurance coverage to 10 times the standard limit at a single bank. More information on this titling process is available at http://bankdeals .blogspot.com. You can determine the level of insurance available on your accounts, based on how they're organized and titled, directly with the FDIC at www.fdic.gov/edie.

ADDITIONAL RESOURCES

* Vanguard is one of the best places to invest, and their general investing page at www.vanguard.com allows you to create a new taxable account online.
* Http://bankdeals.blogspot.com is a good place to keep track of high-yield savings account and CD information, for those who are willing to move their money around to chase higher yields.

- The FDIC offers a useful calculator at www.fdic.gov/edie for deter-mining the level of insurance available on your accounts, based on how they're organized and titled.
- Information is also available on the www.bogleheads.org/wiki.

CHAPTER SUMMARY

Taxable investing is the most straightforward way of holding investments, although often not the best way. You should first take advantage of all of your tax-advantaged options before investing in a taxable account. Tax loss harvesting is a cost-free way of taking advantage of the losses that will inevitably occur in your investments to help lower current taxes. It is important to place your most tax-efficient assets in your taxable account—particularly international equity funds, but also domestic equity and municipal bond funds. Taxable accounts are also typically used to hold emergency funds and nonretirement investments, like savings for a house down payment. Savings accounts, money market funds, and CDs are good savings options that avoid putting your principal at risk. They offer different trade-offs of safety, liquidity, and return.

CHAPTER FOUR

Individual Retirement Arrangements

Jim Dahle A.K.A. EmergDoc

INTRODUCTION

An individual retirement arrangement (IRA), commonly referred to as Individual Retirement Accounts is one of the best ways an investor can save for retirement. The advantage over a taxable investment account (see Chapter 3) is that the assets in an IRA grow without being taxed each year, leaving more money to compound for your benefit. The advantages over an employer-sponsored retirement savings account (see Chapters 5 and 6) include lower fees and more investment choices.

An IRA allows the individual investor to minimize the two biggest drags on investment returns: taxes and expenses. Jack Bogle has said, "In investing, you get what you don't pay for. Whatever future returns the stock and bond markets are generous enough to deliver, few investors will succeed in capturing 100 percent of those returns, simply because of the high costs of investing—all those commissions, management fees, investment expenses and taxes."

47

IRAs are so attractive that the U.S. government has set maximum limits for annual contributions. As recently as 2001, the contribution limit was a mere $2,000 per person. This limit has been raised in recent years, and if possible, investors should take advantage of the higher limits.

IRAs DEFINED

If there was an investment account where you could invest in nearly anything you want, pay no fees or taxes when you change your investments, pay no taxes on the annual returns, and get an up-front tax break on contributions, would you be interested? Of course you would. In fact, you'd probably be wondering what the catch was. There is no catch. Washington wants people to put money away for retirement, and Congress created tax incentives to help. Instead of individual retirement accounts, they could be called tax savings accounts.

Before we get into IRA nitty-gritty, you should understand the difference between an investment account and an investment. An account is nothing more than an empty box for holding your investments. Examples of accounts are trusts, personal, joint, 401(k), traditional IRA, and Roth IRA. Investments are held in an account. Examples of investments include certificates of deposits (CDs), mutual funds, stocks, and bonds. Think of an investment account as a piece of luggage and investments as your clothes. Your clothes go in the luggage.

The luggage might be a backpack, useful for carrying a load through the woods; a nice big rolling suitcase, useful for a week at Aunt Betsy's; or a small carry-on. They all serve the same function of holding your stuff, but each type of luggage has different advantages and disadvantages. In this chapter, you'll learn how to better use your luggage to get your stuff safely to your destination and back.

CONGRESS MAKES IRA LAW

The laws governing the use of IRAs are enacted by Congress and revised periodically. The first IRAs were established in 1974 with a maximum annual contribution limit of $1,500 per year. Any money placed into your IRA was deducted from your taxable income, reducing your immediate tax liability. IRA withdrawals were subject to ordinary income taxes. There was also a 10 percent tax as a penalty if the funds were withdrawn before age 59½.

For the first few years, IRAs were limited to those who didn't have a retirement plan at work. However, in 1981, Congress made them available to all Americans. At the same time, Congress raised the contribution limit to $2,000 and established a spousal IRA for nonworking spouses. The maximum annual contribution limit to a spousal IRA was $250 per year. In 1986, Congress placed an income cap on those who could contribute to the accounts so people earning over a certain amount could no longer deduct their IRA contributions from their taxes. In 1996, Congress raised the spousal IRA contribution limit from $250 to $2,000, matching the contribution limit for employees. In 1997, income thresholds were raised, allowing those with higher incomes to deduct contributions, especially if they did not have a retirement account at work. In 2002, contribution limits on traditional IRAs were increased, and catch-up contributions for people age 50 and over were allowed for the first time. Congress also instituted a retirement savings tax credit that gave low-income people cash to put money away for retirement.

Congress also established the Roth IRA in 1997. It allows for after-tax contributions and tax-free growth and withdrawals, which means that both growth and income in Roth IRAs are completely tax-free. In 2006, income limits for contributions to Roth IRAs were raised.

There is no doubt that the IRA will continue to evolve in future years, and the prudent investor will pay attention to the changes. However, it is unlikely that Congress will take away the special advantages of IRAs anytime soon.

SPECIFIC IRA RULES AND BENEFITS

Remember how a typical taxable investment account works to best understand the advantages of different IRA accounts. As explained in the previous chapter, there are several investment-related taxable events. We will now go through each type of IRA to explain the rules of each and the unique ways they reduce taxes. To review, income taxes are paid by individuals under four scenarios:

1. When you earn the money (ordinary income taxes)
2. As investments pay out cash (taxes on interest and dividends from all investments and capital gain distributions from mutual funds)
3. When you realize a gain on the sale of an investment (capital gains tax)
4. When you withdraw money from a tax-deferred account (ordinary income taxes)

Traditional IRA Rules

Traditional IRAs have many rules regulating money going in and out that must be followed carefully. You must have U.S. taxable compensation to use one of these accounts. Compensation is defined as wages, salaries, and alimony but not dividend, interest, or capital gain income. The money must be received during the same year as the contribution, although you can make the contribution as late as April 15th of the next year. This rule applies to all types of IRAs.

You can contribute to the account only if you make less than a certain amount of money. The IRS uses the modified adjusted gross income (MAGI) to determine if you make too much to use an IRA. The adjusted gross income is just the last line on page 1 of your 1040 form. To get the MAGI, you have to add back a few of the deductions you took elsewhere on your taxes. It tends to get a little complicated, but most people are either well below the limits or well above them and so don't have to make the calculations. If you do, consult the IRS instructions or your favorite tax adviser. The limits have a phase-out range, where you can't take the full deduction, but you can still take a partial deduction. The MAGI limits for 2009 for a traditional IRA are $53K–63K for those single filers and $85K–$105K for joint filers (the deduction is phased out over the specified ranges). Bear in mind these limits *do not* apply if you do not have a retirement account at work. If you have a plan available at work but elect not to use it, the limits do apply. Also, keep in mind that even if you cannot deduct an IRA contribution, you can still make one. This is called a non-deductible IRA and will be discussed later.

You can contribute only a certain amount of money. You cannot contribute more than you make, but assuming you earn more than the annual limit, your maximum contribution in 2009 is $5,000, with a special $1,000 catch-up contribution for those 50 and over. You can have as many different IRA accounts as you like, but the total contribution across all accounts (traditional and Roth) for the year is still $5,000 per person.

You cannot contribute once you reach age 70½, and you must open the IRA at an institution approved by the IRS, generally a bank, credit union, brokerage, or mutual fund company. You can often do it online or by mail, but even if you open it in person, it usually involves only a couple of pages of paperwork.

Remember that this account is for retirement. Although some exceptions are made, you really shouldn't plan on touching this money until you are at least 59½. The IRS will charge you not only the taxes that would normally be due on your withdrawal but also an additional 10 percent as a penalty to discourage the withdrawal. So think twice before taking money out early. The exceptions to avoid the additional 10 percent tax include disability, death of account holder, first-time homebuyer, health insurance premiums, health-care expenses, educational expenses, tax levies, or retired early and taking substantially equal payments (SEPP). More information about SEPP can be found in Chapter 13. To claim one of these exceptions, you must have had the IRA at least five years, or the 10 percent penalty applies.

You have to take the money out of the account. Uncle Sam isn't too keen on you *never* paying taxes on this money, so, beginning at age 70½, you'll have to start taking out required minimum distributions (RMD). For the first few years, the RMD is about 4 percent of the account, but by the time you are in your 90s, it is about 10 percent of the account value. Do not forget to take this out every year, or you will pay a very stiff penalty; 50 percent of what you should have taken out will go to the IRS!

Finally, you cannot borrow money from an IRA. A withdrawal is a withdrawal—you must pay any applicable penalties and you cannot pay it back later.

Roth IRA Rules

Roth IRAs were introduced as part of the Taxpayer Relief Act of 1997. They were originally called American Dream Savings Accounts but were later renamed after their chief advocate, Senator William Roth of Delaware. The individual investor owes Senator Roth a great deal of gratitude for his work on our behalf. The Roth IRA is perhaps the greatest gift ever given to the American investor.

The rules are slightly different from a traditional IRA, however. You still need to have U.S. taxable compensation to use the Roth account. However, the income limits (again, using MAGI) for Roth IRAs are much higher than for traditional IRAs, $105K–120K for single filers and $166K–176K for joint filers in 2009. The contribution limits are the same as for a traditional IRA, and the same catch-up contribution and spousal contribution are also allowed. An additional benefit is that more after-tax money can be sheltered in a Roth IRA than in a traditional IRA. For example, if your marginal tax bracket is 25 percent, $5,000 put in a traditional IRA is really only $3,750 after tax (the government owns the other $1,250 in the form of a tax liability at withdrawal), whereas $5,000 in a Roth IRA is $5,000 after tax for you.

The rules on withdrawals are similar to those for traditional IRAs, with some notable exceptions. You shouldn't touch the money until age 59½ (the same exceptions apply), and you can't borrow the money in the form of a loan. But there are *no* required minimum distributions. You never have to take the money out of your Roth IRA if you don't want to. In fact, if you leave it in your will to a great-grandson, that money can be sheltered from taxes for a period of time upward of 150 years. This particular tax-reduction strategy is known as a stretch Roth IRA, and we'll discuss it later. Because of these very favorable rules, a Roth IRA should be one of the first places you put money for retirement and one of the last places you withdraw it from. But even if you do decide you want to take your money out, that's easier with a Roth, too. The 10 percent penalty and the five-year holding rule that apply to early traditional IRA withdrawals apply only to the *earnings* for a Roth IRA. The original contribution can be withdrawn tax- and penalty-free at any time, including the day after you contributed it, if you really need the money.

Self-Employed Plans

Although employer-based retirement accounts will be covered in another chapter, the employer-based retirement accounts for a self-employed person essentially function as big IRAs. There are four types of accounts that a self-employed investor might consider: a solo 401(k), a Roth solo 401(k), a SEP-IRA, and a SIMPLE IRA.

Solo 401(k)

The 401(k)s first came on the scene in 1978, when section 401(k) of the tax code was written. They were popular with employers because they cost less money than traditional defined contribution plans, and they were popular with employees because of the matching funds and the control offered to employees over their financial future. But they did not serve self-employed individuals very well. It wasn't until 2001 that changes were made to benefit the self-employed, and, thus, the birth of the solo (or self-employed) 401(k).

As with a traditional IRA, you must have U.S. taxable compensation, but the advantage is that there is *no* income limit for contributions, and there is a much higher contribution limit. In fact, it is possible to shelter up to $49K in 2009, $54.5K if you are 50 years old or older. Of course, to put that much away, you must have sufficient income. To max out a solo 401(k), your pretax profit must be at least $205K in 2009. You can defer your first $16,500 into the solo 401(k) as the employee's contribution, but additional money comes as the employer's contribution. This amount is limited to 20 percent of your net business income (including the employer's contribution but not the employee contribution) after subtracting half of your self-employment tax.

The withdrawal rules are exactly the same as with a traditional IRA, except you can borrow up to $50,000 (or 50 percent, whichever is less) of the amount. Borrowing from a 401(k) isn't a good idea because the borrowed money is no longer growing, but at least the interest you pay goes to you instead of a bank. A solo 401(k) can also be rolled over into a traditional IRA, should you so desire, although there is really not a huge advantage to doing so (unless you plan a Roth IRA conversion), because solo 401(k) fees are so low, especially at companies such as Vanguard, Fidelity, and www.401kbrokers.com.

Roth Solo 401(k)

This option became available in 2006. Like a Roth IRA, the Roth portion of the solo Roth 401(k) is an after-tax contribution, which then grows tax-free and allows for tax-free withdrawals in retirement. The employer contribution, however, is always traditional, meaning it has an up-front tax deduction and is taxed upon withdrawal in retirement. The income limits and contributions limits are otherwise exactly the same as with a solo 401(k), although you are effectively sheltering more money by using the solo Roth 401(k) than with the traditional solo 401(k). Vanguard, the mutual fund company favored by Bogleheads for its low costs, recently added the Roth option to its solo 401(k).

SEP-IRA

Prior to the advent of the solo 401(k), this account was the best way for a self-employed high-income earner to shelter income from taxes in a traditional manner. The maximum contributions are exactly the same as with the Solo 401(k) for a high-income earner, except that they come from the employer, not the employee. The result is that you actually need a higher income to max out a SEP-IRA than a Solo 401(k). In 2009, you need an income of $255K, $50K more than with a solo 401(k). When you also consider that SEP-IRAs have no Roth option, smaller catch-up contributions, and no option to take out a loan, there really is very little reason to choose a SEP-IRA over a Solo 401(k). SEP-IRAs used to be more available and significantly cheaper than a solo 401(k) plan, but that is really no longer the case, with companies such as www.401kbrokers.com and Vanguard entering the fray. A SEP-IRA can always be rolled over into a solo 401(k), of course, should you change your mind or want to switch from an existing SEP-IRA.

SIMPLE IRA

SIMPLE stands for Savings Incentive Match Plan for Employees. It was designed as a less-expensive, less-hassle alternative to a typical 401(k) for a small business (less than 100 employees). However, a solo 401(k) is so easy to use that there is little reason to use a SIMPLE IRA if you have no employees (or just a spouse as an employee). Compared with a solo 401(k), a SIMPLE IRA has a lower contribution limit ($11,500 in 2009), a lower catch-up contribution limit ($2,500 in 2009), higher fees, more paperwork, no Roth option, no loan option, and no ability to roll over a traditional or SEP-IRA into it. Like a 401(k), a SEP-IRA, or a solo 401(k), you can eventually roll over the money into a traditional IRA. Although a case can still be made for a small business to use a SIMPLE IRA, there is no reason for a sole proprietor to do so.

More IRAs

There are a few additional types of IRAs that are really just variations of the types already discussed. You are likely to encounter one or more of these along the path to retirement bliss. You should also know how to change your IRA from one custodian to another and understand the contribution limits of each type of IRA.

Spousal IRAs

Being a stay-at-home spouse does not preclude you from having an IRA. Spousal traditional or Roth IRAs require only a marriage certificate and sufficient income to make both contributions. If you are over age 50, you get the catch-up contribution, too!

Rollover IRAs

Many investors have IRAs even though they have never actually made an IRA contribution or inherited an IRA. Whenever you leave a job, you will usually want to roll over your 401(k), 403(b), 457, or other employer-based defined contribution retirement plan to an IRA. Although you lose the ability to take a loan from the savings (which a wise investor doesn't do anyway), you'll enjoy more freedom to choose investments and, almost always, significantly lower investing costs, while preserving the tax benefits. In fact, you should usually contribute even to a poorly designed 401(k) so that it can eventually be rolled over into your IRA. SIMPLE IRAs, SEP-IRAs, and solo 401(k)s can also be rolled over into an IRA, if you so desire. Although the benefits aren't necessarily as large, you can often save a few fees and simplify your finances by doing so.

To initiate an IRA rollover, you just need to contact the custodian (such as Vanguard or Fidelity) where you want to hold the IRA (or where you already hold your IRA) and fill out a couple of pages of paperwork. They'll do the rest.

Stretch (and Other Inherited) IRAs

If I told you there were a way to make your heir a millionaire for only $2,000 today, would you be interested? What if I told you I could also arrange for your descendants to be billionaires in just a few generations at the same time? It involves a completely legal inherited Roth IRA tax scheme called a stretch Roth IRA. Imagine an 18-year-old man who starts a Roth IRA with $2,000 today. He gets married at age 53 to someone 20 years his junior. He dies at 73 and leaves her his Roth IRA, which she lumps into her own. She dies 40 years later at age 93, and leaves the Roth IRA to her great-grandchild, who is 2 years old at the time of her death. The child begins taking the required minimum distributions, which at that age is just over 1 percent of the balance, much less than the amount the Roth IRA is likely to be growing each year, even after inflation. Assuming the child lives a long, healthy life (let's say age 95) and never withdraws more than the RMD, this IRA will have provided tax-free growth for 188 years, and he will *still* leave tax-free money for heirs. Assuming a 9 percent return, the original $2,000 would be worth $229,000 at the time of the man's death. When his wife dies, 40 years later, it would be worth $7.2 million. And 93 years later, this same IRA would have provided millions of dollars in distributions to the great-grandchild, who can leave further millions to his heirs. If he is able to invest the original IRA and reinvest the distributions at 8 percent, he could leave behind more than $9 billion. Now that's an estate tax problem.

When you combine the magic of compounding with tax-free growth and a healthy disinclination to spend, truly amazing things are possible, all for a mere $2,000. Of course, this assumes our country and its current tax laws are still around in 200 years, but even if the benefits are only a fraction of what I've illustrated here, it is still the investing deal of the century.

A traditional IRA can also be stretched, but it is much more difficult to leave a large sum of money behind because of the relatively large RMDs in the last few years of the original owner's lifetime. The pesky issue of your heir having to pay a large amount of taxes with each distribution also rears its ugly head. But you still get some tax-free growth for a large number of years. You should also note that you cannot convert an inherited traditional IRA to a Roth IRA, unless you inherited it from your spouse.

Health Savings Accounts (the Stealth IRA)

A health savings account (HSA) was originally designed to help people pay for medical care, but savvy investors use it as an extra IRA. You are eligible only if your health insurance is a high-deductible health plan that meets IRS rules. Contributions are deductible, just like a traditional IRA, and withdrawals are tax-free, just like a Roth IRA, if you use them for health care. Unlike a flexible spending account, the money does not have to be used up in that particular year. So if you don't spend it, it just keeps growing for decades. In retirement, you can use this money for health care, tax-free, or, after age 65, you can use it for anything, but you'll have to pay tax on it at your marginal tax rate, just like a traditional IRA.

Most HSA plans offer either mutual funds or a brokerage account. The 2009 contributions limits are $3,000 for an individual, $5,950 for a family, and an extra $1,000 if you are over 55. If eventually used to pay for health care, an HSA is better than a traditional or Roth IRA, because it eliminates not just three of the four taxable events discussed earlier, but all four of them! The benefit of tax-free growth is so great that you should preferentially pay for health care with current income or taxable savings to keep this money growing until retirement. Remember that if you itemize your taxes, any amount above 7.5 percent of your adjusted gross income (AGI) that you spend on health care qualifies for an additional tax deduction!

Nondeductible IRAs

If you make too much money to deduct a traditional IRA contribution, you should contribute the money to a Roth IRA. But if you make too much to contribute to either, you can still contribute to a nondeductible IRA. This is simply a traditional IRA without the initial tax break. Your money grows tax-free, and when you eventually withdraw the money, the earnings are taxed at your marginal tax rate. Your original contribution is not taxed again.

The paperwork to keep track of the tax basis (what you originally contributed) through the years can be a pain, and if tax-efficient investments such as stock index funds are held in the account, you may be paying your marginal tax rate on income that would have been taxed at the lower capital gains rate if you had used a taxable investment account instead.

It takes many years of tax-free growth to make up for that higher tax rate at withdrawal. Use a nondeductible IRA under only two circumstances: first, if you need more tax-protected space to hold tax-inefficient investments such as REITs or TIPS (see Chapter 10 for more on this subject) and second, if you plan to convert the nondeductible IRA to a Roth IRA in the near future.

ROTH IRA VERSUS TRADITIONAL IRA

Many investors, even knowledgeable and sophisticated ones, struggle with deciding whether to use a traditional or Roth IRA (or a traditional or Roth 401(k)). Although there are times when the decision is quite obvious, there are so many factors involved that it is sometimes impossible to predict which one will lead to greater tax savings over the years. Using *either* of them is likely to be significantly better than using a taxable investing account, and this difference will increase the longer the money stays in the IRA.

Will your marginal tax bracket be higher now or at the time when you withdraw the money from the retirement account in the future? If you are just starting your career and have a relatively low salary, you should favor paying taxes now while you're still in a low tax bracket by using a Roth IRA. On the other hand, a highly paid attorney at the peak of his career earnings curve will probably be in a lower tax bracket in retirement and should choose the traditional IRA. Although it is nearly impossible to know what Congress will do with the tax code a few decades from now, if you believe tax rates will be much higher in the future, then choose a Roth option and pay taxes now while rates are low, or vice versa if you believe tax rates will fall in the future. Also, if you are concerned that Congress will somehow change the law so Roth IRAs become taxable in the future (although I confess I feel this is unlikely), you should take your tax break now in the form of a traditional IRA.

Other considerations for making this decision include your ability to maximize contributions to the account, estate planning issues, tax diversification, and possible withdrawals. As mentioned earlier, a Roth IRA allows you to effectively shelter a larger percentage of your income from taxes because the contribution is made after tax. But if you cannot save enough to max out the account anyway, this is less of a consideration. If you are a low-income earner, eligible for a significant retirement savings credit, you will be required to save a lower percentage of your after-tax income to get the same amount of money as a tax credit if you use a traditional IRA.

You should also consider estate planning issues when choosing an IRA. It is possible to leave a lot more money to an heir via a Roth IRA than via a traditional IRA. Money that you intend to leave to heirs should be in a Roth IRA, if possible.

Tax diversification refers to a strategy that allows you to have less regret no matter what happens to your personal tax rate in the future. If taxes rise, you'll be glad you put some in a Roth. If you end up having less income than you thought (or if tax rates go down), you'll be glad you didn't pay all your taxes beforehand. By having some money in both traditional IRAs and Roth IRAs, you have the option of reducing your taxes by withdrawing from the traditional IRA only up to the amount that allows you to stay in the lower tax brackets, and then withdrawing any additional needed income from the Roth account.

Having both types of accounts also allows you to do traditional IRA to Roth IRA conversions (we'll get to these later) at a relatively low tax rate, if you stop working for a few years before you begin taking Social Security or pension payments. Last, if you need to withdraw some of your money from your IRA prior to retirement age, it is much easier to withdraw it from a Roth IRA, since the contributions can always be withdrawn without paying taxes or penalties.

IMPORTANT ADDITIONAL INFORMATION

Contribution Limits

Some types of IRAs have an income limit, and all IRAs have a contribution limit. These limits frequently change either on account of changes in law or because they are indexed to inflation, so check with the IRS or your tax adviser every year to stay up-to-date. Table 4.1 explains the 2009 income and contributions limits.

Roth Conversions

The best way to minimize RMDs is to take the money out of a traditional IRA prior to age 70. Of course, when you do this, you lose the benefit of tax-free growth unless you immediately roll over the money into a Roth IRA. Many fully or partially retired investors opt to convert part of their traditional IRA to a Roth IRA in an effort to lower their future RMDs. Although you have to pay taxes at your marginal tax rate on the money withdrawn from the traditional IRA (or equivalent), you will never pay taxes on it again. This tactic can be especially useful in a year where your earnings were particularly low. If you can convert your traditional IRA to a Roth IRA at the 10 percent or 15 percent rate now, but anticipate being in the 25 percent plus bracket later, you can see the wisdom in this move. Others choose to convert some of their IRAs to a Roth IRA in an effort to tax-diversify. They may have never had an income low enough to contribute to a Roth IRA in the past but want some of its benefits in the future.

Nondeductible IRA holders are also prime candidates for Roth IRA conversions. In fact, many high-income investors have been contributing to a nondeductible IRA for the last few years to take advantage of an upcoming change in tax law that allows high-income investors to do

TABLE 4.1 2008 IRA CONTRIBUTION LIMITS

	INCOME LIMIT	ANNUAL CONTRIBUTION LIMIT	CATCH-UP CONTRIBUTION (AGE 50+)
Traditional IRA	$53–63K single, $85–105K joint	$5K	$1,000
Roth IRA	$101–116K single, $159–169K joint	$5K	$1,000
Nondeductible IRA	No limit	$5K	$1,000
Inherited IRA	No limit	No contributions allowed	No contributions allowed
Rollover IRA	No limit	No contributions allowed	No contributions allowed
Roth IRA Conversion	$100K single/joint—No limit in 2010	No contributions allowed	No contributions allowed
Solo 401(k)	No limit	$49K	$5,500
Roth Solo 401(k)	No limit	$49K	$5,500
SEP-IRA	No limit	$49K	$1,000
SIMPLE IRA	No limit	$11K	$2,500
Health Savings Account	No limit	$3,000 Single, $5,950 Joint	$1K (Age 55+)

Source: U.S. Internal Revenue Service

a Roth conversion. It is, in essence, a back door into a Roth IRA. The tax paperwork for a nondeductible IRA can be substantial, but a planned Roth conversion can make it worthwhile.

Factors that should encourage you to do a Roth conversion include (a) not needing the money in the Roth for at least five years, (b) expecting to be in a higher bracket later, (c) meeting the MAGI limits now but not in the future, (d) having the ability to pay the additional tax out of current earnings or a taxable account, and (e) anticipating that you will never need to spend this money. Factors that should discourage you from doing a Roth conversion include (a) needing to pay the additional tax due out of the IRA, (b) the added income affects other items on your tax return because of the higher AGI (such as deduction phase-outs, exemptions, or tax credits), (c) expecting to be in a lower tax bracket later, and (d) fearing Congress will start taxing Roth IRAs despite current rules.

IRA Transfers

Some investors initially open an IRA at an institution with either high fees or poor investment choices and later realize the error of their ways. Luckily, you can easily correct this by contacting the institution (such as Vanguard) to which you plan to transfer the IRA, doing a couple of pages of paperwork, and letting them do the rest. IRA investments can be transferred in kind or liquidated (sold for cash) prior to transfer. But since there are no tax consequences to liquidating, you'll usually end up paying only a few small commissions and an exit fee to escape from the situation.

ADDITIONAL RESOURCES

* IRS Publication 590, the official copy of the rules on IRAs.
* IRS Publication 560, the IRS publication on retirement plans for small businesses.
* Bogleheads Wiki. This online resource has continuously updated pages on every subject in this chapter, as well as IRA distribution tables useful for determining your RMD. (See www.bogleheads.org, and click the Wiki link.)

CHAPTER SUMMARY

People are always looking for a legal tax shelter, and many people are missing out on one of the best by not contributing to an IRA. To truly minimize your taxes and maximize your newfound tax shelter, make sure you are choosing the right IRA for your needs. If you have low income, take advantage of the retirement savings credit to further increase your savings. You might even be eligible for an extra $1,000 return on your first $2,000 of retirement savings if your income is less than $30,000 per year!

CHAPTER FIVE

Defined Benefit Employer Retirement Account

The Finance Buff A.K.A. TFB

INTRODUCTION

Employer-sponsored retirement plans are divided into two types: defined benefit plans and defined contribution plans. Defined benefit (DB) plans provide a promised monthly benefit to employees at retirement. Defined contribution (DC) plans do not promise a specific benefit at retirement. Instead, contributions are made to individual accounts for the employees. An employee's benefit at retirement depends on the amount of those contributions and the investment gains and losses on the contributions.

The focus of this chapter is on defined benefit plans. Less than 40 percent of Americans in the private sector are covered. That is a stark decline from the 60 percent coverage 25 years ago. Nonetheless, DB plans still serve a very important role for the retirement security of millions of people. This chapter will show you what these DB plans are, how the benefits are determined, and how you should incorporate them into your retirement planning.

DEFINING DEFINED BENEFIT PLANS

A DB plan is commonly referred to as a pension plan. A DB plan is a program sponsored by an employer to provide income to employees when they retire. The income benefit is calculated according to a specific formula. The inputs to the formula typically include a salary history, years of service with the employer, age, and when benefits begin.

Here is an example: Acme Corporation's defined benefit plan provides 1.5 percent of the final salary for each year of service at age 65. Susan earned $50,000 a year before she retires at 65. She has worked for Acme for 40 years. Susan's retirement benefit is determined by a formula. After she retires, Susan will receive an annual pension of $30,000 from Acme's defined benefit plan ($50,000 × 1.5 percent × 40).

Defined contribution plans are discussed in detail in Chapter 6. For the sake of clarity in this chapter, a defined benefit plan is different from a defined contribution in that the DB plan life-long income benefit is a function of a formula, whereas the DC benefit is simply the total value of an employee's account at retirement, whatever that value happens to be. DC plans also typically pay a lump sum at retirement rather than an income benefit.

HOW DEFINED BENEFIT PLANS WORK

According to the Employee Benefit Research Institute, as of 2005, 37 percent of private-sector employees were covered by a DB plan. That number is down from 84 percent in 1979, but it still translates to more than 20 million active workers in the private sector. Typically, employers who sponsor a defined benefit plan are larger, more established companies in traditional industries.

If you are represented by a labor union or are employed in the public sector, you are more likely to be covered by a DB plan. The public sector includes federal and state governments, police, fire, and the military, public education, and county and local governments. If you work in a nonunion private-sector position, chances are you are not covered by a DB plan. Ask your employer's human resources department if you are not sure.

Private sector defined benefit plans must comply with the Employee Retirement Income Security Act of 1974 (ERISA) to qualify for favorable tax treatments. ERISA is a federal law that sets minimum standards for most voluntarily established pension and health plans in private industry to provide protection for individuals in these plans.

The law requires plans to provide participants with plan information including important information about plan features and funding, provides fiduciary responsibilities for those who manage and control plan assets, requires plans to establish a grievance and appeals process for participants to get benefits from their plans, and gives participants the right to sue for benefits and breaches of fiduciary duty.

The ground rules for all plans are set by ERISA, and those that comply are called qualified plans. The similarities between plans are due to ERISA requirements. While the outline of the plans can be similar, every plan is different because employers are given some freedom in how they can design their plan.

Benefit Determination

Most defined benefit plans give pension benefits based on your years of service. The longer you work for the employer, the higher your pension benefit. For each year of service, you earn a pension credit. The credit can be a fixed dollar amount or a percentage of your pay. For example, if a plan using the fixed dollar formula pays $500 per year of service, an employee with 40 years of service will receive $20,000 a year after retirement. Most plans, however, don't use the fixed dollar formula. They tie the pension benefit to your pay. The basic formula for most defined benefit plans is:

$$\text{Annual Retirement Benefit} = \text{Pay} \times \text{Benefit Percentage} \times \text{Years of Service}$$

Every component in the basic formula is rigorously defined in the plan rules. The pay in the formula can be defined in many different ways. It can mean your pay in the last year before you retire, the average pay of your final X years, the average pay over your entire tenure with the employer with or without adjustment for inflation, or the average of your highest pay in X years, typically three to five years.

The benefit percentage in the formula does not have to be flat. An employer can reward long-tenured employees with a graded benefit percentage: the more years of service, the higher the benefit percentage. Some plans are integrated with Social Security. For compensation over the Social Security wage base, where the Social Security tax stops, the benefit percentage can be higher. This is called permitted disparity. The current and historical numbers for the Social Security wage base can be found on the Social Security Administration's web site at www.ssa.gov.

The retirement benefit calculated by the formula is usually payable at a *normal retirement age,* which is typically age 65. If you retire early, you may have to wait until age 65 to collect your full pension, or you may choose to receive a reduced pension because you are collecting the benefits for more years. Some plans encourage early retirement by giving the full pension before age 65, if the employee meets a minimum years of service requirement.

The early retirement benefit can be integrated with Social Security, too. Some plans provide a supplement before age 62, when the retiree becomes eligible for Social Security. The idea is that with the supplement, retirees can receive a relatively stable income before and after they are eligible for Social Security.

Because of the way benefits accrue under the basic defined benefit formula, a defined benefit plan gives much higher benefits to long-tenured employees. An employee who works for several employers during his or her career, even if all the employers have identical defined benefit plans, would receive much less in benefits under all employers than what he or she would receive working for a single employer.

Finally, there is a completely different breed of defined benefit plans called cash balance plans. A cash balance plan is a defined benefit plan, but it goes by a formula that's similar to a defined contribution plan like a 401(k) or 403(b) plan. For each year the employee works for the employer, the employer promises the employee a certain amount, typically a percentage of pay, as a cash balance credit. The employer then credits interest to the cash balance at a predefined rate, for example, 5 percent or the 10-year Treasury yield. The retirement benefit is expressed as the sum of the cash balance credits over the years, plus accumulated interest. The formula is:

$$\text{Cash Balance at Retirement} = \text{cash balance credits} + \text{accumulated interest}$$

The promised cash balance and interest credits do not necessarily equal the assets held by the plan, so a cash balance plan falls under the defined benefit plan category.

Funding

A defined benefit plan in the private sector is typically funded entirely by the employer. The money in a defined benefit plan is placed in a trust account. The plan's assets are for the exclusive benefits of the plan participants. The trust is separate from the employer's other assets and is not subject to claims by the employer's creditors. If the employer runs into financial difficulties, it cannot take money from the pension plan assets. The plan's trustees and administrator are held to fiduciary responsibilities for the employees and retirees. They are responsible for managing the plan and investing the money.

Each year an actuary calculates the plan's projected liability and compares that with the plan's assets and their projected growth. That calculation determines the funding level of the plan. There are legal limits to the minimum required funding and the maximum allowed funding. The employer then contributes to the plan within the range between the minimum and the maximum.

The employer typically hires outside investment management companies to invest the plan's assets. Some plans' investments are managed in-house. The assets can be invested in almost anything, including stocks, bonds, real estate, and commodities. Unlike a 401(k) or 403(b) plan, employees and retirees do not control how the money in a defined benefit plan is invested because regardless of how the investments in the plan perform, the employer maintains the same promise to the employees. The employees' retirement benefit accrual does not depend on how well the investments do. If the plan invested poorly, the employer will have to come up with extra cash to meet the plan's minimum funding level. If the plan's investments do really well, then the employer does not have to contribute as much.

In addition to taking the investment risk, the employer with a defined benefit plan (except a cash balance plan) also takes the longevity risk. Because the promised retirement benefit is expressed as a sum of money paid out every year as long as the retiree lives, the pension plan has to keep paying. The retiree receives a lifetime income that never runs out. It is much more secure and easy to plan when you know you have a guaranteed income stream after you retire.

Vesting

Vesting refers to having a nonforfeitable right of receiving benefits from the plan. A defined benefit plan can require a minimum number of years of service before an employee is eligible to receive any benefit under the plan. If you leave the employer before you are vested, you will not receive any benefit from the defined benefit plan. ERISA imposes maximum vesting periods.

A plan qualified under ERISA has two choices for its vesting schedule. Under the first choice, the vesting schedule cannot be worse than a five-year cliff vesting schedule, shown in Table 5.1. Under this option, an

TABLE 5.1   FIVE-YEAR CLIFF VESTING

YEARS OF SERVICE	VESTED PERCENTAGE
Less than five	0%
Five or more	100%

TABLE 5.2   THREE- TO SEVEN-YEAR GRADUATED VESTING

YEARS OF SERVICE	VESTED PERCENTAGE
3	20%
4	40%
5	60%
6	80%
7	100%

employee is not eligible for any benefits before working a certain number of years in service (no more than five). Once you are vested in the plan, your accrued benefits under the plan cannot be taken back by the employer if you terminate.

The employer's second choice is a graduated vesting schedule. Graduated vesting is when an employee's benefits are vested over time, although no more than seven years. If the employer makes this choice, the vesting schedule cannot be worse than the vesting schedule shown in Table 5.2.

Receiving Benefits

The most common scenario for receiving benefits under a defined benefit plan is retiring from the employer, although there are also a few other ways to receive benefits before you retire. The benefit from a defined benefit plan is usually offered as an annuity that provides guaranteed income, year after year. There are several types of annuities. If you are married, the plan must offer you a choice of joint and survivor annuity, which provides a surviving spouse no less than 50 percent of the benefit. A joint and survivor annuity pays the benefit year after year until you die.

After you die, your surviving spouse also receives a percentage of your pension until he or she dies. A 50 percent joint and survivor annuity pays 50 percent of your pension to your surviving spouse. The plan may also offer a 75 percent or 100 percent joint and survivor annuity, which pays your surviving spouse 75 percent or 100 percent of your pension after you die, although the pension amount you receive while alive under a 75 percent or 100 percent joint and survivor annuity will be lower than what you would receive under a 50 percent joint and survivor annuity. If you are single, the plan typically offers a single life annuity that pays only you over your lifetime.

Some defined benefit retirement plans can include cost-of-living adjustments (COLA). In such cases, the benefit will increase with the cost of living after you start receiving your benefit. The COLA can be automatic, tied to a predefined index such as the Consumer Price Index (CPI), or it can be ad hoc, to be announced at the discretion of the employer or negotiated between the employer and a labor union. If your plan does not have a COLA, your pension benefit will be a fixed amount after you retire. The purchasing power of fixed benefits will be eroded over time by inflation.

Some defined benefit plans also offer retirees a choice of a lump sum payment or an annuity. If you choose a lump sum payment, you can roll the lump sum into an IRA and invest it on your own, potentially generating more retirement income than the annuity pays. However, you also run the risk of investing poorly and not generating as much income or, worse, running out of money. Which would you choose? That is a very complex and difficult question to answer.

To answer the question of whether to take a rollover or annuity payments, start by seeking quotes from insurance companies to determine what the lump sum can buy in the form of an annuity purchased outside of your employer. It makes sense to take the lump sum and purchase an annuity if you can purchase an annuity with a higher payout from an insurance company than you can receive from your retirement plan. Be sure to compare apples to apples, because the features of the annuity affect the annuity payout value. For example, a joint and survivorship annuity is different from a period certain annuity. Joint and survivorship means both you and your spouse receive payments as long as either of you are living. Period certain means the insurance company will guarantee payments for a fixed number of years, whether the recipient is living or not. You may want to use the service of a fee-only adviser to make this decision, as long as the adviser who helps you has no prospect of managing your lump sum. Otherwise, the adviser may be biased toward a lump sum.

Defined Benefit Contingencies

What if you quit, die, divorce, or become disabled before you retire? If you quit and you have already met the vesting requirement, you will have a deferred pension from your former employer. You may have to wait until you reach the normal retirement age (typically 65) or until you meet another early retirement milestone defined by the plan before you can collect your pension benefit. It may very well be 10 or 20 years from the time you left your former employer. Don't forget about your deferred pension!

A benefit may be payable to your surviving spouse if you are married but die before you retire. If you die after retirement eligibility, a plan typically will treat it as if you chose the default joint and survivorship annuity and then died immediately. The plan will then pay the survivorship benefit under the joint and survivorship annuity. If you died before meeting any early or normal retirement eligibility, your surviving spouse may have to wait until you would have met the early or normal retirement eligibility before collecting a survivor pension from your vested benefit. A defined benefit plan typically does not pay any benefit if you die while you are single.

Your pension benefit may become a part of your divorce settlement if you get divorced. The court must issue a qualified domestic relations order (QDRO), which stipulates how your benefits will be divided between you and your ex-spouse. Your pension plan then records the QDRO and follows it accordingly. You will probably have to wait until your ex-spouse is eligible to retire before you are eligible to receive a pension benefit from your ex-spouse's plan (more on this in Chapter 19).

If you become disabled while working for the employer, assuming you have long-term disability coverage, you will receive income under long-term disability. When you reach the normal retirement age, you then start receiving pension benefits from your defined benefit retirement plan. Some plans will calculate your years of service up to when you became disabled; some plans will credit you years of service as if you continued working at the same rate of pay.

Pension Guarantees

Your pension plays a very important role in your retirement planning, but how can you be sure it will be there when you need it? The employer can discontinue the defined benefit plan at any time. That does not mean you will lose the benefits you have accrued; however, you will stop accruing more benefits.

There are two layers of safety nets for the benefits you already earned. The first is the plan's assets, which are held in a trust, separate from the company's other assets. The plan's trust is a separate legal entity that holds assets for the plan participants. The employer is legally required to maintain the plan's funding level. If the employer goes out of business, the plan's assets are still available to provide the benefits the employer had promised.

What if the plan is underfunded when the employer terminates the plan or goes out of business? The second layer of safety net is a government agency called the Pension Benefit Guaranty Corporation (PBGC). PBGC collects insurance premiums for all defined benefit plans in the private sector. If a plan is terminated, PBGC takes over the liability of paying the plan benefits. However, this guarantee has a limit. The limit depends on when the plan is taken over by PBGC, your age, and whether the benefit is a straight-life annuity for a single person or a 50 percent joint and survivor annuity for a married couple. PBGC publishes the limits every year. For example, for plans terminated in 2009, the PBGC maximum guarantee for a 65-year-old is $4,500 a month for a straight-life annuity or $4,050 a month for a joint and survivor annuity, assuming the spouse is also 65 years old. The maximum guaranteed amounts for a 60-year-old are $2,925 and $2,632.50, respectively.

The maximum guaranteed amounts may be much less than what the participants had anticipated from their pension plan for participants with higher accrued benefits. If you are counting on your pension in your retirement planning, you must also take into consideration the possibility of the plan being discontinued by your employer or taken over by PBGC. The current PBGC maximum monthly guarantees can be found on PBGC's web site at www.pbgc.gov.

TRENDS IN PRIVATE-SECTOR DEFINED BENEFIT PLANS

Defined benefit plans in the private sector have been in decline in the last 30 years. The number of private-sector defined benefit plans dropped by almost two-thirds, from 148,000 in 1980 to 47,000 in 2004, according to the Employee Benefit Research Institute.

Few defined benefit plans are being created, and many more are being closed. Some employers with an existing plan are not offering it to new employees, while previously hired employees continue accruing benefits. Some employers froze their plan and do not allow existing employees to accrue more benefits. Some terminated their plan altogether. Some converted their plan to a cash balance plan. The motive behind these moves is usually cost savings.

A defined benefit plan is very expensive for the employer. If the plan's investments do not perform well, the employer has to make up the shortfall with additional contributions to the plan. That typically occurs at the same time the economy turns down and the employer's own business is not doing well. Often, retiree longevity assumptions are wrong, and they live longer. That creates a shortfall for future retirees. The pension plan must keep paying the monthly pensions for longer periods of time than the plan's actuary originally projected. Count yourself lucky if you still have a defined benefit plan, but also keep in mind that it may go away in the future.

PUBLIC-SECTOR PLANS

The trend for public-sector defined benefit plans is different than the decline in private-sector plans. Most public-sector employers still offer a defined benefit plan. However, a new trend is developing in the public sector to offer defined contribution plans in addition to, not in lieu of, defined benefit plans. That reduces the cost to the employer in the long term.

A key difference between public-sector defined benefit plans and private-sector defined benefit plans is that the public-sector plans are not covered by most provisions of ERISA. Public-sector employers do not pay taxes, so the federal government cannot induce them to design plans in a certain way in order to qualify for favorable tax treatment. Public-sector employers have more freedom in designing their plans, and there are large variations among public-sector plans. Many public-sector plans are created by legislation or ordinance. Changes to those plans are done through the legislative process.

Public-sector defined benefit plans are not insured by PBGC, the agency that insures private-sector defined benefit plans. Many think the public-sector plans are still safe because public-sector employers have taxing authority and the benefits are guaranteed by state or local laws and ordinances. However, that may not be true if the plans are underfunded. A recent study by two researchers at the National Bureau of Economic Research conservatively predicted that among all state pension plans, there is a 50 percent chance of aggregate underfunding greater than $750 billion and a 25 percent chance of at least $1.75 trillion. When public-sector employers cannot adequately fund the pension plans, they will need to increase taxes, require additional contributions from employees, cut benefits, or institute a combination of several solutions.

Federal Government Plans

The civilian employees of the federal government are primarily covered under two defined benefit plans. The Civil Service Retirement System (CSRS) covers employees hired through 1983, and the Federal Employees Retirement System (FERS) covers employees hired after 1983. CSRS participants are not covered by Social Security, whereas FERS participants are covered by Social Security. As a result, the benefits under CSRS are higher than those under FERS. Both CSRS and FERS provide postretirement cost-of-living adjustments, disability pensions, and survivorship benefits.

The retirement benefit under CSRS follows the basic formula:

$$\text{Annual Retirement Benefit} = \text{Pay} \times \text{Benefit Percentage} \times \text{Years of Service}$$

Pay in this equation is defined as the high-three average salary, which is the highest average basic pay earned during any three consecutive years of service. The benefit percentage is 1.5 percent for the first 5 years of service, 1.75 percent for the next 5 years of service, and 2.0 percent for years of service over 10. The normal retirement age under CSRS is 62 with 5 years of service, 60 with 20 years of service, or 55 with 30 years of service. There are special provisions for specialty occupations (air traffic controllers, law enforcement, and firefighters) and for employees who terminated employment because of major reorganizations. More information on CSRS can be found at the U.S. Office of Personnel Management's web site, www.opm.gov.

Participants are not covered by Social Security. However, if they become eligible for Social Security based on their spouse's work, their Social Security benefits may be reduced by up to two-thirds of their CSRS benefits. This is called government pension offset (GPO). You can find more information about GPO from Social Security Administration Publication 05-10007, available online at www.ssa.gov.

If CSRS participants become eligible for Social Security based on their work outside their federal government job, their Social Security benefits can also be reduced according to a complex table published by the Social Security Administration. This is called the windfall elimination provision (WEP). You can find more information about WEP from Social Security Administration Publication 05-10045, available online at www.ssa.gov.

The retirement benefit under FERS follows the same basic formula:

$$\text{Annual Retirement Benefit} = \text{Pay} \times \text{Benefit Percentage} \times \text{Years of Service}$$

Pay is also defined as the high-three average salary in the FERS formula. The benefit percentage is straight 1.0 percent unless you retire after age 62 with 20 or more years of service, in which case the benefit percentage becomes 1.1 percent. The normal retirement age is 62 with 5 years of service, age 60 with 20 years of service, or age 55–57 (depending on your year of birth) with 30 years of service. There are also special provisions for air traffic controllers, law enforcement, and firefighters. FERS participants who retire before they are eligible for Social Security may also receive a supplemental benefit until they become eligible. The U.S. Office of Personnel Management's web site about FERS is at www.opm.gov.

Career members of the military service are covered under two slightly different military retirement systems. You must serve at least 20 years in the military to become eligible for military retirement. The high-three system pays 2.5 percent of the highest three-year basic pay for each year of service. The REDUX system pays 2 percent for the first 20 years and 3.5 percent for years between 20 and 30, with the benefits adjusted back to the high-three system at age 62. In exchange for lower benefits before age 62 and a lower COLA rate, members who chose the REDUX system receive a $30,000 career status bonus at their 15th year of service (think of it as an advance from the pension). You can find more information about military pension benefits online at www.defenselink.mil.

State and Local Government Plans

According the Census Bureau, as of 2006, there were 2,654 state and local government retirement systems covering more than 18 million members and 7.3 million beneficiaries receiving monthly benefits. About 90 percent of these members and beneficiaries belonged to 221 state systems. Suffice it to say that each system has its own complex rules. Within each system, there can be hundreds of participating agencies using different benefit formulas. For example, California Public Employees' Retirement System (CalPERS) is one of the largest state employee retirement systems in the United States. It covered 1.6 million employees, retirees, and their families in 2008. Within CalPERS, there are 13 different benefit formulas and 57 optional contract provisions. Some employees receive 3 percent of their final pay for each year of their service at age 50. Other employees receive only 1.25 percent of their final pay for each year of service at age 65. It's impossible to generalize the benefits under state or local plans. If you are a member of a state or local retirement system, you should find out exactly how your plan works.

KNOW YOUR PLAN

If you are fortunate enough to be covered by a defined benefit plan, it's important to know exactly how you qualify for benefits so you do not lose what is due to you. If you work in the private sector, your employer is required by ERISA to provide you with a document called the summary plan description (SPD). The SPD is an important document that specifies in plain English how you accrue benefits, when you become vested, and how you will receive benefits under the plan. If you didn't keep the SPD your employer gave you when you first joined the company, you should ask for a new copy now and put it in your files.

Every time the plan is amended, your employer is required to send you another document, the summary of material modifications (SMM). File the SMMs together with the SPD. Read the SPD and SMMs, and try to understand what they say. Make an appointment with a human resources representative if you do not understand the documents, and ask them to explain the forms to you. If you work in the public sector, your employer usually has similar handbooks that describe the plan. Make sure you understand how the plan works.

After reviewing your SPD or benefits handbook, try to answer at least these questions:

* Are you already vested in your defined benefit plan?
* If you are not vested yet, when will you become vested?
* What is the earliest time you will become eligible for retirement benefits from your plan?
* How much will you receive if you retire at the earliest possible time?
* When will you become eligible for a full pension?
* How much will you receive if you retire with a full pension?
* How much more will you receive if you postpone your retirement after you become eligible for a full pension?
* How much less will you receive if you decide to retire early?
* Does your pension have a COLA? If yes, is it automatic or ad hoc?
* If you die before you retire, what does your plan provide to your survivors?
* If you die after you retire, what does your plan provide to your survivors?

If you find yourself unable to answer these questions, you will have to read your plan materials again or chat with a human resources person. Write those answers down. They will help you plan your retirement.

Your employer may also send you annual benefits statements. These statements show you how much you've already accrued in benefits. Because your date of hire and any changes to your employment status or position may be factors for determining what your retirement benefits will be, be sure to verify and document the relevant dates. Save all your W-2s because your compensation history is used in the retirement benefits calculation. Over the course of many years, it is possible that your employment or compensation records were misplaced or recorded incorrectly. If you have your own records, it will be much easier to verify whether your benefits are calculated correctly.

If you are thinking of leaving your employer before you are eligible to receive retirement benefits, you should take into consideration your retirement plan's vesting and benefit accrual schedule. If by staying a few more weeks or months, you can become vested in your pension benefit or accrue one more year of credited service, postponing your departure will mean a higher retirement benefit in the future. Because of the way benefits accrue in a defined benefit plan, leaving an employer when you are close to retirement will reduce your pension benefit by quite a bit. Make sure you take that into consideration when you make job change decisions.

If you are eligible for a deferred pension in the future from a former employer or from a divorced or deceased spouse's employer, be sure to keep the employer's contact address and phone number. Due to company mergers and acquisitions or perhaps even bankruptcy, it's likely the company's contact information will change. When you move, you should also notify the company. You've earned the pension. However small it may be, it's yours. Don't lose it.

ADDITIONAL RESOURCES

- U.S. Department of Labor, Employee Benefits Security Administration. *What You Should Know about Your Retirement Plan,* www.dol.gov. This booklet, published by the Department of Labor, helps answer the most common questions about private-sector retirement plans.
- U.S. Office of Personnel Management provides information on pension benefits for federal government employees at www.opm.gov.
- National Association of State Retirement Administrators at www .nasra.org. This nonprofit association of state public retirement

systems publishes surveys and reports on state public pension programs. Find them in the Resources and Research section of its web site.

* Employee Benefit Research Institute at www.ebri.org. This nonprofit, nonpartisan research and education organization publishes research data and issue briefs on the latest developments in employee benefits, including defined benefit pension plans.

CHAPTER SUMMARY

If you are a participant in a defined benefit pension plan, congratulations! You have a valuable benefit many Americans do not have. Hopefully, you now have a better understanding of how a defined benefit pension plan works. More important, you should understand specifically how your plan works and what you can expect to receive when you retire.

CHAPTER SIX

Defined Contribution Plans

Dan Kohn

INTRODUCTION

A defined contribution plan provides an individual account for each participant. The benefit received at retirement is determined by the contributions over time, the total return of the assets, and the fees the plan imposes. Contributions to a defined contribution plan can be made by the employer, the employee, or both, depending on the type of plan.

The most important benefit of a defined contribution plan is that it is a tax-advantaged account. You typically have money deducted pretax directly from your paycheck, after Social Security and Medicare are taken out. When you eventually withdraw money from the plan in retirement, you owe income taxes on the full amount you receive. The exception is a Roth 401(k), where after-tax money was contributed.

TYPES OF DEFINED CONTRIBUTION PLANS

Defined contribution plans include, but are not limited to, the following:

* 401(k), 403(b), 457, and TSP plans
* Profit-sharing plans
* Money purchase pension plans
* Target benefit plans
* Employee stock ownership plans

Basics about 401(k), 403(b), and TSP Plans

The 401(k), 403(b), and TSP plans are very similar. The 401(k) plans are usually offered by private business, 403(b) plans are offered to public education and nonprofit employees, and the thrift savings plan (TSP) is offered to federal government workers. The 401(k) plans, 403(b) plans, and TSP now have essentially identical contribution limits, withdrawal requirements, and other terms.

In a 401(k) plan, 403(b) plan, and TSP, employees select the funds they want to invest in from a list of options available in the plan. The employer may offer matching contributions for some or all of the employee's contribution.

Size and Matching

Table 6.1 lists the maximum contributions to defined contribution plans in 2009. These figures may adjust each year because of tax law changes and inflation. Check with your tax adviser to ensure you are not taking more than the maximum benefit.

TABLE 6.1 CONTRIBUTION LIMITS OF DEFINED CONTRIBUTION PLANS FOR 2009

	AGE 49 & BELOW	AGE 50 & ABOVE
Employee contribution to 401(k), 403(b), 457, or TSP	$16,500	$22,000
Maximum combined contribution of employee and employer across all plans	$49,000	$54,500

Source: U.S. Internal Revenue Service

The IRS limits for 401(k)-type plans allow contributions up to $16,500 ($22,000 if you're over 49) every year in a tax-deferred account. (That's the amount for 2009; it increases in $500 increments to match inflation.) This allows investment gains to compound year after year, and you pay taxes only when you withdraw the money.

Many employers offer matching funds for some amount of your investment, such as 50 percent of the first 4 percent of your salary that you contribute. The matches often vest over three or four years to encourage you not to switch jobs. Because it is essentially free money, 401(k) matching is one of the best investment options anywhere.

Although you're limited to employee 401(k) contributions of $16,500, your total defined contribution plan limits are $49,000 ($54,500 if you're over 49). You can reach this higher figure either with a 401(k) plan that offers a 200 percent match, by investing in a 457 plan as well as a 401(k), or through a defined contribution plan that also allows employer contributions.

Getting Your Full Match

If you plan to contribute the IRS maximum ($16,500 in 2009, or $22,000 if you are older than 49) to your 401(k) and you receive a match, be careful not to exceed the annual contribution limit before your final pay period, which could cause you to miss out on part of the match. Many employers pay matching funds spread out in all pay periods. Stopping your contributions by reaching the limit early in the year also stops matching contributions. As such, you can subtract the amount you've already contributed from $16,500 and divide the balance by the number of pay periods you have left in the year. This will maximize your annual contribution without forgoing a match.

Responsibility Is on the Employee

401(k)-type plans are always fully funded, which means you own the money as soon as it is deposited in your account. Your employer cannot decide to take it back. By contrast, with defined benefit pension plans, an employer's bankruptcy can affect your portion of the account even decades after your retirement. That can be devastating. When United Airlines went into Chapter 11 bankruptcy in 2005, some pilots and their widows had their payments cut by as much as 75 percent.

In 401(k)-type plans the employer is not responsible for funding and selecting investments in your account. You are. The responsibility lies with you. Employers can make the process much easier by offering low-cost funds and selecting prudent automatic investments for new employees who are not familiar with investment principles (see the following).

Rollovers

One of the great benefits of a 401(k)-type plan is your ability to take your money with you when you leave a company. Compared with traditional pension plans, 401(k)s are a better fit for the modern workplace, where most people will have 5 or 10 different employers over a career. With a 401(k), each time you leave a company, you can roll over your retirement account into an individual retirement account with no tax consequences. Unfortunately, a large number of 401(k) plans have truly atrocious investment options, with fees 10 or even 20 times higher than is reasonable. But even those plans are generally worth investing in, especially if you get a company match. They allow you to build up the tax-advantaged accounts that will dramatically improve your returns over the subsequent decades by enabling you to defer taxes or have your investments grow tax-free. Every time you switch jobs, you should generally roll over the full balance of the 401(k) into an IRA, as described in Chapter 4.

The 401(k) packet you receive from your employer when you start a new job may urge you to roll over your existing IRA or the 401(k) held with your previous employer into your new 401(k). This is rarely a good idea. With an IRA at a low-cost company like Vanguard, you can hold the Total Stock Market Fund for an expense ratio of 0.15 percent, or as low as 0.07 percent if you invest $100,000. Very few 401(k) plans offer such low-cost funds, so it is rarely a good idea to transfer money into them.

Cutting-Edge Features

The best-designed 401(k) plans leverage the latest behavioral economics research to nudge employees into making good choices. Unfortunately, well-designed plans are the exception because a vast majority of 401(k) plans today provide employees with a list of extremely confusing investment options. Worse, the funds selected by 401(k) providers tend to highlight past performance numbers, which are not at all predictive of future returns.

The Pensions Protection Act of 2006 encourages the use of what are called automatic 401(k) or autopilot 401(k) plans. This feature tries to leverage the inertia that many employees feel in making a saving decision. The strategy is to use the inertia in favor of saving, rather than against it.

In an automatic 401(k), new employees are automatically enrolled to invest a portion (often 3 percent or more) of their salaries into their 401(k). When they receive a raise or cost-of-living adjustment, some or all of the increase is automatically added to their 401(k) contribution rather than to their take-home paycheck. That way, employees feel like they are making the same or slightly higher income while their 401(k) contributions see a significant increase. Automatic 401(k) plans normally select a good default investment choice, such as a low-cost, age-appropriate target date fund.

Withdrawals

You can withdraw your 401(k) holdings without penalty at age 59½ or at age 55 if you leave your employer. Ordinary income taxes are due on all withdrawals.

Loans and Early Withdrawal

One advantage of a 401(k) over an IRA is your ability to take a loan from your 401(k) account for up to $50,000 and five years. Although this kind of loan is not recommended, it is superior to borrowing at credit card interest rates. If you do not repay the loan on schedule, or if you leave your employer prior to repaying the entire loan, it converts to an early withdrawal. Early withdrawals from a 401(k) incur a 10 percent penalty in addition to the ordinary income taxes due.

Opt Out

Finally, employees have the option to opt out at any time. The idea of an automatic 401(k) is to nudge employees toward good behavior rather than force them. The opt-out makes employees more comfortable about accepting the automatic increases in their savings rate.

401(k) Plan Issues

The basic problem with 401(k) plans is that the fund menu is selected by the employer, who often does an extraordinarily bad job. A whole industry of consultants is on hand to recommend expensive, actively traded mutual funds for the plans, often based on what has performed well recently. Many 401(k) plans offer no index funds at all or just a single, overpriced fund tracking the S&P 500. Expense ratios in many 401(k) choices are obscenely high. One to 2 percent is common, and some plans charge 3 percent or more, when all fees are taken into account. By contrast, Vanguard index funds are available for 0.2 percent or less, either through an IRA or through a reasonably administered 401(k) plan. The difference might not seem like much, but compounded over 20 years, this means that hundreds of thousands of dollars that should be available for your retirement instead went to overpriced fund companies.

It can be incredibly difficult to find out how high the fees are that you're actually paying. Although many plans provide the ticker symbols for their funds, they don't always list the additional fees (such as asset management fees) that they add on top of the fund charges. Many plans offer proprietary funds that have no ticker symbol, making them impossible to track through publicly available information. Your company's human resources staff has a legal obligation to provide you with information on your plan options, but all too often, they are not well informed and are overtaxed with other benefit issues.

Finally, most 401(k) plans are still designed with an overwhelming number of options. The default contribution level is generally zero, and the default fund selection is generally a money market account that probably won't even keep up with inflation. The automatic 401(k) has barely begun to be implemented.

403(b) Plan Issues

Some of the very worst plans seem to be 403(b) plans for teachers. For historic and completely obsolete reasons, these plans put funds inside expensive annuities. Since the 403(b) is already a tax-deferred account, adding an annuity wrapper adds cost without providing any additional tax-deferral value. Unfortunately, a large number of school districts have locked their teachers into selecting only between high-cost annuity providers.

The dominant 403(b) provider to colleges and universities, TIAA-CREF, is somewhat of an exception. The CREF mutual funds are a much better value than the high-priced annuities found elsewhere. Most important, TIAA-CREF does not lock in employees with surrender fees. However, their expense ratios are still generally two to three times what Vanguard offers for comparable funds. The web site http://403bwise.com offers detailed information on 403(b) plans, including how to lobby your school board for better plan options.

457 Plan Specifics

The 457 plans are a way for government and nonprofit employers to provide additional tax-deferred retirement opportunities, generally on top of an existing 401(k) or 403(b) plan. They allow early withdrawal without penalty but do not allow loans. In general, you should first contribute the maximum to your 401(k) and IRA. If you have more savings available and you qualify for a 457 plan offered by your employer, it is a great alternative to saving in a taxable account. The maximum allowable contribution is $16,500, which is in addition to the $16,500 that can be contributed to a 401(k) or 403(b).

457 Plan Issues

Many 457 plans have problems similar to the 401(k) and 403(b) issues. Specifically, it can be difficult to find out how high the fees are that you're actually paying, the investment choices are poor or limited, and some plans put funds inside expensive annuities. Many 457 plans offer no index funds or just one high-cost fund that tracks the S&P 500. If you find yourself in a bad plan, contact the trustees and state your discontent.

Federal Thrift Savings Plan (TSP) Specifics

The federal thrift savings plan, or TSP, is a retirement savings plan for civilians who are, or previously were, employed by the U.S. government and for members of the uniformed services. The TSP encompasses many millions of investors and has substantial assets.

The TSP is a defined contribution plan administered by the Federal Retirement Thrift Investment Board. In most ways, the TSP closely resembles the dynamics of 401(k) plans. The retirement assets derived from a TSP account depend on how much has been contributed to the account (both by the employee and, if applicable, his or her agency) during the account holder's working years and the earnings on those contributions. The government makes automatic and matching contributions for certain Federal Employee Retirement System (FERS) civilian employees, based on the employee's contributions. The FERS employees receive two different types of contributions: automatic contributions and matching contributions. The government automatically contributes 1 percent of basic pay to the TSP for each employee. In addition, for employees contributing their own money to the plan, the government contributes matching funds for the first 5 percent of pay each pay period. Contributions are matched dollar for dollar on the first 3 percent of pay and 50 cents on the dollar for the next 2 percent of pay.

Employees under the CSRS (Civil Service Retirement System) may participate in the TSP but are not eligible for matching contributions. Military members are generally not eligible for matching contributions.

The government did nearly everything right in developing this offering. They provide indexed funds covering domestic stocks (large and small), international stocks, and bonds. They have target retirement offerings that they call lifecycle (L) funds. These funds let investors make a single selection that automatically rebalances and adjusts their holdings to become more conservative over time. But most important, the government leveraged the fact that they have the largest retirement plan in the world to negotiate the very lowest fees anywhere. The fees for TSP funds are 0.015 percent; some 401(k) plans make their employees pay 200 times more. The fees are the lowest available to any retail investor and actually lower than what many huge institutions pay to invest their money.

Roth 401(k)

One option that is beginning to appear in some plans is a Roth 401(k). Like the difference between a traditional IRA and a Roth IRA, a Roth 401(k) lets you invest after-tax money. One big advantage is that $16,500 in after-tax money is equivalent to $22,000 in pretax money if you're in the 25 percent tax bracket. So, a Roth 401(k) lets you save much more in a tax-advantaged account. Roth 401(k)s are particularly well suited to younger workers who are currently in a low tax bracket but expect to be in a higher bracket at retirement.

However, it's impossible to know what marginal tax rates will be in retirement, since Congress has consistently changed the laws every few years. Also, a Roth 401(k) is taxed at your (high) marginal rate today, whereas a traditional 401(k) will be taxed at your (lower) average rate when you retire. Since there are so many unknowns, one reasonable approach is to split your savings 50/50 between a traditional IRA and a Roth 401(k). However, if you are already in a higher tax bracket, you should probably skip the Roth 401(k).

Also, if you are close to the Roth IRA cutoff limits, the traditional 401(k) may be a better option. The Roth 401(k) does not reduce your taxable income, possibly pushing you over the limits and preventing Roth IRA contributions. By contributing to the traditional 401(k), you reduce your taxable income.

OTHER DEFINED CONTRIBUTION PLANS
Profit-Sharing Plans

A profit-sharing plan is an incentive-based compensation program designed to reward employees by giving them a percentage of the company's profits. It can be a company's only retirement plan, or it can be offered in addition to a 401(k) or other plan. Some plans let you manage your own account, but most select the investments for you.

You have access to the money after a fixed number of years or when you leave employment. Both the contributions and the returns you earn are tax-deferred until you withdraw the money. When you leave employment, you can roll over the money to an IRA to preserve the tax-deferred status of the money.

The big advantage of profit-sharing plans is that they provide a way for a company to make substantial tax-advantaged payments to employees when the business is doing well. For 2009, these contributions can be as high as $49,000 or 25 percent of your salary, whichever is lower.

If you are able to manage the money in your account, treat it like a 401(k) plan and select the best (or least bad) investment choice. If your employer invests the money for you, you have no control but should still understand how your employer invests the money and take it into account when building the portfolio that you control.

Age-Based Profit-Sharing Plan

An age-based profit-sharing plan uses both age and compensation as a basis for allocating employer contributions among plan participants. All of the basic requirements that apply to profit-sharing plans also apply to age-based plans. This type of plan typically has a contribution formula that gives the employer flexibility over the amount of the contribution to be made each year. Since age is a primary factor in the contribution amount, age-based plans tend to favor older employees who have fewer years to accumulate assets for retirement.

Money Purchase Pension Plans

A money purchase pension plan is a defined contribution plan where your employer's contributions are mandatory. It works like a profit-sharing plan, except that your employer can owe a penalty tax if it doesn't make the required contribution. Like other defined contribution plans, the amount of retirement benefits for employees is based on the amount in the participant's account at the time of retirement.

Employers normally must make contributions to a money purchase pension plan regardless of profitability, although there are generally no unfavorable consequences to the employer if contributions stop completely. However, if the employer desires to maintain a money purchase pension plan in the future and start making contributions again, failure to make a contribution continuously could result in the imposition of a penalty tax on the years when contributions were not made. Consult your tax advisor if you have questions about an existing plan.

Target Benefit Plan

A target benefit plan is a defined contribution plan that has similarities to a defined benefit plan. The target benefit is the equivalent of a pension in a defined benefit plan. Your employer makes annual contributions based on a formula that would be sufficient to provide the target benefit, assuming an interest rate and other actuarial inputs.

Unlike defined benefit plans, money allocated to your target benefit plan is not pooled among employees. It is yours. However, if the assumptions used provide more or less money than needed for the target benefit, the result is that you receive more or less than the target benefit. So, you, not your employer, bear the consequences if your investments do not perform as well as expected.

Target benefit plans are similar to money purchase pension plans, except rather than a fixed amount based on your compensation, a target benefit plan provides contributions with the goal of providing a fixed benefit. This favors older employees, who have less time to have their benefits funded.

Employee Stock Ownership Plan

An employee stock ownership plan (ESOP) is a defined contribution plan (or a part of one) designed to invest primarily in the stock of the employer. If you participate in an ESOP, it is essential that you diversify away from company stock as quickly as possible. Many employees of large firms hold their employer's stock in an ESOP or in their regular 401(k). This is a mistake. There is a high probability that employees will lose all those savings if the company goes bankrupt. Since your personal financial risk of a layoff is already highly correlated with the fate of your employer, you need to diversify your retirement portfolio. These risks are even greater when a private company uses an ESOP, since diversification of private shares can be much more challenging.

MANAGING YOUR ACCOUNT
Investing a Self-Directed Account

Some people have great difficulty in trying to manage their own portfolio. This section should help you get started.

The best way to begin evaluating what fund(s) you should hold in your self-directed 401(k), 403(b), or TSP is to sort the options by expense ratio and look for the least expensive funds. If you have access to low-cost target retirement options and all of your investments are in tax-deferred accounts, just choose the appropriate age-based target retirement fund. If you have a TSP account, just choose the L fund with the date closest to your planned retirement.

If you have a taxable account as well, you'll probably want to invest in the lowest cost intermediate-term bond fund in your plan. That is, most investors should begin by placing tax-inefficient bonds in their plans and IRAs, so that they can put tax-efficient equity funds in their taxable account.

You should look for a bond fund that targets the Barclays Capital Aggregate Bond Index (formerly known as the Lehman Aggregate Index). Vanguard's Total Bond Market fund tracks this index, which represents a good mix of investment-grade, intermediate-term bonds. Funds that hold short-term or intermediate-term Treasury Inflation-Protected Securities (TIPS) are also good bond holdings. Finally, PIMCO Total Return is a well-regarded, reasonably priced bond fund that's offered in many plans. If your plan offers Fidelity funds, stick to the Spartan funds or the Four-in-One, which are indexed funds with costs comparable to Vanguard's.

If you're selecting bond funds from the TSP, you should use the G fund (rather than the F fund) for most of your bond holdings. Although the F fund is a great option (it tracks the Barclays Index previously mentioned), it can't compare with the G fund, which offers an unrivaled value proposition:

- The G Fund is invested in risk-free Treasury securities.
- The yield is reset monthly to reflect longer-term Treasury yields.
- Like a money market, and unlike Treasuries, its price never goes down.
- Because the G Fund resets interest monthly, it provides some inflation protection.

If you are unlucky enough to have only high-cost options, your lowest-cost fund will probably be one that tracks the S&P 500. You can start with that and build the rest of your portfolio around it.

Some plans offer windows to allow you to purchase any stock or mutual fund, not just the ones on the preapproved menu. In principle, this could make a plan as flexible as an IRA and provide an alternative to expensive, actively traded funds. In practice, most fund windows are a gimmick. The problem is that the fees associated with using the window are so high that they make the overpriced fund menu options look appealing. If you do use the window, it may be most cost-effective to allocate your plan contributions to a money market or stable value fund and then just make your purchases using the fund window once or twice a year to minimize transaction fees.

If you are able to purchase any stock, exchange traded funds (ETFs) offer a low-cost way to hold the entire world's stock markets and track the bond markets. The lowest-cost ETFs are Vanguard Total Stock Market ETF (VTI), Vanguard's FTSE All-World ex-US ETF (VEU), Vanguard Total Bond Market (BND), and SPDR Barclays Capital TIPS (IPE). Those four ETFs can satisfy the complete needs of many investors' portfolios, but only if they're available at a reasonable cost.

What to Do about Poor Investment Options

When I became responsible for a 401(k) plan as a result of a company merger, I learned just how bad many defined contribution plans can be. Employees of our small firm were paying tens of thousands of dollars per year in unnecessary fees. Each employee would have 17 percent less money in 20 years under that plan than in a more reasonable plan built around low-cost mutual funds. Assuming the maximum contribution for 20 years, switching to a better plan would mean an additional $200,000 for each employee (including me!) in retirement. Needless to say, I switched our plans.

Unfortunately, there is no reliable process to convince your employer to switch to a better 401(k) plan. The 401(k) industry is rife with shady dealings and payoffs that drain away part of your retirement savings each year. The common practice of revenue sharing (a type of kickback) means that fund companies pay record keepers, administrators, and advisers a portion of their fees. The kickbacks create a disincentive to recommend switching to a better, lower-cost plan.

What's so strange about bad plans is that the plan trustees (often the chief operating officer and vice president of human resources) are stuck paying the same high fees for their investments as well. There are much better options available, and switching costs are not very high. Unfortunately, very few 401(k) trustees like to be told how bad their plans are. You can write a letter and get your coworkers to sign on, but your managers may not be happy with you for doing so.

More information on getting your employer to improve its plan is available at the Bogleheads Wiki, www.bogleheads.org.

ADDITIONAL RESOURCES

- The Bogleheads Wiki at www.bogleheads.org has information on all defined contribution plans.
- Vanguard offers a 403(b)(7) plan; see https://personal.vanguard.com.
- Employee Fiduciary at www.employeefiduciary.com administers the lowest-cost 401(k) plans available to small and medium businesses.

CHAPTER SUMMARY

A defined contribution plan provides each participant benefits based on the contributions of you and your employer over time, the total return on the assets, and the fees the plan imposes. Contributions to a defined contribution plan can be made by the employer, the employee, or both, depending on the type of plan.

There are many different types of defined contribution plans. The most common are profit-sharing plans, money purchase pension plans, target benefit plans, employee stock ownership plans (ESOPs), and 401(k) type plans. Each plan has unique features that employees should understand.

A 401(k)-type plan lets you divert a portion of your paycheck to a tax-advantaged retirement account. Your employer may match a portion of your investment, and you should always take advantage of the match. When you switch employers, you can roll over your defined contribution account into an IRA that gives you complete control of the funds you want to use.

CHAPTER SEVEN

Single-Premium Immediate Annuities

Dan Smith A.K.A. Dpbsmith

INTRODUCTION

A fixed single-premium immediate annuity (SPIA) can pay you and your significant other an income for life. That helps solve the problem of how to budget for retirement when you do not know how long retirement will last. Payouts are set by contract and, like a traditional pension, do not fluctuate, making retirement planning a little easier. Payouts are significantly higher than you can obtain from any comparably safe investment because part of your monthly payment includes a return of part of your principal.

An SPIA is a pure insurance product and provides protection against outliving your portfolio. The amount of money you receive is not connected to the stock market or any other investment, like a variable annuity or an equity-indexed annuity. With a SPIA, there is a risk that the insurer might fail, and that risk should not be ignored when you are choosing a carrier. If the insurer fails, state guaranty associations will provide some protection, but that protection is limited.

SPIA BASICS

The word *annuity* means any regular series of payments, and many different financial products are called annuities. This chapter is about life annuities, a kind of insurance product that works like your own private pension and pays you—and, often, a joint annuitant—income for as long as you live. It is not about the high-cost investment products called variable annuities or equity-indexed annuities, which are products to be avoided. Life annuities, on the other hand, solve the problem of how to budget for a lifetime when you do not know how long you will live. If you rely only on your personal investments, you must budget for the possibility that you could live beyond age 100. You cannot budget for your average life expectancy, but an insurance company can.

Single-premium immediate annuities are also known as life annuity products, lifetime payout income annuities, fixed immediate annuities, and immediate income annuities. You purchase an SPIA for a lump sum of money (the single premium), and the insurance company agrees to make regular monthly payments to you for the rest of your life. It is like buying your own private pension.

The terms of an SPIA are a contract with an insurance carrier to make specified payments. These payments do not fluctuate, except in the case of an inflation-adjusted annuity, where the fixed payment adjusts to the inflation rate. The income is as safe as the claims-paying ability of the insurer. State guaranty associations provide a limited safety net in case the insurer runs into financial trouble.

Table 7.1 shows a sample payout rate for a single premium of $100,000 for a husband and wife (joint annuities) of the same age.

These payouts look attractive compared with bond or CD interest rates. The reason they are high is that the payouts are not interest only. Part of the payment is the premium being returned to you. Since the payments continue for only the life of the annuitants, it is quite possible that if you die young, the total amount paid out will be less than the original premium. Your heirs do not collect the remaining premium. In contrast, you can collect much more than your premium if you live a long time. Thus, with an SPIA you accept the risk of losing money that you do not need in exchange for getting extra money when you do need it.

Single-premium immediate annuities are a form of insurance. You give the insurance company enough money to make regular payments back to you over a period corresponding to your *average* life expectancy. The insurance company then makes regular payments to you for your *actual* lifetime, which may be more or less than the average. Think of an SPIA as insurance against the possibility of running out of money, should

TABLE 7.1 SAMPLE ANNUAL PAYOUT, $100,000 PREMIUM FOR A 60-YEAR-OLD COUPLE, 2009

Age of Couple	Annual Payout as a Percent of Premium	Monthly Payout	Year of Birth
60	6.56%	$546.44	1949
65	7.08%	$590.39	1944
70	7.83%	$652.43	1939
75	8.88%	$740.14	1934
80	9.90%	$825.26	1929
85	11.71%	$975.49	1924
89	13.29%	$1,107.72	1920

you be fortunate and need to fund a retirement lasting longer than you expected.

Most retirees in the United States receive longevity insurance in the form of Social Security. But fewer and fewer of us have longevity insurance in the form of traditional defined benefit pensions (see Chapter 5). An annuity allows you to create your own defined benefit pension. A risk-averse person who faces uncertainty about length of life should consider this option, yet most studies show that few consumers voluntarily annuitize their retirement savings.

If you can support yourself entirely from the interest and dividends from your portfolio without invading the principal, then you do not need to think about an SPIA. But if your portfolio is only large enough to take care of you comfortably for your expected life span and not large enough to stretch the range of your possible longevity, then you should consider whether SPIAs deserve a place in your retirement planning toolkit. When comparing annuities with other options, consider these decision factors:

Weighing in Favor	Weighing Against
Lower retirement savings	Higher retirement savings
Not concerned with money going to heirs	Important to leave money to heirs
Concerned about financial independence if very long-lived	Willing to accept help in very late life if needed
Risk-averse	Risk-tolerant

(Continued)

WEIGHING IN FAVOR	WEIGHING AGAINST
Older age	Younger age
Good health with family history of longevity	Poor health (unless medical underwriting can be obtained)
Willing to commit money irrevocably	Unwilling to lose control of money
Willing to trust an insurance company	Skeptical about insurance companies
Expect 10-year Treasury interest rates to fall in future	Expect 10-year Treasury interest rates to rise in future
Main concern: how many dollars a month will I get?	Main concern: how many dollars total will I get back over my lifetime?

HOW ANNUITIES WORK

The premiums that you and everyone else who bought an annuity paid are pooled together and managed by the insurance company. The insurance company grows the pool by investing it, makes payments to everyone who has paid in, and pays themselves for management and administration. Thus, there are four different stakeholders in your decision.

1. You (and often a joint annuitant), because it is your premium being committed, and you who will receive payments
2. The insurance company, which takes full control of the premium, invests it, redistributes it to you and other annuitants, and is paid for doing so
3. Other people who have bought annuities at the same time, because, to a large extent, the extra payments that must be made to the longer-lived annuitants come from money the shorter-lived annuitants contributed and didn't receive back
4. Your estate, because if you are a shorter-lived annuitant, your remaining premiums are used to fund payments to longer-lived annuitants instead of becoming part of your estate

The payouts from an annuity come from three sources:

1. Your premium being paid back to you. It is prorated over your life expectancy and makes up a percentage of each payment you receive.
2. Interest on your principal, which the insurer earns by investing the pool of money in the sorts of safe investments insurers are allowed to invest in.
3. Unused portions of premiums from shorter-lived annuitants, which are used to fund the extra payments needed by longer-lived annuitants.

This leads to several conclusions about annuities. First, they pit your interest against the interest of your heirs. Annuities are the ultimate die-broke strategy. They allow you to spend more per month and insure you against outliving your money, even if you live to be 105, but they leave nothing for the estate if you die soon after buying the annuity. (However, see the discussion of guaranteed periods and premium refunds later in this chapter.)

Second, the advantage of an annuity—that the fortunate people who enjoy a long retirement get more than they put in—is paid for by the unfortunate people who do not and who get back less than they paid in. From a consumption standpoint, annuities are viewed as valuable insurance because they guarantee a certain income, but from an investment standpoint, annuities are a risky asset because the payoff depends on an uncertain date of death and the health of the insurance company in the future. If you think about monthly income that you cannot outlive, annuities look great. But if you think about dollars paid in versus dollars paid out, annuities look uncertain.

Third, because the insurance is charging a hidden load, annuities are actuarially unfair; when adjusted for the time value of money, if you choose to regard it as a bet between you and the insurance company as to how long you are going to live, on average the insurance company is always going to win. This should not necessarily be an objection, any more than it is with any other kind of insurance.

The Annuity Wineglass Analogy

Imagine two similar neighboring islands, Decima and Lachesis, where the inflation rate and the interest rate are 0 percent. Every year, on each island, 1,000 islanders reach their retirement age of 50, and need $20,000 a year in retirement. Where Decima and Lachesis differ is in their mortality statistics. In Decima, everyone lives exactly 100 years. (Whether this is a happy situation is a matter for philosophers, but it certainly simplifies retirement planning.) In Lachesis, the mortality statistics are just like ours.

How much money does it take to support the two populations in retirement? Figure 7.1 takes its cue from Omar Khayyám's metaphor of a Cup of Life filled with the Wine of Life.

The glass on the left in Figure 7.1 represents Decima. The width of the glass represents the number of people surviving at age 50, 60, 70, and so forth. The glass is equally wide all the way down, and represents the same number of people—1,000—at age 50, 60, 70, and so forth.

F I G U R E **7.1**   T H E W I N E O F L I F E

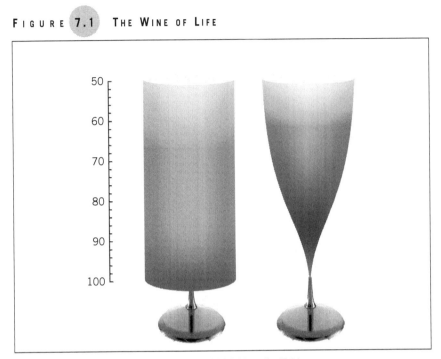

Source: Commissioner's Standard Ordinary 2001 Mortality Table

The glass on the right in Figure 7.1 represents Lachesis. The number of people surviving decreases with age, so the glass tapers. The diagram is based on the Commissioner's Standard Ordinary 2001 Mortality Table for females; the linear width shown on the page has been made proportional to the survivorship curve, despite the three-dimensional appearance.

The total amount of money needed to fund retirement on each island is represented by the amount of liquid needed to fill the glass. In Decima, everyone knows that they will live 100 years, and filling the glass requires 50 years worth of income for 1,000 retirees, a total of $1 billion—$1 million per Deciman.

In Lachesis, some live to be 60, fewer to age 70, fewer to age 80, and so forth. The glass tapers. The average retiring Deciman will live another 50 years, but the average retiring Lachesian will live only 30. It takes only about 60 percent as much wine to fill the Lachesian glass, or $600 million total—$600,000 per Lachesian.

Here is where annuitization comes in. Each Lachesian can choose to go it alone or join a pool of annuitants. If they decide to annuitize, each of them can pay $600,000 to some agency—a private insurer, perhaps—who will have enough to fill the glass and fund every retiree for life.

What if a group of Lachesians does not want to give up the control of their money and prefers to manage each of their individual savings separately? Then they face the same dilemma a real-life retiree faces. Each of them will need more than $600,000. Only some of them will live past age 80, but none of them knows who it will be. Any one of them could live to 100, so every one of them needs to set aside $1 million, just as in Decima.

A Lachesian who has $1 million could well decide not to annuitize, because if she lives only to, say, age 80 and uses only $600,000, then the extra $400,000 will go to her children instead of staying in the wineglass to fund the payouts for other annuitants. But a Lachesian with $600,000 is faced with the prospect of holding back and using only $12,000 dollars a year instead of the $20,000 she needs, even though on the average her $600,000 savings should be enough. By annuitizing, she raises the amount she can safely spend by $8,000 per year. The annuity pays her 67 percent more than she could spend by relying on her savings. This is not interest, because the interest rate in Lachesis is 0 percent, and it is not an investment yield—but it is just as useful in paying the monthly bills as if it were.

SPIA Choices and Options

There are some wonderful tools available online for understanding and exploring SPIA options. Time spent on these web pages is time well spent, regardless of whether or where you choose to buy an SPIA. Berkshire Hathaway's BRK Direct offers one good choice. Vanguard annuity experts who can provide information and quotes are available at 800-462-2391.

Any quote system you use will ask for certain facts about your situation. There are several factors that will influence the amount you would receive monthly. This section highlights some of those factors.

Gender

Gender affects annuity premiums because women live longer, on average. For a 65-year-old man or woman, the same $1,000/month annuity costs $132,321 or $143,109, respectively, or more than 8 percent more for the woman. Couples usually opt for a joint annuity, which pays out as long as either member of the couple survives; in this case, the premium rises to $158,002.

Medical Underwriting

Existing medical conditions that may measurably shorten your life expectancy would cause you to overpay for an annuity you bought based on normal life expectancy. You should seek out insurers that offer medical underwriting. This option offers a reduced premium in exchange for proof of reduced life expectancy. Medical underwriting generally covers serious conditions like cancer, heart disease, and multiple sclerosis. Of course, you need to provide proof of the medical condition to the insurer.

One Boglehead who applied for medical underwriting with AIG found the procedure to be straightforward. She received an impaired-risk letter offering a rated age one year older than her real age and received about a 2.5 percent reduction on a $100,000 premium.

Qualified versus Unqualified Investment

An SPIA can be bought with after-tax dollars (unqualified) funds, or it can be bought with dollars that are in a qualified tax-advantaged retirement account, such as a 401(k), profit sharing plan, and traditional IRA. If you use money from a tax-advantaged retirement account, you would usually opt to buy what is called a qualified SPIA. Buying an SPIA with qualified money is like doing an IRA rollover. The premium money passes directly from the current custodian to the insurance company. You will not owe income tax on money withdrawn and transferred from the retirement account directly into an SPIA. Withdrawing money from a qualified plan and taking personal possession of it before you buy an SPIA could have serious tax consequences. Speak with your tax adviser.

A qualified SPIA distribution is considered to meet the required minimum distribution (RMD) for that portion of a qualified plan. However, distributions from nonqualified SPIAs are not part of your IRA RMD. Check with your tax adviser when confusion arises about what is taxable and what is not.

Single versus Joint

A single life annuity provides payments for the lifetime of a single individual. The annuity payments stop when the annuitant passes away. That works for a single person.

Most couples would probably opt for a joint annuity. A joint annuity names two annuitants and provides payments for as long as either of them is alive. Joint annuities commonly offer the option of reducing payments when only one of the annuitants is still living. Naturally, reducing payments reduces the premium. For example, one quotation for $1,000 per month for a 65-year-old couple shows that electing a two-thirds benefit to the survivor reduces the premium by 8.5 percent.

If your analysis shows one person can live more cheaply than two, and you want to lower your premium by buying no more than you and your joint annuitant need, then you might consider electing such an option. Figure 7.2 illustrates the benefit reduction for a two-thirds benefit election.

FIGURE **7.2** BENEFIT REDUCTION FOR A SURVIVOR

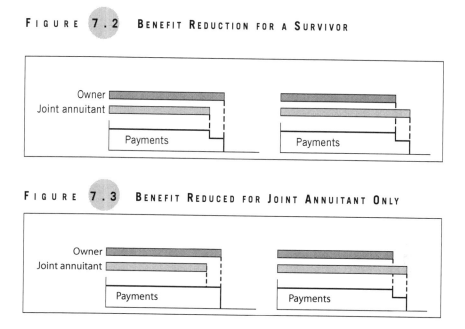

FIGURE **7.3** BENEFIT REDUCED FOR JOINT ANNUITANT ONLY

Or this option can mean that payments are reduced only when the survivor is the joint annuitant but not if the survivor is the annuity owner—a seemingly unfair situation. If you consider this option, be sure you understand what your insurer means by it. See Figure 7.3 for a visual reference.

If you were planning to buy separate annuities in your name and your spouse's name, perhaps to maximize Guaranty Association protection, it might be worth observing that you can create your own custom reduced-survivor benefit by combining annuities. For example, a joint SPIA paying $400 per month with no reduction, plus a single-life annuity paying $300 per month to you, plus a single-life annuity paying $300 per month to your spouse, equals $1,000 per month with 70 percent benefit to either survivor.

Guaranteed Periods and Premium Refunds

In a basic SPIA, payments continue only while you live. In the case of a joint annuity, payments continue as long as either annuitant lives. If you bought a single-life annuity and you die the day after your first annuity payment arrives, that first payment is the only payment you get. The insurance company keeps the rest of the premium. This is not as big a windfall as it sounds because it is expected to happen on occasion, and that premium is needed to fund payouts to other annuitants.

You could opt for a guaranteed period. This option is also called a period certain or term certain. It guarantees a certain number of payments to your heirs if you die. For example, if you choose a 10-year guaranteed period, payments continue to your heirs until 10 years of payments are made. The payments are made to the annuitants' named beneficiaries or estate. Another similar option is known as premium refund or guaranteed minimum payment, which provides for payments to continue until an amount equal to the original premium has been paid out. A short guaranteed period does not cost very much and provides some peace of mind regarding the possibility of wasting most of the money spent on the annuity.

When exploring the effect of a guaranteed period, ask for quotations that provide identical payouts and compare the premiums. You can say that a five-year guarantee period reduces a $1,000 monthly payout by $14 a month, or you can say that it adds $1,800 to the cost of the annuity. These amount to the same thing—a 1.4 percent difference—but considering it in relation to the premium shows you the total number of dollars that are really at stake. Opt for a guaranteed period if you want one. But be aware that it does cost money.

Inflation

If you buy an annuity at age 65, it will hopefully pay out for a long time. Over periods of two or three decades, the effect of inflation on an annuity that pays out the same number of dollars every month can be devastating. From 1942 through 1971, a period of very low inflation, the value of a dollar was reduced to $0.56. From 1966 through 1990, the value of a dollar was reduced to $0.24. A level payout may be acceptable to an older annuitant, but it subjects a younger one to serious inflation risk.

Some insurance companies offer SPIAs that adjust for inflation over time with payment increases. They can be directly indexed to the consumer price index (CPI), or they can provide payments that increase at a specific rate that you choose. A CPI-indexed annuity adjusts your income upward by the same percentage amount as the CPI.

The purpose of an annuity is to reduce longevity risk. An annuity frees you from having to guess about your life span. An inflation-adjusted SPIA also protects your lifelong income from the corrosive effects of inflation. Unfortunately, only a few companies offer CPI-indexed SPIAs. Vanguard's inflation-adjusted SPIA product is underwritten by a subsidiary of AIG. A similar product by Elm Annuity Group is underwritten by the Principal Financial Group.

Many companies offer a graded payout option that increases the payout every year by a specific percentage that you select. It is usually a compounded increase. If you buy an annuity with a $1,000-a-month payout and a 3 percent graded compound increase, it will pay $1,000 per month in the first year, $1,030 per month in the second year, $1,061 per month in the third year, and so forth. Since this is a fixed increase rather than a variable increase based on inflation, whether your payment keeps up with inflation or not depends on how good you were at guessing future inflation when you chose the policy.

Annual payment step-ups cost you money. Over time, these annuities are expected to pay out more than a level-payment annuity, so they cost more. Assume annuitants live more than 18 years. By the end of that time, a 4 percent graded increase would double their payouts. It should come as no surprise to find that such an increase can add 50 percent to the premium.

Table 7.2 compares an example of premiums quoted recently by one insurance company for a joint annuity for a couple, both age 60. The payments start at $1,000 per month and increase according to different schedules. The premiums change regularly based on interest rates.

This insurer example in Table 7.2 charges about the same for CPI-U indexing as it does for a 3 percent per year compounded increase. If you buy an inflation-indexed product and there is little inflation—or no

TABLE **7.2** THE COST OF INCREASING PAYMENT OPTIONS

PAYOUT SCHEDULE	SAMPLE PREMIUM
Level payment	$160,675.49
Increasing 1% per year compounded	$176,948.14
Increasing 2% per year compounded	$195,846.70
Increasing 3% per year compounded	$217,890.58
Increasing 4% per year compounded	$243,714.00
Increasing 5% per year compounded	$274,093.10
Indexed by CPI-U	$220,359.07

Primary Annuitant Age 60, M
Joint Annuitant Age 60, F
Payments per Year: 12
Initial Payment Amount: $1,000.00

inflation—you will receive a smaller number of dollars than if you had purchased a nominal product that pays a defined numbers of dollars.

Since inflation-indexed annuities pay less at the beginning and more later on, you must wait longer for the return of your money. The break-even point—when the number of dollars paid out equals the premium—occurs later. But the point may be moot. From the point of view of the consumption frame, the usefulness of an annuity should be measured by how well it protects against longevity risk—how well it supports longer-lived annuitants—rather than the total number of dollars it pays out.

CHARITABLE GIFT ANNUITIES

A charitable gift annuity (CGA) is a type of SPIA. It can be an attractive way for a person of moderate means to help a charity. A CGA enables you to transfer cash or marketable securities to a charitable organization in exchange for a current income tax deduction and the organization's promise to make fixed annual payments to you for life. Annuity payments can begin immediately or be deferred to some future date. In 2002, a *New York Times* writer called them "the hottest thing in giving."

More than 1,000 charities offer CGAs. If you are of retirement age and belong to a church or alumni association, you may have already received a mailing about a CGA. The following guide compares CGAs with single-premium annuities.

	CHARITABLE GIFT ANNUITY	SINGLE-PREMIUM INCOME ANNUITY
Buying motive	Help a charity.	Income to you.
Income paid	Lower payout, perhaps 40% less.	Maximize payout.
Tax consequence	May qualify for a tax deduction.	Less favorable tax treatment.
Safety	Not protected by state guaranty association; may be exempt from state insurance laws.	Protected by state guaranty association; regulated by state laws.
Shopping	Virtually all charities follow ACGA suggestions and offer identical rates.	Shop around (but consider insurer strength).
Purchase options	Only choice is single life versus joint and survivor. Men and women get identical rates. Fixed payouts.	Many options, notably option for increasing payouts over time to counter inflation.

TABLE 7.3 A SAMPLE COMPARISON OF MONTHLY PAYOUTS ON A $100,000 INVESTMENT

EXAMPLES OF DIFFERENT PAYOUTS	SPIA FROM COMMERCIAL INSURER	CHARITABLE GIFT ANNUITY	CGA PAYS OUT
65-year-old woman	$606	$475	22% less
75-year-old couple	$681	$500	27% less
84-year-old woman	$1,138	$717	37% less
84-year-old man	$1,225	$717	41% less

How Much Less Is the Payout?

The payout for a CGA is a lot less than for an SPIA. Table 7.3 provides an example assuming a $100,000 investment.

The payouts from charitable gift annuities are deliberately set to be low and noncompetitive. The American Council on Gift Annuities (ACGA) is a qualified nonprofit organization. It was established in 1927 to stem rate competition between providers, so there is no point in shopping around. All providers offer identical rates. A 1995 lawsuit challenging this as price-fixing was resolved when Congress exempted CGAs from antitrust law.

How Safe Are CGAs?

The low payout rates on CGAs provide a safety margin for the charity. Since about half of the premium is expected to become a gift to the charity, the charity is receiving twice as much as is needed to make payments to annuitants.

Most states have little regulation of charitable gift annuities because they are not considered insurance and are not regulated as such. They require the annuity contract to contain disclosure language such as "a charitable gift annuity is not insurance under the laws of this state, is not subject to regulation by the State's insurance division, and is not protected by any State guaranty fund." Only 15 states (Alabama, Arkansas, California, Florida, Hawaii, Maryland, Montana, New Hampshire, New Jersey, New York, North Carolina, North Dakota, Oregon, Washington, and Wisconsin) require charitable gift annuities to maintain a segregated reserve fund. Five states (Delaware, Michigan, Ohio, Rhode Island, and

Wyoming) and the District of Columbia have no laws addressing charitable gift annuities at all.

It is worth mentioning that, as with all investments marketed to seniors, it is unfortunately necessary to be alert to the possibility of fraud in the CGA marketplace. This is not a problem with CGAs in particular, but investment scams take many forms, and phony CGAs are among them. The Mid-America Foundation pretended to offer CGAs and took in more than $54 million before the Ponzi scheme was uncovered in 2001. A Ponzi scheme pays a high income to investors with the only funding for that income coming from new investors, not actual returns on investments. Eventually the pyramid collapses.

How Much Help Does the Charity Get?

The CGAs are important donation vehicles, and you are really giving the charity worthwhile help when you buy one. The ACGA says that the payout rates are "computed to produce an average 'residuum' or gift to the organization at the expiration of the agreement of approximately 50 percent of the amount originally donated under the agreement." That is, if you pay $100,000 for a charitable gift annuity, from the charity's point of view, it is about the same as an outright donation of $50,000.

Tax Consequences

The ACGA states that taxpayers who itemize deductions can claim a charitable deduction for a portion of the original gift. The present value of those payments is determined by using IRS tables (see www.IRS.gov). There is also software that provides accurate tax calculations. All charities that offer gift annuities can provide these calculations to individuals who are exploring whether a gift annuity is appropriate for them, and many of those charities have calculators on their web sites that allow potential donors to enter basic information and see how their income tax situations might be affected by a charitable gift annuity agreement.

With regard to the income payments, if the gift annuity is funded with cash, part of the payments will be taxed as ordinary income and part will be tax-free. The charity that issues the annuity will send a Form 1099-R to the annuitant. This form will specify how the payments should be reported for income tax purposes. The ACGA website at www.acga-web.org provides additional information.

An illustration generated by an online calculator suggests that for a couple age 65, a gift of $100,000 would qualify for a charitable deduction of $20,866.78 when the gift was made, and that $2,221.96 of each year's $5,400.00 payments would be taxable. For an 80-year-old couple, $40,625.08 is shown as deductible, and $1,924.81 of each year's $6,600.00 payments as taxable.

ANNUITIZATION STRATEGIES

If you have been accumulating money in an investment account and decide to annuitize, you would contract with an insurance company to start paying you income. When you make the choice to annuitize, you also decide how the payments should be structured.

When to Annuitize

Mortality credits are the additional return derived from pooling assets and giving up residual estate value. They increase with age and at an exponential rate. Figure 7.4 illustrates this phenomenon. At around age 75, the mortality credits appear to be sufficient to overcome the various costs of annuitization. The mortality credits are always positive, so theoretically

FIGURE 7.4   MORTALITY CREDITS INCREASE WITH AGE

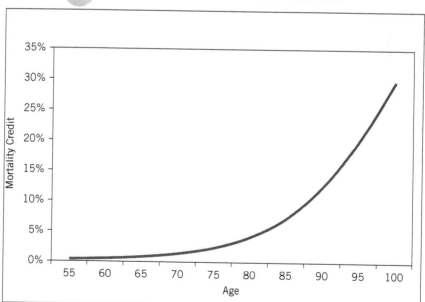

Source: Moshe Milevsky, *If Not Now, When?* www.ifid.ca

(so long as you don't care about leaving an estate), for a given investment return, you should always be better off with an annuity than without one, but in reality you must first exceed the difficult-to-determine, embedded costs of the annuity before you see any net benefits.

In theory, the earlier you annuitize, the more benefit you should get from mortality credits. Before about age 60, the benefit is small, but there is a benefit nevertheless. So in a world where you could be totally confident in your decision to commit funds to an annuity, where the price of an annuity never fluctuated, and where there was no risk of insurer default, the earlier you annuitized, the better.

None of these things is true, so these risk factors weigh against annuitization by younger people. It is a balancing act made difficult by the fact that these risk factors are hard to evaluate. Personal preference—one's degree of risk tolerance or risk aversion—weighs in the balance, and so do financial circumstances, specifically the need for secure income and the ability to meet it solely from one's portfolio.

Several experts believe that age 65 is the youngest someone should be before using an immediate annuity, while waiting until the age of 90 is obviously too late. The experts are hesitant to advocate a single optimal age at which an investor should convert his or her savings account into an irreversible income annuity, given the many trade-offs involved in this decision and numerous sources of uncertainty.

Many experts suggest that immediate payout annuities should generally be purchased after retirement in staggered purchases because annuities are irreversible purchases that partially lock in investors' asset allocations and reduce bequests.

Other things being equal, annuity payouts depend on the prevailing interest rate—roughly following the interest rate on the 10-year Treasury bond, as illustrated in Figure 7.5. Mortality credits are the amount by which the payout of an annuity exceeds the prevailing interest rate. Staged purchases help to dollar cost average across varying interest rates.

Because investment income forms only part of the annuity payout, a decline in a bond interest rate does not decrease annuity payouts proportionately. In fact, a calculation based on a life table indicates that an annuity could pay a 75-year-old man about 8 percent of the premium per year even if the insurance company earned no interest at all on its investment.

How Much to Annuitize

A simple answer to the question of how much you should annuitize is enough to provide for 100 percent of your minimum acceptable level of

FIGURE 7.5 TEN-YEAR U.S. TREASURY NOTE YIELD

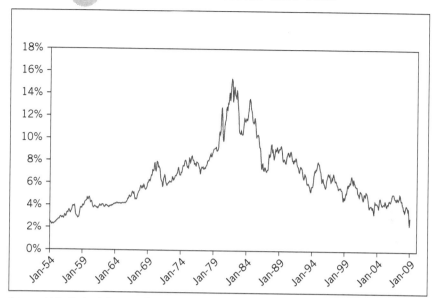

Source: U.S. Federal Reserve Bank

retirement income from all annuitized income sources, including Social Security and pensions. That immediately raises the question, What is 100 percent of your minimum acceptable level of retirement income? It is different at different stages of life. People in their 60s tend to spend more money than people in their 80s. So the correct answer may be that it depends when you annuitize. MetLife offers some help with a simplified online guide at www.metlife.com. Search for "Income Annuities Guide."

The economic models invariably demonstrate that the risk of not being able to cover basic living expenses far exceeds the benefit from the potential upside of taking on additional equity exposure. In calculating how much to annuitize privately, subtract the minimum from what is expected to be needed each month from the amount you will be getting from Social Security and any pension benefits you may have accrued. Then annuitize a sufficient amount of your assets to provide for the remainder of monthly income you will need to reach that threshold level.

There is a strong case to be made for annuitizing your absolute minimum living expenses. These are steady expenses that you must meet during all phases of retirement, whether you are newly retired or well on in your years. The SPIA represents an irrevocable commitment of funds, and a loss of control over them, so use an SPIA sparingly to fill the income gap between your other annuitized income streams and your expected lifelong minimum monthly expenses.

THE SAFETY OF SPIAs

Donald Rumsfeld memorably commented: "There are known unknowns. That is to say, there are things that we now know we do not know. But there are also unknown unknowns. There are things we do not know we do not know." The big unknown is whether you will outlive your annuity insurance company. If they go belly-up, you may be out some income. There are other unknowns that weigh against SPIAs. One is the possibility of buyer's remorse. Rising interest rates after you buy mean better deals on SPIAs available in the future. Opportunity cost is a factor. Once money is put into an SPIA, it not available to use on anything else such as a vacation, a second home, education for the grandchildren, a business opportunity, or an emergency.

This section focuses on an important unknown, the risk of your insurer becoming insolvent. Purchasing an SPIA puts a sum of money into the hands of an insurance company irrevocably. You become partners forever. You cannot get your money back in a lump sum, and there is no cash value to borrow against. An SPIA owner relies on the long-term strength of the insurer, much like a pensioner relies on the financial strength of a former employer to continue making pension payments.

How big is the risk? Few annuitants have taken a loss on fixed annuities, but it has happened. Two relatively large insurance companies ended up paying only 70 cents on the dollar after they got into trouble as a result of bad investments. Mutual Benefit Life, which failed in the early 1990s, left hundreds of thousands of annuity holders with only limited access to their money for some eight years. The web site of the National Organization of Life and Health Insurance Guaranty Associations (NOLHGA) indicates that between 1991 and 2007, eight insurance companies have simply gone out of business, and there were 55 others for which guaranty association intervention was required.

In 2008, many unknown unknowns have made headlines. The safety of annuities has been thrown into the spotlight by the problems of American International Group, Inc. (AIG). Although it is not yet clear how the problems of the holding company affect the safety of its insurance subsidiaries, it has certainly reminded everyone that the safety of even the largest insurers cannot be taken for granted.

Annuities are backed by the state guaranty associations to a point and by the strength of the insurer. In every state, annuities are protected up to a dollar limit—often $100,000—by the state guaranty association. Insurance companies are regulated by states, not by the federal government, so the law is different in every state. Following some large insurance company failures during the 1980s, the insurance industry formed NOLHGA. The organization worked to create guaranty associations in every state and to make the law more uniform across states. You can and should look up the specific details for your own state, via the NOLHGA web site at www.nolhga.com.

Unfortunately, NOLHGA protection is almost a secret because most states prohibit insurance companies from explaining it to you. Banks have FDIC placards, brokerage statements mention SIPC insurance, but insurance brochures never mention the guaranty association. The insurance industry would like you to obtain your information about the program directly from the guaranty association—even though you are not told the guaranty association exists!

Insurers, particularly the stronger companies, have an interest in seeing this protection downplayed because of moral hazard, the danger that consumers could gravitate toward better deals from weaker companies. It is similar to shaky banks offering exceedingly high FDIC-insured certificate of deposit rates.

Here are a few points about the NOLHGA safety net worth noting:

* High rates are not necessarily honored. Many states limit the guaranty association's obligation based on criteria, such as subtracting 2 percentage points from the Moody's average corporate bond yield.
* Insolvencies are handled by and subject to the laws of the state in which you are living at the time of the insolvency.
* What is protected is the present value of the annuity contract, which is calculated by actuaries and diminishes over time as a result of payouts.
* All states have language capping the total amount that the guaranty association will pay for any insured life. NOLHGA notes: "The overall benefit 'cap' in most states for an individual life is $300,000."
* California protects only 80 percent of the insurer's contractual obligations, not the full amount. (The 80 percent obligation is further capped at $100,000.) This partial protection appears to be unique to California.

The aggregate cap deserves special attention because it applies to several different kinds of insurance. A consumer with modest amounts of whole life insurance and long-term care insurance and a life annuity could very easily exceed the limits.

Protection on each individual kind of insurance, such as annuities, is usually per owner per member company. In a state with $100,000 annuity protection, if a complete list of the life, health, and annuity policies you own is two annuities, each valued at $90,000, with two different companies, you are fully protected.

The situation with respect to the aggregate cap is less clear. In New York, where the aggregate limit is $500,000, if an insured had three separate individual life insurance policies, each with a death benefit or cash value of $500,000 or more, with three different insurance companies, is the protection provided by the Guaranty Corporation to the individual $500,000 per company (in this case $1.5 million) or $500,000 in the aggregate, regardless of the number of companies or contracts?

A 2008 document issued by the Office of General Counsel of the New York State Insurance Department posed that question and answered: "Under the hypothetical presented, the protection afforded by the Guaranty Corporation would be $500,000 under each contract, for an aggregate coverage, should all three life insurers become insolvent, of $1,500,000." (Source: www.ins.state.ny.us.)

Each state has different regulations and insurance limits, and there are often multiple agencies involved when corporations fail. Consult legal experts if you have questions about your particular state.

Ratings: A Screening Tool

Five agencies that rate insurers are A. M. Best, Fitch, Moody's, Standard & Poor's and Weiss. Each agency ranks the financial strength of insurance companies using a proprietary scale, outlined in Table 7.4. There's no way to compare ratings between different agencies. The rating methodologies are too diverse. For example, it is difficult to compare A+ from Best to an Aa2 from Moody's. Thus, it is best to look at all the ratings and form a composite view.

Major ratings companies assign not only a letter grade but an outlook. A. M. Best uses positive, negative, and stable, and other modifiers or comments as well. A. M. Best uses *u* meaning "under review," a warning that the rating may change.

These ratings are only a screening tool, not a guarantee. Walter Updegrave, *Money* magazine senior editor wrote: "These ratings are hardly foolproof. Rating agencies can get it wrong. And rapidly deteriorating markets can make what was a sound company weeks ago vulnerable today." During 2004, AIG Life Insurance held S&P's highest rating, AAA.

TABLE 7.4 THE SCALES USED BY MAJOR INSURANCE RATINGS
AGENCIES

Insurance Company Ratings Used by Major Rating Agencies (Best to Worst)

A.M. Best	FITCH	MOODY'S	S&P	WEISS
A++	AAA	Aaa	AAA	A+
A+	AA+	Aa1	AA+	A
A	AA	Aa2	AA	A−
A−	AA−	Aa3	AA−	B+
B++	A+	A1	A+	B
B+	A	A2	A	B-
B	A−	A3	A−	C+
B−	BBB+	Baa1	BBB+	C
C++	BBB	Baa2	BBB	C−
C+	BBB−	Baa3	BBB−	D+
C	BB+	Ba1	BB+	D
C−	BB	Ba2	BB	D−
D	BB−	Ba3	BB−	E+
E	B+	B1	CCC	E
F	B	B2	CC	E−
—	B−	B3	R	F
—	CCC+	Caa	—	—
—	CCC	Ca	—	—
—	CCC−	C	—	—

111

Then it slipped to AA+ a year later, and then it dropped three levels, literally overnight, in September 2008. On September 17, 2008, U.S. regulators seized control of the company.

Martin D. Weiss criticizes the other rating agencies for being too closely tied to insurers, while claiming that his own company, Weiss Research, is independent. In 1992, the *New York Times* said of Weiss that "life insurance companies do not like him much" and that "assigning low grades to large, well-known life insurance companies has become something of a trade-mark for Weiss Research." The 20 top and bottom performing insurance company ratings are available at no cost from www.thestreetratings.com.

What is an acceptable rating? Definitive answers are hard to find. Babbel and Merrill wrote in *Rational Decumulation* (http://fic.wharton.upenn.edu/fic/papers/06/0614.pdf) that "if a default is going to occur, it occurs on average about 25 years after the annuity purchase from an insurer with a claims paying rating of single-A at the outset." In *The Guru Guide to Money Management,* authors Joseph H. Boyett and Jimmie T. Boyett suggest demanding an A or better from Best, AA or better from S&P, and a B or better from Weiss.

Buying SPIAs

Fees: What You See Is What You Get

If the quotation says that you pay $168,418.26 and receive $1,000.00 every month, then you pay exactly $168,418.26 and you receive exactly $1,000.00 every month. But how much does the insurance company make? Somewhere between 2 and 15 percent.

Some researchers claim that in 1999 a typical retiree with average mortality prospects faced an embedded transaction cost of 5 to 20 percent if he or she purchased an individual annuity from a commercial insurance carrier. By 2006, researchers found the range to be much better, from 3 to 5 percent.

It is a misconception that companies with a higher financial strength rating charge higher premiums. Typically, the rating of the company does not influence the level of monthly payment. Last year, a set of quotations was obtained from a firm that specializes in immediate annuities from major companies. Seven quotes were obtained from companies with S&P ratings from AAA to AA−. The quotes for a premium paying $1,000 a month to a 62-year-old woman showed a spread of $18,580 between the low-cost provider at $151,620 and the high-cost provider at $170,200. The low-cost provider's rating was in the middle of the pack.

AN IMPORTANT NOTE ABOUT INCOME FROM SPIAs

Income from an SPIA will usually be taken into account by any means-tested programs, such as public housing assistance and Medicaid. The specific rules for such a situation might create conditions under which spending a sum of money to buy an SPIA would be less favorable than retaining the same sum as unspent assets.

Medicaid considerations vary from state to state and are beyond the scope of this book. An eldercare law expert must be consulted with regard to any specific situation. Various forms of annuities have figured in the legal battleground between individuals seeking ways to sequester assets from Medicaid and the authorities seeking to recover them. This much can be said:

* Some annuities *can* be countable Medicaid assets.
* Annuities meeting certain conditions—irrevocable, nontransferable, with payments not extending beyond the annuitant's life (no guaranteed payments or term certain) *might* not be.
* Using any kind of annuity as part of a deliberate Medicaid estate-planning strategy will put you in the middle of the aforementioned legal battleground, so consult a lawyer.

MANAGED PAYOUT FUNDS

Vanguard's managed payout funds are relatively new, having been introduced in April 2008. These mutual funds are *not* annuities, and they offer no guarantee of income. Nor does Vanguard guarantee the safety of principal. So why are they being discussed in this chapter on immediate payout annuities? Because the funds have been the subject of great interest and some controversy on the Bogleheads' forum, and they need explaining.

As mutual funds pay dividends and interest, you are given a choice to have that income distributed to you as the fund pays it or to reinvest the income by purchasing more shares of the fund or another fund. The managed payout funds are essentially mutual funds with a built-in automatic withdrawal strategy. Instead of paying out interest and dividends, they pay out a calculated amount based on a moving average of the three previous years' return. Here are the basics:

* Like any other mutual fund, and unlike an SPIA, an investor retains full ownership of the fund and full access to it. The investor can buy or sell at any time and can take money out and put money in.

On your death, the value of the fund becomes part of your estate (which would be substantial if the stock market performed well enough to meet the fund managers' stated goals for the fund).

- Like any other mutual fund, and unlike an SPIA, nothing about managed payout funds is guaranteed. The stated goals are merely goals, not promises, as stated in the fund's disclaimers.
- The funds do not take age into consideration, and they do not address the situation of a retiree who would like to spend down assets to $0 but doesn't know how long he or she will live.
- On a 1 to 5 risk-level scale, with 5 being riskiest, Vanguard positions their managed payout funds at 3 on account of market fluctuations. An SPIA is not subject to market fluctuations, and if it was placed on the same scale, it would probably be less risky, with the only risk being the health of the issuer.

ADDITIONAL RESOURCES

- National Organization of Life and Health Guaranty Associations, www.nolhga.com. This is a comprehensive source for everything relating to guaranty association protection, from consumer FAQs to summaries of state laws.
- Berkshire Hathaway "EZ-Quote" at www.brkdirect.com. Another helpful tool for exploring what-if questions about annuities.
- The web site of annuity broker Hersh Stern, www.immediatean nuities.com. A request for an annuity quotation brings a very useful package of material, including a great deal of information on SPIAs in general.
- American Council on Gift Annuities (ACGA), www.acga-web.org. Detailed information on charitable gift annuities, including rate schedules.

CHAPTER SUMMARY

Single-premium immediate annuities (SPIAs) are a valuable retirement planning tool because they provide a higher stream of income than any equivalently safe investment. Some experts suggest that they are underutilized. SPIAs are simple products that are easy to understand and compare. They are pure insurance products, without any investment plan mixed in. SPIAs do have drawbacks that need to be understood. One is that SPIAs provide more income for you at the expense of leaving a smaller legacy to your heirs. Another is the risk of insurer default, which is very hard to quantify. Financial strength ratings mean less than you would wish. Backup protection from state guaranty associations exists and is important, but it has limits.

The SPIAs are most useful to retirees whose savings are marginal. If you are planning your retirement, you should know that they exist, understand how they work, and evaluate what they can do for you.

PART III

MANAGING YOUR RETIREMENT ACCOUNTS

Basic Investing Principles

Bob Davis A.K.A. CyberBob

INTRODUCTION

Investing is simple if you follow a few basic principles: reduce your risk by widely diversifying your investments including a reasonable allocation between stocks and bonds, maximize your return by minimizing fees and expenses, and stick with your plan long enough to experience the power of compounding. Jack Bogle said it all in these few words: "Simplicity is the master key to investment success."

DIVERSIFY TO REDUCE THE RISK OF A LARGE LOSS

Every investor dreams of finding the next Google before the stock skyrockets in value. Putting all your eggs in one basket and hitting the jackpot is one of the quickest ways to get rich. Unfortunately, it is also one of the quickest ways go broke. That investment you expect to skyrocket could also plummet, becoming the next Enron or Lehman Brothers. Diversification—or spreading your assets across a variety of different types of investments—eliminates the risk of a total loss and lowers the risk of a large loss.

The reason for diversifying is fairly simple. By including different investments that have different types of risks in your portfolio, the portfolio should be less volatile than if you put all your money in one type of investment with one type of risk.

Diversification creates a risk-reduction advantage because the returns on each unique investment tend not to be perfectly synchronized. That means the investments in a well-diversified portfolio generally do not move in the same direction at the same time or by the same magnitude. Each investment in the portfolio responds uniquely to changes in the economy. Accordingly, if you own several different investments with different risk profiles, a decline in one investment may be offset by a rise in another. There are times when all investments move in the same direction at the same time, but those periods are rare in financial history.

Specific Risk and Systematic Risk

Specific risk is the risk that comes from fluctuations in the price of a particular stock, whereas systematic risk is the fluctuation in price that is attributed to the entire asset class. For example, having money invested in a few individual stocks or bonds exposes you to specific risk. If one company does poorly, your entire investment does poorly. The more stocks you have in a portfolio, the more the portfolio sheds specific risk and takes on the characteristics of systematic or market risk. Risk in this sense is defined as the variation in return from one period to another.

If you are unlucky enough to own only a few stocks and they all do poorly, it can result in devastating losses to your investment portfolio. But the more stocks you own, the greater the chance that you will have some that go up to offset losses from those that are losers. Diversification reduces the risk of a large loss. Even in the terrible stock market of 2008, there were firms that did well and saw an increase in their stock price. In the end, the market did better than many individual stocks on the market, particularly financial stocks.

The solution for diversifying away the specific risk of a stock is simply to hold as many stocks as possible. Two stocks are better than one. Four is better than two. And ultimately, the widest diversification possible is simply to own every asset in the particular market. A total-market stock fund, for example, offers the most diversification for the equity asset class.

Diversification across Asset Classes

Owning a large number of stocks lowers the specific risk of any particular company, but it will not protect you from the systematic risk of the entire stock market. To reduce the risk of a market, investors should consider diversification on two levels. The first level is to reduce specific risk by diversifying among many different investments of one particular asset class, such as U.S. common stocks. The second level in diversification is to reduce the systematic risk of asset classes by spreading investment across different asset classes, such as stocks and bonds. Stocks and bonds often act differently during different economic conditions, and asset class diversification can help your overall portfolio against the systematic risk of a particular asset class.

Volatility in the stock market is an inherent risk that can't be eliminated by owning more stocks. But that risk can be tempered by owning different asset types. Having part of your portfolio in assets that have potential for high returns and another part in investments that produce more stable returns helps protect your overall portfolio from the ups and downs caused by any single event.

Multiple Asset Class Portfolios

Diversification among asset classes lowers risk and means potentially higher returns in the long term. This is efficiently done using mutual funds and exchange-traded funds. However, simply holding many funds does not guarantee diversification. You can hold several blue chip U.S. stock funds that do little to increase your diversification because they all invest in the same companies. A better allocation would be between stocks, bonds, and cash.

Here are three major classes that can then be subdivided:

Stocks
* By region: United States, Europe, Pacific rim, emerging markets
* By size: large capitalization, mid capitalization, small capitalization
* By style: growth, value, blend

Bonds
* By type: government, corporate, mortgage-backed
* By maturity: short-term, intermediate-term, long-term
* By quality: investment grade, high yield (a.k.a. junk)

Cash
* Bank savings accounts
* Certificates of deposit
* Money market funds

There are times when all asset classes advance and times when all of them retreat, but over the long run, they tend to not be perfectly correlated. Since it isn't possible to know which asset will do best at any particular time, holding a variety of asset classes that move differently moderates the effects of any one asset class and is protection against any single plummeting asset in your portfolio. A well-diversified portfolio should be diversified within asset classes so that specific risk is effectively eliminated and diversified across asset classes so that the risk of the portfolio is consistent with your risk tolerance.

Modern Portfolio Theory (MPT)

Everyone wants to identify a few investments with the greatest opportunity for growth coupled with the least downside risk. But good individual assets meshed together do not always make a good portfolio. Something can go wrong with a few of the investments, and then the entire portfolio performs much worse than the market. Rather than focusing on a few individual investments that appear to have above-average risk-reward characteristics, modern portfolio theory is all about building a broadly diversified portfolio with acceptable risk-reward characteristics for your situation.

Risk is a fundamental part of return. Higher returns are not possible without taking some risk. However, it is possible to construct portfolios that maximize expected return for a particular level of risk. These optimal portfolios occur along what is called the efficient frontier. Plotting differing combinations of assets results in an efficient frontier curve where you can see that for every level of return, there is one portfolio that has historically had the lowest possible risk, and for every level of risk there is a portfolio that has historically had the highest return. If you can construct portfolios that are on the efficient frontier in the future, then you have found MPT nirvana.

Figure 8.1 illustrates an efficient frontier curve of two assets: U.S. stocks and international stocks from 1970 to 2008. The chart plots U.S./international combinations in 10 percent increments. Over the time period represented in the chart, the 100 percent U.S. portfolio had a higher return than the 100 percent international portfolio. During the same period, the international portfolio was riskier because it had a larger variation of year-to-year returns.

Looking at Figure 8.1, you may wonder why anyone would invest in international stocks at all if the returns were lower and the risk was higher. It does not always occur this way. First, the risk and return of any asset

FIGURE **8.1** EFFICIENT FRONTIER FOR U.S. AND INTERNATIONAL
STOCKS, 1970–2008

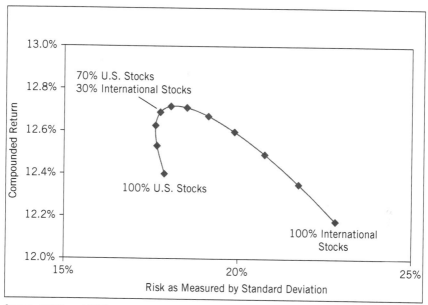

Source: MSCI and S&P

class depend on the time period measured. Second, the return of the combined 70 percent U.S. and 30 percent international portfolio was higher than either asset class alone, with the added benefit of less risk than either asset class by itself. A portfolio that includes multiple types of assets has different risk and return characteristics than the individual assets in the portfolio. A multiple-asset allocation reduces the impact on your overall portfolio from the big ups and downs of one single type of asset.

Modern portfolio theory explains that portfolios on the efficient frontier are best because they offer the highest expected return for any given level of risk and the lowest risk for any given return level. The portfolios on the efficient frontier naturally tend to be the ones that are the most diversified. Less diversified portfolios tend to fall short of being the most efficient.

REBALANCING

A portfolio's asset allocation between stocks, bonds, and cash determines the portfolio's overall risk and return characteristics. Historically, stocks have returned more than bonds, so more of a tilt toward stocks should mean higher expected long-term returns. There is, of course, a trade-off. Stocks have also historically been more volatile than bonds, so more of a tilt toward stocks also means larger short-term ups and downs. As 2008 demonstrated, some of these downs can be very large.

Over time, your portfolio of stocks, bonds, and cash will probably drift from the allocation targets you set. That means your portfolio will have a higher or lower stock-to-bond ratio than you originally intended. In turn, the portfolio's risk and expected return will also have changed, sometimes significantly. Since your portfolio's target allocation should change only when your investment goals change, the portfolio needs to be put back in line. Rebalancing is the primary method used to realign a portfolio with its stated risk and return objectives. Rebalancing means adjusting your portfolio to restore its original target allocation.

During a strong bull market in stocks, a 60 percent stock and 40 percent bond portfolio might become a 70 percent stock and 30 percent bond portfolio because of the high return on stocks. This means that your portfolio value has grown, but it also means your portfolio is now riskier, and you have more to lose if stocks go into a bear-market downturn. Rebalancing back to your original 60 percent stock and 40 percent bond position will bring your portfolio back to your desired risk profile.

In a different year, during a bear market, your balance may tip in the other direction, with your stock allocation dropping from 60 percent to 50 percent. Your portfolio has now become more conservative than your original target. You would then have less money invested for growth, possibly lowering your future returns. So again, rebalancing back to your original 60 percent stock and 40 percent bond allocation will bring your portfolio back to your desired profile.

Rebalancing also has the added advantage of forcing you to buy low and sell high. As an asset class falls in price, rebalancing means you buy more. As an asset class rises in price, rebalancing means you take some profits. Investors without a rebalancing plan often react emotionally and do just the opposite—buy high and sell low—to the detriment of their overall portfolio value.

When to Rebalance

Rebalancing controls risk, but when should you do it? There is no one-size-fits-all strategy. The optimal time to rebalance is different over different time periods, and it is not possible to know in advance what rebalancing strategy will be optimal. There are some considerations.

Rebalancing may involve costs (as described in the costs section later in this chapter), and these costs have to be weighed against your tolerance for risk, relative to your target allocation. Generally, though, there are two major methods: rebalancing after a certain time period (by the calendar) or after your allocation changes by a certain amount (percentage bands).

Rebalancing by the Calendar

A straightforward time frame to use for checking if your allocation is out of whack is once a year. Waiting longer means you run the risk of letting your allocation percentages drift too far from their targets and your desired portfolio risk level. This method is simple and requires little time to implement. Rebalancing more often runs the risk of making changes in reaction to temporary market moves.

Another advantage of using time-period rebalancing is that you don't have to constantly monitor your portfolio. Not looking at your portfolio every day may help you stay the course, limiting your temptation to panic-sell during a bad market downturn.

Rebalancing Using Percentage Bands

After a year has gone by, you may find that your portfolio is not far out of balance. This may have occurred because the markets did not move much or because you have been rebalancing when making contributions or withdrawals throughout the year. If a certain time period has elapsed and your portfolio is only slightly out of balance, it often brings up the question of whether it's even necessary to rebalance at all.

Rather than rebalancing by the calendar, many people make changes only when their portfolio allocations are off by a certain percentage. A commonly used number is 10 percent, meaning that someone with a 60 percent stock and 40 percent bond portfolio would rebalance if their stocks went up to 66 percent or down to 54 percent (10 percent of 60 percent equity is a 6 percent band). They wouldn't make any change if the stock percentage had changed only a little, say, up to 63 percent or down to 59 percent. Using this method allows your allocation to fluctuate enough that rebalancing may actually be required less often. This would be especially beneficial in a taxable account, as rebalancing less often would mean fewer potential taxable transactions. A disadvantage of using a percentage rebalancing method is that it requires more effort to implement, as you need to continuously monitor your portfolio, rather than just looking at it once or twice a year.

A popular compromise between the two methods is to use annual monitoring with actual rebalancing done only when the balance has tipped outside a percentage threshold. This creates a balance between controlling the portfolio risk and minimizing any rebalancing costs.

Rebalancing Considerations

The method for doing rebalancing really doesn't matter as long as you are consistent. In addition to deciding when to rebalance, it's important to consider how to rebalance, so as to minimize any potential tax consequences.

For both taxable and tax-advantaged accounts, if you are still making contributions to your investment accounts, the simplest way to rebalance is to use new money to purchase shares of the asset class that is most underweighted. Each time you have new money to invest, simply look at your asset percentages and put the money in the one that needs a boost to bring it back to its normal weighting. This will generally mean that you are purchasing the asset class that has either appreciated the least or has even gone down recently, so you are buying low. This is also a very tax-efficient way to rebalance, as it doesn't involve any selling of assets, which could result in a taxable capital gain.

If you are no longer making contributions to your investment accounts and are in retirement and taking withdrawals, you can use this method to rebalance by just doing it in reverse. Each time you need to withdraw money from your investments, simply look at your asset percentages and take the money out of the one that is overweight. This will generally mean that you are selling the asset class that has appreciated the most recently, so you are selling high, which is a good thing.

In a taxable investment account, it's especially important to be aware of how any rebalancing may affect your tax liability. If you sell shares in a taxable account to move money to another fund, you may realize a capital gain and be required to pay taxes. So in a taxable account, it's best to keep any selling to a minimum. One way to rebalance a taxable account is to use the cash that the account is already generating through fund distributions. Any time a fund pays a distribution in a taxable account, you have to pay taxes on it, whether you reinvest the money or not. So if you choose to not reinvest distributions back into the same funds that paid them, you can instead use the money to rebalance, by purchasing shares of your underweighted asset classes. The amount of the distributions may not always be enough to totally rebalance, but it will at least lessen the number of shares you may have to sell from the overweight asset class, minimizing tax consequences.

In a tax-deferred portfolio such as an IRA or 401(k), taxable events aren't an issue. When it comes time to rebalance your portfolio, simply sell shares of the assets that are over their target percentage, and use that money to buy shares of those that are under their target. But in a taxable portfolio, every sale of shares in one of your mutual funds is something that gets reported on your tax return and potentially increases your tax liability. So, while selling shares to rebalance is straightforward, a taxable-account investor should aim to limit tax liability and use this method only after the others have been exhausted.

COST CONTROL

All investing involves costs and paying expenses of some sort, either directly or indirectly. These costs come out of your investment profits. And taxes paid further reduce your gains. The investment profit you actually keep equals your investment gains minus expenses, minus fees, minus taxes. Lower overall costs—in the form of expenses, fees, and taxes—allow you to keep more of the profit that your investments have earned.

Unavoidable Expenses

Anyone investing in a mutual fund pays a share of the costs necessary for the day-to-day operation of the fund. If a brokerage firm holds your investments, you may also pay a transaction cost to buy or sell no-load mutual fund shares. Shares held directly with a no-load fund company will not be charged a trading commission.

Basic Expense Ratio

The expense ratio is the cost incurred by the fund to operate. It includes the cost of paying the manager of the fund and the costs of services to the clients of the fund. Client services can include providing fund prospectuses and annual reports, monthly or quarterly account statements, and a toll-free telephone number for contacting the fund. The basic expense ratio of the fund is disclosed in the fund's prospectus.

Indirect Fund Trading Costs

An expense that is not directly spelled out in the prospectus but is born by the shareholders is the indirect cost of trading securities in the fund. The cost of transactions in a fund is based on the turnover of securities and the trading spread of those securities. Mutual funds that buy assets in relatively illiquid markets may find that even though the actual commission to buy is low, the trading spread between the buy and sell prices is high. And if a fund is attempting to buy or sell a particularly large quantity of any security, the fund's own buying and selling may result in a price movement of that security. That market impact cost is not measured in the prospectus. Trading costs are minimized by low-turnover funds such as index funds.

Exchange-traded funds avoid market impact cost by creating and redeeming securities in kind rather than in cash. However, when buying or selling ETFs on an exchange, there is a spread on the fund itself that represents the liquidity of the ETF.

Individual Tax Liability on Fund Dividends

A third unavoidable expense for someone investing in a taxable account is individual tax liability on any fund distributions. Even low-turnover funds that distribute few capital gains to shareholders will probably have to distribute dividends. Bond funds distribute an especially high level of dividends. And in a taxable account, these dividends are subject to tax in the year you receive them, even if you reinvest them. Although receiving these dividends is generally unavoidable, it may be possible to minimize the tax implications by holding the fund in a tax-advantaged account.

Avoidable Expenses

With the thought in mind that your investment profit is reduced by every expense, there are several that are avoidable. Here is a list:

Sales loads: You can divide mutual funds into two overall segments: pure no-load funds and load funds. Pure no-load funds can be purchased directly from the fund company without paying a commission. Load funds are purchased from a broker or other financial services salesperson by paying a so-called load. The load is simply a commission paid to the salesperson. It may be a front-end load, which is taken out of your initial investment amount when you buy, or a back-end load, which is deducted from your proceeds when you sell. There are some funds with front-end loads as high as 8.5 percent. That means that if you make a $10,000 investment in that fund, only $9,150 actually makes it into your account and $850 goes as a commission to the salesperson. That means you need to earn more than 9 percent on your $9,150 investment just to get back to even. Avoid the salesperson, invest directly with the fund company in pure no-load funds, and keep all of your investment money working for you.

12b-1 fees: A mutual fund with a 12b-1 fee charges an extra expense to fund holders to use for advertising and promotion of the fund.

This fee is paid by current shareholders in order to gather new shareholders. Although new shareholders would mean more money flowing into the fund, resulting in more profit for the fund managers, it's generally not beneficial to the current shareholders. In fact, when a fund gets too big, it may start to resemble an index fund and move along with the market, negating any special advantage the fund may claim to have had when it was smaller. A 12b-1 fee is essentially another expense that further lowers the fund return that the individual shareholder gets to keep. Especially egregious are the mutual funds that are closed to new investors yet continue to charge shareholders the 12b-1 fee for advertising. Many load funds also come in a no-load version, but the no-load version charges a 12b-1 fee. That is the difference between a no-load fund and a pure no-load. The pure no-load fund has no 12b-1 fee.

Abnormally high expense ratios: High expense ratios are inversely related to fund performance. The higher a fund's expenses, the lower the investment gains the shareholders get to keep. A low expense ratio is the single most important reason a fund outperforms similar funds. For the long-term investor, these higher expenses can be very significant. Consider two funds that both return 10 percent a year before expenses. The low-cost fund with expenses of 0.2 percent would then have a net return of 9.8 percent. But the high-cost fund with expenses of 2.2 percent would have a net return of only 7.8 percent. Over a 30-year investment horizon, that would mean $10,000 invested in the low-cost fund would grow to $165,000 while in the high-cost fund it would grow to only $95,000. That's a difference of $70,000, or seven times the original investment. Costs definitely matter.

Direct brokerage commission trading costs: Buying mutual funds directly from the fund provider is the cheapest route. But many people hold funds and exchange-traded funds (ETFs) through a brokerage account of some kind. This has the advantage of allowing you to hold funds from multiple fund families, while still keeping everything consolidated in one account. The drawback is being charged a commission every time you buy or sell something. Purchasing ultra-low-expense ETFs through a brokerage account may seem like a sure way to savings, but if you are paying a commission for every transaction, it can quickly get expensive. That $9.99 commission may seem reasonable, but on a $1,000 transaction it adds another full percentage point to your costs. And don't forget you have to pay the $9.99 to sell, too. So while the 0.1 percent expense ratio of that ETF looks cheap, after paying the two commissions, your actual first-year expense looks more like 2.1 percent, making it no bargain. Many brokers are now advertising commission-free transactions to bring in new customers. However, no-commission trading is not the same as no-cost trading. These brokers often earn a handsome profit from the trading spread and reciprocal trading agreements with other brokerage firms.

DIFFERENT STROKES FOR DIFFERENT FOLKS

Many investors transitioning into retirement also transition their expectations of their portfolio from growth to providing income. After decades of growing a portfolio to be as large as possible in anticipation of retirement, retirees often focus on having their portfolio generate as much income as possible. But completely abandoning growth for income overlooks the capital growth aspect of investing that can be as beneficial in a retirement portfolio as it was in the preretirement portfolio.

Income Portfolio

An income-oriented portfolio focuses on incoming dividends and interest and is generally viewed as a lower-risk retirement portfolio. The goal is often to construct a portfolio where one can spend just the income and leave the principal amount intact. This can be a viable strategy if your withdrawals are small in relation to your portfolio size. However, many people find that the yield on a 100 percent bond portfolio may be less than their desired withdrawal—especially in a low interest rate environment. Yield can often be increased by trading some investment-grade bonds for high-yield bonds. But while these bonds may increase the yield, they are also likely to increase the overall portfolio volatility and risk. They don't call them junk bonds for nothing.

Many people would be surprised to know that an all-bond portfolio does not have the lowest long-term risk as measured by year-to-year volatility. Historically, a portfolio with 10 to 15 percent stocks has lower year-to-year volatility of returns than one made up of 100 percent bonds. Some stocks in a portfolio also increase the longevity of a portfolio by adding growth that the all-bond portfolio does not provide. The differing correlations between stocks and bonds, as well as the greater long-term growth potential of stocks—even a relatively small amount—both increase the return and decrease the volatility. Depending on your tax status, an all-bond portfolio may also increase your tax liability, as bond dividends are less tax-efficient than capital gains.

Total-Return Portfolio

In contrast to an income-focused portfolio, a total-return portfolio maintains a balance of both stocks and bonds and focuses on income as well as the appreciation of asset values. Although it assumes spending principal as well as dividends, the growth potential of a more balanced portfolio has historically been better than an all-bond portfolio, more than making up for having a lower overall portfolio yield. An investor who reduces exposure to stocks is making a trade-off. Increasing bonds means having higher income now, but because of lower growth potential and the relentless advance of inflation, it means higher risk to your future spending power.

Philip L. Cooley, Carl M. Hubbard, and Daniel T. Walz are professors of finance in the Department of Business Administration, Trinity University, San Antonio, Texas. In the February 1998 *AAII Journal*, they published "Retirement Savings: Choosing a Withdrawal Rate That Is Sustainable." The article highlighted their findings in a comprehensive study on sustainable withdrawal rates in retirement.

Chapter 12 has much more on withdrawal rates. However, the Trinity University study did stress the importance of retaining some growth focus in retirement. Using actual historical stock and bond returns from 1926 through 1995, the study determined that at a 4 percent inflation-adjusted withdrawal rate, an all-bond portfolio had only a 20 percent chance of surviving over a 30-year retirement period. On the other hand, a total-return portfolio made up of half bonds and half stocks had a 95 percent chance of survival. Clearly, focusing solely on generating income from your portfolio significantly decreases your portfolio's ability to sustain that income over the long run.

COMMON INVESTING MISTAKES

The Bogleheads believe that people can enhance their investment portfolio with some simple changes. Some of those changes involve avoiding common investing mistakes. Here are a few mistakes to avoid.

No Written Plan or Investment Policy Statement (IPS)

Just as a cross-country car trip should start with planning a route, long-term investing should start with planning a strategy. Investing without a plan means you're more likely to make many financial wrong turns. Creating an investment policy statement means putting your investment strategy in writing and committing to a disciplined plan. The plan should be reviewed and updated annually, or as events in your life change that may change your plan. See Chapter 9 for more information on investment policy statements.

Investing Too Conservatively

Many people are afraid to incur any loss in their investment portfolio at any time. Consequently, their investments tend toward low-risk certificates of deposit, money market mutual funds, or savings accounts, where principal values do not fluctuate. This is quite common in 401(k) plans. Participants tend to choose the lowest risk option, even though that is a high-risk selection from a retirement-planning standpoint. Cash-type investments provide short-term security, but over the long term, they are risky because they do not grow at the rate of inflation. Low-risk investors often find their purchasing power declining each and every year, although they never experience a loss of principal. Doing everything you can to avoid a loss may seem like the sensible thing to do, but you also may be cheating yourself out of any chance for real long-term growth.

Ignoring the Impact of Total Cost

Investment costs erode investment returns. But most people don't see what they're missing because expenses aren't specifically broken out on monthly statements. How much of a drag on performance costs really are can be easy to overlook.

Calculate your total investment costs. Total investment costs include the expense ratio of your mutual funds, all trading costs, and your adviser's fee if you choose to hire an adviser. If you are paying more than 1 percent in total costs, then it might be time for a change.

Chasing Performance

Nothing attracts assets like last year's winning strategies, and nothing destroys wealth as fast. Don't chase the performance of funds that have had great recent returns. Last year's hot fund is just as likely to do poorly this year. There is a strong tendency for poor performance to follow good performance, as investment styles tend to rotate over time. Selecting a fund based on its recent short-term performance has historically been a losing proposition. Instead of chasing performance, simply own the entire market through an ultra-low-cost index fund, and hold for the long term.

Trying to time your investments by switching frequently between different funds is also a losing plan. That strategy leaves you open to buying a fund too soon or too late. You can guess correctly some of the time, but that does not prove you to be smart or skilled, just lucky. Successful investing involves leaving your money in place long enough to benefit from the long-term average of the asset class.

Allowing Emotions to Control Your Investment Decisions

People become very brave in a bull market and scared to death in a bear market. After stocks go up in value, people want to buy, and after stocks go down in value, people want to sell. Both of these emotional decisions are quite common and understandable, but they are also counterproductive to your investment wealth. Buying after the market has had big gains means you are buying at more expensive prices. And selling after the market has had big losses means you are selling at cheaper prices. So, you are buying high and selling low. That is the exact opposite to rational decision making.

Instead of reacting to market moves, create an investment plan appropriate for your situation and risk tolerance. Follow a rebalancing plan to keep your allocations at your target levels. Rigorously following this rebalancing plan will mean you will be buying asset classes low and selling them high—a much surer way to increase your overall long-term portfolio return.

ADDITIONAL RESOURCES

* *The Bogleheads' Guide to Investing* by Taylor Larimore, Mel Lindauer, and Michael LeBoeuf (Wiley, 2006). The first book in the Bogleheads series provides easy-to-understand guidance on investing.
* *The Little Book of Common Sense Investing* by John Bogle (Wiley, 2007). The investing wisdom of Vanguard founder John Bogle distilled into one small, easy-to-read volume.
* *The Smartest Investment Book You'll Ever Read* by Daniel Solin (Perigee, 2006). Create a low-cost, widely diversified investment portfolio with just three Vanguard index funds.
* *The Lazy Person's Guide to Investing* by Paul Farrell (Business Plus, 2006). Easy-to-understand and simple-to-start investment portfolios, using low-cost mutual funds.
* *Making the Most of Your Money* by Jane Bryant Quinn (Simon & Schuster, 1997). Reliable and practical advice on virtually every financial topic.

- *The New Coffeehouse Investor* by Bill Schultheis (Penguin Group, 2009). Solid financial advice presented in a casual and easy-to-read format.
- *Serious Money, Straight Talk about Investing for Retirement* by Richard Ferri. This free online book can be found at www.PortfolioSolutions .com.

CHAPTER SUMMARY

Market returns are out of your control as an investor, but many things are within your control that can greatly increase the odds of growing your portfolio over the long haul. Create an investment plan appropriate to your individual needs and stick to it. Lower your overall portfolio risk by diversifying as widely as possible. Keep the risk and reward characteristics of your portfolio in line by rebalancing when things drift too far from your planned allocation, and remember that *costs matter!* Every expense or fee that you pay is that much less your investments will return. Keep investing simple and you will be wealthier and happier for it.

CHAPTER NINE

Investing for Retirement

David Grabiner and Alex Frakt

INTRODUCTION

Retirement is expensive, and you need a viable plan to achieve your retirement goals. Just like heading out on a cross-country road trip without directions and a map is foolhardy, you shouldn't set out on your journey toward retirement without having a road map that lays out the route to your future. Your plan should balance your need, ability, and willingness to take risk. Previous chapters provided information on the different types of personal, employer, and employee investment accounts and other available products that can help along the way. This chapter focuses on creating the road map to a solid investment plan.

INVESTMENT POLICY STATEMENT

The most difficult part of investment planning is getting started, but it is also the most important. Start with a reasonable plan, and revise it later as necessary. If you start with a good plan, you will find it easier to continue to make good investment decisions. Most investors do this backward by starting with investment selection, usually choosing from lists of top-performing mutual funds. The portfolio gets pieced together with the flavor of the month. While these returns may appear tempting, does investing in an African gold fund or a U.S. real estate fund really fit into your long-term plan? Without first developing that plan, you begin the journey into your future by looking in the rearview mirror, almost guaranteeing that, like a car driven forward by using only the rearview mirror, your portfolio may well crash.

A good way to make and follow a plan is to write an investment policy statement (IPS). An IPS is simply a written document that defines your general investment goals and objectives. It describes the strategies you will use to meet these objectives, contains specific information on subjects such as asset allocation, risk tolerance, and cash requirements, and sometimes lists individual investments.

Every investor can benefit from having an IPS. It provides the foundation for all of your investment portfolio decisions and keeps you focused on longer-term objectives. It can provide a way to monitor the investment performance of the overall portfolio, as well as the performance of individual funds. If you are using a financial adviser, an IPS should define the relationship between you and your adviser. An IPS provides a reference to see whether your portfolio is achieving your stated goals and objectives. Any proposed changes to your investments can also be evaluated and reviewed against your overall objectives by using your IPS. An IPS can be referenced in those times when you need to bolster your long-term investment discipline to help you avoid overreacting to short-term market fluctuations.

Investors who don't have a written policy frequently base decisions on day-to-day events and often wind up chasing short-term performance that may keep them from reaching their long-term goals. They also have more difficulty staying with a long-term asset allocation, especially during turbulent markets or exuberant times.

Sign your statement after you write it. If you share your financial decisions with somebody else, such as a significant other or financial adviser, both of you should sign it. Even if it is just your own statement, signing it expresses your commitment to the plan.

Sample Investment Policy Statements

Here are sample investment policy statements, based on the Boglehead principles of investing. The Deferrals need to make annual adjustments to their portfolios because they do not have life cycle funds, which help automate the execution of investment plans, available to them. In the second example, Captain Susan Saver uses the excellent life cycle funds available to her. These investment policy statement examples are deliberately simplified; your own statement may well be longer because you may want to record your reasons for many of your decisions. These investors appear again as examples in Chapter 10.

David and Donna Deferral

Investment Philosophy: We would like a well-diversified, moderately aggressive portfolio with the minimal cost for each asset class we invest in. We will manage it ourselves but would like to keep the management simple. We hope to retire in 10 years, when we both turn 60.

How Much to Invest: We got off to a late start and need to invest 25 percent of our salaries, which is $2,500 a month. The money will be withheld from our paychecks automatically and invested in David's 401(k) and Donna's 403(b).

What to Invest in: The investment options in David's 401(k) are better than those in Donna's 403(b), so we will max out David's 401(k), including catch-up contributions, before investing anything above the 5 percent that Donna's employer matches. Since we expect to retire in the 15 percent tax bracket and are in the 25 percent tax bracket now, the 401(k) and 403(b) are better for us than a Roth IRA would be.

We will allocate our ages minus 10 percent to bonds, and the equities will be 60 percent U.S. large-cap, 20 percent U.S. small-cap, and 20 percent foreign. We plan to choose the least expensive diversified options available for each asset class, which will initially be 40 percent bonds, 36 percent U.S. large, 12 percent U.S. small, and 12 percent foreign stock.

Donna's entire 403(b) will be invested in the S&P 500 stock index fund, which is her only moderate-cost option. David will hold Vanguard's Total Bond Index, 500 Index, Small-Cap Index, and International Growth, which are all low-cost and are the best choices available in his plan. The combined totals will fill our asset allocation.

Rebalancing: We will rebalance to the target allocation, including the 1 percent increase in bond allocations, every July, which is during Donna's summer vacation and David's birthday.

Reviewing This Statement: This statement will be reviewed whenever there is a substantial change in our financial situation and annually when we rebalance. If there are no substantial changes in our financial situation, we will wait at least three months between changing the asset allocation in this statement and actually implementing those changes to our investments. We plan to review any changes in this statement again at that time.

Captain Susan Saver

Investment Philosophy: I would like a broadly diversified portfolio at minimal cost. It should also be as simple as possible to manage; I will trust professional management decisions about appropriate investments for someone born in 1979 who expects to retire around 2040.

How Much to Invest: I am currently investing $500 a month, which is about 10 percent of my pay. I will maintain the same percentage every year as I get a pay increase and invest half my raise when I receive a longevity increase or get promoted.

My investment will go automatically to the TSP. If I am deployed to a combat zone and my pay becomes tax-exempt, I will invest in a Roth IRA instead up to the limit and will have the contribution withdrawn automatically from my checking account on the first of every month.

What to Invest in: My TSP investments will be in the Lifecycle (L) 2040 Fund. My Roth IRA investments will be in Vanguard Target Retirement 2040 Fund.

Rebalancing: As long as I use life cycle funds, rebalancing will be done for me automatically. If I choose to manage my own funds in the future, I will rebalance in January every year, setting my bond allocation to my age minus 10 percent and my international stock allocation to 30 percent of my total stock allocation. (This is approximately the allocation strategy of the L 2040 fund.)

Reviewing This Statement: This statement will be reviewed whenever there is a substantial change in my financial situation and annually in January. If there is no substantial change in my financial situation, I will wait at least three months between changing the asset allocation in this statement and implementing those changes to my investments. I will review the changes in this statement again at that time.

IMPLEMENTING AND FOLLOWING YOUR PLAN

Now that you have a plan, it needs to be implemented and followed. Invest your first dollars according to your plan, make future investments automatic, and protect against procrastination. Your IPS will serve as a reminder of the decisions you've made so that you can carry them out as appropriate. Human nature, procrastination, and overreaction are common causes for concern; a good plan will make it less likely that any of these failings will derail you. Automating your investing means you never have to ask about market conditions. *Now* is always a good time to invest automatically.

Investing Your Dollars

If you are not already regularly investing for retirement, the most important thing you can do is to get started now. Compounded growth is your greatest ally when it comes to reaching your investing goals. It is important to get started right away, even if you are not sure exactly what to buy.

Whether you are early in your career and a new investor, or a mid-career investor just beginning to focus on your looming retirement, when you get started with your investing plan is much more important than what you actually buy. Where you invested your first $5,000 probably won't make that much difference to your final retirement income.

When you start a job that offers a 401(k) or similar retirement plan, contribute at least enough to get the full match from your employer. That is free money to you. If your employer does not match your 401(k) contributions, contribute to either the 401(k) or an IRA as soon as you are in position to contribute.

If you aren't yet sure of your investing risk tolerance or are in the process of working it out, then start investing conservatively. Your first investment should go into something very safe, such as a money market or Treasury bond fund. Select a date, probably a few months in the future, when you will start moving to more aggressive investments. Follow your IPS and include that date in your IPS.

Pay Yourself First

It is easier to avoid spending money if you don't receive the money in the first place. A 401(k) type plan does this for you automatically by taking a fixed percentage or dollar amount from every paycheck and depositing it into your 401(k). Most investment firms allow you to make automatic investments in a similar way in any type of account. For example, if you plan to contribute $3,000 to your IRA annually, you could schedule an investment of $250 on each monthly payday. Making this an automatic part of your regular budget similar to mortgage payments is a very efficient way to save.

Unfortunately, Vanguard does not allow you to open an account with automatic investments. You must make an initial investment of $3,000 or more in most funds, and after that you can do automatic contributions. (The Vanguard STAR fund requires an initial investment of only $1,000.) Therefore, if you decide to have a Vanguard IRA, you would need to start it with $3,000, but then you could continue your future yearly $3,000 contributions by adding $250 a month.

When you receive a raise, consider increasing your 401(k) or IRA contribution by half the amount of the raise or until you reach the maximum allowable contribution amount. That way you are putting away at least half of the raise before you have a chance to spend it.

Dollar-Cost Averaging

Paying yourself first by making regular contributions to your retirement account from every paycheck has a name: it is called dollar-cost averaging (DCA). DCA means investing an equal amount at regularly scheduled intervals. When you do DCA, you are buying in at the average price during the year, and that ensures that you will not be adding your total annual contribution at a market peak. One month you would buy a fixed-dollar amount when the market is down, and the next month you invest the same dollar amount when the market is up. By doing this, you lower your average cost per share.

You may decide to dollar-cost average a newly acquired large sum of money, such as an inheritance. If you have a large sum of money to invest, you may want to move the money that is going into equities in equal amounts over a period of several months. For example, if 80 percent of the money is going into equities, you might invest 10 percent of the total in equities every month for eight months. Many investment firms will let you schedule these transactions automatically.

The advantage of DCA is that you are more likely to stick with the plan because you will have gone through the market's ups and downs with only part of your money invested. The disadvantage of voluntary dollar-cost averaging is that you are not fully invested in the market initially and may miss a strong rally. It is a tough call. The psychology of investing plays a critical role here. On average, you would be best off investing everything at once, since markets go up more often than they go down. However, if you are unlucky enough to be investing in the roughly one out of three years when markets decline, you are unlikely to find much comfort in the average. There's no one right answer for everyone, so you'll have to decide whether dollar-cost averaging or investing the entire amount immediately is best for you.

Even if you do decide to DCA, you should invest the entire amount that is going into bonds as soon as you start investing. High-quality short-term and intermediate-term bonds are unlikely to fluctuate in price enough to make DCA advantageous, so it is best to get the money in and start earning higher interest

The Annual Checkup

Just as you have a regular health checkup to be sure your body is healthy, you should have a regular portfolio checkup to be sure your investments are working according to your plan. You should check your allocation to see if you need to rebalance. Your IPS should have your rebalancing schedule. If your workload varies by season, the rebalancing date should be in the quiet season to make it easier to manage your investments. Otherwise, use an easy-to-remember date, such as every January when you make your IRA contribution, every April after you file your taxes, or your birthday.

You should review your rebalancing plan even if rebalancing is automatic in the balanced mutual fund you selected. Your financial situation may have changed, and perhaps you need a new asset allocation. Perhaps you got a new job, had children, received an inheritance, or had a large unexpected expense. Revisions to your statement should represent where you are now and where you are going in the long run. You might include in your statement a sentence such as "If there is no substantial change in my financial situation, I will wait at least three months between changing the statement and making the corresponding change in my investments, and I will review the change to the statement again at that time."

SOME WORDS ABOUT RISK

Your risk tolerance is the maximum amount of account variability that you can stand during the worst market conditions. To determine your risk tolerance, you must consider your ability and need to take risk. Bear markets such as 1973–1974, 2000–2002, and 2007–2008 can cut the value of a stock portfolio in half; therefore, your stock allocation should be no more than twice the amount you can tolerate losing. Risk and return are directly related. Your asset allocation should balance your *need* to take risk with your *ability* to withstand the ups and downs of the market. *Need* can be determined via basic financial planning formulas. If you're young, you have the benefit of many years of compounding, so your need to take risks is low. On the other hand, if you are older and your portfolio size is small, your need to take risks is high because you will need a higher return to achieve your retirement goal. Now, the opposite is true for ability to take risks. Young people can take more risks because they have many income-earning years ahead. On the other hand, older people have less ability to take risks because their working years are shrinking.

For people closer to retirement, it may be possible to more closely determine need. First, estimate approximately how much income you will need annually after retirement. For example, assume you need $100,000 per year. Next, look at any pensions or Social Security benefits that will provide a source of income. If a pension provides $30,000 per year and Social Security provides an additional $20,000 per year, then the portfolio would need to provide an extra $50,000 each year. Using the 4 percent withdrawal rate discussed earlier, to generate $50,000 per year at 4 percent requires a minimum portfolio size of $1.25 million. How close are you to your goal? Chapter 12 covers planning for withdrawals and calculating spending patterns in more detail.

Turning to *ability*, this is your ability to withstand the ups and downs of the market without getting nervous and making changes to your asset allocation. Selling in the face of a decline is probably the worst thing you can do. Figure 9.1 is a table portfolio based on a severe bear market,

FIGURE **9.1**   EQUITY TO TOLERABLE LOSS STARTING WITH **$100,000**

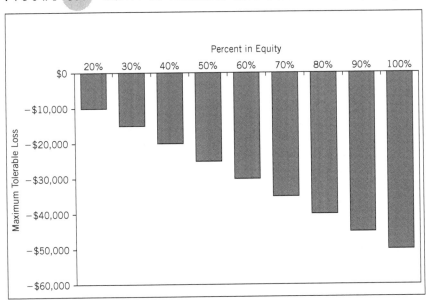

Source: Morningstar, Inc.

showing the loss that should be expected on a $100,000 portfolio for various stock/bond allocations when the next deep bear market occurs.

You can also get help in determining your asset allocation by utilizing the online risk assessment tools available at www.vanguard.com. In addition, there are simpler ways to determine an asset allocation. Vanguard founder John C. Bogle recommends "your age in bonds." For example, if you are 40 years old, hold 40 percent in bonds and the rest in stocks. There are other variations:

* Equities equals 110 minus your age ($110-40=70$ percent in stock)
* Equities equals 120 minus your age ($120-40=80$ percent in stock)

CHANGING ALLOCATIONS OVER TIME

Your investment plan should reflect a lowering of risk as you approach the amount needed at retirement. There are several ways of doing this. The simplest way is to use an age-appropriate life cycle mutual fund such as one of Vanguard Target Retirement Funds. A target retirement fund lowers risk automatically over time by decreasing equities and increasing fixed income. A common way to manage risk is to do it yourself. If you're a younger investor, you will probably want to start with a relatively high allocation to stocks because of the trade-off between risk and expected return and then gradually reduce the stock allocation as you approach your retirement goal. However, we do not recommend more than 90 percent in equities even for young investors.

During a bear market, how much your account will lose in value depends on how much money you have invested at the time and your asset allocation. If you are in midcareer with $500,000 invested, a 20 percent decline in the financial markets will cause a decline in your assets of $100,000. If you are about to retire with a $1 million portfolio, a 10 percent decline in the markets will cause a decline in your assets of $100,000. Either way, a bear market took away the same amount of value. In this scenario, if you suffered the 20 percent loss midcareer, you haven't lost any more money than if you suffered a 10 percent loss prior to retirement.

No one wants to sustain a 10 percent loss, let alone a 20 percent loss. That is why time *in* the market is important. The more time you have to invest, the greater the likelihood that you will benefit from the long-term growth of the stock market. Table 9.1 shows that the U.S. stock market has many bad periods as measured in real returns (returns adjusted for inflation). There have been 26 negative real return periods over rolling 5-year periods since 1871, and 11 negative real return periods over

TABLE 9.1 WORST U.S. STOCK INDEX RETURNS, 1871–2008, ADJUSTED FOR INFLATION

WORST REAL RETURN:	1 YEAR	5 YEARS	10 YEARS	20 YEARS	30 YEARS
Annualized	−36.74%	−10.03%	−4.45%	0.64%	3.11%
Cumulative	−36.74%	−41.04%	−36.55%	13.65%	150.88%
Worst years	2008	1916 to 1920	1999 to 2008	1962 to 1981	1892 to 1921
Periods with a loss	44 of 138	26 of 134	11 of 129	0 of 119	0 of 109

Source: Robert Shiller, www.econ.yale.edu

10-year rolling periods. But there has not been a 20-year negative real return period since 1871.

The implication for these numbers are that if you have 20 years left to invest, then you should have at least some money in stocks. Even if you are nearing retirement, you hopefully have 20 years left to live, and if you don't, your heirs may. Accordingly, you should still have the growth potential of equities in a portion of your retirement portfolio. The money you are planning to spend in the next few years should be in low-risk investments, but at least a portion of the remaining funds should be in stocks.

If you are considering retiring but do not have the resources, you might choose to delay retirement. This would give you more time to contribute to your retirement savings and allow the portfolio to grow, and that combination will increase the number of years you can stay solvent in retirement. For example, assume you have $500,000 at age 65 and retire. If your portfolio earns 6 percent per year and you take out $40,000 per year, you will run out of money at age 87. In contrast, if you work for one more year and save an extra $5,000, plus 6 percent growth in your portfolio, you will have $535,000 at age 66. If you then retire and take out $40,000 per year, you will not run out of money until age 93. One year of extra work and savings extended your retirement solvency for six years.

How Life Cycle Funds Work

Many investment companies now offer life cycle funds, also called target-date funds. They are designed to adjust their allocation automatically from an aggressive allocation to a less aggressive allocation as the target retirement date approaches. Typically, these funds are very well diversified, investing in U.S. stocks, foreign stocks, and bonds. There are many different life cycle funds available, and they all follow different glide paths to reduce equity exposure over the years. It is wise to understand the glide path used on the fund you are considering.

It is usually easy to tell whether life cycle funds are available in a retirement plan. They generally have a name such as Target Retirement 2030. Funds without a date in their name are usually not life cycle funds. The prospectus of a life cycle fund should also explain how its glide path will decrease risk over time. Figure 9.2 shows the equity allocations from two providers of low-cost life cycle funds, the Thrift Savings Plan (TSP) L Funds and Vanguard's Target Retirement Funds.

If you have the option of using life cycle funds in either your 401(k) or your IRA, they are a great way to invest. A small investment can give

FIGURE 9.2   GLIDE PATHS FOR TSP L FUNDS AND VANGUARD TARGET RETIREMENT FUNDS

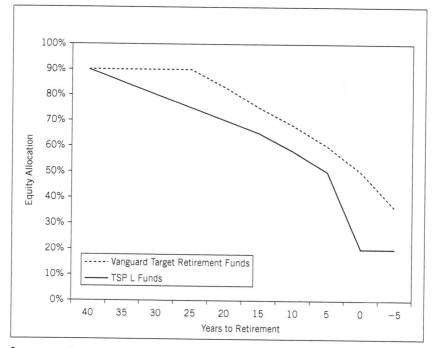

Source: www.tsp.gov and www.vanguard.com

you a broadly diversified portfolio, and you do not need to meet the minimums in individual asset class funds. Plus, you do not need to spend time rebalancing among multiple funds each year. Even if you do not plan to use these life cycle funds over the long-term, you can start with them at first and then branch out into individual asset class funds as your portfolio grows.

Make sure you are comfortable with the asset allocation of the particular life cycle fund you select. Many life cycle funds have very large allocations to equity for the more distant target dates, such as 2040 and 2050. Both the TSP L and the Vanguard Target Retirement Fund that are 40 years out have 90 percent stock. Not all investors are comfortable with that much risk. If you want to take less risk, you can always choose a life cycle fund with a target date earlier than your expected retirement date.

Life cycle funds do have disadvantages. Target-date funds are not very tax-efficient. They include taxable bonds that generate dividends taxed at high ordinary income tax rates, and the frequent rebalancing generates short-term capital gains. As a result, life cycle funds do not work well if you have a mixture of taxable and tax-advantaged accounts. If part of your portfolio is taxable, you want to manage your portfolio to minimize taxes, which means putting tax-efficient funds, such as total stock market index funds, in your taxable account, and tax-inefficient funds, such as bond funds, in your tax-advantaged accounts.

Life cycle funds are designed to provide the investor with a nicely diversified portfolio with a single fund. Therefore, they work well only if they are all or almost all of your portfolio. If a significant part of your portfolio is in a non-life cycle fund, then you will have to adjust your overall asset allocation at least annually to get the portfolio in balance, thus defeating the benefit of automatic rebalancing.

TAXES AND YOUR INVESTMENT PLAN

Taxes are often the biggest expense that investors pay. To help minimize the tax bite, you should view all of your investment accounts as one unified portfolio. A common problem investors face is how to efficiently invest a portfolio that is spread across tax-advantaged accounts such as an IRA or 401(k) and taxable accounts. It can be helpful to place the most tax-inefficient assets in your tax-advantaged accounts while holding the most tax-efficient investments in your taxable accounts. The advantage of placing assets in the right account is to defer paying taxes for as long as possible, while minimizing the taxes you do pay. The disadvantages are the increased complexity of rebalancing and the risk of actually increasing your taxes as the tax laws change.

Certain types of investments are, by their nature, more or less tax-efficient than others. Taxable bond funds tend to pay out interest at a higher rate than a stock fund pays dividends. More interest in a portfolio means more current tax liability, which makes taxable bond funds tax-inefficient for people in a high income tax bracket. Most stock dividends are taxed at a lower qualified dividend rate. So it makes sense to put stock funds in your taxable account and taxable bonds in your tax-advantaged account. Interest on municipal bond funds is tax-exempt, so they go in a taxable account. However, interest rates paid on municipal bonds are lower than on other bonds, so you pay a tax cost in lower returns rather than paying it directly to the IRS.

Table 9.2 lists various types of mutual funds in general order of tax-efficiency. Any fund in the Efficient category is fine in a taxable account. In the Moderate category, you should consider an alternative but not necessarily use one; in particular, if you have to hold bonds in a taxable account in order to meet your target allocation, you should hold them. Holding funds that are in the Inefficient category in a taxable account means you will pay higher income tax rates on distributions from those funds.

A fund that has a high turnover rate from frequent trading of securities in the fund typically has short-term capital gains, which are taxed at your ordinary income tax rate. There may also be long-term capital gains, but

TABLE 9.2 THE TAX EFFICIENCY OF VARIOUS MUTUAL FUND TYPES

Inefficient	High-yield bond funds Real estate funds (REITs) High-turnover active stock funds
Moderately Inefficient	Actively managed U.S. stock funds Actively managed international stock funds Government, mortgage, or investment-grade corporate bond funds (consider municipal bonds instead in taxable accounts)
Efficient	Value index funds (relative to active value funds) Small-cap index funds (relative to active funds)
Most Efficient	Emerging market index funds (relative to active funds) Broad market, large-cap, or growth U.S. index funds Broad market, large-cap, or growth international index funds Tax-managed equity funds Municipal bond funds

Source: Morningstar

these are taxed at a lower capital gains rate. In contrast, a stock index fund or exchange-traded fund (ETF) may have no or very little capital gains distributions because the turnover in those funds is low. In the case of ETFs, the fund operations are such that fund managers are able to distribute low-cost basis stock to a third party, so rarely are gains distributed to shareholders. Gains in the value of ETF shares grow tax-deferred until you sell your shares.

Ideally, the preferred approach to overall portfolio tax management is to place the most tax-inefficient assets in tax-advantaged accounts while placing more tax-efficient investment in taxable accounts. As an example, most portfolios consisting of stock and bond funds are best allocated by placing bond funds in your tax-advantaged accounts and tax-efficient stock funds in your taxable account.

Tax location strategies are not always practical. When frequent contributions or withdrawals are being made to or from only the taxable account or only the tax-advantaged account, it complicates the strategy significantly. Asset allocations quickly become skewed to one asset class or another. Trying to balance between different taxable and tax-advantaged accounts can quickly become convoluted and frustrating. In that case, don't try to tax-locate every asset class. Have the same stock and bond allocation in the taxable account as in the tax-advantaged account. That makes rebalancing easier. You could avoid using REITs and high-yield bonds in the taxable account because they are very tax-inefficient and perhaps substitute municipal bonds for taxable investment-grade bonds.

NONINVESTMENT ASSETS

Your retirement plan should also take into consideration any noninvestment assets that will help provide for your retirement. These assets can provide income, decreasing the amount you'll need from your own investments.

A pension provides the same amount of spending power throughout your retirement, so you will need less from your investments. Captain Susan Saver, who will receive a COLA military pension, uses the appropriate life cycle fund that takes this into consideration. A cost-of-living adjustment (COLA) is a benefit that is adjusted annually for the rate of inflation. Social Security payments have a COLA, and you will get annual increases in benefits as long as that system remains solvent.

If you have a pension that is not adjusted for inflation, the income will provide less spending power over time as inflation increases. One way to hedge a fixed pension is to invest in Treasury inflation-protected securities (TIPS) as part of your bond holdings. TIPS provide some ordinary income from interest and increase in value as inflation rises.

A home can provide additional money for your retirement. Assuming you have equity in your home, you could move to a smaller house or retire to an area where real estate prices are lower. Your home could provide a safety net in an emergency. You have the option of taking out a home equity loan against the equity or using a reverse mortgage to provide monthly income. If you own other real estate or a business, you will draw income from them during retirement and then eventually sell the assets and invest the proceeds in stock and bonds.

ADDITIONAL RESOURCES

* *Your Money and Your Brain*, by Jason Zwieg, discusses the psychology of investing and what you can do about it. It also includes a detailed sample IPS.
* *Spend 'Til the End*, by Scott Burns and Larry Kotlikoff, gives advice specific to life cycle investing and other life cycle-related financial decisions.
* Fairmark's online tax guides (www.fairmark.com) on capital gains and mutual funds provide more information on IRS rules for tax-loss harvesting.

CHAPTER SUMMARY

The key to successful retirement investing is developing a good investment plan, implementing that plan, and then following through on your commitment. Record your plan in an investment policy statement to document your progress. Your plan should include an adjustment of your asset allocation over time, similar to the glide path used in a life cycle fund. Keep your portfolio growing by making automatic contributions. If you invest in both taxable and tax-advantaged accounts, try to be tax-efficient by holding the least tax-friendly investments in your tax-advantaged account. You will be well on your way to a financially stress-free retirement after implementing these recommendations.

CHAPTER TEN

Funding Your Retirement Accounts

David Grabiner and Ian Forsythe

INTRODUCTION

The time has come to pull all the knowledge and planning together and begin to implement your investment policy statement (IPS) to enable you to achieve your retirement goals. This is surprisingly easy, and in a few short steps you can be building a low-cost, tax-efficient, broadly diversified portfolio.

There are many different accounts that can be funded. Which one do you fund first? Which has the best return on dollar invested? Those are the questions this chapter sets out to answer. It is devoted to helping you make an informed decision from among the various types of accounts available to you. It also presents other strategies with the goal of turning every dollar you save while working into as many spendable dollars as possible for your retirement.

PRIORITY OF ACCOUNT FUNDING ORDER

You have many different types of investment accounts to choose from. Several earlier chapters in this book covered taxable accounts and tax-advantaged accounts. Table 10.1 summarizes the characteristics of various types of accounts used for retirement investing.

First Priority: Get the Match

If you are eligible to contribute to an employer-sponsored retirement plan and your employer offers matching contributions, your first priority should be to contribute enough so that you claim the full amount of your employer's matching contributions. When your employer offers you extra money without asking for anything in return, take the money!

Assume your employer matches 100 percent of your contributions to a 401(k) plan up to 3 percent of your salary. Then you should contribute a minimum of 3 percent of your salary to get the full match. Your contribution is tax-deductible and has the added advantage of lowering your income tax expense. By receiving the full match, you get an immediate 100 percent return on your investment. Even if the investment options in your employer's plan are poor, make the minimum contribution to receive the maximum match. Never be dissuaded from taking free money.

Your employer's matching contribution is not included as part of your taxable income, so you get no deduction for that. However, all funds in the account remain tax-deferred, whether you put the money in or your employer does. Only when you take money out do you become liable for income tax. You will be able retain the tax-deferred status even if you leave your employer or retire. When you separate from an employer, simply roll the account into an IRA rollover account with a broker or mutual fund company. IRA rollovers shelter your money from taxes until you are ready to start taking distributions.

Second Priority: Pay Off High-Interest Debt

Paying off high-interest debt is not retirement investing in the strictest sense, but it is your best return on investment. You should seriously consider reducing or eliminating high-interest debt as an integral part of your retirement savings plan. Paying off high-interest debt and revolving credit card balances offers the greatest risk-free, tax-free return on your money. By investing in high-interest debt repayment, you will earn an unbeatable guaranteed after-tax return on your investment, equal to the interest rate on the debt.

TABLE 10.1 CHARACTERISTICS OF ACCOUNT TYPES USED IN RETIREMENT SAVINGS

ACCOUNT TYPE	TAX-DEDUCTIBLE CONTRIBUTION	CONTRIBUTION LIMITS	TAX-DEFERRED GROWTH	TAX-FREE WITHDRAWALS	INCOME LIMITS	EMPLOYER SPONSORED	UNLIMITED INVESTMENT OPTIONS
Taxable account	No	No	No	Partial	No	No	Yes
Traditional IRA	Yes	Yes	Yes	No	Yes	No	Yes
After-tax IRA	No	Yes	Yes	Partial	No	No	Yes
Qualified Annuity	Yes	Yes	Yes	No	No	No	No
Non-qualified Annuity	No	No	Yes	Partial	No	No	No
Small business plans	Yes	Yes	Yes	No	No	Yes	No
Roth IRA	No	Yes	Yes	Yes	Yes	No	Yes
Roth 401(k)	No	Yes	Yes	Yes	No	Yes	No

Reducing or eliminating high-interest debt also frees up cash flow for investing in the future. When the debt is gone, the payments can be redirected toward additional retirement contributions. There is also a psychological benefit: many people enjoy peace of mind from being free of high-interest or consumer debt. You may also find yourself spending less and living within your means, freeing up even more money to invest for retirement.

Third Priority: Tax-Deductible Retirement Accounts

Tax-deductible retirement accounts are very powerful tools that can shield your earnings from relatively high marginal income tax rates while you are working and allow them to grow tax-deferred until they are withdrawn in retirement. Following retirement, the funds are likely to be taxed at lower income tax rates. The difference between the two tax rates can result in dramatic tax savings.

To understand just how powerful tax-deductible retirement accounts can be, you must first understand the progressive nature of the income tax code; the more you earn, the more income tax you pay (see Chapter 2 for complete details). That sounds obvious, right? Well, there's more to it than that. As your income increases, not only do you pay more income taxes, but you pay an increasingly larger percentage of your income in taxes.

Different segments, or brackets, of your income are taxed at different income tax rates, and the rates increase as your income increases. Every additional dollar that you earn at the margin falls within your marginal tax bracket and is taxed at your marginal (highest) tax rate. By contributing to a tax-deductible retirement plan during your peak earning years, you avoid paying income tax on income that would otherwise be taxed at your marginal income tax rate. For example, if the top of your working income falls in the 28 percent marginal income tax bracket, and you contribute $1,000 to a tax-deductible retirement plan, your income tax will be reduced by $280. In other words, you can buy $1,000 in a tax-deductible retirement account for only $720. That's a pretty good deal, and you should take it.

Saving Taxes on Withdrawals

Income tax rates that you will pay when you withdraw tax-deductible funds in retirement are likely to be lower than the income tax rate that you saved when you made the contributions. There are two reasons for this: First, you are likely to find yourself in a lower marginal tax bracket in retirement, even if you spend just as much money. (In a recent survey, 45 percent of retirees reported that they spent less in retirement than before retirement, and 33 percent reported that they spent about the same.) Second, the withdrawals from your tax-deductible retirement accounts are likely to be spread across your lower income tax brackets, so that the effective income tax rate on the withdrawals will be lower than your marginal income tax rate when you made the contributions. The difference can result in dramatic tax savings.

To illustrate the potentially dramatic tax savings, let's consider David and Donna Deferral, who developed an investment policy statement in Chapter 9. They are a married couple who are both 50 years old and who plan to retire at 60. David and Donna earn a combined $120,000 per year, and they file a joint income tax return. They claim the standard deduction and do not claim any dependents. The couple contributes a total of $30,000 to their retirement plans. They pay $10,200 in income taxes, $7,440 in FICA taxes, and $1,740 in Medicare taxes, which results in an after-tax net income of $70,620. David and Donna know that they will not receive a traditional pension and that they will be too young to qualify for Social Security when they retire, so they plan to withdraw money from their retirement accounts to fund their retirement.

David and Donna wisely deferred income taxes while they were working by taking income off the top of their preretirement income—income that would have been taxed at their marginal tax rate of 25 percent. Then, when they retire, they will withdraw $78,800 in the first year of their retirement from their tax-deductible retirement accounts. Those withdrawals will be spread across all of their postretirement tax brackets. The first $18,700 of retirement withdrawals will be taxed at 0 percent, the next $16,700 will be taxed at 10 percent, and the remaining $43,400 will be taxed at 15 percent, for a total income tax of $8,180 on the $78,800 withdrawn.

Since David and Donna will no longer have to pay Social Security or Medicare payroll taxes, they will pay $8,180 in tax and have the same $70,620 to spend after taxes. The result is an average or effective tax rate of only 10 percent on all of the withdrawals. They saved $19,700 in taxes on the first $78,800 they contributed but paid only $8,180 in taxes on the same amount withdrawn in the first year. As Figure 10.1 illustrates, that's a tax savings of $11,520!

David and Donna realized a dramatic tax savings in part because they dropped into a lower marginal tax bracket when they retired. It is likely that you will, too. There are a number of reasons you should be paying lower taxes in retirement. First, you will no longer have to pay Social Security or Medicare payroll taxes, which is an immediate savings of 7.85

FIGURE 10.1   DAVID AND DONNA'S TAX SAVINGS IN RETIREMENT

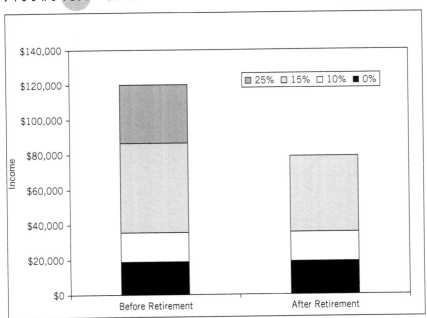

percent, and double that if you are self employed. Also, you will no longer have to save a portion of your income for retirement. Assuming you save 10 percent of your gross income for retirement, the savings on retirement and taxes alone will reduce your required gross income in retirement by almost 18 percent. If you pay state income taxes, the savings may be even greater because your state may not tax retirement withdrawals as income, or because you may retire to a state that does not have state income tax. Other expenses may also be reduced or eliminated, such as work-related expenses, a mortgage payment, and college expenses for your children. Of course, if you receive less taxable income after you retire, you will owe less income tax as well. All totaled, you will probably be able to maintain the same standard of living after retirement with less gross income than before retirement.

You will probably drop into a lower marginal income tax bracket in retirement, and that will also save on taxes. It depends on how retirement withdrawals are spread across all income tax brackets. If your adjusted gross income (AGI) is pushed lower because of the way you are taking money out of your retirement accounts, that will result in a lower effective tax rate on the withdrawals.

Saving Money by Spending Tax-Free Retirement Income

Tax-deductible retirement accounts may provide even greater tax savings if the withdrawals are combined with tax-free retirement income. By replacing some of the withdrawals from tax-deductible retirement accounts with tax-free income, you can maintain the same level of spending in retirement while further increasing the tax savings and further reducing your income tax bill in retirement. For example, withdrawals from a Roth IRA are tax-free, and withdrawals of previous contributions to taxable investment accounts, including savings accounts, money market accounts, and certificates of deposit, are also tax-free because those funds have already been taxed. Money received from selling assets such as stocks, real estate, or mutual funds is also tax-free to the extent that you get back your original investment, while the gains are usually taxed at the long-term capital gains tax rate. Gains on the sale of your main home are also usually tax-free.

Assume David and Donna withdraw $10,000 from a money market account instead of their tax-deductible retirement account. They will reduce their income tax obligation by an additional $1,500, in which case they would pay a total income tax of just $5,512.50, for an effective income tax rate of only 9.17 percent! If they withdraw $20,000 from a money market account instead of their tax deductible accounts, they could reduce their income tax obligation by $3,000, for an effective income tax rate on the tax-deductible withdrawals of only 8.03 percent! Remember that David and Donna saved 25 percent in taxes on every dollar that they contributed to their tax-deductible retirement accounts while they were working.

Qualify for Additional Tax Credits and Deductions

Contributions to tax-deductible retirement accounts provide yet another tax benefit that other accounts do not—they reduce your AGI so that you may be able to qualify for certain tax credits or tax deductions. Examples include the child tax credit, the earned income credit, and the student loan interest deduction. Even if you already qualify for those or other tax credits or tax deductions, your tax-deductible retirement contributions may actually increase the amount of the tax credits or tax deductions to which you are entitled. Assume a married couple with at least one child files a joint return. They will receive the full $1,000 child tax credit so long as their AGI does not exceed $110,000. The credit is reduced by $50 for every $1,000 of AGI above that level. If the couple earned a combined $120,000 and contributed $10,000 to a tax-deductible retirement account, they will effectively increase the amount of the child tax credit by $500 and correspondingly reduce their tax bill by the same amount, in addition to the $2,500 they will save by deferring the income tax due on the tax deductible contributions.

Reducing your AGI provides another potential tax benefit: you may become eligible to contribute to a Roth IRA. A single person with an AGI of $121,500 can become eligible to contribute the full amount to a Roth IRA by contributing $16,500 to a 401(k) and thereby reducing the AGI to $105,000, the threshold at which a person is allowed to make a full Roth IRA contribution.

Convert Tax-Deductible Contributions to a Roth IRA Later

Contributions to a tax-deductible retirement account provide another tax benefit. You will retain the option of converting some of the tax-deductible contributions to a Roth IRA at lower marginal tax rates in the future, and you can time these conversions to get the best possible trade-off between paying current and future taxes. For example, assume you have sufficient savings to fund all of your retirement expenses in any given retirement year. You will probably not owe any income taxes at all, assuming no other sources of taxable income. The withdrawal of previously taxed funds from savings accounts or taxable accounts are completely tax-free. You will then have the option to convert some of the funds in your tax-deductible accounts to a Roth IRA without paying any income tax at all!

Consider David and Donna Deferral in the year they retire. If they sell their house for $300,000 and buy a smaller house for $200,000, they will have $100,000 to pay for living expenses—more than enough to fund their first year in retirement. With no other taxable income, they can then convert $35,400 from their rollover IRA into a Roth IRA. The first $18,700 is not taxed and will grow tax-free for the rest of their retirement. The next $16,700 is taxed at 10 percent, so they pay 10 percent tax now to avoid paying 15 percent tax later on the same money. They pay only $1,670 in tax and the rest of the money will cover part of next year's living expenses.

Potential Disadvantages of Deferring Income

If you will be in the fortunate position of receiving so much taxable income after retirement that you will be in the same marginal tax bracket after retirement, the tax savings just described would be eliminated. It is even possible that you could have so much taxable retirement income that you will be pushed into a higher marginal tax bracket in retirement as a result of tax deferrals. In that case, if you withdraw funds from a tax-deductible retirement account, you would actually owe more tax than if you had paid the income tax when you were working at the lower marginal tax rate.

Required distributions from IRA accounts start at age 70½. The distribution period for a 71-year-old is 26.5 years, and that means you will need to withdraw 3.6 percent of your IRA balance and pay income taxes on the distribution. The amount goes up over the years. When you are 81 years old, the distribution period is 17.9 years, and the distribution rate is 5.6 percent, which requires you to pay taxes on a larger amount. Here is the shocker: when you are 91 years old, the distribution period is 10.8 years. That means you must distribute 9.3 percent of your account balance and pay taxes on the entire amount. The older you get, the larger the required distribution and the more taxes you have to pay. Couple larger RMD distributions with the potential of higher income tax rates in the future, and retirees with substantial savings are going to be writing extremely large checks to the IRS in their later years.

Many people expect income tax rates to increase in the future to pay for the huge federal deficit we are accumulating. If marginal income tax brackets are indeed higher when you retire, the expected tax savings that you will realize from contributing to tax-deductible accounts may be reduced, but they're unlikely to be eliminated because the progressive tax system is likely to be retained and expanded. The effective tax rate applicable to the withdrawals from your tax-deductible retirement accounts will probably be less than your marginal tax rate during your peak earning years, assuming higher income tax rates prevail after you retire. Recall that David and Donna saved 25 percent of every dollar that they contributed to their tax-deductible retirement accounts, but the effective tax rate on the withdrawals in retirement was only 10 percent, and even the last dollar was taxed at 15 percent. If the lower tax brackets are increased to 15 percent and 20 percent before they retire, they will still realize a net tax savings because they saved 25 percent of every dollar that they contributed while they were working.

Fourth Priority: Roth IRA

If you are in a moderate or high marginal tax bracket, study the difference between tax-deductible investing and tax-free investing in a Roth IRA, or in a Roth 401(k) if your employer offers one. If you are in a high tax bracket, the tax savings from tax-deferred savings might be substantial. But if you are in a very low marginal tax bracket, you should prefer a Roth IRA over tax-deductible investing because the income tax that you would save now by investing in a tax-deductible retirement account is likely to be less than the tax you will pay when the funds are withdrawn in retirement. In addition, you may use a Roth IRA as a supplement to your retirement plan because your employer plan may have no choice or a poor choice in some asset classes, or you may need additional tax-advantaged investing space.

Roth IRAs offer a significant tax benefit. Anyone who qualifies to contribute to a Roth IRA should consider including this vehicle as part of a well-rounded retirement savings plan. The tax benefits of a Roth IRA are the mirror image of the tax benefits of tax-deductible retirement accounts. Contributions to a Roth IRA are not tax-deductible, and they do not reduce your AGI, but withdrawals in retirement are tax-free.

The tax-free Roth account offers a form of protection against future income tax rate increases in retirement. Retirement income from Roth IRAs reduces the amount of Social Security benefits that are subject to income tax, because the income is not included in your AGI that is used to calculate how much of your Social Security benefits are subject to income tax. Of course, there is also a small risk that Congress will change the rules and make Roth IRA withdrawals partially taxable, or limit the amount of tax-free withdrawals by some form of means testing, with high earners paying more in taxes per dollar withdrawn.

As an illustration, consider Professor Young, who takes advantage of his low tax rate. Professor Young is a 30-year-old assistant professor at a state college who earns $45,000 per year. He expects to earn a higher income later in his career when he becomes a full professor. His college enrolled everyone in the 403(b) plan by default with a 6 percent employee contribution and a 3 percent matched contribution. Professor Young is in the 15 percent tax bracket, with adjusted gross income of $42,300. His AGI is reduced by the $2,700 contribution to the college 403(b) plan.

Professor Young expects to be in the 25 percent marginal income tax bracket in the future and when he retires. He has invested his 403(b) with a low-cost investment provider, and as long as he is in the 15 percent bracket, a Roth IRA is better for him than an unmatched contribution to the 403(b).

Comparing Costs

The cost of a Roth IRA is easy to compute. It is the expense of the investments, compounded over the number of years you hold the fund. The effective cost of a tax-deductible investment must also include the tax benefits of the deduction and the taxes paid later. Table 10.2 gives examples of the cost comparison, illustrating why an investor who expects to retire in a higher tax bracket should prefer a Roth over an unmatched 401(k), while an investor who expects to retire in a lower tax bracket should usually prefer a 401(k) unless the 401(k) has higher costs which negate the tax advantage. To estimate the cost difference, compound the difference in expenses for as long as you stay with the employer; an extra 1 percent a year is a cost of 10 percent if you leave the employer in 10 years and then roll over the 401(k) to an IRA.

As an illustration, consider Frank and Francis Frugal, who minimize their costs. A married couple, both 45 years old, Frank works for the U.S. government, and Frances works at a hospital. Each earns $90,000 a year. Their state tax bracket is 6 percent, and they expect to retire in the same state. Frances has a mediocre 403(b) plan.

Their first investing priority is to get the employer matches. Frank and Frances both get a match on the first 5 percent they contribute to their TSP and 403(b) plans. Frank has a health savings account (HSA) as part of his health insurance and adds his own money to contribute the maximum to the account. (See Chapter 4 for a discussion of health savings accounts.) Frank and Frances can be in either the 25 percent or 28 percent marginal tax bracket, depending on how much they reduce their income with retirement contributions and deductions. After accounting for state taxes, they are in the 29.5 percent or 32.3 percent combined marginal income tax bracket. They plan to retire in the 25 percent tax bracket in the same state and plan to take the standard deduction in retirement, so they will be in a 31 percent bracket. Since these brackets are close, they should prefer to save in the lowest-expense plans.

Frank's TSP charges 0.02 percent a year in expenses and is a great deal. That is better than the low 0.2 percent on their Roth IRAs and

TABLE 10.2 RELATIVE VALUES OF ROTH AND
TAX-DEFERRED PLANS

CURRENT TAX BRACKET	TAX BRACKET IN RETIREMENT	$1,000 OUT OF POCKET BECOMES X IN TAX-DEFERRED	AFTER-TAX WITHDRAWAL VALUE
25%	15%	$1,333	$1,133
28%	25%	$1,389	$1,041
25%	25%	$1,333	$1,000
15%	25%	$1,176	$882
15% with 100% employer match	25%	$2,353	$1,765

much better than the 1.0 percent expenses on Frances's 403(b). Based on all this information, if they have $15,000 to save after getting the matches and HSA contribution, they should contribute the maximum allowed to Frank's TSP, which is an additional $12,000, and then contribute $3,000 to a Roth IRA. This is their most advantageous allocation, based on current taxes and fees.

Fifth Priority: Taxable Accounts

Taxable accounts are any accounts that are not tax-free or tax-deferred, and they include general investment accounts, brokerage accounts, savings accounts, money market accounts, certificates of deposit, and any other form of account that is funded with after-tax money and is subject to income tax or capital gains tax each year. The tax treatment is detailed in Chapters 2 and 3. You should consider investing in taxable accounts as part of your retirement plan if you have exhausted the previous options. It is unlikely that you will want to invest for retirement in taxable accounts if you still have tax-deferred options, even if they are poor. If a taxable account loses 30 percent to taxes, a 401(k) charging 1.5 percent a year in extra expenses is still worth more after tax, unless you expect to stay with the employer for more than 20 years.

Moving Taxable Money into Tax-Advantaged Accounts

If you invested money in a taxable account before reading this book and realizing that you may have made a mistake, or if you invested a windfall inheritance or a large bonus in your taxable account, you may be wondering if it's worth transferring this money to tax-advantaged accounts over time. Any tax you pay on capital gains will be much less than the tax you'll save by getting the money into tax-deferred accounts. This strategy assumes you are not currently able to maximize all tax-advantaged retirement accounts available to you or your spouse, using your current income. This strategy involves immediately making the maximum annual contribution to your IRA.

Most 401(k) plans let you contribute 100 percent of your salary to your 401(k), up to the plan limit, but prohibit transferring funds from non-401(k) accounts. You could immediately change your payroll deductions to maximize all contributions to employer-sponsored retirement accounts. By doing this, and using taxable money to cover your daily living expenses, you are effectively transferring the taxable money into your tax-advantaged 401(k) account. Your spouse can do the same, halving the time it takes to transfer the money to tax-advantaged accounts. When the taxable money is gone, reset all retirement account deductions back to levels that can be supported by your income.

As an example, after Professor Young made the plan in the previous section, his grandmother died, leaving him $100,000 in taxable money. He wants to use this money for retirement savings. He should temporarily hold the inheritance in a taxable account and max out both his Roth IRA and 403(b). He would then withdraw enough from the taxable account every year so he can continue to max out the retirement accounts.

Sixth Priority: Nondeductible IRAs and Annuities

We have now reached the lowest priority for your retirement investing: nondeductible IRAs and annuities. They are distinct account types, but their tax treatment is similar: you get no income tax deduction for the contributions, the account grows tax-deferred, and you pay tax on the gains at your full income tax rate when you withdraw the money. This income tax treatment—and the high fees on annuities—make them poor investment choices for most investors. Variable annuities have a variety of options, including some that guarantee a level of return. Some annuities have stable-value funds, which pay a fixed return that is determined every year; others have an option to guarantee a certain minimum return. The single-premium immediate annuities (SPIAs) covered in Chapter 8 are not the same as variable annuities. Do not confuse them.

Taxable accounts are preferable to nondeductible IRAs as long as tax-efficient investments are selected. In a nondeductible IRA, you defer taxes, but when you pay tax on all your gains, you pay the tax at your full income tax rate even on your capital gains rather than the lower capital gains tax rate. This is the potential disadvantage of a nondeductible IRA compared with a taxable account.

A nondeductible IRA might be a reasonable choice if you would otherwise have to hold tax-inefficient investments, such as bonds, in your taxable account. A stock index fund is likely to do better in an ordinary taxable account than a nondeductible IRA.

Variable annuities have the additional significant disadvantage of higher costs. The fees associated with most variable annuities are very high—2 percent fees are common. Even low-cost providers such as Vanguard charge significantly more for their variable annuities than for their comparable mutual funds. In addition, most variable annuities have surrender charges, which force you to either pay the high fees for a long period or pay the annuity provider a fee to compensate them for the high fees you avoided paying by leaving early. A typical surrender charge structure might be 7 percent if you redeem in the first year, decreasing by 1 percent a year until you have already paid 14 percent or more in total annual fees by holding the variable annuity for seven years.

Even a low-cost variable annuity is not likely to cost less than a comparable taxable investment. The only situation in which a low-cost variable annuity might make sense is if you need to hold something tax-inefficient, such as REITs, and you have no way of holding it in one of your other tax-deferred accounts. If you already have a high-cost variable annuity, it may well make sense to pay any surrender fees. The surrender fee is likely to be less than the total cost of staying until the fees go away. Switch to a low-cost provider such as Vanguard or TIAA-CREF, and then invest it the same way you would invest in an IRA. If you have a high-cost variable annuity inside your 401(k) or 403(b), roll it over to an IRA when you leave your employer. Since the rollover doesn't have to be to another annuity, you'd then have the entire range of low-cost investment options available to you in your rollover IRA.

Timing Contributions for Tax Benefits
Susan Saver, age 30, has served eight years in the U.S. Army and is now a captain earning $63,000 a year. Like Professor Young, she expects to make more later in her career. The Army does not match contributions to the TSP. Instead, it provides her with a pension. Therefore, her choice is between unmatched contributions to the TSP and Roth IRA contributions.

Her tax situation has one special consideration. Most military pay in a combat zone is exempt from taxes. Therefore, she is in the 25 percent bracket if she spends most or all of the year in the United States. However, if she spends half the year in a combat zone, she'll pay only 15 percent on her U.S. pay and 0 percent on her combat pay. Tax-exempt contributions to the TSP work like a nondeductible IRA; she will pay tax at her full tax rate but only on the gains. She won't retire in a combat zone, so she expects to retire in the 25 percent tax bracket. Her state bracket is 5 percent and will be the same 5 percent in retirement.

When she expects to spend most of the year stateside, she prefers the TSP to a Roth IRA because of the TSP's lower expenses, since she is in the same tax bracket now as at retirement. If she will be deployed for part of the year, then the Roth IRA becomes the better choice, since she expects to retire in a higher tax bracket than her tax bracket for that year. The Roth IRA is clearly better for tax-exempt pay. If she learns that she will be deployed in November, she will want to make sure to get all her TSP contributions made by October so that they are deductible and then contribute only to the Roth in November or December if she has more to contribute. If she learns that she will be deployed in July, she should max out her Roth IRA while deployed and take the rest of her contributions to the TSP from her taxable pay.

ADDITIONAL RESOURCES

* The IRS web site, www.irs.gov, is the natural place to look up the income limits or tax rates on various sources of income. It was the source for all of the tax information in this chapter.
* Fairmark, www.fairmark.com, online investment tax guides.
* TurboTax, TaxCut, and TaxAct software, useful tools for tax questions. Enter your tax data into this software to see how all of the deductions, phase-outs, and limitations interact.

CHAPTER SUMMARY

Carefully consider the types of accounts available for your retirement investments and the order in which you choose to invest in those accounts. Taking an employer match and paying down high-interest debts should be easy decisions. Then take full advantage of tax-deductible retirement accounts unless you are in a low marginal tax bracket or the investment options available in that account are very poor. A Roth IRA also deserves serious consideration, especially if you are in a low marginal tax bracket or need additional tax-advantaged investment space to supplement any plans available through your employer. If you are in the fortunate position of contributing the maximum to all available retirement plans and you would like to contribute additional funds for your retirement, you should then contribute to a taxable account. A nondeductible IRA should be considered only if you have a considerable amount of taxable savings. A variable annuity is almost never a good choice.

PART IV

THE RETIREMENT PAYOFF

CHAPTER ELEVEN

Understanding Social Security

Dick Schreitmueller

INTRODUCTION

Social Security is the primary source of income for many retirees in the United States, yet few of us know much about this vast program. How much will your benefits be? When can you start to receive them? Should you apply for benefits as soon as possible? Must you pay income tax on these benefits? What happens to the money deducted from your pay for Social Security? Will the program run out of money, and what happens if it does?

Social Security's formal name is Old-Age, Survivors, and Disability Insurance (OASDI). Federal law specifies the main features of Social Security, which only Congress can change. The Social Security Administration (SSA) issues detailed rules and forms, communicates with you, and pays benefits. The Internal Revenue Service (IRS) collects the taxes that support Social Security.

This chapter answers some basic Social Security questions about retirement benefits for workers and their spouses. Chapter 14 will explain how Social Security protects workers and their families before retirement age with disability and survivor benefits. The information in this book can only act as a guide. The best source for detailed information is the Social Security Administration.

HOW MUCH WILL YOU GET FROM SOCIAL SECURITY?

Social Security laws are vast and complex. The system covers a wide range of recipients who receive hundreds of billions of dollars per year from the government. Generally, people are familiar with old-age benefits; however, the law covers much more, including disability benefits; benefits for a surviving spouse of a deceased worker, surviving child of a deceased worker, or surviving parent of a deceased worker; benefits for a spouse of an old-age or disability benefits recipient; and benefits for children of an old-age or disability benefits recipient. This chapter concentrates on Social Security old-age benefits.

Who Is Covered

Social Security covers about 95 percent of American workers, including nearly every worker in private employment. The noncovered workers include some railroad workers and employees of a few state and local governments that opted out of the program years ago. A relatively few other workers are excluded by law because of special occupations, religious beliefs (such as the Amish), and other reasons. Household workers or family members are excluded if their annual wages are very small.

Social Security covers uniformed members of the military, as well as most others within the federal government. It covers civilian employees who (a) are elected or appointed officials or judges, (b) were hired after 1983, (c) were rehired after 1983 following a break in service of more than a year, or (d) elected to transfer to a federal retirement program that includes Social Security. By about the middle of this century, all federal government employees will be under Social Security.

In state and local government, most employers elected to cover their employees by Social Security during the 1950s. Noncovered state and local employees are those who never came into the program and certain formerly covered groups whose employers elected to terminate coverage before 1984. Congress changed the rules in 1983 to prevent any more groups from dropping out of Social Security. About 70 percent of state and local government employees are now covered.

Retirement and Survivor Benefits

The amount of your Social Security retirement benefit is based on your year of birth, your age when your benefits begin, and the earnings on which you paid Social Security payroll taxes—not on the amount of taxes you paid. This section explains the benefit rules and has numerical examples. References given later list computer programs for estimating your benefit or calculating it exactly.

Social Security isn't adequate for most people to maintain a comfortable standard of living in retirement. It is designed to provide a floor, a minimum level of income to partially replace earned income. Social Security provides a base that you can build on with employer plan benefits, personal savings, and part-time work. Retirement income from Social Security has the extra benefit of an automatic cost-of-living adjustment (COLA) that increases your payments annually to keep pace with inflation.

You should apply for benefits about three months before you want them to begin. It also helps to discuss your situation with a Social Security representative about a year before you apply.

Eligibility for Benefits

You may apply for your benefits to begin between the ages of 62 and 70 if you have at least 10 years of coverage. A retired worker's spouse can apply for benefits at age 62 or later. A surviving spouse of a worker or retired worker can apply at age 60 or later.

A divorced spouse who was married to a retired worker for at least 10 years and is unmarried may start benefits at age 62 or later. Benefits payable to your ex-spouse do not affect the benefits payable to you or your current spouse. If you apply for two benefits, for example, as a worker and a spouse, you get only the larger one. Federal law now defines marriage as between one man and one woman for purposes of all federal programs. Social Security recognizes common law marriages but not same-sex marriages.

YOUR ANNUAL SOCIAL SECURITY STATEMENT

Workers and former workers receive a personal statement from SSA by mail each year after age 25 or on request at any age. Your statement shows year-by-year earnings on which you have paid Social Security taxes. It also summarizes the estimated benefit amounts you and your family may get as a result of those earnings. The statement is a handy guide to your benefits. It also gives you a chance to correct any errors in the official record of your earnings.

Benefit Amount

Your basic benefit amount as a worker (sometimes called the primary insurance amount) is computed by a very complex set of formulas. The formulas go through these four steps:

1. Compiling a history of your earnings for each year you worked under Social Security.
2. Indexing each year's earnings to make them reflect historical levels of average national wages. This generally raises the amounts of your prior years' earnings to be used in the benefit calculation.
3. Averaging the indexed earnings for the 35 highest years, which may include years with zero earnings.
4. Applying a graded set of percentages to the average indexed earnings. The percentages decrease as your earnings go up, so that higher-paid workers get proportionately lower benefits as a percentage of their earnings.

The resulting basic benefit amount gets adjusted annually after age 62 to keep up with inflation, based on changes in the consumer price index (CPI). For more information, see "Your Retirement Benefit: How It Is Figured" at www.ssa.gov.

For a worker's spouse, the basic benefit is half of the worker's benefit while both spouses are alive. For a surviving spouse, the basic benefit is equal to the deceased worker's benefit. The basic benefit for a worker, spouse, or surviving spouse is reduced if it begins before the individual's full retirement age.

Full Retirement Age

Full retirement age is the age when you can get a full benefit—an important milestone. Social Security retirement benefits that begin sooner are reduced, and benefits that begin later are increased. If you were born after 1942, your full retirement age is in the range of 66 to 67, as shown in Table 11.1.

Once you reach full retirement age, there's no limit on how much income you can earn without any reduction in your benefit by the retirement earnings test (explained later). Table 11.2 illustrates the amount of a worker's basic benefit at full retirement age 66 in 2008, based on four different patterns of preretirement earnings.

Note that as a worker's earnings go up, the benefit amount increases, but the percentage of preretirement earnings decreases. For workers who

TABLE 11.1 FULL RETIREMENT AGE

Year of Birth	Year You Reach Age 62	Your Full Retirement Age
1943–1954	2005–2016	66
1955	2017	66 and 2 months
1956	2018	66 and 4 months
1957	2019	66 and 6 months
1958	2020	66 and 8 months
1959	2021	66 and 10 months
1960 and after	After 2021	67

Source: 2008 OASDI Trustees' Report, Table V.C3

TABLE 11.2 SAMPLE BENEFITS AT FULL RETIREMENT, AGE 66

Earnings Level	Benefit Amount	% of Earnings
Low earner	$10,252	55.7%
Medium earner	$16,893	41.3%
High earner	$22,383	34.3%
Maximum earner	$26,455	28.4%

Source: 2008 OASDI Trustees' Report, Table VI.F.10

retire after 2008, these same percentages will apply at their full retirement age, with earnings patterns and benefit amounts adjusted to 2008 dollars.

HOW OTHER SOURCES OF INCOME AFFECT BENEFITS
Working after Benefit Begins

If you work while you get a Social Security retirement or survivor benefit, the retirement earnings test may reduce your benefit temporarily.

This rule counts only money you earn from working, not income from investments.

- If you are under full retirement age for the entire year, $1 of your benefit is withheld for every $2 you earn above an annual limit ($14,160 in 2009)
- In the year you reach full retirement age, $1 of your benefit is withheld for every $3 you earn above a higher limit ($37,680 in 2009). This formula counts only earnings before the month when you reach full retirement age.
- After full retirement age, you get your benefit without any limit on your earnings.

At full retirement age, SSA automatically recalculates your benefit and gives you credit for any months when your benefit was reduced or withheld. Thus, if the retirement earnings test takes away some of your benefit, you get it back later. Your benefit will also increase if your latest earnings were high enough to raise your 35-year average earnings record.

Pension from Noncovered Employment

Your Social Security benefit may be reduced if you get a pension from work not covered by Social Security. In that case:

- The windfall elimination provision may reduce your own Social Security retirement benefit.
- The government pension offset provision may reduce or eliminate any Social Security spousal benefit that's available to you because your spouse worked under Social Security.

Software for estimating an individual's Social Security benefit often disregards both these provisions and thus may overstate your actual benefit.

THE TAXATION OF SOCIAL SECURITY BENEFITS

The rules are very complex for determining whether any of your benefit is taxable as income and how much is taxable. There are two considerations: the amount of Social Security benefit that is taxed and the marginal rate you pay on that amount. The income you earn from other sources has a direct impact on the amount of Social Security benefit subject to tax and the marginal tax rate you pay on the benefit. The information that follows is a basic overview. Chapter 2 provides more information on marginal rates.

Basic Rules

The IRS treats up to 85 percent of an individual's Social Security benefit that is above a base amount as taxable income. For most taxpayers receiving Social Security, the base amount is high enough that none of their benefit is taxed now. But the base amount doesn't go up with inflation, so in future years, more and more retirees will pay tax on their Social Security benefit.

State and local tax treatment varies widely. Most of the states with an income tax do not tax Social Security benefits. Most of those states that do tax benefits offer a deduction or other relief rather than taxing the same amount as the IRS does. Detailed information on state tax policy as it relates to Social Security is available at the AARP web site, www.aarp.org.

How Much of Your Benefit Does the IRS Tax?

Table 11.3 gives a very rough approximation of the amount of your benefit that will be subject to tax. The percentage of your benefit that's reportable as income for tax purposes can vary from zero to 85 percent, depending on how much other income you have. Provisional income in Table 11.3 is the sum of your adjusted gross income (excluding Social Security), any tax-exempt interest, and half of your Social Security benefit.

TABLE 11.3   PERCENTAGE OF BENEFIT SUBJECT TO INCOME TAX

YOU ARE A:	AND YOUR PROVISIONAL INCOME IS	THIS MUCH OF YOUR BENEFIT IS TAXABLE
Single taxpayer	Less than $25,000	None is taxable
	$25,000 to $34,000	Up to 50%
	Above $34,000	50 to 85%
Couple filing jointly	Less than $32,000	None is taxable
	$32,000 to $34,000	Up to 50%
	Above $34,000	50 to 85%

Calculating the exact amount of your benefit subject to federal income taxation takes some doing. Fortunately, tax preparation software such as TurboTax or TaxCut will do all the work. Following are the steps usually needed, omitting a few refinements that are rarely encountered.

First, let's note some special items used in the computation:

- Adjusted gross income: From your federal tax return, excluding Social Security.
- Provisional income: From your federal tax return excluding Social Security. It is your adjusted gross income plus tax-exempt interest plus half of your Social Security benefits (including Tier 1 railroad retirement benefits).
- Base amount: $32,000 for couples filing a joint return, $25,000 for a single taxpayer.
- Higher base amount: $44,000 for a couple ($34,000 for a single).
- Constant amount: $6,000 for a couple ($4,500 for a single).

The computation goes like this (did we mention that it's very complex?):

a. If your provisional income exceeds the base amount, then you must include in taxable income 50 percent of the excess of provisional income over the base amount or, if less, half of your benefits.
b. If your provisional income exceeds the higher base amount, then you must instead include in taxable income 85 percent of your benefits or, if less, the sum of (A) 85 percent of the excess of provisional income over the higher base amount and (B) the smaller of the amount computed in step a or the constant amount.

Putting all this together, Table 11.4 goes through all the steps in a sample calculation of taxable Social Security benefits.

Table 11.4 is adapted from an example in the 2008 edition of IRS Publication 915, at www.irs.gov. Publication 915 is an excellent source of information on the details of Social Security benefit taxation.

WHERE DO SOCIAL SECURITY DOLLARS GO?
Income and Outflow

Income to Social Security was about $808 billion in 2009. Most came from payroll taxes paid by workers and their employers. During 2009, employers and employees each were taxed at 6.2 percent on wages up to $106,800.

TABLE 11.4   SAMPLE CALCULATION OF TAXABLE SOCIAL
              SECURITY BENEFITS

ASSUMPTIONS FOR THIS EXAMPLE:	
Couple is filing joint return	
Adjusted gross income excluding Social Security = $40,000	
Social Security benefits received in the year = $10,000	
Tax-exempt interest = $500	
Other Amounts to Be Used in the Calculation:	
Provisional income = $40,000 + ½ of 10,000 + $500 = $45,500	
Base amount = $32,000	
Higher base amount = $44,000	
Constant amount = $6,000	
1. Does provisional income ($45,500) exceed the base amount ($32,000)?	Yes
If No, you're finished: report zero taxable Social Security income. **If Yes,** keep going.	
2. 50 percent of this excess (50% of $13,500) or, if less, half of benefits (½ of $10,000)	$5,000
3. Does provisional income ($45,500) exceed the higher base amount ($44,000)?	Yes
If No, you're finished: report the amount from line 2 as taxable Social Security income. **If Yes,** keep going.	
4. 85 percent of the excess of provisional income ($45,500) over the higher base amount ($44,000)	$1,275
5. The smaller of line 2 ($5,000) or the constant amount ($6,000)	$5,000
6. The smaller of line 4 ($1,275) or line 5 ($5,000)	$1,275
7. The smaller of line 6 ($1,275) or 85 percent of benefits ($8,500)	$1,275
8. Add line 2 ($5,000) and line 7 ($1,275). Report this amount as taxable Social Security income.	$6,275

Source: IRS Publication 915

Additional income comes from interest on trust fund assets and from part of the income taxes that get paid on Social Security benefits.

Expenditures from Social Security were about $686 billion in 2009. That covered benefits to 50 million people, plus the cost to administer the program. Administrative expenses were a little under 1 cent for each dollar of benefits paid.

The Trust Funds

Any excess of income over expenditure, currently about $120 billion per year, goes into the Social Security trust funds. These funds amount to more than $2.5 trillion at the end of 2009. They are invested in a special type of U.S. Treasury bond underwritten for the fund. Treasury uses this money to pay for other government programs, while crediting interest on the bonds held in the trust funds. In other words, the cash is spent as soon as Treasury gets it, and Social Security holds a growing stack of government IOUs.

Social Security's cash surpluses in every year from 1984-2009 have made a substantial contribution toward reducing the government's annual budget deficit. However, cash expenditures in 2010 are expected to exceed tax receipts for the first time since 1983. The projected cash deficit of $41 billion in 2010 (which excludes interest income) is attributable to the recession and to an expected $25 billion downward adjustment to 2010 income that corrects for overstatement of payroll tax revenue in earlier years. This deficit is expected to shrink substantially in 2011 and to return to small surpluses in 2012-2014 due to the improving economy. After 2014, cash deficits are expected to grow rapidly.

Although the thought of the government taking all the money out to pay for other programs sounds ominous, the process is not much different from any pension fund that invests in U.S. Treasury securities as part of an asset allocation. The money invested in Treasury bills, notes, and bonds goes to fund the day-to-day business of the government.

Financial Outlook

Social Security's official annual projections of long-range income and expenditures indicate trouble ahead. The best actuarial estimates show expenditures rising rapidly, exceeding income after 2016. From that point on, Social Security will need increasingly large amounts of cash from Treasury to pay benefits. By about 2037, Treasury will have repaid all the money borrowed from Social Security; that is, the trust funds will be used up. After that, under current law, Social Security income would be enough to pay only about 74 percent of the scheduled benefits.

Causes of the long-range financial problems are mainly demographic. Large numbers of baby boomers born between 1946 and 1964 are reaching retirement age over the next two decades, while relatively few young people are entering the workforce. At the same time, the longevity of retirees is gradually increasing. As a result, the number of workers for each Social Security beneficiary is expected to shrink from 3.3 in 2009 to 2.2 in 2030 and to stay at about that level indefinitely. More information on the health of Social Security and Medicare can be found at www.ssa.gov.

SOCIAL SECURITY REFORM

A strong economy helps Social Security's finances by boosting the number of workers, their wage levels, and their payroll taxes. Unfortunately, economic downturns have the opposite effect on Social Security. Also, Treasury had to meet huge demands for funds to help the economy recover from the recession in 2008 and 2009. Meanwhile, Medicare's financial problems are much larger, more urgent, and harder to fix than Social Security.

There's virtually no chance that Congress will let this popular program run out of money to pay scheduled benefits. Social Security will get fixed, though the timing and methods may fall within a wide range. Social Security reform is better done sooner than later. However, that will require political leadership to form a consensus in Washington, and there has not been any on this issue in recent years.

Possible reforms include higher full retirement ages, gradual reductions in the growth of benefits with inflation, tax increases on employers and workers, means testing to reduce or eliminate benefits to high-net-worth individuals, and even general-revenue subsidies from Treasury. Diverting Social Security funds into the stock market has also been discussed, but it is not popular. Benefits for existing retirees will probably be protected against reduction.

MINIMUM AND MAXIMUM RETIREMENT AGES

Social Security retirement benefits can begin at any age from 62 to 70. Lifetime benefits go up each month you wait. This section explains how you can increase your monthly benefit as a worker or spouse for the rest of your life by waiting to apply.

Earliest Age to Receive Benefits Is 62

Workers and their spouses may receive retirement benefits as early as age 62. Surviving spouses can begin benefits at 60. Benefits are permanently reduced if they begin before full retirement age. The amount paid at age 62 to a worker born after 1959 is 30 percent less than the full benefit. The comparable reduction for a spouse is 35 percent.

Mandatory Payment at Age 70—Delayed Retirement Credit

If you were born after 1942, your basic benefit increases by a delayed retirement credit of 8 percent for each year that you wait past full retirement age, up to age 70. Years ago, when the credit was only 3 percent for each year you waited, it made perfect sense to start benefits by your normal retirement age or before. Despite what you may have heard, that's no longer true, especially with retirees living longer than ever.

The delayed retirement credit is on top of the automatic cost-of-living adjustments that are added to your available benefit each year after age 62 while you're waiting. There is nothing to gain by waiting beyond age 70, so it's essentially mandatory for you to start benefits by age 70.

Benefits to a spouse are computed from the basic benefit earned by the worker married to that spouse. So a married couple can both gain when one of them waits until 70 to build up a larger benefit. Table 11.5 shows the percentage of your basic benefit that's available if you apply either before or after full retirement age.

Suppose you were born after 1959 and your estimated basic benefit is $1,000 a month at your full retirement age of 67. The last line in the table indicates that your benefit at age 62 would be $700 and that it would be $1,240 if you waited to age 70. The increase would be even more if additional earnings, credited while you're waiting to apply, increase your basic benefit.

When Is the Ideal Time to Start Collecting?

One of the most asked questions is "When is the best time to apply for Social Security benefits?" There is no simple answer to that question. First, you need to decide when you have enough financial resources to retire and are comfortable about taking that big step. Do not quit work and apply for Social Security before doing the math because you may discover that your benefit does not provide enough money. Of course, many workers have little choice about when to stop working because of poor health or job loss.

You can start Social Security as early as age 62 and get lower monthly payments for life or start as late as 70 and maximize your monthly payments. Each month you wait between 62 and 70 increases your monthly

TABLE 11.5 PERCENTAGE OF BASIC BENEFIT PAYABLE
AT VARIOUS AGES

YEAR OF BIRTH	AGE 62	AGE 66	AGE 67	AGE 70
1943–1954	75.0%	100.0%	108.0%	132.0%
1955	74.2%	98.9%	106.7%	130.7%
1956	73.3%	97.8%	105.3%	129.3%
1957	72.5%	96.7%	104.0%	128.0%
1958	71.7%	95.6%	102.7%	126.7%
1959	70.8%	94.4%	101.3%	125.3%
After 1959	70.0%	93.3%	100.0%	124.0%

Source: 2008 OASDI Trustees' Report, Table V.C3

benefit. Whether you start early or late, your lifetime benefits, including cost-of-living increases, have about the same expected value. If your wife or husband receives a benefit as your spouse or surviving spouse, that amount will be based on your benefit. Still, as discussed in the following, your own situation may make a difference:

* Take into account you and your spouse's expected longevity, based on personal and family history. That's only common sense if you're deciding when to start receiving payments from an annuity or pension. Someone who expects to live a long time may prefer to wait and receive higher lifetime payments; someone in poor health may want to start collecting right away.
* If you plan to work part-time, learn how the retirement earnings test may reduce your benefit temporarily and make you consider deferring receipt of your benefit.
* You may want to consider certain SSA rules about starting and stopping benefit payments to a worker or spouse. Sometimes, following these rules carefully allows you to receive extra benefits.

The following are strategies for individuals and married couples to consider in deciding when to start their Social Security benefits. Some of these approaches take advantage of little-known SSA rules for claiming benefits as a worker or spouse. The discussion here assumes no change in the 2008 Social Security program or federal income tax code.

Strategy 1: Start as Early as Possible
Some workers want to retire as soon as Social Security is available. But if you're in good health, consider waiting past 62 before applying for Social Security so you can build up more retirement income. Many retirees live into their 80s and 90s, when Social Security may provide most or all of their income. This is especially true for women, who have a longer life expectancy than men. However, a married spouse with relatively low Social Security benefits is an exception to this rule if she would later get a larger spousal benefit anyway.

Another exception is an unmarried worker with below-average life expectancy and earnings. The shorter your life, the more it pays to start benefits as soon as possible. You also may make out better from the partial tax-free treatment of Social Security benefits.

Strategy 2: Start When You Stop Working Full-Time
Simply begin Social Security when you quit working full-time regardless of age (if you are age 62 or older). It makes sense for many workers who know when they can afford to retire and don't want to use some other strategy explained here.

Strategy 3: Start as Late as Possible
Waiting a few extra years to retire is a powerful way to make retirement more affordable. Consider waiting until age 70 to apply for Social Security if you're in good health and have enough other income to get by for that long. Applying for Social Security at 70 instead of 62 raises your monthly benefit by more than 75 percent. You may also save on income taxes by increasing your Social Security benefits that receive favorable tax treatment while spending down some of your taxable retirement savings. The disadvantage of waiting until age 70 is that you have a shorter life expectancy at that age and will collect fewer payments over your lifetime.

Strategy 4: Start at 62, Reapply at 70
Some individuals may want to take advantage of a SSA rule that lets you apply for benefits, say at age 62, then withdraw the application retroactively at a later age such as 70 and reapply. To do this, you must file SSA Form 521 and repay all benefits you've received without interest. It becomes an interest-free loan to you. Between ages 62 and 70, invest the money, and then keep the interest earnings when you repay the loan. If you paid income taxes on benefits that you're repaying, IRS Publication 915 explains how to recover such taxes as either an itemized deduction or a credit.

This strategy may appeal to a disciplined person in good health who can afford to invest the benefit money received before age 70 instead of spending it right away. What if your health and longevity deteriorate before you reach 70? In that case, you may simply choose not to repay the benefits and be glad you applied at 62.

Even if you're still in good health, there's no guarantee you'll live long enough to come out ahead by reapplying at 70, but your chances are good. Also, there is no guarantee the government won't change the rules, such as by making you repay the benefits with interest or by giving you only a short time to reapply after payments begin.

Strategy 5: Start Retirement Benefit, Grow Survivor Benefit

This method is for working couples wishing to maximize survivor benefits for the lower earning spouse. For example, Mary, the spouse with lower earnings, starts Social Security at 62 while her husband John waits to apply until age 70. John thus maximizes his retirement benefit, which would be Mary's potential benefit as a surviving spouse. This method may work well if Mary outlives John by many years.

What if John stops working before 70? In that case, the couple may need to draw down significant amounts of retirement savings until John's Social Security kicks in. The couple must plan their various sources of retirement income carefully. They need to make sure adequate income is available, no matter how long either spouse lives.

Strategy 6: Start Spousal Benefit, Grow Spouse's Retirement Benefit

This method may appeal to working couples, especially those with fairly similar earnings histories. For example:

a. John, the older spouse, starts his Social Security before Mary reaches her full retirement age (FRA).
b. At her FRA, Mary applies for just a spousal benefit, not a worker's benefit. Social Security rules allow such a limited application only by a person who has reached FRA. If Mary wants to keep working, the retirement earnings test won't reduce her spousal benefit after her FRA.
c. At age 70, Mary applies for her own retirement benefit.

Using this method, Mary eventually gets her full retirement benefit as a worker. Her spousal benefit is extra, a reward for following the benefit rules carefully.

**Strategy 7: Start Spousal Benefit, Grow Worker's
Retirement Benefit**

This method is for couples who want one of them to get spousal benefits
while the other waits to collect retirement benefits. Normally, SSA doesn't
allow this, but a special SSA rule makes it possible by letting a worker
who is getting benefits and has attained FRA suspend payment. Here is
an example:

1. John applies for Social Security at FRA.
2. His wife, Mary, applies for a spousal benefit.
3. John tells SSA to suspend payment of his benefit. These three actions
   may all take place at the same time or within a short period of time.
4. While John's benefit is suspended, he earns credit for waiting, just as
   if he'd never started his benefit.

More information on strategies 4, 6, and 7 is in the paper "Unique
Claiming Strategies" at http://crr.bc.edu. More information on strategy 5
is in Jim Mahaney and Peter Carlson's paper "Rethinking Social Security
Claiming in a 401(k) World." See www.pensionresearchcouncil.org.

BENEFIT CALCULATORS AVAILABLE FROM THE SSA

The Social Security Administration has links to benefit calculators for
various purposes on their web site. The most accurate calculators use your
actual earnings history, not earnings data that you enter or some kind
of rough estimate. Accuracy is very helpful when you're near retirement
but not too important when retirement is far away. Here's what SSA has
available online.

Retirement Estimator: This produces accurate benefit estimates at different retirement ages. It uses your official earnings record from SSA files.

Quick Calculator: This makes rough estimates based on just your current earnings plus assumptions about your past earnings. It also will
estimate disability or survivor benefits payable if you were to die or
become disabled today.

Online Calculator: This gives closer estimates than the quick calculator by using the earnings data you enter for past years.

Special Online Calculator: Unlike other calculators, this one includes
the windfall elimination provision that can reduce benefits of workers

with government pensions earned by service not covered under Social Security.

Detailed Calculator: This one is very powerful, able to compute almost any Social Security benefit. To use the program, you need to install it on your computer.

ADDITIONAL RESOURCES

- *The Social Security Handbook* explains Social Security rules in detail. Also, the "Annual Trustees' Report for OASDI" contains 75-year financial projections, plus a great many other tables and technical explanations. Search under www.ssa.gov.
- The Bogleheads' Wiki has links to Social Security resources and discussions. See www.bogleheads.org, and click the Wiki link.

CHAPTER SUMMARY

This chapter has given you an overview of Social Security information relevant to retirement planning. The system covers a wide range of recipients from old age benefits to disability payment to benefits for a surviving spouse and children. It is not possible in this chapter to cover all the contingencies, but it does give you a good start. For the foreseeable future, the viability and benefits of Social Security will keep playing an important part in determining how early you can afford to retire and how comfortably you'll live in retirement.

CHAPTER TWELVE

Withdrawal Strategies

Carol Tomkovich

INTRODUCTION

The end result of your retirement plan is to provide stable income in retirement that is high enough to maintain the lifestyle you wish to live. Part of that process will include making a number of decisions that will affect your lifestyle and your financial security as you approach the end of the accumulation phase of life.

While working full-time, you probably opened and funded several different types of accounts to assist in saving for retirement. One decision you will make as you enter retirement is how to efficiently take money out of those accounts. That is not always a simple decision because taxes play an important role. There are tax-efficient ways to withdraw money and tax-inefficient ways. The withdrawal decision is not as straightforward as it seems because a tax-efficient strategy in the short term may be a very tax-inefficient strategy in the long term. There are many things to consider. This chapter will provide you with the necessary tools.

BUDGETING FOR RETIREMENT

The amount you need to withdraw each month in retirement depends directly on the amount you anticipate spending in retirement. Your first order of business as you approach retirement is to do a budget.

Your budget or spending plan in retirement will be somewhat different than your budget while working full-time. Some expenses will increase, and others will decrease. You are likely to spend more money doing things you enjoy, such as travel and hobbies. Perhaps your medical costs will increase if you have to pay a greater portion of the premium or change insurance carriers. On the other hand, you will not be contributing to a retirement plan any more or paying Social Security taxes. Perhaps your clothing budget will also change. Taking time to estimate how these spending changes will affect the amount you need in retirement is a worthwhile endeavor.

Most people pay far lower taxes in retirement than they paid when working, and saving for retirement is curtailed or eliminated. For example, if soon-to-retire Sally earned a salary each year, paid employment and income taxes, contributed to her 401(k), and put money into savings each year, her retirement spending wouldn't include the employment portion of her taxes, nor would it include the 401(k) contributions or bank savings.

Two Ways to Estimate Spending

Estimating spending in retirement does not have to be difficult. You can either keep a detailed budget or do a rough, back-of-the-envelope estimate.

If tracking spending has never been a top priority for you, it is a good idea to attempt the exercise at least one year prior to retirement. Start by listing all of your normal expenses as they occur. That means writing down *everything* from mortgage to food, insurance, utilities, transportation, medical insurance premiums, charity, clothing, and so on. There are numerous budgeting tools available on the Internet by searching for the phrase. Much of your spending information can be found by looking over bank statements and credit card statements. Don't forget to include things that only occur once or twice per year such as property taxes and magazine subscriptions. Leave out income taxes for now.

After documenting your annual spending while working, make estimated adjustments for spending in retirement. You may not need to buy a lunch each day or buy dinner for the family because you are late getting home from work. New retirees tend to spend more fixing up their homes and doing repairs that they have been intending to do for years. A good rule of thumb for repairs is 1 percent annually of the value of a new home, or 2 to 3 percent annually of the value of an older home. Then there are the big expenses. If you purchased a new $25,000 car every 5 years while working full-time, perhaps you can stretch that to 7 or 8 years because you will not be driving as much.

A second way to estimate spending is to simply subtract your annual savings amount from your after-tax income. Write down your annual pre-tax income, total income taxes paid, and your net contributions to savings accounts for the past few years. Subtract your taxes and savings from your pretax income. This is the amount you spent. Once you have an idea of your spending while you are working, make adjustments for estimated spending changes in retirement, as stated earlier.

Taxes in Retirement

When you have documented your spending and estimated adjustments in retirement, it is time to address income taxes. Recall from Chapter 10 that marginal tax rates tend to fall in retirement. You are earning less taxable income, and that reduces income tax considerably. You also can select the accounts you withdraw retirement money from in retirement, which means you have control over the amount you pay in income taxes. In addition, no Social Security or Medicare taxes are paid on employer retirement benefits or withdrawals from tax-advantaged retirement accounts.

The easiest way to estimate your taxes in retirement is to use a commercially available tax program such as TurboTax or TaxCut. Plug in your retirement income (Social Security, pension, dividends, interest, etc.) and any deductions to get an estimate of your new postretirement tax liability. If you are skilled with taxes and spreadsheets, create your own tax spreadsheet tailored to your specific situation and compare different scenarios side by side, or use financial tracking software like Quicken to run different scenarios. Of course, you can always use the tax forms available directly from the IRS.

Your Personal Inflation Rate

A hidden expense in retirement is inflation. You should estimate how inflation may affect your income needs. Inflation affects different people in different ways, depending on housing needs, health issues, and the amount of travel you anticipate in retirement. One calculation you can do is to estimate your personal inflation rate. That is done by comparing your annual spending year-over-year and analyzing the differences.

Make adjustments for large purchases such as automobiles and vacations. For example, if your budget this year was $65,000 and your budget next year is $67,500 your personal inflation rate is 3.85 percent.

Your personal inflation rate may be higher or lower than the government-calculated change in the consumer price index (CPI). Housing is a large part of the federally calculated inflation rate. If your home is paid off or you have a fixed-rate mortgage, and your property taxes are capped, your housing inflation rate is likely to be lower than the national average that includes rentals. On the other hand, if you have health issues, it is possible that your personal inflation is higher than the national average.

Estimating your retirement budget and personal inflation rate will assist you in forming a long-term retirement plan. These calculations do take a lot of work, but this is the rest of your life we are talking about.

LUMP SUM OR ANNUITY

People who have a defined benefit (DB) or defined contribution (DC) plan at work will need to make an important decision when they retire (see Chapter 5 for information on DB plans and Chapter 6 for information on DC plans). Upon retirement, you may be given the choice of taking a lump-sum cash distribution and rolling it into an IRA account (see Chapter 4) or receiving income from an annuity (see Chapter 7). The annuity may come from your employer directly or from a third-party insurance carrier.

If you take a lump-sum distribution, you should first open an IRA account and then roll the money into that account directly from your employment account. That will allow you to defer paying income tax on the lump-sum rollover amount until you begin withdrawals from the IRA during retirement. If you annuitize the account, then you will get steady income for life, although you will not be able to change this option once you make that decision.

Reasons to Choose a Lump Sum
* You want full control of your money.
* You want full control of your taxes.
* You do not need fixed annuity income.
* There is no inflation adjustment for the pension or annuity. That means you'll need to withdraw more money each year from your other investment accounts to make up for inflation.
* You are worried about the financial health of your employer or the insurance company that is underwriting the annuity.

Be aware that income taxes are due on all annuity income and on any lump sum that is not rolled into an IRA. A lump-sum distribution to a taxable account may well put you in a higher tax bracket. However, if you were born before 1936, you may qualify for 10-year income averaging. Consult your tax adviser.

Reasons to Annuitize

* Hassle-free income for life.
* You will depend on this income and cannot take any risk with it.
* You believe you have a longer-than-average life expectancy.
* You are not concerned with leaving the money in an inheritance (see Chapter 7).

Before making any decision on rolling over a lump sum into an IRA or taking an annuity payment you must be *thoroughly* familiar with the advantages and disadvantages of both. Part of that includes a complete understanding of benefits that go to your heirs. Once you annuitize, you cannot go back. If you take a lump sum, you can always take a portion of that amount and buy an SPIA, perhaps with a higher payout rate than is offered by your employer.

INCOME FROM OUTSIDE SOURCES

We are not ready to decide on withdrawal strategies just yet. First, you need to determine what income you have coming in before taking any money out of savings. Also, we will look at alternative retirement income sources that do not add to your taxable income.

Social Security

Chapter 11 offers a great summary of Social Security benefits, and this is simply a recap. As discussed in Chapter 11, your benefits depend on when you retire and your earnings record over the years. When you are paid benefits, up to 85 percent of those benefits may be taxable. The taxation of Social Security creates a tax hump in that if you are normally in the 15 percent bracket, your marginal tax rate can go from 15 percent to 27.75 percent during a certain income level and then back down to 15 percent. If you are below or in the middle of the Social Security tax hump, it may be best to avoid increasing taxable income by not taking distributions from IRA accounts and other accounts that may cause higher taxable income. However, once you are past this hump and still within the

15 percent bracket, you might as well use up the 15 percent bracket by taking taxable income out of tax-deferred retirement accounts. All these scenarios should be discussed with your tax adviser or calculated on your own with tax software.

Income from Your Home

Converting equity in your home to retirement income creates tax-free income. You can downsize to a less expensive home or area of the country. That could provide an immediate tax-free gain of up to $500,000 for a couple or $250,000 for a single person. A second option is to take out a home equity loan or reverse mortgage. That will provide you with tax-free income without having to sell your home. All of these maneuvers should be considered carefully.

Before retiring, spend some time thinking about housing. It often makes sense to downsize. You may no longer need that five-bedroom house on an acre of ground. Often, a two-bedroom townhouse will meet your needs nicely, and you'll reduce a long list of expenses, including property taxes, utilities, insurance, and home maintenance expenses. Also consider location. If you do not already live near your family, you may want to relocate to be closer to your children and grandchildren. Or you may want to move to a warmer climate and/or a state with low taxes. You'll also want to look toward the future when deciding where to live and consider how difficult it might be for your children to care for you long distance. Here is an example: if you own a fully paid-for home valued at $300,000 and you sell it to buy a new $200,000 home, the extra $100,000 can be used to generate income for retirement. If you move to a less expensive home, your housing expenses for electricity and property taxes should also go down.

If you are in a cash crunch and need steady income, a reverse mortgage provides you with a tool to access your home equity without having to move. Here's how it works: a lender agrees to lend you money, and the amount you get is based on the equity in your home, your age and the age of your spouse, and current interest rates. The money can be paid out in one lump sum, paid out in monthly checks, drawn on as a line of credit, or some combination of these. If you choose monthly payments, these usually continue for as long as you live in the house. You do not have to make any payments. The interest on the loan compounds over the life of the loan. The loan is due when you die or when you sell the house. After the house is sold and the loan paid off, you or your heirs get to keep anything that is left. In most cases, if the value of the house goes down and more money was paid out than can be recovered by selling the house, you or your heirs are not liable for any shortfall.

There are disadvantages, and due to these disadvantages, a reverse mortgage is recommended only as a last resort. The money you get from a reverse mortgage is not free money; it just enables you to access a portion of your home equity. Your home equity is the difference between the value of your home and how much (if any) you owe on it. All banks and lenders are in business to make money, and a reverse mortgage lender is no different. Reverse mortgages are more expensive than traditional home loans. The reverse mortgage lender, not you, is taking on the risk that you live to be 100 years old because, for that entire time, they cannot ask for a payment from you. You usually need a lot of equity to qualify for a reverse mortgage. Reverse mortgage lenders do not offer you the full amount that your house is worth—after all, they're not buying your home. You do not have unlimited amounts of home equity, and a reverse mortgage does not change that. It is merely a means of tapping into the home equity that you do have. You will qualify for a given amount of money up front. Once you use up that money, it is gone, although you will not owe any monthly payments. If you are concerned about running out of money, then you should choose the tenure income option, which guarantees you a monthly amount.

Consider Paying Off Your Mortgage

If you are retiring and have a mortgage, and you have excess savings available in your taxable account, consider paying off the mortgage. If you have owned your home for 20 or 25 years, there is a good chance a significant portion of your monthly payment is principal anyway. And since your retirement income puts you in a low tax bracket, you may no longer be getting a meaningful tax deduction on the mortgage interest. Many retirees take the standard deduction rather than itemize. Paying off the mortgage is the same as receiving a risk-free rate of return equal to the mortgage interest rate.

Paying off the mortgage also reduces risk. During significant market declines, one critical tool available to retirees is the ability to temporarily reduce spending. A monthly mortgage payment limits the amount of spending that can be reduced.

Inheritances

Although you may not count on receiving an inheritance, if you believe you have one coming, you may want it to play an important role in your retirement plan. You may or may not know the specifics of the financial situation of your parents or whoever is leaving you money, and even if you do, you don't know the timing of the inheritance. Also, those leaving you money could suddenly need their money or decide to give much of it to charity. Only if you are the trustee over your parents' assets or the beneficiary of an already funded trust should you count on an inheritance as a retirement fund source. Since receiving an inheritance is not a sure thing, the best thing to do is ignore it when planning unless you are guaranteed to receive it and confident of the amount.

TAKING WITHDRAWALS

Finally, we have come to the key question: How much should I withdraw, and which accounts should I take it from? There is not a one-size-fits-all answer. Some retirees have enough income from pensions and Social Security that they have no need for a fixed withdrawal from their portfolio. Others have no income from pensions and depend on their portfolio to provide the majority of their future income.

There are at least two different ways to think of withdrawing your assets. The first is a minimum tax scenario where you spend down most of your taxable money first and may end paying higher taxes later on. The second is where you pace your tax payments over time by taking money out of both taxable and tax-advantaged accounts.

Tax Consequences from Taxable Accounts

Investments in taxable accounts generate taxable income, unless they are tax-free municipal bonds. Taxable bonds or bond mutual funds provide taxable income. Most stocks and stock mutual funds pay dividends that are taxed at a preferred dividend rate. You will owe taxes on income and dividends even if you don't take the income out for expenses.

Investments in taxable accounts may not generate enough interest and dividend income to cover your liabilities. In that case, you can withdraw principal to supplement your income by selling some investments. That could generate a capital gain, on which you will have to pay taxes but at the more favorable capital gains tax rate.

Tax Consequences of Tax-Advantaged Accounts

There are no taxes due on tax-advantaged accounts unless you take money out. With Roth IRAs, there is never a tax due unless you take money out before age 59½ and pay a penalty. Traditional and rollover IRA accounts have required minimum distributions (RMDs) starting at age 70½. That means you must start taking out a minimum distribution and pay ordinary income tax on that amount, whether you want to or not. For more information, see IRS Publication 590.

The required amount is calculated by taking the value of your IRA as of December 31 of the previous year, divided by your life expectancy. If you have a spouse who is more than 10 years younger than you and is the sole beneficiary of your IRA, then you can use a joint life and last survivor expectancy table that will lower the minimum amount of the distribution. In a sense, our government is giving a tax break to people who marry a much younger person.

For example, John is 80 years old. The value of John's IRA as of December 31, 2007, was $185,000. According to the uniform lifetime table, his life expectancy was 18.7 years, so his RMD for 2008 was $8,893 ($185,000/18.7). Now, if John's wife was 30 years his junior, then the joint life expectancy is 33.6 years and his RMD for 2008 is only $5,500 ($185,000/33.6). Assuming John is in the 25 percent federal tax bracket, he would pay $848 less in federal taxes each year because his wife is 30 years his junior. The purpose for this is so that the IRA is made to last longer to support a younger spouse.

It is extremely important that you take your RMD each year because the penalty for not taking the RMD is 50 percent of the amount you should have taken. However, due to a poor stock market in 2009, the penalty for not taking an RMD was waived, effectively meaning that there are no RMDs in 2009 and no penalties for not taking a withdrawal.

How Much to Take

If you have done budgeting for retirement and have calculated all the sources of income you will have from Social Security, pension plans, and perhaps rental property or as a silent partner in a business, then the shortfall in income must be replaced by investment withdrawals. How much is a safe withdrawal amount so that you do not outlive your money?

There are many Internet-based calculators that can help you decide on a sustainable withdrawal rate in retirement. The rule of thumb is 4 percent in early retirement. However, the true safe rate of withdrawal will depend on your life expectancy, your spending habits through retirement, and how your portfolio investments perform. For most of us, life expectancy is an unknown number, and there are no guarantees concerning how the investments in your accounts will perform in the future.

These historical return studies do not take investment expenses into account. If your safe withdrawal rate is 4 percent based on market returns, but you are paying a wrap fee of 1 percent and average fund expense ratios of another 1 percent, your actual safe withdrawal is only 2 percent. The same $100,000 now provides only $2,000 in income after 2 percent fees and expenses. It makes a lot of sense to reduce your investment expenses at any time, and it is particularly important in retirement.

The greater the amount you take over 4 percent in withdrawals, the less your heirs are likely to inherit when you pass away. Of course, the markets may be good to you and your heirs, but you should not count on a bull market to make your retirement plan work.

Many retirees end up withdrawing only part of their principal and leaving the balance to their heirs or to charity. You really need to ask yourself if you want to live frugally and leave the maximum amount to your heirs and/or charity, or if you want to enjoy your remaining years in style. The choice is up to you.

The 4 percent withdrawal rate can be used in two different ways in planning for retirement. The first is to withdraw 4 percent of the portfolio value in the first year and then increase that dollar amount by the rate of inflation each year. The second is to take 4 percent of the portfolio each year based on each year's beginning value. The first method, where 4 percent is used initially and then annually adjusted for inflation, could jeopardize the long-term viability of your portfolio if the investments significantly decrease in value early in your retirement. The second method, withdrawing 4 percent of the current value of the portfolio each year, will result in your income varying along with your portfolio value, sometimes dramatically.

Spending more in some years and cutting back in others sounds reasonable, but if your portfolio declines by 20 percent on account of poor market conditions, that translates into a 20 percent reduction in income from your investments. It might be difficult to reduce expenses by that amount. A variation on this would be to smooth out income by setting aside any excess in the up years so that it's available to you in the down years.

In summary, the shortfall between your expenses and other sources of income will dictate how much you will need to withdraw from your retirement accounts each year. The 4 percent safe withdrawal number is a reasonable estimate of the amount you can take each year without running out of money. It is a good start when planning. Also plan to have enough money to live 10 years past the age your oldest parent or grandparent lived, but don't plan on living 40 years past that age. You do need to be conservative, but you do not need to be the richest person in the graveyard.

Which Accounts Should You Withdraw From?

After using Social Security, any pension or annuity payments, and RMDs from your traditional IRA for living expenses, the least taxing way to withdraw money is in the following order:

1. Taxable Accounts—Since any money you receive from taxable interest, dividends, or capital gains is taxable anyway, spend that money first. If you still need more, withdraw principal from your taxable account. If you believe you will need principal from your taxable account, keep enough money available in liquid money market funds or very short-term bond funds to last a year or more. That avoids being forced to sell stocks or stock mutual funds during a down market.

2. Roth IRA—Since money left in a Roth IRA builds up tax-free until removed and has no RMD requirement, it is the most tax-efficient source of capital you have. Unfortunately, Roth IRAs usually have a small amount of money in them, compared with taxable accounts and tax-deferred accounts. Therefore, use the money in a Roth IRA as a safety net rather than as a regular source of retirement income.

3. Tax-Deferred Accounts—If you need substantially more income and do not have adequate assets in your taxable accounts, take a distribution from your traditional or rollover IRA. Leave the amount you don't need in the account. You will have to take an RMD after age 70½ and pay taxes on the distribution.

When Paying Taxes Makes Sense

If you have sufficient income from other sources and do not need to take an RMD from an IRA distribution, it may make sense to take an IRA distribution anyway. If your tax bracket is low, you can do an IRA rollover into a Roth IRA. True, you may have to pay some income tax on the distribution, but once the distribution goes into the Roth, you will never have to pay income taxes on the interest or gains that money earns.

There are two benefits to voluntarily taking an IRA distribution. First, the taxes you will pay are going to be negligible because you are going to do this only if you are in a low tax bracket. Second, taking money when you do not have to lowers the amount you have in the IRA at age 70½, reducing the amount you are required to take as an RMD.

The goal in retirement is not to avoid taxes but rather to control taxes. You will probably pay some income tax each year, but at least you have your hands on the levers that control how much you pay and when you pay it.

It is helpful to plan years ahead in retirement. Consider your probable tax bracket now and in future years. Try to minimize your income in the years you are in a high tax bracket and increase your taxable income in years when you are in a low tax bracket. Here's an example: assume you retire at the age of 62 and stop receiving a salary. You are not required to take an RMD from your traditional IRAs until you turn 70½. In the meantime, you will have less taxable income, so you could take this opportunity to do Roth conversions each year, to fill up the 15 percent tax bracket. Late in the year, estimate your taxable income for the year. If it looks like you will have room left in the 15 percent bracket, use up the rest of the 15 percent bracket.

Here is another example: assume a married couple filing jointly in 2008 had $45,000 of taxable income. The top of the 15 percent bracket was $65,100, so the couple could have converted $20,100 of their traditional IRA (assuming they made no after-tax contributions) to a Roth and would have paid only 15 percent tax on the entire conversion amount. Another way to use up the 15 percent bracket would be to sell savings bonds that have a large amount of built-up interest.

Potential Future Tax Law Changes

Keep in mind that this information is based on the current tax laws. Tax laws change frequently and can be difficult to keep up with. It's not possible for anyone to accurately predict how the tax laws will change in the future, so the best you can do is plan by using the current tax laws and try to keep abreast of any changes that might affect you.

PUTTING IT ALL TOGETHER

Once a year, sit down and do a little planning. Create some budgeting worksheets as you approach retirement, and then update them annually. Many budgeting worksheets are available free on the Internet. After you complete these worksheets for the first time, updating them each year will be much easier. Paper copies work fine, but it is easier to create spreadsheets on your computer. Follow these five steps.

1. Update your budget worksheet to determine income needs for the coming year.
2. Update your income worksheet to determine how much additional income you will need, if any.
3. Update your net worth statement to get an overview of your financial status. If you are attempting to keep most of your principal intact, your net worth should be the same or larger than it was last year. If you plan on using up some or most of your money, your net worth may well decrease each year. Large stock market fluctuations may make your balances larger or smaller.
4. Estimate your taxes. Use a commercially available program such as TurboTax or Tax Cut, or have your tax preparer do it for you. If this year's information is very similar to last year's, your taxes will be similar to last year's, unless there have been major changes to the tax laws.
5. Update your asset allocation worksheet.

Now, you have all of the information you need to plan your withdrawals. Check your asset allocation and, if possible, withdraw money from those accounts that have a higher-than-desired percentage. For example, if your target allocation is 25 percent stocks and 75 percent bonds, but the stock market has risen recently and you now have 30 percent stocks and 70 percent bonds, specify that your RMD be taken from the stock funds within your IRA.

If your account needs further rebalancing, whenever possible rebalance within your tax-deferred account to avoid selling anything in your taxable account.

ADDITIONAL RESOURCES

* An excellent resource for tax issues is www.fairmark.com, which includes online tax information guides and discussion boards.
* *Capital Gains, Minimal Taxes* by Kaye A. Thomas (Fairmark Press, 2009) is a plain-language guide to handling capital gains, dividends, and other issues investors deal with.
* IRS Publication 590, "Individual Retirement Arrangements," discusses the rules concerning RMDs.
* These three web sites discuss withdrawal rates:
      http://bobsfiles.home.att.net/trinity.htm
      www.retireearlyhomepage.com
      www.quantext.com

CHAPTER SUMMARY

Advanced planning and annual monitoring of your financial situation is crucial to a successful retirement. Spend some time before you retire planning out your budget, estimating changes to your spending, and analyzing your housing situation, asset allocation, investments, and taxes. Then all that's needed is a little time, once a year, to plan withdrawals. Enjoy the rest of the year, knowing you have planned your finances for the year. In addition, you may even want to consider long-term, generational planning by taking into account the amount you may want to leave your heirs, if any.

CHAPTER THIRTEEN

Early Retirement

Jeff McComas A.K.A. Jeff MC

INTRODUCTION

Early retirement! Who doesn't like the sound of that? The Bogleheads' path to early retirement is similar to the Bogleheads' path to a normal retirement: create a viable plan, execute the plan, and *stay the course!* The earliest age that will be considered for retirement in this chapter is 40. We will describe several strategies and sources of bridge income that can support you during the interim between your last day of full employment and your first Social Security payment sometime in your 60s. A case study in each section will assist you in visualizing your needs when writing your own successful early retirement plan.

Perhaps after reading this book, you will realize that you already have enough resources to retire early. You pick a retirement date two months out, calculate how to bridge your income, make your final list of to-do items, and then tender your resignation. You go on to enjoy early retirement immensely, secure in the knowledge that you will have enough resources to weather any financial storm. Your only regret is that you didn't retire earlier. You go on to live a full, satisfying life during an extended retirement. If you save early and often, live below your means, and do not go off on a rock star lifestyle, there's no reason you should not be able to retire early, on your own terms. So, let's go figure out how to make that happen.

WHAT IS EARLY RETIREMENT?

Historically, retirement meant quitting a full-time job around age 65. A longtime employer gives you a retirement party and a gold watch or a clock, and then you spend endless days puttering around the house, traveling more, and perhaps enjoying hobbies such as golfing or fishing. It is an idyllic scene from the classic movie *On Golden Pond*.

That was your father's retirement. Now there is a new option available that can be called a soft retirement. A soft retirement has several differences with the traditional definition. It can be an easing of employment from full-time to part-time to none at all; it can mean a paid or unpaid sabbatical every few years, followed by a return to part-time or full-time work; it can mean becoming a self-employed consultant with a flexible schedule, preferably part-time; or a complete change of careers to an occupation that satisfies your spiritual needs rather than your financial needs. Whatever form soft retirement takes, it will not be the abrupt change of going from 100 percent full employment to no employment at all on your 65th birthday.

There are also a few windfall early retirees. They are the lottery winners, Hollywood celebrities, professional athletes, young entrepreneurs who sold their businesses, and people who received large inheritances or lawsuit settlements. Receiving a rags-to-riches windfall is a dream we all have, but they are few and far between. This chapter is primarily written for the other 99 percent of the population who are researching early retirement without the aid of a lucky lottery number or a 100 mph fastball.

There are millions of American military personnel who enlisted at 20, worked 20 years, and retired at 40 with a full pension and medical benefits. However, if you are not working and are younger than 40, let's just say you are in between jobs. Even though the Social Security Administration (SSA) considers age 67 the new retirement age, nobody considers retiring at 65 to be early retirement. While some people are able to retire prior to 40, and there are octogenarians working full-time, we will define early retirement as that sweet spot from age 40 to 64.

CASE STUDY: TOM

Tom is 45 years old. He retired at 41 from the technology industry. His wife is still working. They live on her income and try not to touch their $1.4 million nest egg. They have three children under 18. Tom has no regrets about early retirement, except that he wishes he could have retired even earlier by saving more when he was younger. He spends his time with his children and on his hobbies: woodworking, gardening, and volunteering. He will never seek gainful employment again unless it is absolutely necessary.

CASE STUDY: THERESE

Therese is 54. She quit the rat race at 48 to follow her passion for art. She retired from a Fortune 500 company and started creating and selling her art in the Midwest. After a bumpy start, with few paying customers and expensive overhead, she now sustains her art business year-round. Her partner is now her second and only employee. In retrospect, Therese wishes she had overlapped her old career as an attorney with her new one as an artist to avoid the drastic drop in cash flow and fear of business failure. She also underestimated her need to develop a client list. But that is past. She has succeeded and never intends to retire from this new career. It does not feel like work.

IMPORTANT AGES TO CONSIDER

There are important ages to consider when working on your plan for early retirement. Table 13.1 lists some of those important ages.

In addition to the age information in Table 13.1, you may be affected by other age-related events. For example, your employer's pension may offer an early retirement option after a certain age or according to a work-plus-age formula. Your employer may also offer medical coverage until Medicare starts.

Your pension benefits may be a significant factor in determining your retirement date. Typically, employees are not fully vested in their pension plans or stock options until they turn 60 or 65. However, prospective early retirees are eligible for an increasing percentage of these pension benefits as they approach their full retirement age. This makes the early

TABLE 13.1   KEY AGES FOR EARLY RETIREMENT

Age 50	Catch-up provisions allow additional funding of IRAs and 401(k) plans
Age 55	May be able to withdraw 401(k) funds if still with employer until 55
Age 59½	Can withdraw earnings from IRAs without penalty
Age 62	Eligible for early Social Security (SS) benefits
Age 65	Medicare becomes available
Age 65	Full SS retirement benefits for those born in 1937 or before
Age 67	Full SS retirement benefits for those born in 1960 or later
Age 70	Should start taking SS benefits, as they stop increasing beyond age 70
Age 70½	Required minimum distributions (RMDs) begin for traditional IRA and 401(k) accounts
Never	Mandatory distributions from Roth IRA or Roth 401(k) accounts

retirement decision difficult and stressful. Delaying early retirement by one year often means an additional 5 to 10 percent in pension benefits. Delaying by two years means an additional 10 to 20 percent. And so on. You must weigh the pros and cons of delaying retirement by a year to get the extra benefits, and then do the same analysis each year.

MORE FACTORS TO CONSIDER

While you are contemplating early retirement, there are three H factors to consider in addition to how much you have in the bank. They are health care, household, and globe-hopping.

Health Care

Health-care costs are a growing concern for many early retirees. In fact, health care is often the determining factor in their decision-making process. Most households cannot afford a financially catastrophic health-care event without sufficient insurance. Not only are they unable to afford the medical bills but also they often cannot return to work to bring in needed income.

Because Medicare does not begin until 65, this becomes the de facto retirement age for many, superseding the importance of Social Security or pensions.

Household

Other factors to consider are the magnitude and variability of your household expenses. How much money will your household spend in a year? What is the variability? Can you (and a possible significant other) live on a fixed budget? Do you have an emergency fund for unexpected costs, such as home repairs, auto accidents, or a child returning to your once-empty nest? The other side of your balance sheet is income and its possible variation. Do you have the appropriate asset allocation? Is part of your nest egg annuitized either through a pension or an investment vehicle like an annuity?

Globe-Hopping

What do you expect to do in early retirement? Hobbies and traveling can be expensive. Deciding on an acceptable standard of living is crucial. Will you stay in your current home or downsize? Will you move to a cabin by the lake or travel the country by RV? Will a spur-of-the-moment cruise get booked?

SAFE WITHDRAWAL RATE

George Foreman had it right: "The question isn't at what age I want to retire, it's at what income." Early retirement comes down to the income you need to cover your cost of living. Is $25,000 a year enough? Is $100,000 enough? How much do you need to have saved to pay yourself that amount?

CASE STUDY: DENNIS

Dennis is an early retiree wannabe. He's 51, with a 53-year-old home-maker spouse. Dennis planned to retire soon, until the bear market in 2008 caused him to rethink his plans. In retrospect, he thinks he had too much of his nest egg in equities, and now health care costs also worry him. Although he still has a nice seven-figure nest egg, he now plans to continue working "until the market rebounds." He wonders if this is the right decision. Should he wait for the markets to recover?

Most people love the sound of early retirement, but many are not emotionally prepared when it arrives. Realize that most of your peers will still be working full-time. You may not be ready for retirement cruises or the silver plate special at the diner. And while you may need to be a millionaire as you enter early retirement, you certainly cannot afford to live like one. In early retirement, it's important that you live within your means and have a plan for daily activities to avoid boredom.

To answer the key question of this chapter, "Can you retire?" you will need to run the numbers. A good rule of thumb is the generally accepted 4 percent historically safe withdrawal rate (SWR) mentioned several times in earlier chapters. This means that when you retire, you can safely withdraw 4 percent of your nest egg for the first year. This 4 percent needs to include investment costs and taxes, as well as living expenses. Then, revise this initial 4 percent withdrawal rate upward by inflation for future years. So, if you retire with $1 million, you can withdraw 4 percent ($40,000) in your first year. In your second year of retirement, withdraw 4 percent plus inflation. Assuming an inflation rate of 3 percent, you can withdraw $41,200 ($1 million × 4 percent × the 1.03 inflation adjustment). In year three, you can withdraw $42,400, and so on.

The 4 percent SWR is assumed to be generally safe for someone 65 years old with 30 years in retirement to look forward to. But if you want to retire at 40, you will need to withdraw less than 4 percent a year because you are likely to have more than 30 years in retirement. As a general rule, although a somewhat conservative model, you should reduce your safe withdrawal rate if you retire younger. (See Figure 13.1.) Thus, if you want to retire at 55, you should plan to withdraw 3.3 percent or less of your nest egg per year. To retire at 45, you should plan to withdraw no more than 3 percent of your nest egg. What may be alarming to the prospective early retiree is that to retire at age 40, you should be able to live on only 3.0 percent of your nest egg.

These data may be depressing. What if you do not have $1 million or cannot live on 4 percent a year of your nest egg? What if your annual expenses are $60,000, but the SWR allows you to withdraw only $40,000 per year? The 4 percent SWR ignores other sources of income. This is where annuities, Social Security, pensions, rental income, and part-time jobs enter the picture to close that income gap.

Another withdrawal strategy to ensure your nest egg lasts as long as you do is to live off only dividends and interest, and leave the principal intact. This is a less precise strategy, because different stock sectors and company sizes offer different levels of dividends. For example, small high-tech company stocks historically offer little or no dividends, and

FIGURE 13.1   SAFE WITHDRAWAL RATES AT DIFFERENT
                RETIREMENT AGES

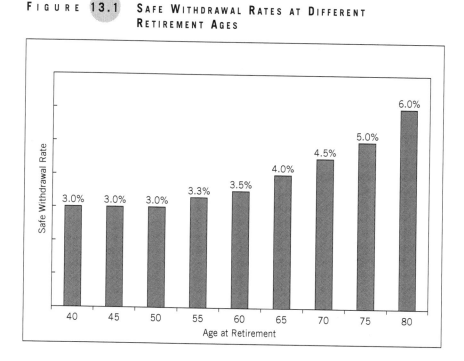

large utility companies historically offer high dividends. Fixed-income investments have interest and dividend variability that will cause a retiree's annual income to fluctuate each year. Also, this strategy does not provide an inflation hedge. Depending on its size, it may not be possible to leave the initial principal intact over the years, as inflation erodes the purchasing power of the dividends and interest.

There are some excellent, free Internet calculators to help you determine withdrawal strategies and chances of success. One of the best calculators is FIRECalc, available at www.fireseeker.com. FIRECalc uses very sophisticated (Monte Carlo) methodologies to predict your cash flow, based on user-supplied input.

FAMILY RELATIONSHIPS

Singles retiring early face unique issues. There is no income buffer provided by a significant other, and they cannot rely on a partner's health-care plan. Also, being single and retired at 45 is no guarantee that you will still be single and able to stay retired at 55. A new partner could bring significant debt or have dependent children. On the other hand, singles are more mobile, need less living space, and have more flexibility to pursue their own interests, hobbies, and jobs without interference. In addition, singles often have larger annuity and/or pension payouts because they do not need to consider survivor benefits.

Half-retirement is when one partner has retired early and the other one continues to work full-time. This arrangement can create built-in conflicts. Vacation schedules, household duties, budgeting, resentment issues, and the sharing of free time must be worked through, preferably before early retirement begins. However, this is not a marriage counseling book (whew!), and this chapter will not delve into strategies for healthy relationships during half-retirement.

As with most issues, clear communication prior to the retirement party and during early retirement will make all the difference. The first year of early retirement is a lot like the first year of marriage or the first year with a newborn. You determine what works best through trial and error as your new normal takes root and lifestyles adjust. But do not be fooled. The first year of early retirement is not always one long, happy honeymoon.

Another family dynamic involves children and other dependents. College bills have delayed many early retirements. However, there is an old saying: pay yourself first. Nobody is going to finance your retirement, but you and your children can finance college. Dependents often incur other costs in addition to college. Weddings, home down payments, and children still living at home can put a strain on your early retirement plans.

At the other end of the dependent spectrum are elderly parents. Just as college bills have delayed many retirements, so has elder care. Unless managed correctly, a pending inheritance or your own retirement nest egg can shrink from significant medical costs, assisted living, nursing home care, and the day-to-day costs necessary to support aging parents. Deciding between early retirement and supporting your parents is usually an easy decision. The parents win.

HOW TO RETIRE EARLY

So, how can you retire early? A key is to live below your means. Spend less money than you make. To do this, you must know how much money you bring in (this is the easy part), as well as how much goes out (it's usually more than assumed). A good strategy is to track your spending for an extended period. Chapter 12 discussed developing a retirement budget. The same techniques apply to building an early retirement budget.

If you have children nearing college age, think about retiring before they start the application process. This may seem nonintuitive, but when applying for college aid via the Free Application for Federal Student Aid (FAFSA) form, parents are asked about their current income and assets. The lower your income and assets, the more your child may receive in financial aid. Therefore, you may want to retire four years earlier than conventional wisdom suggests.

CASE STUDY: CHUCK

Chuck is 39, as is his wife, Rebecca. They plan to both retire at 50, when the first of their two children enters college. Alternatively, they may work part-time or pursue flexible work schedules. So far, they're on track. They live below their means and have managed to adequately save for retirement. Both work in stable, well-paying careers. They have inexpensive hobbies, are debt-free except for a mortgage, and drive their cars into the ground. Their nest egg is invested in an aggressive but appropriate asset allocation suitable for Boglehead-minded folks. They have no financial regrets and do not feel as though they are sacrificing for their future. Both are frugal by nature and good savers.

Bridging Your Income

Let's get down to the nuts and bolts of early retirement. How can you make it happen? What successful early withdrawal strategies can be used? How can you most efficiently tap your retirement nest egg prior to the traditional retirement age? A key enabler of early retirement is to bridge yourself from when you stop working until the traditional sources of income start, such as Social Security, 401(k), and IRA withdrawals. As discussed elsewhere in this book, annuitizing a portion of your nonretirement assets is often a good idea. See Chapter 8 for details. Following are some additional strategies that can be used solo, or in concert, to help bridge your income gap.

The IRS has created a magnificent (but underutilized) loophole that allows anyone to tap their IRA without any penalties: the 72(t) exception (also known as SEPP, substantially equal periodic payments). At any age, you can begin taking withdrawals from your IRA by initiating a five-year or longer program of substantially equal periodic payments (SEPP) and continue these payments until you turn 59½. The beauty of this IRS rule is that you avoid the 10 percent early withdrawal penalty, and you pay income taxes only on the withdrawals. There are three withdrawal calculation methods (annuitization, life expectancy, and amortization) and it can be difficult to determine the optimal method for your situation. Visit www.irs.gov or meet with your tax professional to determine the logistics and best strategy to implement a SEPP program. Following is a simplified, hypothetical SEPP program withdrawal scenario.

CASE STUDY: HUNTER

Hunter is 40, just retired, and wants to use a SEPP program to tap his $800,000 traditional IRA. Actuarial tables assume he will live 40 more years. So, he withdraws 1/40 of the $800,000 IRA, or $20,000 a year. Once he starts these SEPPs, he must continue them until he is 59½. Although he is free to rebalance his IRA, he must maintain constant annual withdrawals for the entire 20-year period. This is regardless of the value of the underlying IRA, which will certainly fluctuate over the years. There are no penalties if the IRA runs out of money prior to age 59½.

Roth accounts can also offer a good source of bridge income. Roth IRAs allow you to withdraw all contributions (but not earnings) at any time, for any reason, without any penalties or taxes. For Roth IRA funds that were converted from a traditional IRA, you must wait at least five years before withdrawing these funds tax- and penalty-free. For example, if you rolled over a 401(k) to a traditional IRA and then converted this to a Roth IRA at age 35, you could withdraw these funds, starting at age 40, with no penalties and no taxes. And unlike a SEPP program, there are no schedules of withdrawal that you must maintain. You can take out as much as you want, whenever you want.

Of course, once withdrawn, you can deposit funds back into your Roth account only based on annual contribution limits. You must have earned income below the modified adjusted gross income limits to contribute to a Roth IRA. Unlike contributions, your earnings must stay in the account until age 59½, or penalties will be levied (except for special hardship cases). Roth 401(k) accounts behave like Roth IRAs, once you are no longer employed by the sponsoring company. While employed, you cannot withdraw funds from the sponsoring employer's Roth 401(k) account.

Traditional 401(k) plans typically do not allow withdrawals prior to age 59½ without penalty. However, some company 401(k) plans do allow penalty-free withdrawals starting at 55, if you stay employed with the company until age 55. After you turn 55, you must retire from the company to access these funds. As 401(k) plans are widely used, this may be an effective source of bridge income for many early retirees. Review your company plan documents to determine if they offer early withdrawals starting at 55. Taxes are still owed on withdrawals, but no penalties apply.

A 457 plan is similar to a 401(k), except that it is available only to government workers. If you have a 457 savings plan, this presents another potential source of bridge income. Unlike 401(k) plans, you can withdraw 457 funds prior to 59½ without penalty, as long as you are no longer with the employer. You will pay income taxes on any withdrawals, as these funds were invested on a pretax basis.

Bridging beyond Retirement Accounts

In addition to the alphabet soup of retirement accounts, you most likely have assets in after-tax accounts, too. Your after-tax investment funds are available to you whenever they are needed. However, they may have large capital gains (especially any funds or stocks that have been growing for decades), and there may be significant long-term capital gains taxes on your withdrawals. But besides taxes, there are no trigger dates or penalties associated with tapping these funds as a source of bridge income.

Reverse mortgages are another possible source of income for those 62 or older. Reverse mortgages, however, generally have high fees and low rates of return for the home owner. For these reasons, reverse mortgages should be a last resort for providing income. Depending on mortgage interest rates, tapping the equity in your home or real estate via a fixed loan or home equity line of credit (HELOC) may make more sense than a reverse mortgage. However, using home equity is not a prudent source of income for most retirees, especially those retiring early. Your home is more than a piggy bank. In fact, if you need to use your home equity to fund early retirement, you are probably not in a realistic financial position for a successful early retirement. Many early retirees have paid off their mortgages, giving them one less monthly payment in retirement.

Another potential source of bridge income involves possible changes in retirement account laws. Government legislation is periodically proposed to loosen access to retirement account funds due to hardship, economic need, or recession relief. It's possible that before you reach your existing trigger dates, laws could be changed to give you penalty-free access to your retirement accounts earlier than current constraints. However, since these possible changes cannot be planned, it is judicious to assume that existing laws will remain in place.

If the idea of retiring early cold turkey is too scary, you can do a trial retirement. Request a one-year unpaid sabbatical if offered by your employer. This will give you the opportunity to decide if early retirement is the right choice or if you need paid employment for your emotional health or economic well-being. Nobody needs to know that you are toying with the idea of early retirement. As you work out your plan for early retirement, remember that a decision to annuitize or initiate a SEPP program is irreversible.

WINDFALLS, UNEMPLOYMENT, AND DISABILITY

Windfalls, whether they come from the lottery, inheritances, lawsuits, showbiz, sports, or buyouts, carry with them special concerns. The good news is that the same retirement advice applies to windfalls as to other sources of income. It makes no difference if the nest egg was slowly built over 25 years through diligent, regular savings and compounding interest, or if it comes via one comically large check from the lottery office in front of the cameras. What may differ is the mind-set of the early retiree.

Most early retirees have been planning, calculating, and brainstorming for 10 or more years before pulling the trigger. Your challenge is to ensure that the windfall doesn't become easy come, easy go. Today, even a multimillion-dollar lottery jackpot may not be enough for a successful early retirement. Lump-sum lottery payouts are usually half of the advertised jackpot. Taxes consume half of what remains. After buying a new BMW and a McMansion, you may find yourself scraping by, unable to afford the lifestyle you imagined a millionaire is supposed to live.

CASE STUDY: STEVEN

Ten years ago, police officer Steven retired immediately after winning a $2 million lottery at age 48. He had no experience managing large sums of money and became overwhelmed by advice and requests for loans/gifts. His life that first year was far from the happy lifestyle he envisioned. Fortunately, he kept a cool head and did not make rash decisions, except for a few large loans to family and friends. Loans became gifts when family members could not repay. He did not want to lose relationships over the debts. Steve is single and lives on a

> small, fixed budget. He takes two marquee vacations a year (Hawaii and the Bahamas) but otherwise lives frugally. He is considering part-time security work to make his vacations longer and nicer. Although he does not regret winning the lottery, it did not make his life a storybook ending of happiness and freedom from worries. He advises windfall receivers to take it slow, give no loans, and make no significant purchases for at least a year. He suggests that you trust only yourself with your money. Also, be aware that feelings of envy can ruin relationships.

Whereas windfalls may lead to voluntary early retirement, other events may occur to create an involuntary early retirement. Pick your favorite euphemism. Whether you are downsized, rightsized, outsourced, cosourced, fired, or subject to job elimination, layoffs can lead to a long job search. During this search, after realizing that they can handle the economic and emotional aspects of being unemployed, some people simply stop looking for new work. At some point, they stop saying, "I'm an engineer" and start saying, "I'm retired" when asked what they do.

Disability

If you become permanently disabled, you may be an involuntary early retiree. Living on Social Security Administration (SSA) disability presents some challenges. There are two SSA disability programs: disability insurance and supplemental security income. Disability insurance pays benefits to you if you're insured, meaning that you have worked long enough and paid Social Security taxes. The second disability benefit (supplemental security income) pays benefits based on financial need. To receive payments, you need to apply for disability status and be approved. Because Social Security pays only for total disability, no benefits are payable for partial or short-term disability. Disability under Social Security is based on your inability to work.

To determine if you are disabled, the SSA uses a rigorous process, based on five questions.

1. Are you working? If yes, you generally cannot be considered disabled.
2. Is your condition severe? It must interfere with basic work-related activities.

3. Is your condition on the list of disabling conditions? If not, SSA decides if it is of equal severity to a listed medical condition.
4. Can you perform your previous work?
5. Can you perform other types of work? If you cannot adjust to other work, your disability claim may be approved.

Once approved, you remain on disability for the rest of your life or until your condition improves and you can work again. You get an annual raise called a cost-of-living adjustment (COLA). But you cannot work *and* receive disability. Your income is limited for life, which creates restrictions that nondisabled people do not have. Also, you may have health care costs associated with your disability that further constrain your standard of living. (See Chapter 15 for more details.)

UNRETIRING

Life happens. Things change. Even the most dogmatic, organized planner cannot predict all life events. Issues with dependents, health care, partner relationships, accidents, deaths, market crashes, or unexpected natural disasters can put a serious wrinkle in early retirement plans. Perhaps you will discover that living on 3 percent or 4 percent of your nest egg is not acceptable. You may need to *un*retire. Americans are working longer into their sunset years in today's soft retirement world.

CASE STUDY: KEVIN

Kevin retired early as an electrician at 54. He is now 66. He unretired at 63 by picking up a part-time job at a retail store near his home. He started working again not because he needed the income but, rather, because he wanted to help out his heirs and keep himself busy. He wanted enough income to fully fund his Roth IRA that will become a de facto college fund for his grandchildren. At work, he enjoys helping people, has a flexible schedule, and has a feeling of accomplishment, without the headaches and stresses of his earlier career. In retrospect, he thinks he should have worked a few more years to alleviate his worries about running out of money.

There are several nonfinancial reasons that you may unretire and rejoin the work force. Boredom may set in. Interactions with people (coworkers and customers) can be sorely missed. Your batteries may be fully recharged after a few years off, and you may be ready to go back to work with renewed vigor and enthusiasm. Perhaps you've found a new passion and wish to turn a hobby or volunteerism into your next career. Sometimes, when you give up looking for work, your dream job falls into your lap, so you decide to rejoin the workforce.

The good news is that the barriers to unretiring are few. There are no papers to sign, no contracts to rip up, no unretirement parties to attend, and nobody is expecting the gold watch back. Just grab that tie (or hammer, paintbrush, laptop, or car keys) and get back to work. Start rebuilding your nest egg so you can re-retire later at that magical 4 percent safe withdrawal rate.

CHANGING YOUR MIND ABOUT EARLY RETIREMENT

There are several other reasons you may change your mind about early retirement. Your pension and Social Security benefits will undoubtedly be smaller when you retire early. Usually, your salary is at its highest as you are nearing retirement (your 50s and 60s), due to your experience and inflation adjustments. Social Security payments are based on your career earnings. That means your benefits will be higher if you wait. Also, many employers calculate pension payouts based on a formula of your three to five highest annual salaries and your years of service.

The biggest financial reason to remain in the workforce is more obvious: retirement means that you stop making money and need to start spending money. Psychologically, you need to flip the switch between saving and spending, knowing you cannot replenish your nest egg as you have always been able to do. You must be prepared for the potential stress of tapping into money that you've spent a lifetime accumulating. You must get comfortable watching your net worth decrease. However, the good news is that at a 4 percent or less withdrawal rate, you should still experience some years when your net worth increases from above-average annual returns on your investments.

Working full-time has a great side benefit that should not be underestimated. It's difficult to spend much money doing anything else while you're working. With all of your extra free time in retirement, you may spend more on entertainment, travel, hobbies, and that endless to-do list of home improvements. Your utility bills may increase. You may find that you could afford to retire based on your preretirement budget but simply cannot live on 80 percent of your preretirement income before tax. Conventional wisdom has been that you need 80 percent of your preretirement income, but this may not apply to your situation.

Unretiring, or simply not retiring early, may be the most prudent course of action for your circumstances. It's more fiscally conservative to retire at a normal, traditional retirement age. And although it is dangerous to generalize Boglehead behavior, our philosophy is to retire only if you have the resources to remain invested, can weather market downturns, will stay the course, and are able to effectively manage the costs of your retirement.

Feeling empowered and able to retire early is a freeing achievement. It's ironic, though, that many people who are in a position to walk away from their jobs and retire early start finding their career more meaningful and fulfilling, without much of the stress that normally accompanies a 9-to-5 job. You're now free to explore other positions, take a chance with a new company, or volunteer for a risky short-term position. You do not need to grovel for a small cost-of-living raise. You know that if it gets unbearable, you can just walk away. And if your employer knows this, too, you may be treated differently. If your contributions are valued, you will receive meaningful work, making your job a profitable endeavor for both you and your employer.

ADDITIONAL RESOURCES

* www.ssa.gov/planners/calculators.htm is a Social Security page of retirement calculators.
* www.early-retirement.org/forums: Discussion forums on early retirement.
* www.retireearlyhomepage.com: Resources for early retirees.
* www.fireseeker.com: FIRECalc early retirement calculator.

CHAPTER SUMMARY

For many future retirees, retirement will not start as 100 percent full-time employment on Friday to zero percent on Monday following your 65th birthday. Flexibility allows you to dip your toes into the retirement pool without fully plunging in. This same flexibility will allow you to go back to work, if desired, in retirement. Early retirement is really about flexibility and empowerment.

A key enabler of early retirement is figuring out how to bridge your income between your last paycheck and that first Social Security check, Medicare coverage, and traditional pension income streams. As discussed, there are several possible strategies to meet your early retirement income needs. Some combination of the much underused SEPP program, withdrawals of Roth IRA contributions tax- and penalty-free, tapping home equity or 401k or 457 plans early, and annuitizing some of your nonretirement assets are mechanisms to get you out of the office a few years or even decades before your peers.

You cannot lose by preparing your household for early retirement. Once you have that trump card in your back pocket, you can play it whenever you want to end the game called work. Good luck!

PART V

PROTECTING YOUR ASSETS

CHAPTER FOURTEEN

Income Replacement

Lee E. Marshall

INTRODUCTION

Your greatest asset is your ability to earn a living for yourself and your family. As long as you can continue doing so, you may well earn a fortune during your lifetime. A worker earning $50,000 on the average annually over the next 40 years will generate a total income of $2 million. However, that is only if the person is able to work. With life's uncertainties, protecting your earnings from premature death or disability is a necessity. Fortunately, insurance plans are available today to protect against these risks. Winston Churchill said, "If I had my way, I would write the word 'insure' upon the blotting book of every person, because I am convinced that for sacrifices that are inconceivably small, families can be secured against catastrophes which otherwise would smash them up forever."

The focus of this chapter is on life and disability insurance programs and proper ways to implement them. We'll discuss how much and what types of life and disability insurance you need, explore ways to buy coverage including buying tips and how to select insurance agents, and help you avoid some common mistakes. Following these suggestions will help put you in charge of the buying process.

The three main events that can reduce or eliminate your flow of income are death, disability, and retirement. In the United States, a tripod of economic security helps to protect us from the effect of these threats. Government programs, employer programs, and personal insurance and investment programs combine to provide us with a cushion of security. But make no mistake, considering life's uncertainties, maximizing your personal insurance and investment programs should be the foundation of your security. This is the one area where you have the most control. In the final analysis, planning for the known and insuring against the unknown work hand in hand to achieve your financial goals.

LIFE INSURANCE

If you have dependents, are accumulating assets for retirement, or wish to pay for your last expenses such as a funeral, you probably need life insurance. Life insurance is one of the best financial instruments available to meet the needs of your dependents at the time of your death if you have not accumulated a level of wealth that would take care of those dependents. Life insurance provides a specific amount of money, exactly when it is needed, and if paid to a named beneficiary, it is income tax-free. Death benefits are not tied up in probate and are usually received by the beneficiary within a few weeks.

Insurance benefits can be taken as a lump sum or in other available settlement options. If taken as a lump sum, the money should be invested according to the principles set forth by John Bogle as detailed in his books and as outlined in this book and *The Bogleheads' Guide to Investing*. Alternative settlement options include installments of a fixed amount, installments for a fixed period of time, or the proceeds held by the company with interest paid out, or the money can be paid out as a lifetime income annuity (see Chapter 7). Insurance company settlement options can be set in advance by the policy owner if desired. Preset settlement options are a good planning tool to help protect the interests of the beneficiary, including minors who cannot enter into legal contracts or directly receive insurance proceeds.

Types of Life Insurance Policies

Perhaps you're wondering what types of insurance policies are available today. How can you use these products to meet your individual needs? Building a good life insurance program need not be complex. Learn the basics and follow a few simple principles.

The two major categories of individual life insurance policies are term insurance and permanent insurance. Term policies are designed to provide protection for a fixed period of time, such as 10, 20, or 30 years. Permanent policies are designed to provide protection for life. Within each category, there are several types of insurance that you can choose from.

Term Life Insurance

Term insurance is best suited for needs that are temporary, meaning they end at a predictable time in the future. For example, family income needs are typically reduced after your children leave the nest and start providing for themselves. Another example of a temporary need is in the years before you and your spouse become eligible for adequate pension benefits. Still another is prior to inheriting a sizable estate. In these cases, life insurance is wealth replacement. You do not yet have the financial means to take care of your dependents in the case of your demise, and life insurance can fill the gap.

Term insurance is also a good choice to pay fixed obligations such as a mortgage, auto, and credit card debts and for children's education, as well as for an emergency fund. At younger ages, term insurance is inexpensive for most families. For younger breadwinners, term insurance is the only practical way to provide needed protection at affordable costs. It provides pure protection and builds no cash value (to be explained later).

Group term insurance may be available from your employer. It is purchased in an amount equal to your annual income or some multiple of your income. Some employers pay part of the cost, making it less expensive than individually purchased policies. Another advantage of most employer-sponsored life insurance is that you cannot be denied coverage. If you sign up for the insurance at the inception of your employment, you will get the insurance regardless of your health or preexisting medical issues. You'll want to consider enrolling in your employer's plan unless you can purchase it at a lower cost on your own.

Association group term may also be available for those in certain occupations, such as teaching, public accounting, and nursing. Association plans can be less expensive than individual term policies, and they usually have a streamlined underwriting process that may not require a blood test. An Internet search of associations will tell you if plans are available for a group that you belong to or can join. You may also obtain life insurance through your bank if savings bank life insurance (SBLI) is available in the state you live. You'll want to check their rates against individual term.

Level-premium term policies for periods of 10 to 30 years are very competitive for individuals. They are the best way to build the foundation of your insurance program. Premium rates have never been lower, even as life expectancies have increased. It is best to choose a term period that matches your need so that your coverage does not expire and leave you uninsured. If you choose a term policy for a shorter period than you need, you will have to qualify for a new policy bought later on, and it usually will have a higher price.

Permanent Life Insurance

By age 60, term insurance is expensive, and age restrictions may disqualify an individual from obtaining necessary coverage. Permanent insurance is intended to remain in force until the insured dies. It solves the problem when coverage is needed for life. That helps a couple reaching retirement age with insufficient assets to be financially independent, should either spouse die. Permanent life insurance is also useful in many estate planning and business situations, which will be discussed later.

Permanent insurance is available in three major types: whole life, universal life, and variable universal life. They each have unique advantages and disadvantages.

Whole life (WL) insurance has been around for more than a century. It features guaranteed death benefits, guaranteed cash values, and guaranteed premiums until death. It costs much more than term because the insurance company invests a portion of the premium to build policy reserves known as cash value to help pay future death claims. The cash value in these policies is invested primarily in intermediate- and long-term bonds. One benefit of building cash value is that the policy owner may take loans against the amount or obtain a cash distribution upon surrender of the policy.

Policies issued by mutual companies and participating policies issued by stock companies pay nonguaranteed annual dividends. Those dividends can be taken in cash, used to reduce premiums, left to accumulate with interest, or used to buy additional paid-up life insurance. A higher monthly premium is paid for these policies, but cumulative dividends usually exceed the extra premiums. Earnings grow tax-deferred while the money stays in the policy. This results in lower policy costs, or higher death benefits and cash values. One disadvantage of all WL policies is that they do not disclose internal expenses and mortality charges for death claims.

Universal life (UL) policies build cash values that are invested mostly in short-term fixed-income securities. They became popular in the 1970s when cash values invested in these products had higher interest rates than long-term government bonds. UL policies also disclose internal expenses, mortality charges for death claims, and interest rates. The major disadvantage of many UL policies is that they can run out of money if any of these elements perform less favorably than illustrated. If that happens, the policy terminates unless the insured pays in extra money to keep it in force.

In recent years, some ULs can now be purchased with a lifetime premium and death benefit guarantee. With this type of guarantee, the premium is lower than whole life because the policy is designed to provide a lifetime death benefit and not build high cash values. It is the closest thing to a term until death policy on the market today. UL can also be purchased with level or increasing death benefits to counter potential future inflation. You pay a little more for the increasing death benefit option.

Variable universal life (VUL) became popular in the 1980s, when stock market returns were outperforming fixed-interest investments. VUL works basically like UL, but your premiums are invested in your choice of a variety of subaccounts that are similar to mutual funds. This option provides the opportunity for potentially higher returns, thus enhancing death benefits and cash values. VUL policies come with higher potential returns and higher risks, like other equity investments. The policies often project level premiums for life, but if investment performance is inadequate, then future premiums can be much higher or the policy can terminate. VULs are often promoted as investments and are often illustrated to provide a lifetime income at retirement. However, in our opinion, VULs are too risky a product for permanent life insurance needs.

Survivorship life insurance (SLI) policies are designed to pay at the death of the second spouse. Because of an unlimited marital deduction, estate taxes often become due at the second death. The survivorship policy can work well in these situations. These policies can be WL, UL, or VUL, and they are less expensive than individual policies on each spouse. Underwriting older ages is easier because the joint mortality of both insured is used.

PROTECTING YOUR FAMILY

Establishing a life insurance program to protect your family is more complex now than it was in the recent past. Most families before the baby-boomer generation grew up in one-income homes with the father providing the income while the mother took care of the home and raised the children. Insurance companies developed formulas to determine the amount of life insurance needed to provide for these traditional families.

Today insurance underwriting is more complex. Two-income families are more common; the primary breadwinner can be either partner, or both can contribute equally. Unfortunately, more than half of all marriages end in divorce. Single-parent families are on the rise, and the institution of marriage is constantly undergoing changes. Remarriages often result in blended families. Thus, no single life insurance formula can address the needs of all individuals and families of today.

How Much Do You Need?

The amount of life insurance you need depends on your financial goals for yourself and your family. The best place to begin is a thorough and frank discussion with your partner and perhaps other beneficiaries. Address facts and feelings regarding death and its financial impact on their needs. Bear in mind that a lot of emotions regarding death, remarriage, management of proceeds, and help by family members will arise in such a discussion. Disagreements sometimes occur, as thoughts of death and disability are frightening when brought up. Working through this process now, when all parties are healthy, is definitely the best time.

Social Security

If your family includes or will include minor children, your next step is to see how much annual income Social Security survivor benefits will pay after the death of either spouse. The personal statement the Social Security Administration sends you annually shows the estimated amounts that would be payable. Detailed information about eligibility and other factors is in the Social Security Handbook at www.ssa.gov. Income from Social Security can be very helpful to the surviving family, although it's likely to leave a significant gap to be filled by life insurance.

Figuring the Right Insurance Amount

There are numerous formulas to arrive at the amount of insurance you need for your family. Probably the simplest way is to multiply the amount of annual income you want to provide by the number of years desired. Add to this an amount for final expenses, children's education, and an emergency fund, and you'll have a good estimate of the amount of insurance you'll need.

Stay-at-home parents should also be covered. Hiring someone to look after children and to perform the duties of the deceased spouse can be very expensive for the surviving parent. Paying for those expenses on one income adds a load of extra stress at a time when children most need the support of their remaining parent.

If you have no dependents, your only life insurance needs would be for last expenses such as a funeral, any probate costs or legal fees, and any debt repayment. If you are financially independent, you may not need any life insurance at all.

For a more thorough needs analysis, you can seek the help of a professional insurance agent. Most will provide the service at no cost. You can contact an attorney or financial planner for this service, but expect to pay a fee.

Commercial software and insurance web sites are readily available to help you calculate insurance needs. These web sites are for-profit, so we don't make specific recommendations. A simple Google search will provide you with many to choose from.

Regardless of which approach you decide to use, remember to err on the side of a little extra coverage. Inflation is sure to take its toll, and a little extra term insurance is inexpensive for those in good health.

INSURANCE AS A WEALTH ACCUMULATION VEHICLE

We believe that permanent life insurance should not be used as an investment vehicle. Buying the appropriate term policy and investing the difference will almost always result in more wealth accumulation and better insurance protection. We need to emphasize this because the life insurance industry historically has promoted permanent insurance as a good investment for future retirement and other cash needs. Policy illustrations often project unrealistically high earnings and cash value growth up to 40 years down the road. These cash values are touted as providing a tax-free stream of income to educate children, pay for emergencies, and provide for retirement income.

Why is permanent insurance a bad investment alternative? Here are a few disadvantages of going this route:

- Total policy sales charges can be 100 percent of the premium for the first year, and ongoing annual fees and charges can eat up a chunk of the annual premium. Of course, money lost to commissions and loads does not go to work for you.
- Current policy expenses are not guaranteed in some types of permanent insurance, and actual expenses can be higher. Even current mortality charges are not guaranteed in some products, so you may pay more for those in the future.
- Some permanent products transfer risk back to the insured because the policy can terminate if earnings and expense assumptions are not met.
- Your cumulative premiums are effectively locked up for years. Policy termination in the early years will result in forfeiture of all or a large part of your payments.

* It becomes difficult to afford enough protection for your family if you buy permanent insurance for investing. High premiums also reduce the amount of money you have to invest in qualified plans and no-load investments.

Those who benefit most from the sale of permanent policies, sold as an investment, are often insurance agents and the company they work for. Billions in assets held by many life insurers were accumulated during the latter half of the twentieth century, when sales of highly profitable permanent insurance were much higher than they are today. With the rise in prominence of low-profit term insurance, life insurers have increasingly turned to other products to boost their income, such as long-term care and deferred annuities. Our recommendation is to buy term insurance and do your own investing elsewhere. This will improve your own bottom line—not the bottom line of the insurance agent and company.

INSURANCE FOR PENSION MAXIMIZATION

Defined benefit pension plans (see Chapter 5) are subject to the automatic survivor benefit requirements. This law requires that retirement benefits be paid in the form of a qualified joint and survivor annuity unless the employee waives the right and it is agreed to by the spouse. If waived, the employee can opt for other choices, such as a straight life annuity on the retiree only. The joint annuity provides a lower monthly payment than the straight annuity, but all or part of the income continues to the surviving spouse. The straight life annuity provides a higher monthly benefit, although the death of the retiree leaves the surviving spouse with no income.

To address this predicament, the insurance industry developed a marketing concept called pension maximization. This idea suggests that the retiree take the higher payout of the straight life annuity and use the difference in retirement benefits to help pay for a permanent life insurance policy. This arrangement offers the advantages of flexibility to select a new beneficiary at any time or to cash in the policy if your situation changes in the future. The cash value in the policy can be tapped if needed, and the death benefit of the insurance is income tax-free, unlike the joint annuity payments, which are taxable.

Disadvantages include that the premium to buy enough life insurance to match the benefits of the joint and survivor annuity may not be available when the policy is purchased. You also have to qualify for the coverage, and you have to deal with the knowledge that should you die first, your spouse will never receive one dollar of the pension benefits you earned over your working career. Still, there are situations where life insurance might be a good choice. For example, if your spouse has a reduced life expectancy or is older than you, life insurance may make sense. Each situation is different. It would behoove you to evaluate your pension options several years before retirement. You want to have a plan in place before you sign off on the joint annuity.

INSURANCE TO PAY ESTATE SETTLEMENT COSTS

Estate transfer of your property at death may involve shrinkage due to federal estate taxes, state estate taxes, administrative expenses, probate expenses, and payment of debts. If you foresee a need for estate liquidity, you should consider life insurance as a way to help solve this problem. Illiquid estates that include small businesses or closely held corporations are particularly vulnerable to estate shrinkage. These estates often are composed largely of property, machinery, or other assets that cannot easily be converted into cash in a timely manner or at full value. A forced fire sale of a business and other illiquid assets can result in a substantially lower value, thereby reducing the amount available to pay estate settlement costs and the heirs. Federal estate taxes are due nine months from the date of death. They can be paid from liquid assets, from loans if available, or from life insurance earmarked for this purpose.

Advantages of life insurance to pay estate expenses include:

* A known amount of cash is delivered precisely when needed.
* The insurance policy proceeds can stay out of the gross estate by ownership and beneficiary provisions, including the use of trusts.
* The use of life insurance to pay estate expenses can eliminate the need for forced liquidation of assets or borrowing.
* The use of life insurance promotes orderly administration of the estate.
* Life insurance substitutes certainty for uncertainty.

Disadvantages of using life insurance to pay estate expenses include:

* Funds to pay for the cost of the needed permanent insurance may not be available.
* Policy proceeds may actually be less than the amount of cash that could be accumulated by investing the premium amount yourself. An internal rate of return calculation can be provided by the agent to show you the breakeven point.
* The insurance solution may not be available to you because the policy has to be underwritten.

- Estate life insurance placed in an irrevocable trust may be inflexible to changes in personal circumstances and estate tax laws.
- There may be no need for life insurance if your estate is small or if you have substantial liquid assets.

A good way to find a qualified insurance agent who specializes in estate planning is asking for recommendations from trusted friends, estate planning attorneys, and trust officers. You might want to obtain several referrals from each source, interview those who interest you, and select the agent you believe will do the best job for you. These agents are often Chartered Life Underwriters (CLUs), who are trained in estate planning concepts. They can perform estimates of projected estate settlement costs and provide education on the use of insurance trusts and other options that are available to solve these problems. If the agent recommends insurance for your estate needs, we suggest you confirm the recommendation with solid research on your own and by consulting an estate planning attorney, who will write any legal instruments needed. Please note that insurance agents are not attorneys, and they do not provide legal advice. Other professionals, such as fee-only insurance agents, CPAs, or financial planners can perform this work, but you will be charged a fee for their services.

INSURANCE FOR BUSINESS NEEDS

Small business owners commonly use life insurance for business needs to replace potential lost revenue and to resolve ownership interests in the case of death. This is done through buy-sell agreements, key-person insurance, and arrangements for debt coverage in case an owner dies. Buy-sell insurance provides surviving business owners with the cash needed to buy out the share of the deceased partner from his or her heirs. Key-person insurance provides a cash cushion to the company while the business seeks a replacement for the loss of a productive employee. Likewise, insurance to cover business debt provides liquidity when an owner dies. Term insurance is often used for temporary needs, such as debt coverage. Permanent insurance is often recommended by professionals for permanent needs. It is recommended that business owners seek qualified help in the same manner as you would for estate planning.

DISABILITY INCOME INSURANCE

Disability income insurance protects your income against the risks of serious illness or accident. According to the Social Security Administration,

3 in 10 workers entering the workforce today will become disabled before reaching full retirement age. The U.S. Census Bureau says that an illness or accident will keep one in five workers out of work for at least one year. Yet, according to the Social Security Administration, 70 percent of the private-sector workforce has no private long-term disability insurance.

You should consider protecting your earnings with a good disability insurance program above and beyond the meager Social Security benefits for the disabled. Even though you may have some disability income (DI) coverage at work, it may only be short-term disability (STD), or it may be long-term disability (LTD) that does not cover enough of your income. Just ask yourself how long you could go without a paycheck before spending your savings and investments.

How to Figure your Disability Insurance Need

In order to ascertain your DI needs, you will need to take into account government programs, employer programs, and individual coverage. No company will insure 100 percent of your earnings, as there would be no incentive to return to work. Sixty to 70 percent of your earnings is typically the maximum amount you can insure. A good rule of thumb is to insure for the maximum amount available because few of us would feel comfortable taking a pay cut. In addition, disability tends to increase your living expenses with medical and related costs.

Most of us are covered by some combination of disability insurance provided by the government, our employers, or individually purchased plans. A basic understanding of insurance that is available from these three providers will help you implement a program that meets your needs and fits within your budget.

Government Disability Programs

Social Security covers most American workers. The Social Security disability insurance (DI) program pays monthly income to disabled workers and their families. Benefits are based on your earnings record and number of dependents, with annual cost-of-living increases. The personal statement Social Security Administration (SSA) sends you annually shows the estimated DI benefit that would be payable.

You must be unable to perform any substantial gainful work to qualify for Social Security disability benefits. The impairment must be expected to last at least 12 months or potentially result in death. You also must have a history of fairly steady covered employment, especially in the last years leading up to disability. SSA often takes years to resolve a DI claim because the rules for evaluating a disability are complex. A disapproved claim can be appealed several times, and a large backlog of unsettled claims is in the pipeline. Legal representation helps. There are attorneys who specialize in only this area of law.

Benefits begin after a waiting period of five full calendar months and continue for life if your disability doesn't end before full retirement age. You also become eligible for Medicare benefits two years after your DI benefit begins. Detailed benefit information is available in the Social Security Handbook on the Web at www.ssa.gov.

Active-duty military, retirees, and veterans may be eligible for additional disability benefits. Some federal and state employees and railroad workers have their own programs in lieu of Social Security. A wealth of information on alternative programs is available online or from the agencies directly.

Employer Disability Programs

Many employers provide DI protection for eligible employees. Short-term disability (STD) coverage includes sick leave, group disability benefits, and workers' compensation. These plans offer protection for up to 26 weeks. About half the large and midsize companies offer long-term disability (LTD) to their employees. These programs typically replace up to 60 percent of earnings, with benefits lasting for five years or up to age 65. If your employer pays the premium on disability insurance, any benefits will be taxable to you as ordinary income.

The cost of employer group DI is usually less than the cost of an individual policy. This affordability makes these programs popular. However, with the lower cost comes less favorable policy language than is available on individual policies. For example, the definition of disability is often less favorable with group policies than with individual programs. Also, most group policies are not portable if you change employers or become self-employed. You could be without coverage if your insurability status changes as a result of a job change. Additionally, group policies commonly make no provisions for partial disability. They may also limit claims for mental or nervous conditions and for drug and alcohol abuse.

Individual Disability Programs

Though expensive, an individual long-term disability policy is the best way to protect your income. LTD plans may protect up to 70 percent of your income. Benefits are income tax-free when premiums are paid with after-tax dollars. Most long-term disability policies have benefit periods of either two years, five years, or to age 65. These policies are not affected by job or earnings changes, and they offer more favorable definitions and terms than group plans.

Here are the key points you'll want to consider when selecting an individual policy. The first is cost. Disability premiums typically are 1 percent to 3 percent of your income. Premiums are based on your occupation, age, sex, and other underwriting factors. Safer occupations receive the best rates, while riskier occupations pay higher premiums. Blue-collar workers and others doing manual labor often must apply to specialty companies because obtaining coverage is more difficult. Factors influencing policy costs and benefits are length of elimination period, length of benefit period, definition of disability, integration with Social Security, and optional benefits chosen.

Important Definitions When Purchasing Individual DI

Disability

The best definition is own-occupation, which pays if you are disabled and cannot perform the principal duties of the job you now have. It pays even if you can do some other types of work. Note that even an own-occupation definition will vary from company to company, and typically it is offered only to those in certain occupations. The next best definition is modified own-occupation, which pays if you cannot do your own job for two years, after which a less favorable definition applies. Some definitions state that you must not be able to do any work that you are reasonably fitted to do by education, training, or experience. The worst definition is one where you cannot do any meaningful work.

Renewability

Renewability of your policy should be looked at carefully. Consider only those policies that are noncancelable and guaranteed renewable. This means that as long as premiums are paid, the policy cannot be canceled, nor can the premiums ever be increased.

Waiting Period

Also called the elimination period, this is the time between occurrence of the disability and the time benefits begin. Common waiting periods are anywhere from 30 days up to a year. Of course, shorter waiting periods have higher premiums, so carefully consider your short-term disability coverage and any liquid assets you are willing to use before coverage begins.

Optional Riders

Riders can be added to your policy to enhance your protection. These riders include, but are not limited to:

* Residual disability allows you to return to work part-time and collect a partial disability benefit, in addition to collecting part of your salary.
* Cost-of-living adjustment (COLA) becomes active when you are receiving benefits. It ties into the consumer price index (CPI), based on the percentage elected, and it increases your monthly benefit as the cost of living increases.
* Future increase options guarantee the right to increase your monthly benefit at certain intervals, as long as your earnings level increases.
* Automatic increase riders allow you to increase the monthly benefit during the first five policy years, usually by about 3 percent.
* Waiver of premium means that you do not pay policy premiums after you've been disabled, generally for three months.

Some other factors weigh in on the cost and benefits of individual disability policies. One way to reduce the cost is to consider a policy whose benefits are integrated with Social Security. With this type of policy, if you qualify for Social Security benefits, this amount is subtracted from your DI benefit and the company pays you the balance up to the insured amount. If you do not qualify for Social Security, as often happens because of Social Security's strict definition of disability, the policy pays the full insured amount. Either way, you are guaranteed a monthly income at least equal to the full basic benefit amount in the policy. Keep in mind that individual DI policies that are not integrated with Social Security will always pay the full benefit, in addition to any Social Security benefits you may receive.

Another way to reduce costs is to sign up for your employer's long-term disability and then buy a supplemental individual disability income policy. The supplemental policy can increase the percentage of replacement income up to about 70 percent. The supplemental policy will usually have more liberal definitions, and since you own it, it is portable.

HOW TO SHOP FOR LIFE AND DISABILITY INSURANCE

There are two ways to shop for life and disability coverage: do it on your own or find an agent to help with the process. Your premium will be the same regardless of whether you buy from an agent, broker, Internet provider, or directly from an insurance company. This is true for several reasons. First, regulations in many states make it illegal to rebate commissions or negotiate lower commissions to obtain business for individual coverage. Second, there are marketing costs regardless of how and where you buy your insurance. Third, all of these products are ultimately written by a licensed agent somewhere in the distribution system, and of course they are paid either a salary, a commission, or both.

Doing It Yourself

How to shop for insurance is dependent on the type of insurance you are buying. Shopping for term life insurance is simple and can be done online. Shopping for disability income insurance is complex and should probably be done with the help of a knowledgeable agent who brokers insurance with a number of carriers.

Your first step for buying life insurance online is to select one or more Internet web sites that can provide term insurance quotes for a number of companies. You will be asked to provide underwriting information including health history, occupation, avocation, tobacco usage, and family history. This information will lead to a tentative rating class, such as super preferred, preferred, standard, or rated. The web sites will provide quotes based on the length of the term and the amount of protection selected.

You can compare similar policies from different companies and get a feel for which policies are competitively priced and which are not. The better companies will normally be in the same ballpark. You will also want to check on the financial stability of any company you're considering. You can check with A. M. Best Company, Moody's, Standard and Poor's, Fitch Ratings, or Weiss Research. Look for a rating of at least A+ by A. M. Best or its equivalent with the other rating companies.

After selecting a policy, you begin the application process, much of which is done online. The company will set up an appointment for a nurse or paramedic to visit you. On their visit, they will take your physical measurements, collect blood and urine, and perhaps do some other tests. The home office underwriter will check with the Medical Information Bureau (MIB) to see if any pertinent information is available from previous insurance applications.

Next, the insurance company may request medical records from your doctors. They might order an inspection report to check out other risk factors, such as driving record or criminal history. When all the information is received and evaluated at the company, you are assigned a rating class and issued a policy, unless you are uninsurable.

Working with an Agent

An easier way to buy insurance is with the help of a qualified agent who brokers with a number of insurance companies. This is particularly true when you buy complex products such as disability insurance. The agent can perform a needs analysis, estimate your rating class, and pick a quality company that is competitive. If you have any smoking history or medical or other underwriting problems, agents know which companies would be most lenient with your situation. They are very familiar with the marketplace and can save you time and energy. If you are shopping for term insurance, make this clear to the agent up front, and explain that you are not interested in sales talk about permanent insurance.

Choosing a good agent can be a challenge. You want an agent who has expertise in the life and health area and who makes this their primary business. The agent should be experienced and preferably be a CLU. This designation requires a great deal of learning, and CLUs must pass a number of rigorous examinations.

A good way to find a qualified agent in the family market is to ask for recommendations from people you trust. Also, look in the Yellow Pages to find the names of agents and firms that work in your area. Bogleheads normally interview several prospective agents to discuss their needs and preferences before making a choice.

ADDITIONAL RESOURCES

There are a number of excellent web sites where you can learn more about life and disability insurance. Information is also available from federal and state agencies.

- Social Security Administration—www.ssa.gov
- Department of Veteran Affairs—www.va.gov
- Insurance Information Institute—www.iii.org
- America's Health Insurance Plans—www.ahip.org
- National Association of Insurance Commissioners—www.naic.org

CHAPTER SUMMARY

Choosing the life and disability coverages that are best for you and building a solid insurance program are critical components to protect you and your family while you invest for your retirement. Following these simple suggestions can save time and help you select the best coverage at the best prices. Remember that your needs will change over time, so you'll want to review your program every few years.

Insurance planning is not fun because you are addressing the risk of unpleasant outcomes, but it is always necessary. A good insurance plan works hand in hand with a good retirement plan to provide you and your loved ones with security.

CHAPTER FIFTEEN

Health Insurance

Lee E. Marshall

INTRODUCTION

Anyone who has lost their good health even for a little while believes as classical Roman poet Virgil said, "The greatest wealth is health." Our health enables us to use our energies to earn a living for ourselves and our families and to prepare for our retirement and old age. Despite steps taken to lead healthy lives and minimize risk, the odds are high that at some point in time we will suffer illnesses or accidents that threaten our economic welfare.

Health insurance was created in the early part of the twentieth century to help protect our financial well-being from the risk of poor health. Unfortunately, health-care insurance costs have risen dramatically over the last 50 years. Finding and qualifying for affordable health-care insurance is a challenge for many people. Many Americans are shut out of the health insurance market because they either cannot qualify for it or because they cannot afford it.

This does not mean that the segment of the population without health insurance does not get health care; far from it. No one in America

239

is denied health care when they need it. It does mean wiping out the savings of those who do not have coverage before the cost is picked up by hospitals, doctors, charities, and the government. And it does mean that people without health care insurance may not receive the high level of treatment that someone with health insurance would receive.

On the positive side, technological advances in medical procedures and the discovery of new drugs and treatments have resulted in improved longevity and quality of life. Cancer and heart disease was once a death sentence. Now those are treatable diseases. The future holds the promise of cures for many diseases and perhaps the ability to slow down or even reverse the effects of aging itself. There is also an increasing awareness that we are responsible for protecting our own health by improving our lifestyles in the areas of smoking, obesity, exercise, and stress management.

In this chapter, we'll discuss health insurance in two segments. The first is medical insurance, and the second is long-term care insurance. We will provide tips on finding the plan and policy that fit your needs. Health insurance issues are complex and cannot be covered comprehensively in a single chapter. Additional resources are available at the end of the chapter for further research. The time you spend researching health insurance choices can make a huge difference in your final out-of-pocket costs and the quality of your care.

MEDICAL INSURANCE

Medical insurance is obtained primarily through three avenues: employers, government programs, and purchased individually. It helps pay for health-care costs for doctors, hospitals, prescription drugs, home health care, and a wide variety of other services. That availability of health insurance and its costs and benefits vary widely, and it is wise to learn as much as you can before choosing a plan. The medical insurance system is very complex and changes rapidly. There are many terms and acronyms. Familiarity with the jargon can help you understand your choices. Some of the more common terms follow:

- *Copayment* is the amount an insured pays toward the cost of a particular benefit, such as $10 for each doctor visit.
- *Co-insurance* is the percentage of expenses the individual shares with the carrier, for example, 80 percent paid by the company and 20 percent paid by the insured.
- *Coordination of benefits* is the health plan provision that determines the order in which benefits will be paid when an individual is covered

under two medical insurance plans. This prevents double payment of benefits.

* *Deductibles* are the amounts an insured pays annually, before policy benefits are paid. A low-deductible plan might be $100 and a high deductible plan might be $1,000 or more.

* *Exclusions* are expenses that are not covered under a medical insurance plan.

* *HIPAA* is the Health Insurance Portability and Accountability Act of 1996. It's a law that improves portability of health insurance plans.

* *In network* refers to a group of doctors, hospitals, and other providers contracted with a specific health plan. You generally pay less when using an in-network provider.

* *Maximum plan limits* cap an insurer's liability for medical expenses. Plans can have both a yearly and a lifetime maximum dollar limit.

* *Maximum out-of-pocket expense* is the most an insured has to pay during a plan year before the insurer begins to pay all covered expenses.

* *Medicare-approved amount* is what Medicare will pay for medical services. Providers who treat Medicare patients agree to accept this amount.

* *Preexisting conditions* are medical conditions that are known or treated before you enroll in a new plan. Individual plans and some small group plans deny or restrict coverage because of these preexisting medical conditions.

* *Providers* are persons or entities that provide medical care. They include doctors, hospitals, home health agencies, and licensed nursing homes.

* *Preventive care* aims to keep you healthy. It includes physical exams, cancer screening, and flu shots.

* *Primary care physician* is the doctor who manages your health care and authorizes referral to specialists and hospitals.

* *Usual, customary, and reasonable charges* are the amounts that an insurer will pay for services in a particular geographic area. Usually associated with indemnity plans, the insured is responsible for any excess amounts.

The Internet is an excellent resource for a more complete list of terms. Often a plan or policy comes with brochures that explain terminology used in the plan. Health insurance has a language of its own. Take a little time to learn the language before reviewing the many options available in the market.

TYPES OF MEDICAL INSURANCE

The two main types of medical insurance are indemnity plans and managed care plans. The major differences between the two are choice of providers, out-of-pocket costs for covered services, and how bills are paid. Most individual, group, and government plans are one of these types or some combination of the two.

Indemnity Plans

Indemnity plans are also know as major medical plans. They have an annual up-front deductible, after which the insurance company pays a percentage of the charges. When your out-of-pocket payments reach a set maximum for the year, the insurance company pays 100 percent of any remaining costs that year, up to the plan limit.

Indemnity plans allow you to choose your own doctor and provide the greatest amount of flexibility in managing your health care. High-deductible indemnity plans can work well with health savings accounts, as we will explore later in the chapter.

Managed Care Plans

Managed care involves contracts between insurance companies and health care providers. These plans control costs by negotiating fees, limiting choice of providers, and requiring referrals from your primary care physician when you need to see a specialist. Managed care plans usually cost less than indemnity plans but limit flexibility and choices. A variety of managed care plans are available. They include the following:

- Health maintenance organizations (HMO) offer access to a network of participating health-care providers. You choose a primary care doctor from an approved list. Your doctor then coordinates your care and manages referrals to specialists. You are required to obtain your care within the network to receive full benefits. HMOs are the least flexible of all the plans.
- Preferred provider organizations (PPO) allow you to see any doctor within the plan. All or most of your costs are paid for after a small copayment as long as you use network providers. You pay more if you go out of network. The primary advantage is that you do not need a referral to see a specialist.
- Point of service plans (POS) offer several options, including using a primary care physician, using a network provider, or going outside of

the plan. Reimbursement will vary, depending on which option you select.

Medical Care Providers

Medical coverage in the United States is provided by employers, the government, or individually purchased plans. Large employer group plans and government plans typically cover all enrolled participants, regardless of prior health conditions. Small group and individual policies require underwriting and can exclude or limit coverage to unhealthy applicants. It's possible that some form of national health care could be proposed in the next few years. In the meantime, choosing health care wisely remains of paramount importance.

EMPLOYER POLICIES

Many Americans obtain medical insurance through their employers. Negotiated group rates are less expensive to employees because the employer typically pays part of the cost and for underwriting reasons. The benefits of group plans may be better than those offered by individual plans. Larger groups offer even lower premiums, better benefits, and ease in obtaining coverage. With smaller groups, employees pay more for fewer benefit choices, and medical underwriting can severely restrict coverage. Employer health insurance is valuable and can be a factor in an employee's decision to change jobs or to become self-employed.

A federal law called COBRA allows you to keep your group coverage for up to 18 months after you leave a company that has 20 or more employees. If you leave voluntarily, you would be required to pay full price for COBRA. The American Recovery and Reinvestment Tax Act of 2009 includes a 65 percent government subsidy to employees who are involuntarily terminated between September 1, 2008, and December 31, 2009. The employer must first provide this payment and then be reimbursed by the government.

Another choice is to be added to your working spouse's group policy if that option is available. Another federal law, HIPAA, helps workers with preexisting conditions who have lost their group coverage to obtain new coverage with less limiting exclusions. Information on these federal laws can be obtained at the web site of the U.S. Department of Labor at www.dol.gov.

Note that not all employer group plans are created equal. Employers are increasingly passing on a greater share of the cost of health-care insurance to their employees. In some cases, employers subsidize the premium only for the employee, not the family. The full premium an employee has to pay to cover spouse and children can be high. In these situations, it may make sense for the employee to stay with the group and for the family to receive individual coverage. Make sure the individual coverage for the spouse and children is already in place before opting out.

POLICIES FOR INDIVIDUALS AND THE SELF-EMPLOYED

Some people do not qualify for group medical insurance because they are self-employed or work for a small company that doesn't offer insurance. Or perhaps they are unemployed and their COBRA benefits have run out. Individual policies are available from many companies, although getting covered may be difficult if you have serious or chronic medical problems. The insurance company will ask you to answer health questions, request authorization to access your medical records, and possibly require a physical exam to prove insurability. It is extremely important to provide correct and truthful answers to all medical and underwriting questions. At the time of a claim, the insurance company can look back to make sure you did not omit anything on your application. They can deny coverage and cancel your policy if they find out that you lied.

Ask for referrals or look in the Yellow Pages to find agents or brokers in the area. Look for a health insurance broker who is knowledgeable in medical insurance and does business with a number of companies. The best health insurance brokers often specialize and can save you a lot of time by finding the best coverage for your situation. Many Internet sites provide information and quotes if you decide to shop for yourself. Be prepared to do a lot of homework to get up to speed on the subject, as health insurance choices can be quite complex.

GOVERNMENT HEALTH PLANS AND ACCOUNTS

Government health insurance plans are funded at the federal, state, and local level. The major categories of government health insurance are Medicare, Medicaid, the State Children's Health Insurance Program (SCHIP), military health care, the federal employees health benefit program, state plans, and the Indian Health Service.

Medicare is the federal program that helps pay health-care costs for people age 65 and older and for certain people under age 65 with long-term disabilities. The program does not cover all medical expenses or the cost of most long-term care. Medicare is financed by a portion of payroll taxes paid by workers and their employees. It is also financed in part by monthly premiums that are deducted from Social Security checks.

Medicare has four parts:

1. Hospital insurance (Part A) helps pay for inpatient care in a hospital or a skilled nursing facility following a hospital stay. Part A also pays for some home health and hospice care. You automatically get Part A when you sign up for Medicare. Most Americans, age 65 and older, are eligible for free Part A coverage, because they have paid Medicare taxes over the years. Those with less than 40 quarters of Medicare-covered employment have to pay a premium for Part A. A deductible and copay provisions apply, resulting in some out-of-pocket expenses for the insured for hospital and skilled nursing facility stays. In 2009, the hospital deductible is $1,068 for each benefit period. A benefit period begins when you enter a hospital or a skilled nursing facility, and ends when you have been out of the hospital or skilled nursing facility for at least 60 days in a row.

2. Medical insurance (Part B) helps pay some of the costs for doctor bills and for many other medical services and supplies. Part B is optional, but if you enroll, you pay a monthly premium. The monthly premium for 2009 is $96.40 for people with individual income up to $85,000. Higher-income individuals pay more. Deductible and copay provisions apply when you receive services. The deductible for 2009 is $135, after which the insured pay 20 percent of the Medicare-approved amount.

3. Medicare advantage plans (Part C) are available in many areas. They are also known as Medicare replacement plans. People with Medicare Parts A and B can choose to receive all of their health-care services through a provider organization under Part C. Some advantage plans offer prescription drug, vision, hearing, and dental coverage, so the prices will vary, depending on the benefits. Advantage plans replace Medigap policies, which will be discussed a little later.

4. Prescription drug insurance (Part D) helps pay for medications that doctors prescribe for treatment. Part D is available to those who have Parts A and B and are willing to pay an extra premium. There are a number of plans to choose from, and benefits vary. Part D does not pay for all prescriptions, and it is infamous for the doughnut hole—a large coverage gap where the insured pays 100 percent. Premiums, deductibles, copays, and covered drugs will depend upon the plan you choose.

Medicaid is a joint federal-state program that provides some coverage to low-income people with few or no assets. States establish their own eligibility and benefits rules and administer the programs. Medicaid is a means-tested program and not all low-income people qualify. The groups of people served by Medicaid include children, seniors, low-income parents, and those with disabilities. Only your state Medicaid office can tell you if you are eligible for benefits. Their offices can be accessed at www.healthsymphony .com. More information is available at the web site of the U.S. Department of Health and Human Services, listed at the end of this chapter.

Military and Indian health care is provided through several programs, including Tricare/Champus, ChampVa, and the Veterans Administration (VA). Military care is further divided into active duty, retired, and other honorably discharged veterans. Each program is unique and handles health care differently. Historically, some form of medical care has been provided for the military. That dates back to the seventeenth century. However, it wasn't until the twentieth century that federal laws began to guarantee benefits to the military. More information is available from the U.S. Department of Defense Military Health System at www .health.mil.

Indian Health Service (IHS) is an agency within the Department of Health and Human Services that provides care primarily through IHS facilities. Interestingly, Indian health care is probably the oldest program in the United States. It began in 1787 with Article I of the Constitution and has evolved with treaties, laws, Supreme Court decisions, and executive orders. The IHS provides health care to approximately 1.5 million American Indians and Alaska Natives who belong to more than 557 federally recognized tribes in 35 states. More information is available at the Indian Health Services web site at www.ihs.gov.

High-risk pools are available in over 30 states. They were created to catch some of those less fortunate people who fall through the cracks. The pools provide coverage for individuals who have serious medical problems and cannot qualify for other coverage. Premiums are typically higher than for individual plans that are required to insure you. High-risk pools are increasingly important because they provide an element of stability for those who could not otherwise qualify for coverage. Contact information for your state can be found at the web site of the National Association of State Comprehensive Health Insurance Plans at www.naschip.org.

Emergency rooms or emergency departments are required by federal law to provide minimal care to all who seek it. Patients cannot be turned away because of inability to pay. Although it may be a program of last resort, it does provide some level of care for everyone. Many Americans who have no health insurance at all use emergency rooms to access heath-care benefits.

Supplemental Policies for Retirees (MEDIGAP)

People with original Medicare Parts A and B frequently buy a Medigap insurance policy that helps pay the deductibles, copays, and gaps in coverage. These plans pay for additional services not covered by Medicare. New policies no longer cover prescription medicine.

When you sign up for Part B of Medicare, you have an open enrollment period of six months to buy a Medigap policy. During this six-month window, you cannot be turned down, even if you have health problems. You would have to qualify medically for these plans beyond the open enrollment period. Most states have standardized versions for Medigap plans (A–L) making it easy to compare policies. Details on these plans are available at the Medicare web site.

Medigap policies are not available if you have a Medicare advantage plan, as these plans already include benefits typically paid for by a separate Medigap policy. So, if you have a choice, you will want to carefully compare traditional Medicare plans with a supplement to the Medicare advantage plan. We recommend that you seek help from experts in this area because these choices can be complicated. In most communities, there are agencies that help citizens understand Medicare and other issues related to aging.

Health Savings Accounts

Health savings accounts (HSAs) are an alternative way to pay for medical expenses with flexibility and tax benefits. HSAs are accounts in which you or your employer can make tax-advantaged contributions. Money placed in the account can help cover deductibles, copayments, dental care, vision care, and over-the-counter drugs. They can be a very good choice for those who want to manage their own health-care insurance needs.

Individual contributions are tax-deductible, and withdrawals to pay medical expenses are income tax-free. If your payments are through your employer, they are on a pretax basis, and payments for medical expenses are income tax-free to you. Annual inflation-adjusted contribution limits are set by the IRS. For 2009, the annual limit on deductions is $3,000 for an individual and $5,950 for a family. Catch-up contributions and a limited IRA rollover option are also available to those who qualify. The account can be invested in a variety of instruments while you wait to use it, subject to the rules of your plan. More information is available at the Department of the Treasury web site at www.treas.gov.

High-Deductible Health Plans

High-deductible health plans (HDHP) feature higher deductibles and out-of-pocket maximums than traditional medical insurance plans. Your HDHP may be offered as an indemnity plan, an HMO, PPO, or POS. Premiums for HDHPs are less than for traditional plans because the deductible is higher. For 2009, the deductible for an individual must be no less than $1,150, or $2,300 for a family. Annual out-of-pocket maximums for health-care expenses are $5,800 for an individual or $11,600 for a family.

Consider an HDHP if you are healthy and your medical expenses are limited. Plans are available individually and may be offered by your employer. HDHP might also be a good choice for family members with nonsubsidized group coverage. Take time to educate yourself and carefully research all the choices available to you.

Premium savings can be used to help fund your HSA. An individual HDHP with an HSA can be a good way to fund health care for those who can meet the health and underwriting criteria and can afford to pay for smaller, routine medical bills themselves. By law, you must enroll in an HDHP before setting up an HSA, and you cannot be enrolled in Medicare or another health plan.

LONG-TERM CARE INSURANCE

Long-term care insurance (LTC) provides care generally not covered by other health insurance, Medicare, or Medicaid. It typically covers home care, assisted living, adult daycare, respite care, hospice care, nursing home, and Alzheimer's facilities. LTC can pay for home care if home-care coverage is purchased. It will pay for a visiting or live-in caregiver, companion, housekeeper, therapist, or private-duty nurse up to 7 days a week, 24 hours a day (up to the policy benefit maximum).

Paying for LTC is an increasing challenge for millions of Americans. The U.S. Department of Health and Human Services says that 70 percent of Americans age 65 and older will eventually pay for long-term care services. Genworth Financial's 2008 Cost of Care Survey shows the average annual cost of a private nursing home room to be more than $76,000 and rising annually. The annual cost for assisted living averages $33,000, and the cost for noncertified home health aides is $25 an hour. Skilled care costs more.

The focus of this section is on planning for the needs of the elderly, although LTC can also be used at any age for illness, accidents, and periods of rehabilitation.

Bob Hope once quipped, "I don't feel old. I don't feel anything until noon. Then it's time for my nap." While it's good to be able to joke about getting older, it's also wise to make solid plans for the time when we may no longer be able to take care of ourselves. Planning in advance for disability and dependence in later life can help put you in charge of the type and quality of care you'll receive when you need it. Without advance planning, your options will be more limited, and they may be ones you would not like.

Defining Long-Term Care

In the United States, care for the elderly takes place in nursing homes, assisted living facilities, continuing care retirement communities (CCRC), and in the home. LTC is a variety of services, including medical and nonmedical care for people who have chronic illnesses or disabilities and who need help with their activities of daily living. Unlike traditional medicine that is administered to help people get well, LTC provides care for people as they are, even if they are not expected to get better. This care can be provided by skilled professionals, unskilled aides, family members, or friends.

Because LTC has its own language, learning the basic terms can be helpful:

* *Activities of Daily Living* (ADLs) are everyday functions of living, including bathing, continence, dressing, eating, toileting, and transferring. Inability to do two or more ADLs typically triggers LTC policy benefits for those who are insured.
* *Assisted Living Facilities* (ALFs) are living arrangements that provide individuals help with ADLs. These facilities offer more independence of lifestyle and are for those who do not need to be in a nursing home.
* *Cognitive impairments* are mental deficiencies that affect one's ability to function independently. Alzheimer's, dementia, and memory loss are the most common conditions.
* *Coordinated Care* involves the use of a health-care professional who works with an insurance company and a patient to develop and manage a plan of LTC.
* *Custodial Care* is nonskilled care that helps individuals with ADLs. It is provided by health-care aides at home or in a facility.

- *Home Health Care* refers to a wide array of services for health and custodial care received in the home.
- *Hospice Care* is for those who are terminally ill and expected to live six months or less. It can be provided at home or in a facility.
- *Inflation Protection* is a provision in an LTC policy that increases benefits to help pay for increases in the cost of care.
- *Nursing Homes* are residential facilities for people with chronic illness or disability, particularly the elderly.
- *Partnership Policies* are a type of LTC policy that allows individuals to keep more of their assets before Medicaid kicks in.
- *Respite Care* relieves family caregivers for a period of time, giving them a break from providing care.
- *Skilled Care* must be ordered by a physician, and it follows a plan of care. Care is performed or supervised by skilled medical personnel and can be received at home or in a facility.
- *Spend-down* is the term that refers to the requirement that individuals use up most of their assets in order to qualify for Medicaid.

Buying Long-Term Care Insurance

People can provide for their long-term care needs in several ways. Many families take care of their own. Some fortunate people self-insure in that they have the financial resources to pay for care out of pocket and do not need insurance. Other people with very limited income and few assets may qualify for Medicaid. Finally, a large portion of the population cannot afford to pay potential care costs out of pocket, but their net worth is too high to quality for Medicaid, and family care is not an option. These are the people who should look at LTC insurance to help fund their needs.

The main problem for this last group is the cost of coverage, which typically runs from $1,500 to $3,000 annually per individual. There are several methods that will allow you to buy adequate coverage while keeping costs as low as possible. In the final analysis, the decision to buy LTC insurance is highly personal. It requires looking at a number of factors, including family health history, family relationships, personal desires, and your financial situation.

Some large employers offer group LTC plans, including the federal government, and associations you may belong to could offer LTC plans. However, most LTC policies are sold to individuals directly by insurance agents. The complexity of the product and the wide number of choices available typically requires the help of a skilled professional. LTC policy details vary, but your main choices will include the following:

- A tax-qualified policy allows you to deduct some of your premiums if you itemize deductions and your total deductible medical expenses exceed 7.5 percent of your adjusted gross income. In our opinion, you should buy only a tax-qualified policy.
- The benefit amount is usually presented as a daily amount that ranges from $50 a day to more than $250 a day. For example, for a policy with a $200 a day benefit, the insurance company would pay about $6,000 a month or $72,000 a year. One way to lower your premium is to choose a lower daily benefit and then self-insure for part of your need.
- Your benefit period may range from two years to lifetime. Plans with lifetime benefits are the most expensive. You might want to consider a four- or five-year plan, since about 90 percent of all nursing home stays are less than five years.
- The elimination period you choose can range from 30 days up to a year. This is the time period that you pay out of pocket after the benefit is triggered and before the insurance company starts to pay. Choosing a longer elimination period reduces your premium payments but increases the amount you pay up front at claim time.
- Covered services can include nursing home or assisted living care, home health care, hospice care, respite care, and adult daycare. Make sure you select a policy that is comprehensive in coverage and that meets your expected needs. Some policies cover only your state and only certain types of facilities.
- Benefit triggers should not exceed more than two ADLs that you cannot perform. The triggers for benefits in a facility and benefits in your home can be different. Make certain that your policy covers cognitive impairments.
- Inflation protection should be selected for all policies. A policy with a $200 daily benefit and 5 percent compound inflation protection would pay $415 a day in 15 years. Policies with automatic inflation protection cost more than those without it. Nonautomatic inflation protection allows you to increase your coverage periodically. An increase in benefits will increase the annual premium you pay.
- Waiver of premium is an option that relieves you of payments at the time of claim or up to 90 days thereafter. That is a good option to consider.
- Restoration of benefits restores used benefits to the original amount after you have recovered and a stated period of time has passed without your using additional benefits.
- Nonforfeiture benefits guarantee the return of some or all of your premium payments if you cancel the policy after it has been in force

for a defined period of time. This option is usually too expensive for most to consider.

- Exclusions and limitations are part of every LTC policy. Most policies do not pay for alcohol or drug addiction, injury or illness caused by acts of war, attempted suicide, or self-inflicted injuries.
- Renewability guarantees that the insurance company cannot cancel your policy, but they can increase your premiums periodically, on a class basis. Renewability is guaranteed in most states. Make sure your state is one of them.
- Premium payment options vary. Most people pay annually, but single-payment, 10-year-payment, and 20-year-payment plans are available.
- Shared benefit coverage for couples is a smart way to keep costs lower. One policy covers both spouses and provides benefits for both. Be sure to consider this option if you are eligible.

One final thought about buying LTC insurance: some people will recommend that you buy LTC when you are young and in good health because the premiums are low. The problem with this approach is that you have to pay premiums for 40 or more years, with rate increases, and you may never need the benefits. Buying it when you are age 55 to 65 limits the number of years you pay premiums and limits the number of price increases you might expect. If you wait until you are older, you do run a higher risk of being rated or uninsurable. These are tough choices, and each individual must decide what's best.

Medicare, Medicaid, and LTC

Medicare does not pay for complete LTC. Most LTC needs are custodial, and Medicare does not pay for these. It pays only for medically necessary skilled nursing in a nursing home or for skilled home care. Even here you must meet certain conditions to qualify for these limited benefits. You should be aware that some Medicare supplement plans pay a small amount for people recovering at home from illness or injury. However, it is unwise to count on these small benefits in your LTC planning.

Medicaid is a federal and state-funded program that pays for nursing home care for certain eligibility groups. It may pay for limited home care and community services. A recipient must have low income and own few assets. Qualifying for Medicaid depends on the rules of the individual states, and the qualifications vary widely among states.

Many seniors look for ways to keep more of their assets and still qualify for Medicaid benefits. They have worked a lifetime to accumulate their nest eggs, and now they face the prospect of using it up for LTC. Unfortunately, those seeking Medicaid for LTC expenses will have to spend down their assets until they meet eligibility requirements.

Recent federal law has increased Medicaid's look-back rule to five years. If you transferred assets for less than full market value during this period, you will not qualify for Medicaid. Another problem with gifting or giving away assets to family members is that once given away, assets are irrevocably gone. This means you can't get them back if your situation changes or if you change your mind. Putting money in a trust may work, but this is expensive, and restrictions apply. You can contact an elder law attorney to help shed assets, but that also comes with a price tag. In all cases, you should know that it is illegal to hide assets to qualify for Medicaid. Everything must be done with full disclosure and within the scope of the law.

One alternative is a partnership plan. These products are the result of an alliance between a state and insurers that allows participants to hold on to more assets before qualifying for Medicaid. A partnership plan may work like this: you want to protect $100,000 of assets so you buy an LTC policy that pays this amount in benefits. If you become eligible for Medicaid, you keep $100,000 of your assets above Medicaid's limit. Partnership plans are being launched in a number of states. More information on partnership plans is available from your state insurance commissioner and from your Medicaid office.

ADDITIONAL RESOURCES

For those who have access to employer-sponsored health insurance, the first place to look for more information is your human resources department. Ask for brochures. You may also ask to inspect the plan documents themselves. Federal and state employees can obtain detailed information on their agency web sites, as well as from their human resources departments. For individual plans, a wealth of information is available online and from agents. The following web sites are very helpful:

* Life and Health Foundation for Education: www.life-line.org
* Medicare: www.medicare.gov
* National Organization of Life and Health Insurance Guarantee Association: www.nolhga.com
* U.S. Department of Health and Human Services: www.hhs.gov
* U.S. Department of Labor: www.dol.gov
* U.S. Department of the Treasury: www.treas.gov

CHAPTER SUMMARY

Medical and long-term care insurance can help protect people from expenses that most of us could not meet out of pocket. It ensures that we have access to needed care that improves the quality of our lives. The health insurance marketplace is dynamic, and changes occur frequently. The only things we know for sure are choices and costs as of today, and that they will change in the future.

If you have group insurance available or are enrolled in Medicare, study your options carefully before deciding what is right for you. If you need individual coverage, find a broker who specializes in this area and study the recommendations thoroughly. Review your health plans every few years, as new products and changes in the law may present new choices for you.

CHAPTER SIXTEEN

Essentials of Estate Planning

Robert A. Stermer

INTRODUCTION

"In this world nothing can be said to be certain, except death and taxes." Benjamin Franklin (1706–1790) wrote these words in a letter to Jean-Baptiste Leroy in 1789, and they were reprinted in *The Works of Benjamin Franklin, 1817.* Those words are as timeless today as the day they were first penned. No one enjoys discussing death and taxes, but taking the proper steps now to make sure that your family and financial assets are protected in case of tragedy brings a sense of peace. Chapter 3 discussed taxes, and this chapter covers preparation for a crippling disability and eventual death.

Estate planning is the process of deciding who will make your decisions when you are not able to do so because of death or disability. It includes a discussion about what you may or may not want done to preserve your life during a serious medical problem and how your worldly possessions will be distributed after you are gone.

Bogleheads believe in doing the necessary research to learn enough to hold an intelligent conversation with an estate-planning attorney. Many books have been written on estate planning. This chapter covers the basics, and the information is not meant to be sufficient to create your own estate plan. Laws differ from state to state. Consult an estate-planning attorney in the state where you reside to make sure your plan will work in that jurisdiction.

GOALS OF ESTATE PLANNING

Estate planning is twofold. First, it includes the possibility of a severe disability in the future. The disability could be physical, meaning that you may not be able to take care of your own needs, or it could be mental, which impairs your ability to make your own decisions, or it could include both. Second, an estate plan directs what happens to your assets at the end of your life.

Do you wish to have your life prolonged using all available means? Or if death is imminent and inevitable, would you prefer to be allowed to die with no extraordinary measures taken, except for receiving sufficient pain medication to keep you comfortable? These are decisions that should be made while you still have the capacity to make them, rather than having a court make them for you when you are incapable of expressing your wishes.

You may own substantial assets at the time of death, and it may be important for you to specify what will happen to those assets after your demise. Properly drafted estate planning documents can ensure that your wishes are followed.

PROPERTY TITLING

The titling of property has a profound impact on how your assets are treated when you pass away. Proper titling can save your heirs time and money when settling your estate.

Types of Property

Property comes in two types: personal and real. Both types can be owned in a variety of manners. Understanding the various options and consequences of that ownership is key to making the best decision.

Personal Property

Personal property includes your movable assets, such as cars, household furnishings, jewelry, artwork, and other things that can be picked up and moved. Perhaps the easiest way to think of personal property is that it is all property that is not real estate.

Real Property

Real property is dirt and things permanently attached to dirt, such as buildings, and the things permanently attached to buildings, such as decks and a built-in swimming pool, which are known as fixtures. Real property also includes more esoteric forms of property ownership, such as ownership of a unit in a condominium.

Types of Ownership

Individual

Property is commonly held in the name of a single individual. If you title property this way, on your death, property owned in this manner may be subject to probate unless a statute allows you to name a beneficiary.

Tenancy in Common

Property can be owned as an undivided interest in the whole with one or more persons. When property is owned in such a fashion, the owners are known as tenants in common and the form of property ownership is known as a tenancy in common. Upon death, the interest of the deceased party continues and becomes the property of his or her estate. It does not automatically pass to the other person or persons.

Joint Ownership

Property can also be owned jointly with another person. On your death, jointly owned property will usually pass to the joint owner with no further action required.

Tenancy by the Entireties

Tenancy by the entireties property is a special form of joint ownership that can be created only by persons who are married. In some states, tenancy by the entireties property is not subject to the liabilities of either marital partner individually. It is subject only to joint liabilities.

Community Property

There is special ownership for married couples under laws of community property. Each has equal rights to any appreciation or income derived from those assets. Not all states have community property laws. If you live in one of the nine community property states (Arizona, California, Idaho,

Louisiana, Nevada, New Mexico, Texas, Washington, and Wisconsin), property acquired during marriage may be owned in this special kind of joint tenancy.

Ownership by Trustee

You may also transfer ownership of your property to a trustee, who may even be you! If you elect ownership by trustee, property is no longer considered to be owned by you as an individual but is instead owned by the trust. When you die, it is not usually subject to probate.

Life Estates

It is sometimes helpful to think of property rights as though they are a bundle of sticks. One of the sticks is the right to occupy the property during life (the right of the life tenant), and another is the right to the property after the life tenant dies. A person holding the second right is known as a remainderman. On the death of the life tenant, the remainderman automatically and immediately passes into ownership of the property. Life estates come in two flavors: ordinary life estates and enhanced life estates.

Ordinary Life Estate

The ordinary life estate is pretty much as just described. Using a bill of sale for personal property or a deed for real property, the grantor (the person establishing the life estate) transfers the property to the remainderman, reserving the right to make use of the property during life.

Enhanced Life Estate

The enhanced life estate is established in the same manner as the ordinary life estate, but the grantor reserves additional rights. Usually the grantor reserves the right to transfer the property back into his or her name, the right to sell the property and keep the proceeds, and the right to mortgage the property; in most cases, the grantor disclaims any liability for waste, which is the failure to maintain the property. The enhanced life estate is preferable in most instances because of its great flexibility.

METHODS OF PROPERTY TRANSFER AT DEATH

Your heirs will settle your estate after you are gone. All real and personal property must be transferred to a new owner. How this is done varies from state to state.

By Operation of Law

Legislatures in most states have established means by which property can pass automatically to heirs with no action required by the beneficiary other than the production of a death certificate. Some of the mechanisms that have been established are discussed next.

Pay on Death or Transfer on Death Accounts

In many states, it is possible to establish an account as a pay on death or transfer on death account. The person named as the pay on death or transfer on death party has no rights to the account during the life of the original account owner. However, on the death of the original account owner, the pay on death party automatically becomes the new owner of the account. Pay on death and transfer on death accounts apply only to personal property and cannot be used to transfer real property.

Totten Trust

The Totten trust account is an account in which the original depositor deposits funds to be held in trust for a named beneficiary but reserves the right to withdraw the funds during his or her life. In practice, this account functions identically to a pay on death or transfer on death account. Totten trust accounts are used only to hold personal property and cannot be used to transfer real property.

Joint Ownership of Accounts

Joint ownership, also known as joint tenancy with rights of survivorship, means that all of the owners have the current right to make use of any property. On the death of any owner, the remaining owners automatically receive the interest of the deceased owner. Both real property and personal property can be held in this manner.

Homestead

Some states confer a special status on a person's homestead (home and property around it) and provide for its transfer by operation of law upon the death of the owner.

Through Probate

The legal process of probate, discussed in more detail later, provides a court-supervised method of transferring assets at death. The probate process can be expensive, as both the person administering the estate, commonly known as an executor or personal representative, and the attorneys they employ receive a fee for acting on behalf of the estate.

By Transfer to a Trustee
If one establishes a trust and transfers assets to the trustee, the terms of the trust will control the disposition of the assets so transferred.

PROBATE

The technical definition of probate is the process of organizing a deceased party's assets, determining his or her liabilities, paying those liabilities, determining the correct beneficiaries, and transferring whatever is left to the beneficiaries, all under court supervision. A person dying having a valid will is said to have died testate, whereas a person dying without a valid will is said to have died intestate.

Assets Subject to Probate

Assets subject to probate, commonly known as the probate estate, include all of a person's assets with several notable exceptions. Assets are treated differently depending on the type:

Insurance: The proceeds of life insurance policies are not subject to probate unless the estate of the deceased party is named as the beneficiary of the policy, or there is no beneficiary.

Annuities: Proceeds of annuity contracts are excluded from the probate estate unless the estate is named as the beneficiary of the contract, or no beneficiary is named.

Jointly Owned Property: Title to jointly owned property passes to the remaining living joint owner or owners upon the death of any other joint owner.

Tenancy by the Entireties Property: Title to tenancy by the entireties property passes to the remaining living spouse upon the death of the other spouse.

Property Transferred to a Trustee: Property transfer to a trustee passes in accordance with the directions contained in the trust document.

Homestead: The social policy underlying homestead property is to preserve a place to live for the surviving spouse and family. Accordingly, if the person who died was survived by a spouse and children, the spouse takes a life estate in the property and the children take a vested remainder interest. If there are no children, the surviving spouse takes a fee simple interest in the property. The application of the homestead statute can be avoided by owning the homestead as tenants by the entireties.

The Probate Process

This section provides a general overview of what happens during the probate process. Although the procedure differs somewhat from state to state, and different terms are used in different states, this description should provide enough background to understand the tasks that must be accomplished to successfully navigate the probate process under the guidance of an attorney.

If a person dies not having a will, the property will be distributed in accordance with the laws of intestate succession. The intestate succession statute represents the legislature's best guess as to how someone would want property distributed after death. If the statutory distribution is not satisfactory, it will be necessary to have a will to control the distribution of property after death.

The will kicks off the probate process. It is deposited with the probate court, along with a death certificate. The person desiring to be the personal representative, a term synonymous with executor, must be appointed by the court. This is accomplished by filing a petition for administration or similar form.

In testate cases, the will must be admitted to probate. Those having, or potentially having, an interest in the estate are given a chance to contest the validity of the will and the choice of the personal representative. The interested parties must receive notice of the probate to allow them the opportunity to bring forth any objections they might have.

A Supreme Court decision requires that all reasonably ascertainable creditors be given notice of the probate. This is accomplished by mailing all known creditors a copy of a document known as the notice to creditors. This gives creditors an opportunity to put in any claim they have against the estate of the deceased party. It is incumbent on the personal representative to review the deceased party's papers and bank records to determine who might potentially file a claim against the estate and to provide the attorney for the estate with that information as soon as practicable after the commencement of probate. You can help with this process by keeping well-organized documentation as part of your estate plan.

An estate is a separate tax-paying entity. Any trust associated with the estate also becomes a separate tax-paying entity. To get a trust into the system, a form SS-4 should be filed so that a taxpayer identification number can be assigned. The fiduciary should file IRS Form 56 to inform the IRS of the proper contact party. The estate and nongrantor trusts need to file an income tax return, and the personal representative or successor trustee may have to file an estate tax return if the deceased party left a taxable estate.

The personal representative is responsible for gathering the assets of the decedent. They also decide which assets to sell and which assets to keep. That gets the estate into a position to pay creditors' claims and then to distribute whatever is left to the heirs. To that end, the personal representative can sell real estate, securities, and personal property to raise cash. After all creditors having valid claims have been paid, the personal representative distributes the remaining assets to the heirs in accordance with the decedent's will. If there is no will, the remaining assets are distributed in accordance with the intestate succession statute.

When all taxes have been paid, all creditors' claims disposed of, and all distributions made, the estate has been fully administered and can be closed. In an estate not subject to estate tax, the entire process can be accomplished in less than a year. It is necessary to obtain an IRS closing letter in an estate subject to estate tax. That process can take several years.

DIVORCE, MARRIAGE, AND REMARRIAGE

Existing wills are typically administered and construed as if the former spouse had died at the time of the dissolution, divorce, or annulment of the marriage, unless the will or the dissolution or divorce judgment expressly provides otherwise. Simply put, a divorced spouse does not get your money when you die, but any children you had with that spouse may. It is a good idea to revise your will after a divorce to ensure things happen the way you want.

Depending on the state, there is generally no effect on an existing trust as the result of a divorce or annulment unless language providing for those eventualities is included in the trust instrument. Accordingly, trusts should be reviewed after a divorce to ensure that the trust reflects the grantor's wishes.

There is no effect on existing account designations as the result of a divorce or annulment in most states. Accounts should be reviewed after a divorce to ensure that account ownership designations are in accordance with the wishes of the owner. Property rights for property that is held jointly or as a remainder interest are not affected by a subsequent divorce, but property that is held as a tenancy by the entireties is converted to property held as tenants in common after the divorce.

There is no effect on existing beneficiary designations for insurance policies or annuity contracts as the result of a divorce or annulment. Policies and contracts should be reviewed after a divorce to ensure that account ownership designations are in agreement with the wishes of the owner. You may not want your former spouse to receive the proceeds of your life insurance policy instead of your children or a new spouse. Pay close attention to details.

Marriage and Remarriage

Suppose when you were 21 and single, you wrote out a will leaving everything you owned to the three who meant the most to you in the whole world: your mom, your girlfriend Sue, and your faithful golden retriever Gus. Five years later, Mom has remarried and you can't stand her new husband, Joe. Sue ran off with your former best friend and is living in Vegas, and Gus bit the mail carrier and is now living on a farm in upstate New York. In the meantime, you met Greta at a party in Bali and married two months later. You and Greta have a new baby, Gilbert.

Unfortunately for you, one day a wheel falls off an airliner passing overhead, and you are the unlucky one that it hits. You die while en route to the hospital. Your budding career as a pediatric cardiologist is over. Who will inherit your soon to be vast estate? Greta and baby Gilbert are not in your will! Fortunately for them, but not for mom, Sue, and Gus—here comes the law to the rescue. Greta and Gilbert are pretermitted parties. They are people related to you by marriage or blood whom you inadvertently failed to mention in your will. By statute in most states, they will get a share of your estate equal to the intestate share.

If you fail to leave anything to your spouse in your will, even if you do so intentionally, your spouse will still be able to get a share in your estate by invoking the provisions of your state's spousal share law. The spousal share extends to assets beyond those included in the probate estate in most states. That prevents a former spouse from transferring assets with the intention of depriving the current spouse of those assets.

Prenuptial and Postnuptial Agreements

Almost any marriage right can be modified or waived via a prenuptial or postnuptial agreement. A prenuptial is agreed to before a marriage, and a postnuptial is agreed to after a marriage. Rights to property, to inherit, and to spousal share can all be waived or modified by one of these agreements. Nuptial agreements are often used in second-marriage situations to preserve property for the children of an earlier spouse.

BENEFICIARY DESIGNATIONS

Naming individual beneficiaries is usually the best choice for a beneficiary designation. That is the easiest way to ensure those people receive the asset.

Naming a trust as the beneficiary works well when there are issues. For example, the beneficiaries are minors, have a history of alcohol or drug abuse, are deeply in debt, have had a judgment or restitution order entered against them that remains unsatisfied, have a spouse with any of those problems, can't manage money, or there is a desire to benefit more remote descendants.

The more common reason to use a trust, avoidance of probate, is inapplicable in this situation because accounts for which a beneficiary designation is available usually pass directly to the named beneficiary outside the probate system.

Designating the estate as a beneficiary is usually the least desirable choice. By designating the estate as a beneficiary, the account may become subject to claims of creditors. Also, IRAs that might have been withdrawn over an individual beneficiary's remaining life span will probably have to be cashed in within five years.

It is important to keep beneficiary designations up to date. If a deceased spouse remains named as the beneficiary of an IRA, insurance policy, or annuity and no contingent beneficiary is named, the account or policy will become a probate asset and will become available to creditors of the estate. In an extreme case, an asset that would have been completely immune from creditor's claims can become subject to those claims and completely consumed in satisfying the claims.

SELECTING TRUSTEES, ADMINISTRATORS, AND FIDUCIARIES

Give much thought and care to the selection of your fiduciaries, whether they are the agent named in your durable power of attorney or living will, the trustee or successor trustee of your trust, or the personal representative named in your last will and testament. These people will act on your behalf when you are either incapable of acting on your own behalf or have passed away.

When considering a person to act on your behalf, the first question to ask yourself is whether he or she will have the time to devote to your affairs. Managing someone else's affairs takes time, and it must be done prudently. Does the person have the necessary temperament to act on your behalf? It does little good to name a person to act as the agent on your living will to prevent the doctors and hospital from taking unnecessary steps to prolong your life if the person you select is incapable of making the necessary decision. You should also consider whether the person you are considering has the necessary skills to manage your affairs. Will he or she use good judgment in making the necessary financial and legal decisions required to keep your affairs in good order? Finally, is the person you are considering honest? I mean *really* honest? You are entrusting your life and your fortune to this person, so make sure you select someone who can be trusted to not steal you or your heirs blind and who will act in your, or their, best interest.

Institutions as Fiduciaries

Using a trust company to act as the fiduciary may be the best choice if no individual qualifies. You will have to pay them a fee to act for you, but you will gain the benefit of having a trust officer assigned whom you can get to know and with whom you can become comfortable before it is necessary to utilize the trust company's services. If there is any misfeasance or malfeasance in the handling of your account, there is likely to be an errors and omissions insurance policy against which a claim can be made, if necessary. Before selecting a trust company, you should interview several, meet the people who would be working on your account, and understand and approve the fee structure. You should also understand that there are some services trust companies do not provide, such as acting as the agent on a living will.

ESSENTIAL DOCUMENTS

This section addresses the documents you may need to complete your estate plan. Not all documents are required for all plans. Your individual circumstances will dictate the documents you need to accomplish your objectives. Most people will need a durable power of attorney, a designation of health-care surrogate, perhaps a living will, and a last will and testament to meet their minimum needs.

Assets

Begin by generating a list of your assets, insurance policies (all policies, not just life insurance), and trusted advisers (and not-so-trusted advisers) to make administering your affairs less burdensome, should you become incapacitated or die. Include information about who has custody of your money or other assets, including account type, account number, address, and phone number for each institution holding any asset belonging to you. If you have a brokerage account or an account with a mutual fund company, it is not necessary to list each individual security or mutual fund. Simply list the institution's name, the account number, who you deal with on a regular basis, and the address and phone number of the office you use. You should also include a list of any real estate you own. It is a good idea to include statements (updated quarterly) and property tax bill copies in this section.

List each insurance policy and annuity contract, the policy or contract number, the issuing company, and the contact information of the company. Either include the policy/contract or provide directions to where each policy or contract can be found.

Advisers

Include in this section contact information for your attorney, accountant or tax preparer, insurance agents, investment adviser, spiritual leader, and any other person you desire to be notified in the event of your death or disability.

Wills

Your will must meet the technical requirements for a will in order to be valid. The consequence of not meeting those requirements is that you will be considered to have died intestate, and parties other than those you intend may end up inheriting your assets. In some states, a will must be in writing and must be signed at the end and in the presence of two witnesses, who also sign.

Wills typically contain an introductory paragraph, a paragraph directing payment of debts and expenses, a paragraph identifying family or perhaps identifying the beneficiaries, a paragraph naming the personal representative (executor), a paragraph specifying the powers of the personal representative, and one or more paragraphs directing the ultimate disposition of the estate. There may also be paragraphs establishing trusts for minor beneficiaries and a paragraph allowing the personal representative to pay the bequest to any minor or disabled person to a fiduciary or to set up a Uniform Gift to Minors Act account.

If your estate plan includes a living trust, you will have a special kind of will, known in the will-drafting trade as a pour over will, which directs the personal representative to distribute your assets to the trustee of your trust. The trust (more on trusts later) will then control the ultimate distribution of your assets.

There are some common misconceptions regarding wills. The following is a summary of those misconceptions:

* *Wills and Probate:* "If I have a will, does that mean my estate will not have to go through probate?" Despite the common belief, it is not true. Wills are administered through the process of probate, and there is no way to avoid it unless one uses a trust or pay-on-death account or the asset is one that by statute is not subject to probate, such as an annuity.

* *Disclaimers:* Suppose Auntie Edna leaves you all of her $100 million fortune. You are her sole heir. The only problem is, you just sold your Internet start-up company for $475 million, and you really don't need the money. What do you do? Well, you could accept the inheritance and just pass it on to your son when you die. But if you do that, your son will end up paying estate tax on his inheritance. Assuming the maximum estate tax rate will be 60 percent, he could lose 60 percent of the $100 million to taxes when you inherit and another 60 percent when you die and he inherits. A lightning-quick calculation on your part reveals the loss could be $60 million on the first inheritance and another $24 million on the second inheritance, a total of $84 million lost to taxes. Ouch! What do you do? You go to your attorney's office and explain the situation. "Don't worry," says he, and he explains that under the federal tax code, you can disclaim an inheritance by filing a qualified disclaimer, and by doing so, you will be treated as if you died before Auntie Edna and never received the inheritance. He further explains that since Auntie Edna left the money to you per stirpes, a quaint Latin phrase translated "by the roots," the property descends in the family line. If you file the disclaimer, young Jake will inherit Auntie's fortune. Since you did not inherit, the estate tax due on your death will be avoided. Jake will be $24 million richer than he would have been, had you taken the inheritance for yourself. There are many other potential uses for qualified disclaimers—too many to go into here—but their use should always be considered in planning and administering taxable estates. Qualified disclaimers must be filed within nine months of the date of creation of the interest disclaimed and must meet the requirements of the Internal Revenue Code.

Trusts

A trust is an arrangement in which one party agrees to manage assets contributed by another party for the benefit of a third party. Under common law, all the parties had to be separate individuals. By statute, they can now be the same individual, creating a convenient legal sleight of hand that conveys many benefits.

Trusts accomplish three main objectives. First, the assets transferred to a trust during life avoid probate and hence potentially reduce the cost of administration of an estate after the death of the person who originally established the trust. Second, trusts provide a means of providing for the orderly administration of a person's assets when that person, or the person designated to receive the benefits of the assets, is unable to administer the assets for themselves. Third, trusts provide a means of protecting assets and conserving them for the benefit of those designated to receive the benefit of the trust.

The People Involved

The person who contributes the assets to the trust is known as a settlor, grantor, or trustor. The person who manages the assets is known as the trustee. The person for whom the assets are managed is known as the beneficiary or, much less commonly, the *cestui que trust*.

Revocable versus Irrevocable

When a settlor decides to establish a trust, he or she must first decide whether to reserve the power to terminate the trust and, hence, recover the assets from the trustee on demand. If the settlor reserves the right to terminate the trust, the trust is a revocable trust. If the power to terminate is not reserved, the trust is irrevocable. The rule cited is the rule under common law.

In some states, trusts are considered to be revocable unless the trust document specifically states the trust is irrevocable. Irrevocable trusts are often structured to hold life insurance policies on the life of the grantor. Such trusts, known as irrevocable life insurance trusts or ILITs, can be used to pass large sums to beneficiaries free of estate tax if correctly structured.

If the settlor decides to name herself or himself as initial trustee, the trust document is known as a declaration of trust. If the settlor names a third party as the initial trustee or as joint trustee with the settler, the trust document is known as a trust agreement.

A trust in which the beneficiary is the source of the assets contributed is known as a self-settled trust. That term is not used when the source of assets is a third party. In most states, a self-settled trust provides no protection from creditors' claims, but there are exceptions. Consult an attorney for details.

Charitable Trusts

Trusts can be classified by the objective of the trust. A trust is known as a charitable trust if the primary objective is to benefit a charity. There are two common types: charitable lead trusts and charitable remainder trusts.

Trusts in which the charity receives the initial stream of payments from the trust, and after those payments have been distributed, whatever is left is distributed to some third party, are known as lead trusts. The charity leads the way in receiving payments from the trust.

Trusts in which the charity benefits only after one or more intermediate parties benefit are known as charitable remainder trusts. The charity gets the remainder only after a specified series of payments have been paid to the initial beneficiaries.

Two types of remainder trusts are commonly used; the grantor retained annuity trust (GRAT) and the grantor retained unitrust (GRUT). The difference between the two lies primarily in how the stream of payments is determined. In a GRAT, the grantor gets a fixed amount of money over a fixed period of time, usually in payments paid annually or more often. In a GRUT, the grantor receives a fixed percentage of the trust assets for a fixed period of time. The amount to be paid is determined annually.

Charitable remainder trusts are useful when one desires to receive income from an asset during life and wishes to receive a charitable contribution income tax deduction as well. It is even possible to use the money received, and perhaps the tax savings, to fund a separate ILIT to provide additional money to beneficiaries, free of estate taxes. Chapter 17 provides more detail.

Special Needs Trust

A special needs trust is established for a person suffering from some disability, such as a severe physical or mental disorder. The trust serves as the repository for the assets because, if the disabled person received the assets directly, the receipt of the assets might disqualify the disabled person from receiving public benefits. Special needs trusts must be constructed very carefully, so consult an attorney with experience in these types of trusts.

Powers of Attorney

The power of attorney allows the person you name, known as an agent or attorney in fact, to act for you and to take the actions authorized in the power of attorney. Powers of attorney are of two types: regular and durable.

A regular power of attorney is suspended if the principal, the person writing the power of attorney, becomes disabled. By statute in most states, disability will not suspend a durable power of attorney.

A durable power of attorney will allow the attorney in fact to take any action the person making the power of attorney could do if personally present. Typical powers granted—and this is by no means an exhaustive list—include the power to initiate banking and securities transactions, the power to demand and receive, the power to sue or defend lawsuits, the power to apply for government benefits, the power to fund a trust or perhaps even create a trust, the power to make transfers for Medicaid qualification, and the power to make health-care decisions.

Designating a Health-Care Surrogate

The designation of health-care surrogate (DHCS) is an alternative to a durable power of attorney. A DHCS contains health-care provisions and allows a person you name to step in and make medical decisions for you, if you become incapable of making them for yourself. The DHCS form allows the person you name to do anything in regard to your health care that you could do yourself, were you able to do so.

The powers granted in a DHCS usually come into play only after the maker has been declared incapacitated by one or more physicians. Examples of things a person designated as health-care surrogate can do include hiring and firing doctors, selecting health-care facilities, consenting to operations, authorizing other necessary treatment, and consenting to the administration of antibiotics and other necessary medications.

Advance Directives/Living Wills (AD/LW)

A living will prevents you from receiving medical care when your death is inevitable. People typically desire to be allowed to die without the application of heroic measures to prolong the dying process. In rare cases, a living will is structured to require medical care even if the situation appears to be hopeless.

The agent you name in your living will has the power to discontinue treatment measures designed to prolong your life or to prevent those measures from being taken. Before that happens, your physician and one other doctor must agree that you are in a terminal condition, an end-stage condition, or a persistent vegetative state.

Business Buy-Sell Agreements

Failure to plan for a key person leaving a business can result in loss of control by the remaining participants, admission of an outsider to the business, forced curtailment of expansion plans, or even the forced liquidation or sale of the business. Buy-sell agreements allow for the orderly transition of ownership in a business when a participant leaves the business for ill health, retirement, death, or other reasons.

The first thing to decide is who will purchase the business if someone leaves. Among the available choices are all or some of the remaining members of the business, the business itself, or an outsider.

Funding Alternatives

Many buy-sell agreements are drafted with the thought that a key participant in a business might die, and so they are funded with life insurance. If a whole life policy is used (admittedly, an expensive way to go), the policy will build up a cash value over time that can also be used as the basis for a loan to fund a buyout if someone leaves the business for a reason other than death. It may also be possible to fund the purchase with a loan from a third party, but consideration should be given to the likelihood that the death or departure of a key person may affect the ability of the remaining members to obtain a loan or may affect the terms on which a loan would be offered. Finally, the remaining members of the business can personally assume the obligation to buy out the departed member. When they have the obligation to do so, the agreement usually provides for a down payment and the purchase of the departed party's interest over time at a stated interest rate. The departed party usually retains a security interest in the interest sold (which may be released as payments are made) to secure payment for the interest.

As the great Texas football coach Darrell Royal said about passing the football, "Three things can happen when you pass the ball, and two of them are bad." (This quote has also been attributed to General Robert Neyland when he coached at the University of Tennessee, Coach Duffy Dougherty of Michigan State University, and others.) Likewise, many things can happen when one fails to plan for business succession, and most of them are bad.

ADDITIONAL RESOURCES

The following books on wealth preservation are recommended:

* James E. Hughes Jr., *Family Wealth—Keeping It in the Family* (rev. and expanded ed.). Bloomberg Press, 2004.
* Gerald M. Condon, *Beyond the Grave* (rev. ed.). Collins Business, 2001.

- Kathryn G. Henkel, *Estate Planning and Wealth Preservation.* Warren Gorham & Lamont, 1998.

CHAPTER SUMMARY

Estate planning can be complicated, but it is important to address the topic before the emergency happens. Knowing how property can be owned and how it can be transferred at death is an important step in estate planning. Understanding the legal process of probate provides a reason to avoid it if possible. People should have certain documents in order, including durable powers of attorney, living wills/advance directives, wills, and trusts. Trusts are a great way to direct your assets. There are many different types that are used for different reasons. Buy-sell agreements are a crucial consideration for anyone engaged in his or her own business. Estate planning is comprehensive and should be done with the help of a qualified expert who is familiar with the laws of your state.

CHAPTER SEVENTEEN

Estate and Gift Taxes

Robert A. Stermer

INTRODUCTION

"When you're dead, you're dead. That's it." Well, Marlene Dietrich may not have gotten it exactly right because after death it isn't over. The government is not done with you yet, or at least not done with your money. Your heirs may be subject to an ominous estate tax, better known as the death tax.

Planning today for sharing your wealth can save your heirs thousands of dollars in the future. This chapter provides an introduction to estate and gift taxes. It provides a basic understanding of how these taxes work and how to mitigate their damage. Increased understanding will help you arrive at an estate plan that best meets your needs. It will also help you administer an estate more effectively if you are appointed to be a personal representative. However, this short chapter does not have all the answers. Your estate plan should involve a qualified estate-planning or tax attorney.

ESTATE AND GIFT TAX LAW

Malcolm Forbes once said, "I made my money the old-fashioned way. I was very nice to a wealthy relative right before he died." We should all be so lucky. Most Bogleheads will work hard and accumulate assets over a long period. If successful, many people make tax-free gifts to their loved ones to help with college, buying a home, and all sorts of things. At the time of death, these people want to escape government confiscation through taxation and transfer as much wealth as legally possible to their heirs.

Whether you give things away while you are alive or after you die, Uncle Sam wants to spread some of your wealth around. The gift tax is part of the estate tax system and not part of the income tax system. It levies the same tax on transfers that would be assessed after the donor dies and is intended to prevent people from giving everything away while alive and avoiding the estate (a.k.a. inheritance and death) tax.

In 2001, President George W. Bush pledged to get rid of the federal estate tax. He carried through with that pledge to a degree. Congress approved the Economic Growth and Tax Relief Reconciliation Act of 2001 (the 2001 Tax Act), which made substantial changes to the estate and gift tax laws. By 2010, the estate tax would be completely eliminated. Unfortunately, that would be temporary. By 2011, all the changes made by President Bush are to sunset, and federal estate taxes will snap back to their onerous pre-2001 level, and in some cases higher.

The Internal Revenue Code provides a table that tells the levels of taxation based on year. There are two important numbers in Table 17.1. The unified credit is a credit against estate taxes that would otherwise be due as the result of death. It is used in the actual computation of the tax in the estate and gift tax return. The second number is the applicable exclusion amount. That tells you how much you can pass on to your heirs free of tax.

Changes to the estate tax unified credit and the resulting applicable exclusion amount were implemented beginning in 2002. In 2006, the unified credit was increased to $780,800, where it remained until the end of 2008. A unified credit of $780,800 effectively means that estates of less than $2 million are not taxed. The credit is available to the estate of each individual person. So for married couples, if each party through good estate planning preserves his or her unified credit, the value of the assets that can pass free of estate tax is doubled to $4 million. In 2009, the unified credit increased to $1,455,800, resulting in individual estates of less than $3.5 million not being taxed or twice that amount, $7 million not being taxed for a couple using widely available estate planning techniques.

TABLE 17.1   UNIFIED CREDIT AND EXCLUSIONS AMOUNT

Tax Year	Unified Credit	Estate Tax Individual Exclusion	Exclusion for Couple	Maximum Estate Tax and GSTT	Exclusion	Maximum Gift Tax
2006	$780,800	$2 million	$4 million			
2007	$780,800	$2 million	$4 million			
2008	$780,800	$2 million	$4 million	45%	$1 million	35%
2009	$1,455,800	$3.5 million	$7 million	45%	$1 million	35%
2010	Eliminated	Eliminated	Eliminated	Eliminated	$1 million	35%
2011+	$345,800	$1 million	$2 million	55%*		

*5% surtax on estates $10 million+
Source: U.S. Internal Revenue Code

As of this writing, in 2010, the credit will drop to 0 percent, essentially repealing the federal estate tax. On January 1, 2011, the estate tax repeal sunsets. The unified credit will return to $345,800 on estates of more than $1 million for a single taxpayer and $2 million for a couple unless Congress acts to extend or modify the exclusion amount.

Tax Rate Changes

Estate and gift taxes are constantly being tweaked as Washington plays political football. The 2001 Tax Act changed the effective minimum tax rate, the rate applicable after the application of the unified credit, and the top tax rate of estate and gift tax. After the act was adopted, the effective minimum tax rate was increased by virtue of the increase in the amount of the unified credit, and the top rate was decreased by virtue of the statutory changes contained in the act. For 2008 and 2009, the maximum tax rate is 45 percent. That rate will continue in effect until 2010, when the estate tax rate will be 0 percent.

That said, it is very likely that the estate tax will not go away in 2010, as the subject is up for debate again in Congress. Check with the IRS or an estate-planning attorney before making any financial decisions about gifting.

Generation-Skipping Transfer Tax (GSTT)

The generation-skipping transfer tax (GSTT) is a federal tax on transfers of property made to a family member who is more than one generation below the donor; they occur either during life as a gift or at death by will or bequest. The GSTT exemption amount is the same as the estate tax applicable exclusion amount and will continue to be so. The GSTT tax rate continues to be the same as the top estate tax rate during the time period the act is in effect and thereafter. The benefit to a large estate is that the money skips a generation, so it is taxed only every other generation.

Gift Taxes

With such high estate tax rates, perhaps the better option is to gift your money to your children. Not so fast! Congress keeps that loophole closed by limiting the amount you can gift without paying gift tax.

The gift tax applicable exclusion amount is $1 million in 2008, 2009, and 2010. In 2010, when the estate tax and GSTT are repealed, the gift tax will continue in effect. Presumably, this was done so that gifts made in 2010 would not escape taxation, although the maximum tax rate of 35 percent is lower than the estate tax rate would be in 2009, prior to repeal, or in 2011, after the changes sunset, so it may still be advantageous to make gifts, especially of appreciating property (more on that in a minute).

The donor is generally responsible for paying the gift tax. Under special arrangements, the donee may agree to pay the tax instead. See your tax professional if you are considering this type of arrangement.

BASIS RULE CHANGES IN 2010

Under the law prior to passage of the act, assets acquired from a decedent were entitled to a basis value equal to the fair market value on the date of their death. That rule will change for people dying in 2010. The basis of property acquired from someone who died will be essentially the same as for property acquired by gift, which means it is the amount the decedent paid for it. Prior to 2010, a stock's basis is the date of death price. During 2010, it is the decedent's purchase price.

There is some relief from the harshness of this provision in that the law allows the personal representative to allocate $1.3 million of basis to appreciated property, and in the case of a decedent who was married at the time of death, an additional $3 million of basis can be allocated to appreciated property. This provision will apply only to decedents dying in 2010.

Sunset Provision

After 2010, a single individual will be able to pass $1 million free of tax, and married couples will, by preserving both unified credits, be able to pass twice that amount. The highest tax rate will be 55 percent, except that a 5 percent surtax will once again apply to estates in excess of $10 million. This could all change in the future. Consult your tax adviser or estate-planning attorney before making any major gifts.

ESTATE TAX COMPLIANCE AND TAX CALCULATION

This section provides an introduction to the calculation of federal estate taxes. It is calculated by using U.S. Estate (and Generation-Skipping Transfer) Tax Return Form 706, available on www.irs.gov.

An estate tax return must be filed once for all citizens or residents of the United States who die with a taxable estate. The term *taxable estate* refers to gross estate less allowable deductions.

Valuation Date and Alternative Valuation Date

Generally, a decedent's assets are valued as of the date of death. In some cases, the value is interpolated between dates. For example, if a person dies on a weekend, the value of stock can be computed as the average of the close on Friday and the close on Monday. Congress long ago recognized that the value of assets might go into a steep decline immediately after someone died. If that happened, it would be unfair to tax the heirs on the value of the estate at the time of death, when the heirs would not be able to realize value from the estate so quickly. Therefore, the law allows an alternative valuation date that is six months after the date of death.

If an estate declines in value after the death and the alternate valuation date was used, it would serve to reduce the total amount of tax due. Use of the alternate valuation date can sometimes result in substantial tax savings.

What Goes Into the Gross Estate

All of your property owned at the time of death is included in the gross estate. Items such as securities, real estate, mortgages owned, notes and cash, life insurance, and other miscellaneous property, including personal property and money owed to the decedent, are all included.

The Internal Revenue Code also contains a host of provisions designed to limit gray areas on the part of heirs designed to reduce taxes. These include certain property transferred within three years of death, transfers in which some aspect of ownership was retained or in which you retained a reversionary interest, transfers in which you retained the right to revoke the transfer, annuities in which the purchaser retained a right to receive payments, jointly owned property, property that could pass under a general power of appointment, certain life insurance, and a special category of property known as qualifying terminable interest property.

Deductions from the Gross Estate

There are allowable deductions from a taxable gross estate to find the taxable estate. Funeral expenses and expenses incurred in administering property subject to claims (estate administration expenses) can be deducted. Debts including mortgages and liens are deducted. Net losses during estate administration are deducted, as are expenses incurred in administering property not subject to claims. Potentially, this deduction could reduce the estate tax to zero in even the largest estate. Finally, a deduction is allowed for gifts to charities.

Effect of Prior Taxable Gifts

Taxable gifts made after December 31, 1976, must be added back into the estate. A credit given for prior gift taxes paid ensures that is the case. Once gifts are added back, a tentative tax can be computed. Any prior gift taxes paid are then deducted from the tentative tax. This statutory scheme is designed so that all gifts are taxed, but only once.

Subtracting previously paid gift taxes from the tentative tax results in a gross estate tax. From here, some credits are potentially available that may serve to further reduce the tax due. The first of these is the unified credit discussed earlier and highlighted in Table 17.1. The estate is also allowed a credit for foreign estate taxes paid and a credit for estate taxes paid by a prior estate on the assets inherited. The credits reduce the gross estate tax and yield the estate tax due, assuming there are no generation-skipping transfer taxes (discussed later).

There are some important points you should take away from this discussion. Married couples should engage in estate planning to take advantage of both personal exemption amounts while both are still alive. Also, assets that are not included in the gross estate may avoid taxation completely, such as insurance policies held in a properly constructed irrevocable life insurance trust. Finally, don't forget that charitable bequests reduce the estate dollar for dollar and can be used to reduce taxes while simultaneously supporting a cause you believe in.

Your estate planning should focus on the estate limits discussed earlier. If you die in 2009 having close to $3.5 million or in 2011 and beyond with close to $1 million in assets and prior taxable gifts, consult with your attorney and accountant to see if an estate tax return would need to be filed. Anyone having an estate over $1 million, and not planning on dying before 2011, should consult with an attorney to determine what steps would be appropriate to minimize the burden of estate taxes after the act sunsets at the end of 2010.

By the way, the estate and gift tax laws are a political football. The tax code may have changed by the time this book is published. Consult an estate-planning attorney for up-to-date information.

Sources of Liquidity for Taxes

Now that you know what the estate tax liability is, where does the money come from to pay the tax? The most obvious source is from the estate itself. However, those assets may not be liquid. The heirs can also pay the taxes if they have cash or perhaps take out a loan. The Treasury will grant an extension of the time to pay, with interest.

If there are illiquid assets and no cash to pay the taxes, consider establishing an irrevocable life insurance trust (ILIT). As its name suggests, an ILIT is an irrevocable trust created to hold life insurance. Typically, a mother or father would purchase life insurance on their lives for the benefit of children. The annual life insurance premiums are paid with annual gift exclusions and do not count against the lifetime gift exclusion.

The proceeds of the life insurance policy can be borrowed from the trustee of the ILIT, or assets can be sold from the estate to the trustee of the ILIT to raise money to pay the estate taxes upon the death of the insured.

Basis of Property Acquired from a Decedent

Once the tax has been paid and property has been distributed to the heirs, what is the basis of property that is subsequently sold by the heirs? Property acquired from a decedent receives a basis equal to the fair market value of the property at the date of death of the decedent or six months later, whichever is used as the estate valuation date. If it is sold for less than the fair market value at the estate valuation date, a capital loss deduction is potentially allowable to the recipient. If the property is sold at a gain, there will be a capital gains tax to pay (an exception is made for assets sold in a tax-sheltered inherited IRA account). The tax code allows beneficiaries to use a long-term holding period and pay long-term capital gains, even if they have held the property for only a short time.

GIFT TAXES

The Treasury taxes gifts of property from one person to another over a certain annual amount. The reason for taxing large gifts to another person is to protect the tax revenue stream. If gifts were not taxed, you could give away all of your property during life and avoid the estate tax entirely.

Annual Exclusion and Applicable Credit Amount

Congress allowed certain exceptions to mitigate the harshness associated with taxing gifts. Here are three examples:

1. The annual $13,000 exclusion in 2009. You can gift this amount once per year to anyone, and there would be no gift taxes due. The amount adjusts periodically to account for inflation.
2. College and trade school tuition can be gifted in an unlimited amount for any number of beneficiaries as long as payment is made directly to the educational institution. It would be possible for grandparents to pay tuition for a private prep school or pay college tuition for grandchildren without incurring any liability for the gift tax so long as payment is made directly to the educational institution.
3. Gifts can also pay for qualified medical expenses in an unlimited amount for any number of beneficiaries. The gift must be made directly to the health-care provider.

Basis of Property Acquired by Gift

The basis of property acquired by gift is the same as it is for the original owner who gave the gift, with one exception. If the basis is greater than the fair market value of the property at the time of the gift, then for the purpose of determining loss, the basis is considered be the fair market value.

Assume a person gifted you common stock worth $100. If the person giving the gift had a basis of $50 on the stock, then your basis is $50. If the person giving the gift had a basis of $200, then your basis is $100. Your basis is either the original basis or the fair market value at the time of the gift, whichever is lower.

Property Gifting Considerations

There is a great degree of utility in making lifetime gifts. The effective tax rate on gifts is much lower than the effective tax rate on property transferred at death. This fact is not obvious from looking at the tax tables, as the same table applies to both categories of transfers. However, because the tax is not paid out of the gift for transfers occurring at death but is paid by the transferor for assets transferred during life, the effective tax rate is much lower for lifetime gifts.

By transferring property that is appreciating, all the future gain and any income generated are permanently transferred out of the estate of the donor, as long as the donor lives for an additional three years. Otherwise, the gift can be viewed as a gift made in anticipation of death and will be included back in the donor's gross estate. If it is anticipated that property is going to appreciate in value, then it is better to give it at a time when the value is low to take full advantage of the tax code.

Gift Tax Implications and Filing Requirement

A gift tax return must be filed if the succeeding year gifts are made in excess of the annual allowable deductions. No tax will be due, even though a tax return is required, until the amount of lifetime taxable gifts exceeds $1 million. A gift tax will be due on an annual basis once the $1 million threshold is exceeded.

GENERATION-SKIPPING TRANSFER TAX

The GSTT is a separate system of taxation that taxes transfers to a special class of persons known as skip persons. A skipped person is generally the child of a donor. In short, the estate tax skips every other generation in large estates.

Here is a little history. After the adoption of the estate and gift tax, enterprising tax attorneys and accountants came up with a means of partially avoiding it. Congress's plan was that as each generation died, estate tax would be paid on what was transferred from the preceding to the succeeding generation. Needless to say, that prospect was unappealing to persons of substantial means.

To ameliorate the wealth-sapping effect of the estate tax, a new class of trusts, often referred to as dynasty trusts, was invented. In a dynasty trust, assets were placed into trust, and since according to the rule against perpetuities no trust could last forever, the termination of the trust was set for two, three, or perhaps even four generations in the future. In the meantime, the trust paid out all its income to each generation of beneficiaries, but no principal was paid out. As a result, your great-grandfather put his assets into a dynasty trust and provided that income would be paid to your grandfather, your father, you, and finally your children.

On the death of your children, all money in trust would be paid to your grandchildren. That meant that estate tax would be paid only on the death of great-grandfather and again on the death of your grandchildren. No estate tax would be paid on the death of your grandfather, your father, you, or your children.

Thus, with one document, the dynasty trust, great-grandfather denied Treasury four applications of the estate tax. What a wonderful result! However, Congress felt the practice of establishing dynasty trusts to be abusive and enacted the generation-skipping transfer tax to tax transfers to intermediate generations and to preserve the government's revenue stream.

The GSTT is very complicated, and only a broad brush overview can be given, which unfortunately will have to leave out many details and exceptions. For that reason, consult with your tax attorney or CPA if you intend to leave any money to anyone who might be a skip person to see what taxes might be due and to take advantage of any planning possibilities inherent in the tax code.

ADDITIONAL RESOURCES

* Stephens, Maxfield, Lind, and Calfee, *Federal Estate and Gift Taxation* (8th ed.). Research Institute of America, 2002.
* IRS Publication 950, Introduction to Estate and Gift Taxes.
* IRS Publication 551, Basis of Assets, for more information on basis calculation.
* The IRS web site, www.irs.gov, has many other informative publications.

CHAPTER SUMMARY

Many volumes have been filled with explanations of how the tax code works, and it is confusing. However, you don't want to pay any gift, estate, or GST tax that you don't owe. If you think you have sufficient assets that would require tax planning to avoid the estate and generation-skipping transfer taxes, it is wise to read a few books and then visit a qualified estate-planning attorney to investigate legal means to mitigate the impact of these taxes on your estate. Don't delay, as the Reverend Ford said in *Pollyanna*, "Death comes unexpectedly!" and with death, most planning opportunities are foreclosed.

PART VI

FINDING GOOD ADVICE WHEN YOU NEED IT

CHAPTER EIGHTEEN

Seeking Help from Professionals

Dale C. Maley A.K.A. DaleMaley and Lauren Vignec

INTRODUCTION

It can be very hard to be truly objective about money, insurance, and financial planning. Perhaps you need technical advice or someone to help you stay on track. Or perhaps you and your spouse have very different beliefs about money and risk. You may need an objective outside opinion. If so, it might be a good idea to seek the services of a financial adviser.

There are many different types of advisers, and some work better in some situations than in others. This chapter will help you understand different types of financial advisers, how they work, how they are paid, and how to choose one for the need you have.

ADVISERS CAN HELP

Financial advisers can help deal with a wide range of financial issues. Many people have a hard time balancing the desire for spending with the desire to leave an estate. Sometimes people are overly optimistic about how much they can realistically leave for their children or for charity. Other people underestimate how much they need to maintain their standard of living in retirement. If you have difficulty developing or sticking to a plan, a financial adviser may provide the discipline and oversight you need to succeed.

You may also be an excellent saver with a strong moral impulse to save too much and find it stressful spending on the things you need. Or maybe you need help balancing the need to take risk with your willingness to take risk. An objective outside opinion can help.

Often spouses have two very different levels of risk tolerance or spending priorities. These differences can lead to uncomfortable discussions, especially when the risks show up during declining markets. You and your spouse may even have different levels of interest in financial planning, leading to a situation where the interested spouse has total control of the financial planning decisions. If the interested spouse passes first, the less interested spouse may be stuck with a financial estate he or she is not prepared to manage. A good financial adviser can help with all of these situations.

WHO SHOULD GET PROFESSIONAL ADVICE?

There are several situations where investors may need the services of a financial adviser. In some cases, investors simply need technical guidance. For example, investors with large or very complex estates who lack the experience to manage those estates—and realize that fact—work with tax, legal, and financial advisers. Another situation where a financial adviser could be helpful is when an investor basically knows what to do, but just wants help doing it.

People who do not desire or need a particularly complex retirement plan may still benefit from a financial adviser. There are those who lack the time, patience, or discipline to successfully create, implement, and maintain a plan. Others are not interested in investment management or financial planning. People do not always act rationally with regard to their money, and some people hire professionals to keep them from making emotional mistakes. A financial adviser who deals with many investors facing similar difficulties can be helpful.

However, some individuals who would like to delegate their financial planning to a professional might be better off without one. It depends on the adviser you hire and what their real agenda is. You could unknowingly hire an adviser who takes high risks with your money, chases performance, or sells high-cost financial products that benefits the adviser rather than you. For example, an adviser fee of 1 percent or more will drain assets from your accounts, and that lowers the safe withdrawal rate from your portfolio.

Take the time to find a professional who shares your values and understands your goals. If you understand how the financial services industry works, your search for a good adviser will be much easier.

FINANCIAL PLANNING VERSUS MONEY MANAGEMENT

Money management and financial planning are two significantly different services that are often bundled together. Money management services center on investment choices. Financial planning deals with just about everything else.

Money management is usually most attractive to higher net worth investors. Investors who seek money managers often delegate the entire investing process to their manager by giving the manager discretionary authority. This means the manager makes all investment decisions in an account. A discretionary money manager is typically paid a small annual percentage of the account asset value. Other money managers may not have discretionary authority over their clients' accounts. Those managers simply carry out their clients' requests. Nondiscretionary advisers are paid in a variety of ways, such as an annual fee or commissions from the products they recommend.

Many people find that they really need help with the "everything else" not including ongoing discretionary investment management. Financial planners often help their clients invest by creating an investment plan as part of their overall financial plan. However, planners do not actually implement the investment portion. These investors may not want to pay a money manager to implement their financial plan and simply want the planner's help in creating their plan. It is also common for an investor to have a financial planner who helps establish an investment plan and an unaffiliated money manager who implements that plan.

Many advisers do both financial planning and money management. Since the purpose of this book is retirement planning, this chapter will discuss finding a financial planner who only does planning rather than manage money. Most investors need good financial planning to help with that aspect before they decide if they need professional money management. Finding a good money manager is covered in *The Bogleheads' Guide to Investing* and is the subject of many conversations on the Bogleheads' forums.

FINANCIAL PLANNING DEVELOPMENTS

Two distinct trends have driven developments in financial planning: increased life expectancy and replacement of traditional defined benefit plans with defined contribution (DC) plans. Future retirees can expect to spend 20 or 30 years in retirement and will need substantial assets to support themselves. Many DC plans such as a 401(k) shift the responsibility for accumulating a retirement nest egg from the employer to the employee, and all DC plans shift the responsibility for distributing the retirement nest egg from the employer to the employee. Unfortunately, many individuals do not have the knowledge or ability to successfully manage their own retirement assets. See Chapter 6 for more information on DC plans.

The field of financial planning is relatively new, compared with accounting, engineering, medicine, and law. The first book approximating a textbook on financial planning was *The New Money Dynamics*, written by Venita VanCaspel in 1978. An organization of fee-only financial advisers, the National Association of Personal Finance Advisers (NAPFA), was established in 1983. The certified financial planner (CFP) designation came into existence in 1985. College degree programs in financial planning were finally offered on a widespread basis in the 1990s, and at least one college now offers a doctoral program in financial planning.

Many of the breakthrough findings in financial planning have occurred in the last 20 years. Monte Carlo analysis was first applied to the problem of determining a maximum safe withdrawal rate from retirement savings in 1997, when Bengen published his seminal study on 4 percent safe withdrawal rates in retirement. In 2002, Daniel Kahneman was awarded the Nobel Prize in Economics (The Sveriges Riskbank Prize in Economic Science in Memory of Alfred Nobel) for his pioneering work in behavioral finance that had important implications for financial planners in the area of risk control. Eugene Fama and Ken French introduced the three-factor model of investing in 1993, which is used by a growing number of planners in forming retirement portfolios.

Technology also opened up the field of financial planning in new and exciting ways. The Internet, e-mail, and phone calls make it possible to work with an adviser across town, across the state, or even across the country. Perhaps it is pleasant to meet face-to-face with an adviser, but that does not change your financial situation, and time spent face-to-face with an adviser costs you money in higher fees. It may be more practical and less costly to forgo the formality and instead seek a truly competent adviser wherever they are.

More than 78 million baby boomers in the United States will be entering retirement over the next couple of decades. Growing numbers of impending retirees who are depending increasingly on their own investment wits will drive many changes and improvements in the financial planning field in the coming years. Financial planning will expand in clients and scope to keep up with the growing demand and complexity faced by America's largest graying generation ever.

COMPARISON OF FEE STRUCTURES

Financial advisers are paid for their advice and services. There are many different types of fee structures, and no fee structure is right for every person and every situation. This section covers the three major ways financial advisers are paid.

Commission Sales Structure

The oldest fee structure is commission sales. An adviser (or broker) is paid a commission or fee from a company whose financial product they sell to a customer. Some commissions are easily recognized in the sales literature, and those costs are supposed to be explained by the adviser. However, not all product literature provides adequate disclosure about commissions, and not all advisers are forthcoming about these expenses. Some commissions are cleverly disguised as high expense ratios, back-end and level loads, or some combination of the two. The purchaser of these products definitely pays a commission, even though it is not called one.

One of your primary goals as an investor is to minimize expenses. Each dollar you save in expenses is a dollar that goes into your pocket. You should select investments that have no loads, minimum trading expenses, and low annual expenses (expense ratios). Your adviser should also be paid a reasonable amount for services rendered. Unfortunately, the incentives driving the commissioned salesperson are often directly opposed to your interests as an investor. Salespeople are rewarded if they can convince you to buy high-commission investments and trade them often. That is exactly the opposite of what you should be doing.

To further confound this obvious conflict, many commissioned advisers have no fiduciary responsibility to you. That means an adviser who is paid from commissions is not *obligated* to act in your best interest, although securities laws do prohibit them from recommending unsuitable investments. This comes as a shock to many investors. Most investors do not realize that the financial adviser on commission does not have a fiduciary responsibility to them. Once investors understand the extent of the conflict, they generally decide they want no part of it.

Documenting the Conflict between Brokers and Their Advice

The conflict of interest between offering advice and getting paid commissions has been a problem for a long time. It probably began when the U.S. stock exchange was started under the buttonwood tree in 1792. The first book to chronicle such conflicts of interest was Fred Schwed's 1940 classic *Where Are the Customer's Yachts?* The foreword of that book has a great story:

> *Once in the dear dead days beyond recall, an out-of-town visitor was being shown the wonders of the New York financial district. When the party arrived at the Battery, one of the guides indicated some handsome ships riding at anchor. He said, "Look, those are the banker's and brokers' yachts." "Where are the customer's yachts?" asked the naive visitor.*

There are many other books on the subject of brokers and commissions. Thomas Saler documented many adviser conflicts of interest in his 1989 book, *Lies Your Broker Tells You*. For a more humorous recounting of this age-old conflict of interest, read Michael Lewis's 1990 classic, *Liar's Poker*.

High-Commission Products to Look Out For

You should know that the highest commissions are typically paid on the worst investment products. That gives the adviser incentive to sell them. Limited partnerships, variable annuities, equity-indexed annuities, and loaded stock and bond funds all will cost you dearly in commissions and fees. Investments that are good for brokers are usually very poor choices for investors.

The heyday of limited partnerships was in the early 1980s. Commissions between 6 and 10 percent drove salespeople to heavily market these investments. Sales personnel promoted these risky partnerships as a safe way to invest. These partnerships relied on rising oil prices, rising real estate prices, and the federal tax code. The main attraction for investors was generous tax deductions. The Tax Reform Act of 1986 wiped out the federal tax advantages. Declining oil and real estate prices put the final nail into the coffin. Thousands of investors were left with worthless investments that couldn't be sold. It's interesting to note that Wall Street has recently attempted to resurrect limited partnerships, calling them direct participation programs this time around.

The complexity of variable annuities plus sales commissions around 5 percent often lead to abusive, high-pressure sales tactics. The *Wall Street Journal* ran an interesting article in 2002: "Annuities 101: How to Sell to Senior Citizens." It described how advisers and insurance salespeople were trained to use abusive and high-pressure sales tactics. These abuses became so flagrant that the Financial Industry Regulatory Authority (FINRA) had to issue an investor alert in 2003: "Variable Annuities: Beyond the Hard Sell." Visit www.FINRA.org to read the entire article.

Equity-indexed annuities are an onerous variation of a fixed annuity where the interest rate is based on an outside index, such as a stock market index. They offer juicy commissions to sales personnel and marginal returns to investors. Equity-indexed annuities are promoted as investments that achieve some of the higher return of stocks but with limited losses. These are extremely complex investments that most people cannot begin to understand. In general, equity-linked annuities have high commissions, high annual expenses, and steep surrender charges. Because of abusive sales practices involving senior citizens, FINRA issued another investor alert in 2008: "Equity Indexed Annuities: A Complex Choice." The SEC is considering improved regulation of equity-indexed annuities to rein in the abuses. The SEC proposal is to switch from state insurance regulation to federal securities regulation of equity-indexed annuities.

Let's look at a hypothetical example that illustrates a potential conflict of interest between a salesperson/adviser and client. Robert and Rita are a 65-year-old recently retired couple who fortunately have all their retirement living expenses covered by two generous defined benefit pension plans (see Chapter 5). They assume at least one of them will live to age 95. In addition to their pensions, they have accumulated $600,000 in a taxable account and $400,000 in a tax-deferred retirement account that they hope to pass on to their children as an inheritance.

Robert and Rita are seeking financial advice on investments. They first receive advice from an adviser at a major Wall Street firm. The broker recommends investing the $600,000 of taxable funds in a variable annuity, which in turn goes into stock funds. The broker also recommends that the couple invest the $400,000 of tax-advantaged money into an actively managed bond fund. How much will the brokerage firm get if Robert and Rita bite? The brokerage firm would receive a commission of $30,000 for selling the variable annuity (5 percent of $600,000) and $18,000 for selling the bond fund (4.5 percent load on the $400,000). In total, the firm would receive a commission of $48,000. The brokerage firm would split that amount with the broker who sold the products.

Regardless of how long Robert and Rita own the investments, they are guaranteed to pay $48,000 in commissions. But that is not the end of it.

Assume that the variable annuity has an annual expense ratio of 2 percent per year for as long as they own it and the bond fund has an expense ratio of 1 percent for as long as they own it.

Ignoring taxes, the couple would receive a net return on the variable annuity of 8 percent (the long-term stock market average of 10 percent minus a 2 percent expense ratio). Ignoring taxes, the couple would receive a net return on the bond fund of 5 percent (the long-term bond market average of 6 percent minus a 1 percent expense ratio).

We'll assume our couple's portfolio compounds at these rates over their 30-year retirement period. At the end of 30 years, their heirs would inherit $7,386,696. We can assume the salesperson spent 10 hours selling this couple the variable annuity and the bond fund. The couple paid the salesperson $48,000 or $4,800 per hour for this advice.

Now let's assume Robert and Rita hired a fee-only financial planner who believes in low-cost index-fund investing. We'll assume the fee-only financial planner charged $200 per hour. For 10 hours of advice, the fee-only planner's total bill would have been $2,000. The fee-only planner recommends investing $600,000 in Vanguard's Total Stock Market Index Fund. This planner also recommends investing $400,000 in Vanguard's Total Bond Market Index Fund. There are zero sales commissions involved with these investments. Since they'd be investing more than $100,000 into each of these two funds, they'd qualify for Vanguard's Admiral class shares of the two funds. The Admiral class of the Total Stock Market Index Fund has an expense ratio of 0.07 percent, and the Admiral class of the Total Bond Market Index Fund has an expense ratio of 0.1 percent.

Both funds are passively managed (they're index funds). Since they're passively managed, we'll assume they each return 100 percent of their index averages.

Ignoring taxes, the couple would receive a net return on the Vanguard Total Stock Market Index Fund (VTSAX) of 9.93 percent (100 percent of the long-term stock market average of 10 percent minus the 0.07 percent expense ratio). Ignoring taxes, the couple would receive a net return on the Vanguard Total Bond Fund (VBTLX) of 5.9 percent (100 percent of the long-term bond market average of 6 percent minus the 0.1 percent expense ratio).

We'll assume Robert and Rita's portfolio would compound at these rates over their 30-year retirement period. After 30 years, their heirs would inherit $12,504,857. The benefits of following the advice of the fee-only planner versus that of the commissioned salesperson are significant. It would result in this couple leaving $5,118,161 more to their children.

These two cases vividly illustrate the inherent conflict of interest present in the commission-based model.

Percentage of Assets Under Management Model

Many financial advisers use an Assets Under Management (AUM) fee model, where clients are charged a percentage of the portfolio being managed. Advisers using the AUM model are usually registered investment advisers (RIA) under the Investment Advisor Act of 1940. RIAs are bound by law as fiduciaries to act in the client's best interest. Generally, advisers using the AUM model are money managers, although financial planning may also be included under that fee.

Under the AUM model, RIAs typically charge about 1 percent. Some advisers charge more, and some charge much less. Do not assume that you get more services from the ones who charge more. RIAs do not typically include the value of a client's home or business in the quantity of assets being managed because they are very difficult to value accurately and really cannot be managed in the way that stocks and bonds can be managed.

Let's assume an investor has $1 million in investable assets. An RIA with a 1 percent AUM fee would charge the investor $10,000 per year for money management. In some cases, financial planning services are included in the AUM fee, and in other cases, they are charged separately. Do not pay a higher AUM fee for an adviser who automatically includes planning services you do not need or need only occasionally. It is better to negotiate those services separately. Why pay for the complete buffet when all you want is a salad?

Many advisers use a tiered approach to the AUM fee. For example, an RIA may charge 1.2 percent on the first $500,000 under management and then drop to 1 percent for the next $500,000. Investors with more would be charged less than 1 percent per year on the assets over $1 million.

Adviser fees should be clearly explained in writing before you enter into an AUM agreement. Investors would do well to shop around for price and compatibility. Many advisers post their fees on their web sites.

When financial advisers first start in business, they'll often accept any size client. Successful advisers learn that the time required to prepare and implement financial plans turns out to be very similar, regardless of the client's net worth. If financial advisers want to optimize their time and profits, the AUM model usually drives them to higher net worth clients. Often, a successful adviser will attempt to replace the smaller clients with larger clients. At this stage, advisers may increase their minimum asset level per client they accept or increase the minimum annual fee per client. Some advisers direct their existing lower net worth clients to other options, and some continue working with these customers. It depends on the adviser. If you are a smaller client, that would be a good question to ask.

The AUM model eliminates most conflicts of interest. Advisers who charge a percentage fee can align their interests with the client's. Both parties want the client's net worth to increase. Many clients find it comforting that their advisers are actually in the boat with them.

There can be drawbacks to the AUM model. For instance, under a bundled fee approach where the AUM covers financial planning and money management, investors might be paying a lot for planning advice that they use infrequently or not at all. Also, since an adviser is paid based on assets, an unscrupulous investment adviser may recommend investments that are too risky because over the long run, riskier investments would be expected to increase the adviser's assets under management. Unfortunately, those unethical advisers are exposed only in a bear market, after you take substantial losses.

Fees by the Hour or Project

Some advisers offer hourly or project-based billing. Financial advisers who offer planning and investment services by the hour charge $80 to $400 per hour. The hourly fee depends on the experience of the adviser, the geographic location of the client, and the complexity of the financial planning services provided. Other financial advisers charge by using project-based methods. A project-based fee could be $100 or $10,000, depending on the included services. In general, a simple retirement plan would cost about $500. Advisers using the hourly fee or project model are usually RIAs and must act in the client's best interest.

People with limited assets and resources may find hourly and project-based advisers an ideal choice. There is a nationwide network of planners who cater to this market. Sheryl Garrett established a financial adviser program that assists working-class and middle-class individuals. The Garrett Planning Network is composed of independent fee-only financial planners who charge either by the hour or by the project. She contends that most middle-class investors do not need comprehensive financial planning. Thus, it is best to break up financial planning into different and specific elements so that everyone can afford help in the specific area they need. If a client needs another element at a later date, they can work with their planner and pay only for the next element.

Charging by the hour or by the project tends to eliminate most conflicts of interest. But there could still be issues. For instance, hourly advisers may try to log as many hours as possible. That can be pretty frustrating, not to mention a waste of money. These investors should probably investigate other types of advisers. Finally, some planners advertise hourly planning but they promote their AUM asset management services when you go for an appointment. That is a conflict of interest.

Annual Flat-Fee Model

What you see is how much you pay, no more and no less. That is the flat-fee model. The fee is set in advance and does not change. Some years, you may need more advice and some years less, although this does encourage frequent communication and face-to-face meetings. The annual flat-fee model focuses on long-term relationships rather than pay as you go. This model eliminates incentives for the adviser to recommend riskier investments to increase the quantity of assets under management.

Flat-fee advisers tend to dislike the AUM model because that puts their annual income at the vagaries of the stock market. In addition, they do not want their clients to judge them by the performance of the financial markets. The flat-fee adviser wants to be a client's long-term financial person regardless of what the markets do.

Just like all the other methods of compensation, the flat-fee model has a few pitfalls. For instance, a flat-fee adviser may try to do as little work for you as possible and still collect the fee. Also, some flat-fee advisers get kickbacks from the referrals they give to money managers and insurance agents. Make sure your adviser has no conflict of interest.

Mutual Fund Financial Advice

There is a fourth model. Several large mutual fund companies offer limited financial planning services for free or a fee, depending on the amount you have invested with that company. One company that offers this service is the Vanguard Group founded by John Bogle in 1975. This firm is unique among mutual fund companies because the customers own the firm. It is a mutual benefit type of company. Vanguard offers excellent educational materials on their web site and also provides personal portfolio advice.

Vanguard has different customer levels and services, based on the amount each client has with the company. Customers with more than $1 million at Vanguard are called Flagship clients. They receive free portfolio advice, including annual checkups. Customers with $500,000 or more invested at Vanguard are called Voyager Select customers. They get their fee waived for portfolio advice, and annual checkups are included. Voyager customers have $100,000 to $500,000. They pay $250 for portfolio help as needed. All other customers pay $1,000. Free annual checkups are not included for any client with less than $500,000 invested. Even if you do not qualify for free portfolio advice, Vanguard's prices are still relatively inexpensive. There are no face-to-face meetings. You would be talking with your Vanguard financial adviser over the telephone.

As you can see, there is no one fee structure or set of services that's right for all investors. By comparing the various fee structures and services you require, it should be easier to select the fee structure that best suits your needs.

FINANCIAL ADVISER DESIGNATIONS

Financial advisers' designations are a smorgasbord of acronyms. In fact, there are so many different designations that the subject is often compared to alphabet soup.

The field is relatively young but vast. Consequently, there is no single financial adviser designation that covers everything. However, of all these designations, Certified Financial Planner (CFP) is the most prominent for people searching for a financial planner. The CFP designation was first awarded in 1972 by the College for Financial Planning in Denver. In 1985, the International Board of Standards and Practices for Certified Financial Planners (IBCFP) assumed responsibility for CFP examinations. The IBCFP also awards CFP licenses. Currently, there are over 23,000 licensed CFPs, some of whom are also CPAs.

The IBCFP maintains a list of registered educational programs. Some are bachelor's or master's degree programs at colleges and universities around the country. Many others are certificate programs in financial planning and are designed specifically to prepare applicants for the CFP exam. The best-known certificate program is the CFP professional education program offered by the College for Financial Planning. This is a six-part, self-study program that usually takes two years to complete. It is possible, however, for students to accelerate the program and complete it in one year.

The CFP comprehensive certification exam is a two-day, 10-hour exam that includes multiple-choice questions, matching items, and case problems or problem sets with multiple-choice responses. The exam covers insurance, investment, income tax, retirement, and estate planning.

The requirements for acquiring the CFP designation are designed to provide the CFP applicant with the tools needed to provide effective financial planning services.

If you are seeking investment management, the Chartered Financial Analyst (CFA) designation is a high-level money management designation. It is similar to the CPA in accounting. People who seek a career in investment analysis and portfolio management seek the CFA charter rather than the more broadly based CFP. CFA candidates must complete a graduate-level self-study program and pass three extremely rigorous exams. The process generally takes three years, although it can be completed in two and a half. A CFA candidate is tested on financial reporting and analysis, quantitative investment tools, asset classes, wealth planning, and ethics.

There are at least 56 different designations for financial advisers. Except for the CFP and CFA designations just noted, many of these designations are not recognized as meaningful in financial circles. However, they're often used in an attempt to impress potential clients.

Some advisers also list RIA after their names as if it were a designation. It is not. As you recall, RIA stands for registered investment adviser. The requirements for becoming an RIA are not particularly stringent. Typically 40 hours of study is required to pass a Series 65 exam administered by a state securities regulator. The adviser must also complete Form ADV, which includes the fee structure and a written code of ethics. Because RIA is not a designation, the SEC forbids people from putting the letters RIA on a business card next to their names. Unfortunately, that does not stop some less ethical advisers from doing so in an effort to fool the public.

SELECTING AN ADVISER

If you have decided that using a financial adviser is the best decision to help you achieve your financial goals and objectives, then selecting a good one is the next step. You now have the necessary background and understanding of key topics to help make this process easier.

Adviser Compensation

Thoroughly question a potential adviser regarding the various methods of adviser compensation, and get it in writing. For instance, some advisers are hybrids. These hybrid advisers are paid commissions under one business identity and take fees under another identity. It is not possible to overstate the serious conflicts of interest that can arise with this arrangement.

Potential advisers should also be questioned thoroughly about any referral arrangements. Many advisers make a business out of referring their clients to friends or family members for other services they recommend. Unfortunately, some advisers practice the old retail trick of bait and switch. They advertise one type of service when they really want you as a client for a completely different service.

Qualifications

You should inquire into your potential adviser's qualifications. What educational background and professional designations does the adviser have? Ask the adviser for a copy of the ADV Part II, which is filed with either the state or the SEC. The adviser is required by law to provide this document to you before you invest with them. The ADV Part II is genuinely worth reading because it describes in detail the adviser's business. The best way to get an ADV Part II is to call the adviser and ask for it. Many advisers have links in their web sites.

Some people need help in a specific area. Certain advisers specialize in target markets like small-business owners or employees of large corporations. Investors with large taxable accounts are the most obvious example. Other advisers deal with difficult tax situations, including company stock option programs. If taxes are an issue for you, make sure your adviser has the necessary experience and expertise.

Ethics

Ask the potential adviser if your relationship will be a fiduciary relationship. In a fiduciary relationship, the adviser puts the interests of the client first. Ask to see the adviser's written code of conduct. The SEC requires all RIAs to have a written code of conduct that is to be made available to a client or potential client on request. Also contact your state's securities office and make sure your state officials have no outstanding issues regarding this adviser.

Unfamiliar Products

A red flag should arise if an adviser starts recommending investments you are not familiar with. There is a good commonsense rule of thumb about complex products: the more complex the product, the worse it is for you, and the better it is for the adviser. Hedge funds are particularly dangerous. Hedge funds have notoriously high fees and very little transparency.

Also, some advisers may charge what appear to be low fees for complex, unusual investments, but there's usually a catch. They charge low fees because their firm, or a related firm, owns the products being sold.

Finally, be very wary if the adviser asks you to write a check to them for an investment. Most advisers do not take custody of their clients' money. A separate brokerage firm does that function. The only checks you should be writing to an adviser are for management fees.

Risk

There is a simple way to distinguish poor financial advisers from competent advisers. Ask the adviser what risk is. The adviser should have a good answer that you can understand clearly. Beware of advisers who claim that they can avoid risk entirely or who use past data exclusively when discussing risk. Avoid advisers who always talk about returns but not about the risk necessary to achieve such returns.

Advisers who are selling something that seems too good to be true are, indeed, selling something that's too good to be true (anyone remember Bernie Madoff?). Remember, there is no such thing as a free lunch. Many investors in supposedly safe and conservative money market funds that were providing an unusually high yield learned the hard way that they were actually holding risky investments during the market turmoil of 2008. Risk and return are always related, regardless of what your adviser indicates.

Second Opinions

If you have any doubts about your financial plan or planner, there are many good ways of getting a second opinion. You can use the expertise of the members of the Bogleheads Internet forum group. Post the details of your financial situation, and ask the Bogleheads to comment. You can also post your adviser's financial plan and ask the Bogleheads' forum members to comment on the plan. If you don't understand something about the financial plan, feel free to ask the Bogleheads.

If you have an accountant or attorney, you might seek their opinion of the proposed financial plan. However, beware that many accountants and attorneys have conflicts of interest themselves. They are often tied in with insurance salespeople and brokerage firms and receive kickbacks from the products and services you buy through their referral network. You will be led astray if you show your plan to the wrong accountant or attorney. Know where these people stand before asking them for a review.

You could also ask another financial adviser to review the proposed plan. A financial plan from Vanguard is another option. Remember that there is no such thing as the perfect portfolio; there is only a portfolio that is perfect for you.

ARE YOU HIRING A PLANNER OR A MONEY MANAGER?

In a simple world, financial planners do financial planning, and investment managers take care of investment portfolios. Regrettably, the world is not simple. Many people who have a CFP designation call themselves financial planners, but they are actually investment managers or brokers. That is because their main compensation is derived from money management fees or commissions, not financial planning fees. You should ask potential advisers what their primary source of revenue is. If you are searching for a financial planner to do financial planning, you will want one who is paid from financial planning fees, not money management fees or commissions.

Many fine investment management firms do not do detailed financial planning. Those money management firms will not be part of the hourly fee-only Garrett network or have membership in NAPFA. Unfortunately, there is no one-stop shop where you can find someone to manage your portfolio. Finding a competent money manager who charges a reasonable fee and shares your beliefs can require some work on your part.

A good place to ask for help is www.Bogleheads.org. The long-time members of the forum tend to know which advisers you should be talking with. Many money managers who follow a Boglehead philosophy write books and articles that you can often find online or at your library. All the investment advisers have web sites on the Internet, and they tend to publish research articles on those sites. You'll want to read a few books or articles to see if an adviser's investment ideas are aligned with yours.

ADDITIONAL RESOURCES

- www.bogleheads.org—The Bogleheads' Internet forum is an excellent source of information on financial planning, investments, and money managers.
- www.napfa.org—The web site of the National Association of Personal Financial Advisors (NAPFA) offers an excellent list of questions you should ask a prospective financial adviser.
- www.garrettplanningnetwork.com—On the Garrett Planning Network web site, you can find an hourly fee financial planner in your

geographic area. The web site also has an excellent list of questions you should ask a prospective financial adviser.

CHAPTER SUMMARY

Financial advisers come in two general types: financial planners and investment managers. Comprehensive financial planning covers many different fields, including savings strategies, taxation, diversification, investment selection, retirement, and estate planning. It is difficult for many people to gain the broad knowledge required for financial planning. If you lack the time, temperament, or experience to do your own plan, then consider the services of a financial planner. If you are seeking an investment manager to create and manage a portfolio for you, seek out a knowledgeable professional who has the same investment philosophy as you do.

Selecting the right financial advisers to assist you with planning and investing is, of course, extremely important. It's not possible to describe a foolproof selection method that will work for everyone. Hopefully, the information in this chapter will point you in the right direction.

CHAPTER NINETEEN

Divorce and Other Financial Disasters

David Rankine

INTRODUCTION

In the perfect world, everyone following the Bogleheads' guidance in this book will have a happy and secure retirement. Unfortunately, the world is not perfect. In the real world, people lose jobs, good health turns bad, more than half of marriages end in divorce, and other setbacks occur that can ruin a good retirement plan. Few of us will get through life without one serious financial crisis along the way. This chapter discusses how life's problems can impact your retirement plans and what to do about it. Surprisingly, retirement need not be a victim of things going wrong if you are informed about potentially ruinous events and can act to minimize the damage. This means knowing what happens in divorce courts and with creditors when an unpleasant event occurs. The rules may vary from state to state, so know your rights and consult an expert before taking any action.

DIVIDING ASSETS IN A DIVORCE

Divorce is often a painful experience for everyone involved. Part of the pain is coming to a court-approved agreement about how assets will be divided. Divorce courts traditionally have sought to ensure that children are provided for, that spousal support is granted based on need when there was a long-term marriage, and that assets are divided equitably. Traditionally, pensions were future contingencies that were not divided or awarded by divorce courts. Only in the last 50 years have judges across the country sought to value and divide retirement plans.

Retirement Plans Funded during the Marriage

Divorce is governed by the differing laws of the 50 states. The general rule is that property acquired during a marriage is split equally between the spouses at the time of divorce. Thus, a couple with no substantial property other than one spouse's retirement plan should expect a divorce court to divide the plan equally. There are exceptions to this general rule.

The divorce court is not greatly concerned with which spouse was working and whose earnings funded the particular retirement plan. The plan belongs to both spouses in the eyes of a divorce court. This is in recognition of the fact that even if one spouse did not fund the retirement plan, he or she made other contributions to the marriage. The division of a plan between two spouses has no tax consequence.

A couple with two retirement plans of equal value and no other property should expect the court to award each their own retirement plan free of any claim from the other spouse. If one spouse was working and accruing retirement for a period prior to the marriage, the court might award one spouse more than the other in recognition that the portion of the plan acquired during the marriage is only a fraction of the money contributed to the plan.

There are exceptions to equal division of retirement plans. The percentage of a plan going to each spouse can be complicated by other property of the parties. That property, if acquired during the marriage, may affect the percentage division of retirement plans. An example of this is where a couple owned two homes of different value and one retirement plan. The court may give each person one home and then equalize the total division by giving the spouse who received the house of lesser value a greater portion of the retirement plan.

Valuing the Plan Prior to Division

A retirement plan must be given a value before it can be divided. An individual retirement account (IRA) is easily valued. It is the sum of money in the account as shown in a statement. Defined contribution plans (DC) are valued the same way. The pension administrator can report to the court how much is in an employee's account.

The value of a defined benefit plan (DB) is not so easily determined. Recall that those are plans where the benefit is a monthly amount from a pension fund that is not segregated into individual accounts. Perhaps the employee is entitled to $1,000 per month after 20 years of service. The $1,000 payment in the distant future is not going to be worth $1,000 at the time of the divorce. A present value of future benefits must be calculated.

There are numerous ways of calculating future value, and the resulting figures can vary considerably, depending on assumptions in the formula. For example, an assumption needs to be made for the expected rate of return, called a discount rate, along with an assumption about the future inflation rate. This is very difficult and often a point of contention. During a divorce, people can pay expert witnesses thousands of dollars to put a value on a plan. If the experts make different assumptions about inflation or length of service, the resulting figures will differ by a wide margin. Courts try to avoid valuing such plans. In the case of a wide disparity between parties, the judge will decide on a compromise.

Rather than go through a valuation, a common approach to dividing DB plans is to have the plan administrator divide the plan benefits as of the retirement date of the employee spouse. Thus, the divorce court would issue an order requiring the plan administrator to give the nonemployee spouse a fractional share, where the numerator would be the years of the marriage and the denominator the number of years of employment divided by two. For example, if a marriage lasted 10 years, and the employee spouse retired after 20 years, the benefit to the nonemployee spouse would be $250 per month ($1,000 per month x 10 years of marriage/20 years of service divided by 2 to get the nonemployee spouse's share).

Other Factors Influencing the Division

A nonemployee spouse might not want to be awarded a portion of a defined benefit plan. First, if there is a substantial age difference, the nonemployee spouse may need the income before the employee spouse would be expected to retire. Such a spouse would prefer to be awarded some asset that would produce income at an earlier time. Second, the spouse may prefer an asset that can be passed on by inheritance. Payments from defined benefit plans end with the death of the beneficiary. Note that if the beneficiary is the nonemployee spouse, payments will continue until the end of that spouse's life. There usually is nothing to inherit except a death benefit, which usually is not large and may not be reserved for this particular spouse.

QUALIFIED DOMESTIC RELATIONS ORDERS

The divorce court divides a retirement plan by issuing a special order: a qualified domestic relations order (QDRO). A qualified plan is any DC or DB plan. There can be no division of a qualified retirement plan without that order. The order may be issued at the time of separation to prevent a retirement plan from being dissipated. There will be a QDRO at the time of divorce anytime a qualified retirement plan is being divided. A QDRO is not necessary to divide an IRA. In that case, the divorce decree must direct the division.

The QDRO order is a creature of federal law that is applicable in all 50 states. The law prevents divorce courts from modifying pension rights in ways that threaten the tax-free status of retirement funds. It prohibits divorce courts from changing benefits under the plan in ways that might violate retirement law. The plan administrator must approve the QDRO, or it will not have legal affect. Divorce courts do not have jurisdiction to order a plan administrator to do anything he or she does not agree with that the QDRO may require.

In practice, here's how the law works. A divorce lawyer preparing a QDRO usually requests a fill-in-the-blank form from the plan administrator and turns that form into a draft QDRO. That draft is then sent to the administrator, and after the administrator agrees that the QDRO is in proper form, the lawyer sends it to the judge for entry. QDROs are a malpractice nightmare for lawyers. They can charge only a few hundred dollars to prepare the QDRO, and they take on hundreds of thousands of dollars of liability if, for some reason, the QDRO does not protect the client's interest in the retirement plan.

As an example of how things can go wrong, recall the order that divided a defined benefit plan with a benefit of $1,000 monthly between parties who were married 10 years. Suppose that several years after the divorce, the employer is downsizing and offers the employee spouse a buyout where, in lieu of retiring with benefits, the employee is offered cash. If the QDRO does not divide the plan until the time of retirement and the employee elects the cash payment, then the nonemployee spouse's half interest may never come into being and that spouse gets nothing.

Special Rules Exist for Military Plans

The same scenario can happen in a divorce where one spouse is in the military. The Uniformed Services Former Spouses Protection Act (10 USC 1408) allows divorce courts to divide military retirement pay and prohibits the division of disability benefits. The U.S. Supreme Court ruled that a nonmilitary spouse could not prevent the other spouse from accepting disability payments in lieu of retirement pay and that the objecting spouse was not entitled to share in the disability pay elected in lieu of retirement pay.

There are other special rules for dividing military retirement in a divorce. A QDRO is not required. The spouses must have been married 10 years during which the military spouse served 10 years before a court can divide the military pension. The division can never take more than 50 percent of the retirement pay. These rules are explained quite well at www.dfas.mil.

DIVORCE AND SOCIAL SECURITY BENEFITS

Social Security benefits are not divided or awarded in a divorce. Do not expect to receive half of your spouse's Social Security benefits. Recall that the right to receive Social Security is derived from working for a sufficient number of years to qualify. The size of the benefit is based on the length of employment and amount of income.

A spouse may only get survivor's benefits based on the other spouse's employment and income. If you divorced more than 2 years prior to requesting benefits and the marriage lasted more than 10 years, then you may receive benefits based on your former spouse's income. These benefits may be more than you qualify for on your own. If you remarry, you lose the right to apply for benefits based on your previous marriage but may qualify for benefits through your current spouse. Alternatively, you may qualify for benefits based on your own circumstance and employment history, whether you are married or divorced.

AGREEING TO A DIVISION BEFORE MARRIAGE

The general rule that assets acquired during a marriage are divided equally has exceptions that vary from state to state. As mentioned, property acquired prior to the marriage and kept separate is not usually divided, and its value does not enter into the division. Similarly, if one spouse inherits or is gifted property and that property is kept separate, such as funds in a brokerage account in just that spouse's name, then that asset will not usually be subject to division.

A couple can also agree prior to marriage about how property may be divided or remain separate. This brings us to the subject of premarital agreements, which are also known as prenuptial and antenuptial agreements.

They are written agreements between spouses entered before marriage that govern which spouse will have an interest in property the other spouse might claim in the event of separation or divorce.

In the eyes of many, premarital agreements developed an undeserved reputation of being unfair, or that people who entered into them were less dedicated to the marriage than people who do not have them. There are a lot of good reasons for a premarital agreement. Entering into the agreement can help a couple get used to talking about money and property. They can make rules that they prefer to their state's property or inheritance laws. Older individuals may want to keep property separate so it can be given to children of an earlier marriage. Areas where a state's law is vague or unpredictable can be clarified by the premarital agreement. In other words, the couple can plan the economics of their marriage in advance.

In the event of divorce or death, expensive litigation can be avoided. Premarital agreements have an estate planning use even if a couple never divorce. State laws regarding inheritance can restrict the manner or extent that marital property can be given away by a will. Typically, a third to half of marital property must be given to a spouse, or the spouse can elect to receive that much, even if the will has a different provision. These restrictions can be avoided if the property is kept separate by use of a premarital agreement.

All 50 states enforce premarital agreements. To be enforced, they must be fair—that is, not unconscionable or significantly imbalanced. The process of reaching the agreement must be free of coercion, and there must be a full and accurate disclosure of assets, debts, and the effect of the agreement. The agreement must be written. The process by which the agreement is reached is more important than the actual terms. It is wise to have two lawyers involved.

Common provisions dealing with retirement plans may provide that a plan or plans remain separate property, even if the spouse continues making contributions to the plan from marital income. The agreement may specify that if one spouse gives the other money to fund their retirement plan, that gift will not convert the plan to marital property. The agreement may create a fund that will be given to a spouse in lieu of a retirement plan or it may define the spouse's interest in the retirement plan. Another provision may require one spouse to buy the other a retirement annuity to make up for the fact the spouse will not be working, and accruing retirement, while raising children. Child support can never be waived in a premarital agreement. In a number of states, spousal support cannot be waived in a premarital agreement.

If you marry without a premarital agreement, an increasing number of states will enforce postmarital agreements. These agreements can cover the same subjects as premarital agreements. In the event of a dispute, the postmarital agreement is more closely scrutinized to see that it is fair and that the process leading up to it was fair. Involving attorneys in the preparation of a postmarital agreement is a good idea.

REMEMBER TO CHECK DESIGNATED BENEFICIARY

Note that a division of property in a divorce may not be the last word on everything you own that has been discussed in this book. Certain assets, such as life insurance and IRA assets, pass to designated beneficiaries if you die. A divorce decree will not change the designations. If you get divorced, you should immediately review all beneficiary designations to ensure your property is received by the person of your choice.

FACING A FINANCIAL DISASTER

Professionals who counsel people experiencing financial difficulties will tell you that only a minority of them are to blame. Accidents not covered by insurance, job loss, family members who need help, and unanticipated illness can create a financial emergency without anyone being at fault. That means a financial disaster can happen to you. Here is some information that may be of use to you if a financial crisis occurs in your life.

Creditors Cannot Take Your ERISA Plan

The first concern is whether your retirement funds can be taken from you by creditors. Any plan that is covered by Employee Retirement Income Security Act (ERISA) is protected from the claims of creditors and prevents any creditor from going to a plan administrator and demanding either money in your account or payment of any portion of your monthly benefit check. The fact that debt may have been reduced to a judgment does not change the fact that all ERISA plans are exempt from the claims of your creditors. There is no dollar limitation to this protection, and all money in an ERISA plan is exempt from creditor attachments. This is true if you file bankruptcy or do not file bankruptcy. So, the answer to your question about whether your private defined benefit plan, defined contribution plan, profit sharing, 403(b) annuity, or similar plan could be taken from you is *no*.

IRAs Have Some Protection

Although there are state laws that partially protect assets in an IRA from creditors, ERISA does not apply to IRA accounts. About half the states prevent judgment creditors from attaching money in an IRA account. These state laws are called exemption laws. They usually contain a dollar limit such as protecting only the first $100,000 in an IRA, or they limit their protection to amounts reasonably necessary for the support or sustenance of a debtor or dependent. The IRS can always seize money in IRA account regardless of state law.

Savings Accounts and Trust Accounts

Exemption laws do not protect money in personal accounts or brokerage accounts from seizure by judgment creditors. Accordingly, you should maximize money in qualified plans.

Various trust arrangements including charitable remainder trusts have been discussed in this book. The general rule applicable in all jurisdictions is that if you set up and fund a trust, including a charitable trust, the trust will not protect the money you give to it or your right to the trust's earnings from the claims of your creditors. If you are told that setting up a trust will protect assets transferred to it from the claims of the creditors, you need to know that any creditor who wants to go to court can void the trust. This rule is true if you file bankruptcy.

You can provide in a trust you set up and fund for others that the creditors of those beneficiaries cannot invade either the principle or earnings of the trust. This is called a spendthrift clause.

Early Withdrawal from a Retirement Plan

Withdrawing money from your tax-sheltered retirement plan may seem like a good idea in the middle of a financial crisis. The key questions are whether you can or should. You can withdraw money from an IRA tax-free as long as you pay the money back into the IRA within 60 days. If you do not, you will be subject to the early withdrawal tax penalty equal to 10 percent of the withdrawal amount on top of income taxes if you are not yet 59½ years of age. ERISA-qualified plans may allow you to withdraw money as a hardship distribution. These are limited by federal law to withdrawals to keep your principal residence out of foreclosure, for a medical emergency, or to pay for postsecondary education for you or a dependent. You will still have to pay taxes on the withdrawal and may still be subject to the 10 percent penalty. Check with your tax adviser.

Many ERISA plans allow you to borrow money from the plan up to a specified percentage. Assuming you enter into such a loan and pay it back, there is no tax consequence. If you do not repay the loan, amounts outstanding are treated as an early distribution, and you are liable for the taxes on the withdrawal plus the 10 percent penalty if you are not yet 59½ years of age.

Consider This Before Invading Your Retirement Account

Develop a plan that takes you from the beginning of the financial emergency to the end before prematurely withdrawing money from any retirement account to deal with a problem. You should feel certain that the financial emergency will end before it is worth using your retirement account funds to pay creditors. It may be wiser to leave the money in a retirement plan and file bankruptcy if withdrawing money from a retirement plan will not solve your problem. You can take a retirement account through a bankruptcy without losing it.

Be Realistic and Prioritize

As soon as you realize you have a financial crisis, sit down and list all your financial resources and liabilities. Resources include your income and things you might sell. Also include spending you might forgo and amounts other people might give you to help out. Then list all the people you owe now and will owe in the future. You need to budget your way through your financial difficulty.

Be accurate when doing this exercise. Review your checkbook and financial accounts for spending you put on a credit card. You also need to account for expenses that occur intermittently, such as car repairs or annual registration. As an example, most people, if asked how much they spend on food, will give a low figure because they will forget to include restaurant meals.

Prepare a forward-looking budget to find ways to spend no more than the amounts provided in revenue. Generalized resolutions to spend less rarely work unless you have a mechanism to stop expenses before you exceed any item in the budget. You need to prioritize, assuming the budget will not pay all debt when it comes due. Higher priority debt is debt that is secured by some asset you would not want to lose. Your home mortgage and car loan are high-priority debt. Debts that will not go away in a bankruptcy are also priority debts. Child or spousal support falls into this category, as does the IRS.

Differences between Creditors

Home Mortgage Providers

If you have two home mortgages secured by your residence, the first mortgage is a higher priority debt than the second mortgage. The first has greater rights to its collateral, your home. That is the reason the lender on the first mortgage has less of an incentive to work with you than a second-mortgage holder. Do not omit making the payment on the first mortgage and pay the second because that payment amount is lower. If you do this for long, the first mortgage will foreclose, and the holder of the second mortgage will not help you keep the house.

Companies holding first mortgages do not like to receive partial payments and may even mail back your check. If you cannot make a whole payment on a first mortgage, make a payment with the late charge when you can. For example, if all you can afford is half a payment a month, send a full payment and late charge every other month, rather than a half payment each month. If you realize you cannot afford to keep both your house and your car, it is best to decide which you will give up before things get so bad you lose both.

If you miss a payment on your home mortgage, you receive a few calls and letters over a four-month period, and then the lender sends your file to a foreclosure trustee who will take the house from you in one to four months, depending on your state's foreclosure period.

Credit Cards and Other Unsecured Debt

General unsecured debt is not entitled to priority. To understand why this is the case, you need to learn how creditors will act if you don't pay them. If you miss a credit card payment, within a few days you will receive a polite call inquiring whether you forgot to pay. Missing a second payment prompts another call inquiring if you forgot to pay again. About two weeks after that second call, you will receive another call informing you that the account will be turned over to the creditor's in-house collection department if you continue to remain in default. About the time your third payment is due, the credit card company will cancel your card and send your file to the credit collection team.

For approximately nine months, the hardball team will call you and seek to harass, bluff, or terrorize you into making payments. Only after this time has elapsed will the creditor consider suing you. If you do not pay an unsecured debt for up to a year, all that is going to happen is your phone is going to ring. You do not have to answer it. When your financial crisis ends, call your credit card company and make them an offer. A typical settlement is a third to half of the amount owed on debt a year old.

Now contrast what will happen if you stop paying on your car loan. You usually receive two polite calls about the time the first payment and then the second comes due. About the time the third payment is due, the car will be repossessed while parked outside your home or workplace.

It is not a good idea to neglect to pay the IRS. Even if you do not have the money to pay, always file your tax return on time. If you do this, you will still owe interest but will not be assessed penalties for failure to file. Within 30 days, the IRS will send you a letter saying they received your return but could not find the check. At this point, it is wise to fill out the form that will be with their letter and propose payment in installments. It is best if you propose to complete payments before the next April. If you do not respond to this letter, the IRS will send you notices that, if ignored, will allow them to start levying (seizing property). The IRS does not have to sue you before they can levy on your property. They can mail a letter to your bank, and the bank will send them everything in your account, which will cause any outstanding checks to bounce. They can also garnish all but $570 of your monthly pay. Can you live on the $570?

Prioritize your debts based on making a full payment to priority creditors rather than making partial payments to a larger number of creditors. Your credit will be affected whenever you miss payments. However, some debts will show as current if you prioritize the debts. This will have less effect on your credit than if you make partial payments to all, which causes all accounts to show you as delinquent.

Filing Bankruptcy

If your budget simply won't work or if circumstances deteriorate further, there are few financial problems that are not solved with a bankruptcy filing. You do not lose everything if you file bankruptcy. General unsecured debts go away. However, certain priority debts are not affected by the bankruptcy, including child and spousal support, debts for recent taxes, and student loans. These generally survive bankruptcy.

You have already learned that in most places all retirement plans are exempt from the claims of creditors. In a minority of states, only an IRA is at risk of loss in a bankruptcy. Most states also allow keeping a retirement annuity, even if it is not covered by ERISA. State exemption laws usually allow you to keep equity in your home and a car, as well as your clothes and furnishings. Check with your state to know how assets and liabilities are treated.

How to Get Competent Help

Most people experiencing a financial crisis do not know where to turn for financial advice. There are two groups of professionals skilled in giving advice to people with financial difficulties.

The first group, credit counselors, are certified either by the U.S. Department of Housing and Urban Development or the trade group National Federation of Credit Counselors. Their Web pages are listed at the end of this chapter. The Department of Justice (also listed later) certifies credit counselors for prebankruptcy counseling. Most reputable credit counselors will be on these lists.

The second group of skilled counselors are consumer bankruptcy lawyers. State bar associations maintain referral lists. Bar associations usually post their referral numbers at the beginning of the attorney section of the yellow pages. Also, many bankruptcy lawyers are members of the National Association of Consumer Bankruptcy Attorneys and are listed on its web page, www.nacba.org.

Credit counselors advertised on cable TV channels promising to settle with your creditors for pennies on the dollar are usually scams that become apparent only after you have paid a large nonrefundable fee. Don't go there. Also, the creditors who call you on the phone are not a good source of financial advice. Avoid asking them for it.

ADDITIONAL RESOURCES

- www.nfcc.org—National Federation of Credit Counselors for a list of people who do general counseling.
- www.hud.gov—U.S. Department of Housing and Urban Development for information on home mortgage debt and a list of counselors.
- www.usdoj.gov—The Department of Justice certifies credit counselors for prebankruptcy counseling.

CHAPTER SUMMARY

When bad things happen to good people, it does not have to result in financial ruin. Understand what happens under different circumstances, and you will more easily move through the crisis in a way that maintains your sanity and finances.

Your retirement will be divided if your marriage fails, and a special type of court order is needed to secure a share of a retirement plan awarded in a divorce. Some assets are exempt under prenuptial agreements and accounts intentionally separated from joint assets.

In a financial crisis, if you cannot pay those you owe, most retirement funds are exempt from the claims of creditors. Various common types of creditors will use a variety of methods to collect from you if you don't pay them. Prioritize debts to minimize the financial disaster. Seek competent professional help from people who will give you the right answers.

Meet the Bogleheads

Taylor Larimore and Mel Lindauer

INTRODUCTION

Boglehead is the name adopted by investors who follow the beliefs of a remarkable man, John C. Bogle, founder and former CEO of the Vanguard Group of mutual funds. In this final chapter, we will share with you a bit about John C. (Jack) Bogle so that you might understand why we're so proud to be called Bogleheads. You'll learn a bit about what went on behind the scenes of our forums, starting with the original Morningstar Vanguard Diehards Forum and then later at the larger Bogleheads .org forum. The growth and acceptance of these forums have been unparalleled.

The Bogleheads Wiki is a recent addition to the Bogleheads community. It is a valuable reference resource providing in-depth coverage of many of the subjects that are constantly mentioned on the forums. The community extends beyond the Internet into books and nationwide meetings. The Bogleheads' Guide series of books has had phenomenal success, and our annual reunions and local chapter meetings are very well attended. Perhaps you'll join us at one of our meetings?

ABOUT OUR MENTOR, JACK BOGLE

John Clifton Bogle is our distinguished mentor and friend. Jack (as he likes to be called) was born in Montclair, New Jersey, into a genteel, prosperous, and loving family in May 1929, just a few months before the worst depression and bear market in U.S. history. Jack's father enjoyed spending on the good life. Unfortunately, he lost his job, and the family savings rapidly disappeared. Jack began his business career at the age of 10 by selling newspapers and magazines to help out with his family's finances. Some of his later jobs included ice cream dipper, bowling alley pinsetter, waiter, ticket seller, mail clerk, cub reporter, and brokerage house runner.

Jack obtained a working scholarship to Blair Academy in New Jersey with his uncle's help. He graduated cum laude, and Blair Academy would later name Bogle Hall in his honor. Jack's academic record at Blair earned him yet another scholarship that enabled him to attend Princeton University. At Princeton, Jack decided to make mutual funds the subject of his senior thesis. It was a subject that interested him because of the potential for growth. At that time, there were fewer than 70 U.S. open-end mutual funds, held by about 1 percent of families. Today there are more than 8,000 U.S. mutual funds, held by more than 50 percent of U.S. families.

Jack's Princeton thesis included the philosophy that he later implemented at Vanguard: serving investors with efficiency, honesty, and candor; being innovative in developing new funds; opening institutional markets; curtailing advertising abuses; and focusing on costs.

After graduating from Princeton magna cum laude with highest honors in 1951, Jack obtained an interview with the Wellington Fund, a large mutual fund company. Walter Morgan, the head of the fund, had read Jack's 128-page senior thesis. Morgan hired Jack in a clerical position but told associates: "Bogle knows more about the mutual fund business than we do." Jack rose rapidly within the organization. In 1967, at the age of 38, Jack became president and CEO of Wellington.

Jack was fired from Wellington in 1974 after a series of disagreements with the board of directors. He decided to start a new company and organized it like no other mutual fund company ever was. His small upstart company would be owned by the mutual funds' shareholders themselves and operated solely for their benefit. He named his new company Vanguard after Lord Nelson's flagship at the Battle of the Nile, where the British defeated the much larger French fleet.

In 1975, Jack started the first retail index mutual fund, benchmarked to the S&P 500 Index: First Investors Trust. Competitors called the fund "Bogle's Folly" and even "unAmerican." But Jack had the last laugh when his now titled Vanguard 500 Index Fund became the world's largest equity mutual fund by the turn of the century. Vanguard would go on to become the largest mutual fund company in the United States with more than a trillion dollars in assets. As an interesting note, a $10,000 investment in Bogle's Folly at inception was worth $252,684 on December 31, 2008.

Jack worked for the benefit of his investors for many years, despite having the first of his six major heart attacks in 1960. Jack's heart finally gave out in 1996. After 128 days in the hospital and a successful heart transplant, Jack returned to Vanguard as senior chairman. Jack left the board at the end of 1999 and launched the Bogle Financial Markets Research Center, sponsored by Vanguard. The center's mission is to "give ordinary investors a fair shake." Visit www.johncbogle.com for more information.

Jack has had many accomplishments and awards. Here are just a few:

* *Time* magazine's one of the world's 100 most powerful and influential people.
* Awarded *Institutional Investor*'s Lifetime Achievement Award.
* Named by *Fortune* as one of the investment community's "Four Giants of the 20th Century."
* Received Woodrow Wilson Award from Princeton University for "distinguished achievement in the nation's service."
* Named one of the "Financial Leaders of the 20th Century" in leadership in financial services by Macmillan Press Ltd.
* Presented the Award for Professional Excellence from the Association for Investment Management and Research.
* Inducted into the Hall of Fame of the Fixed Income Analysts Society.
* Served as chairman of the board of governors of the Investment Company Institute.
* Named by the Commonwealth's Chamber of Commerce as Pennsylvania's Business Leader of the Year.
* Served as Chairman of the Board of the National Constitution Center from September 1999 to early 2007.
* Received honorary doctorates from Princeton University, University of Delaware, University of Rochester, New School University, Susquehanna University, Eastern University, Widener University, Albright College, Pennsylvania State University, Immaculata University, Georgetown University, and Drexel University.

Investors have purchased more than 500,000 copies of Bogle's books.

- *Bogle on Mutual Funds: New Perspectives for the Intelligent Investor* (Irwin Professional Publishing, 1993) has been a best-selling investment book since publication.
- *Common Sense on Mutual Funds: New Imperatives for the Intelligent Investor* (John Wiley & Sons, 1999) is also a bestseller.
- *John Bogle on Investing: The First 50 Years* (McGraw-Hill, 2000) has met with critical acclaim.
- *Character Counts: The Creation and Building of the Vanguard Group* (McGraw-Hill) was published in 2002.
- *The Battle for the Soul of Capitalism* (Yale University Press) was published in 2005.
- *The Little Book of Common Sense Investing* (John Wiley & Sons, 2007) was given to everyone who attended the 2007 Bogleheads Reunion in Washington, D.C.
- *Enough* (John Wiley & Sons, 2008) speaks to millions of people who are in search of the meaning of money.

Irwin is also the publisher of *John Bogle and the Vanguard Experiment: One Man's Quest to Transform the Mutual Fund Industry*, by Robert Slater (1996).

Jack Bogle resides in Bryn Mawr, Pennsylvania, with his wife, Eve. They are the parents of 6 children and the grandparents of 12. Jack still works full-time helping individual investors.

WHO ARE THE BOGLEHEADS?

Jack Bogle isn't just the namesake of our group. He is an active member who posts messages on the forums from time to time. He has written about the Bogleheads, and here in Jack's own words is what he had to say in his foreword to *The Bogleheads' Guide to Investing* (John Wiley & Sons, 2006):

Two especially notable characteristics mark the Boglehead culture:

One is rationality. These individual investors are awash in common sense, intolerant of illogic, and permeated with a preference for facts over hyperbole. Today's popular investment misconceptions—short-term focus and fast-paced trading, the conviction that exceptional past fund performance will recur, the ignorance of the importance of fund operating expenses, sales commissions, hidden portfolio turnover costs, and state and federal taxes—are anathema to them. Bogleheads have come to accept as the core of successful investing what I have called "the majesty of simplicity in an empire of parsimony."

The second characteristic is, of all things, caring. Bogleheads care about one another. They are eager to help all investors—regular visitors to the Web site and new ones, informed and naive, experienced and novice alike—who have questions on almost any investment subject, and willing to discuss the investment issues of the day, sometimes even the national and global issues, with no holds barred (except for rudeness or coarseness). Fund selection, fund performance, types of investments, retirement planning, savings programs, tax management—none are beyond the scope of this remarkable association of investors who, without compensation or bias, strive to help their fellow investors. If there is a web site that bespeaks the Golden Rule, surely the Boglehead site is its paradigm.

THE BOGLEHEADS' ONLINE FORUMS

The original Morningstar Vanguard Diehards forum began in March 1998. Taylor Larimore posted in Conversation #1, the first of his more than 24,000 forum contributions. Mel Lindauer was another pioneer whose investment and business experience soon made him a forum leader, and he has made more than 15,000 posts. The Morningstar Vanguard Diehards forum flourished. Thousands of investors read and participated in the open forum discussions. It was a very successful forum for many years.

As the number of forum followers grew, Alex Frakt (username "lowwall") created a web page called Conversation Tracker in 2001. It quickly became an indispensable gateway for the regular posters and readers of the Morningstar Vanguard Diehards forum. A few days after announcing his conversation tracker, Alex heard from another forum participant, Larry Auton. Larry was an Internet pioneer and fan of Jack Bogle. He had been in charge of one of the original dozen Internet routers at Bell Labs and had written the software that made moderated Usenet newsgroups possible. Together, Alex and Larry turned the one-page project into a full-featured web site and registered the names diehards.org and bogleheads. org. The two partners decided to manage and fund the project themselves and paid all costs out of pocket. They accepted no advertising to avoid any conflict of interest or commercial bias on the forum. It was their vision to contribute whatever they could to bring Jack Bogle's crusade to the masses and help small investors get a fair shake.

By 2007, the Morningstar Diehards forum was overflowing with ideas and commentary. This led to the grassroots effort to spread the message of Jack Bogle through the creation of a stand-alone web site. The new stand-alone site was created by "Phoenix," another of Jack's followers. The new forum was quickly integrated into Alex and Larry's web site at Bogleheads.org. The broadly expanded capabilities of the new site, made possible by new software, allowed the forum to become a smashing success. The site continues to be financed and administered by Alex and Larry, and it is free to all investors who comply with the forum's policies and etiquette.

At the time of this writing, the Bogleheads.org investment forum had more than 20,000 registered members who have made more than 800,000 posts. There are also a large number of guests online at any one time. Guests can read the forum but only registered members can post. More than 9,000 different individuals visit our web site daily. In any one month, there are more than 100,000 unique visitors making more than 300,000 visits and reading a total of more than 1 million pages. By all accounts, this new forum is a resounding success, and it's now considered to be one of the premier investing web sites on the Internet.

THE BOGLEHEADS WIKI

Bogleheads forum librarian Barry Barnitz and a small group of forum members quickly realized the valuable contribution that a Bogleheads Wiki could make to both the Boglehead community and to the greater investing community at large. A Wiki is a page or collection of Web pages designed to enable anyone who has editing access to contribute or modify content by using a simplified markup language. Wikis are often used to create collaborative web sites and to power community web sites.

Barry undertook this important project and recruited a few other loyal Bogleheads to help create the bones of the Wiki. The bones are slowly being fleshed out by an ever-growing number of Wiki contributors, and this great resource becomes more valuable with each passing day. As envisioned, the Wiki will become a valuable reference source and serve as a repository of informative and helpful investing information. You'll find the Bogleheads Wiki link on the www.bogleheads.org web site.

THE BOGLEHEAD BOOKS

The first book in the series, *The Bogleheads' Guide to Investing*, was a for-profit project by three founding members of the online forum. The success of the first book, and continuing support from publisher John Wiley & Sons, led to this not-for-profit book. It is a community effort under the leadership of the founding members of the forum, Taylor Larimore and Mel Lindauer, along with Richard Ferri and "Queen" Laura Dogu. This book capitalizes on the breadth and depth of knowledge of the many posters on the forum by having some of the members contribute individual chapters.

John C. Bogle, the founder of The Vanguard Group, in his book *Common Sense on Mutual Funds*, sums up what it means to be a Boglehead in 23 little words: "Rely on the ordinary virtues that intelligent, balanced human beings have relied on for centuries: common sense, thrift, realistic expectations, patience, and perseverance." These words permeate the advice given throughout the chapters of this book and the first book. They also come to life daily in the many online postings through the community of investors who follow these beliefs at www.Bogleheads.org.

BOGLEHEADS LOCAL CHAPTERS

Online relationships are great for gathering information, but there's nothing like meeting face-to-face to build camaraderie. There are now 38 local chapters throughout the United States and Europe. Local chapter members meet periodically to discuss investing topics of interest with other members from their area. Locations and contact information for the various chapters can be found at this web site, provided and maintained by Boglehead Ralph Averson: www.lostsprings.com/diehards/chapters/.

THE BOGLEHEADS REUNIONS

Bogleheads reunions are the result of a joint effort between Taylor Larimore and Mel Lindauer to make the online forum relationships even more personal. Originally called Vanguard Diehards reunions, these meetings offer forum participants a chance to meet the people behind the various online usernames.

Attendees also get to meet and mingle with Jack Bogle, popular Boglehead authors, and other Bogleheads they chat with or read about on the forum on a regular basis. Favorite Boglehead authors who have attended previous Bogleheads reunions include Bill Bernstein (*The Intelligent Asset Allocator*; *The Four Pillars of Investing*; *The Birth of Plenty*; and *A Splendid Exchange*), Richard Ferri (*All About Asset Allocation*; *All About Index Funds*; *Protecting Your Wealth in Good Times and Bad*; and *The ETF Book*), Bill Schultheis (*The New Coffeehouse Investor*), Larry Swedroe (*The Only Guide to a Winning Investment Strategy You'll Ever Need*; *What Wall Street Doesn't Want You to Know*; *The Only Guide to a Winning Bond*

Strategy You'll Ever Need; *The Successful Investor Today*; *Rational Investing in Irrational Times*; *Wise Investing Made Simple*; and *The Only Guide to Alternative Investments You'll Ever Need*), and *The Bogleheads' Guide to Investing* authors (Taylor Larimore, Mel Lindauer, and Michael LeBoeuf).

Diehards I: Miami, March 10–11, 2000

On Thanksgiving Day, 1999, Taylor Larimore made a post on the forum titled "A Time to Give Thanks" and listed a number of things he had to be thankful for. In the long list of things he was thankful for, he stated: "*I thank John Bogle and Vanguard, first for their unsurpassed educational tools, second for providing an investment service that is unsurpassed.*" Many Diehards chimed in on that thread, listing things they were thankful for in some very lovely and moving posts. A few days later, Taylor received a beautiful handwritten letter from Jack Bogle, who had read the forum thread. In his letter, Jack stated that he was "inspired" by Taylor's post and all the responses from the other Bogleheads. In his letter, Jack listed a number of things he was thankful for, and concluded his letter with this memorable question: "*Would there be any interest in a Bogleheads conference for a day, at a convenient (non-resort, I think) location?*" The idea of a "conference" or "reunion" was actually initiated by Jack Bogle himself.

Taylor received Jack's permission to post his letter on the forum, and the response to the idea of getting together with Jack Bogle was overwhelmingly positive. Now it was up to Taylor and Mel to figure out how, when, and where they could pull off this event. That opportunity presented itself early in 2000, when Taylor and Mel learned that Jack Bogle was scheduled to be the keynote speaker at the *Miami Herald*'s Making Money Seminar in March. Florida seemed like the ideal place to them since Taylor lives in Miami and Mel spent the winters there.

Jack Bogle accepted Taylor's invitation to join the Bogleheads during his stay in Miami. With very little notice, 22 Bogleheads from around the country arrived in Miami to join Jack Bogle for dinner in Taylor's lovely condo overlooking the night lights of Miami and beautiful Biscayne Bay. (Taylor describes his home as "the house that Jack built," a reference to his benefiting as a long-time investor at Vanguard.)

After a lovely Florida dinner, the Bogleheads sat in Taylor's living room and shared dessert while Jack took questions and chatted with all those who attended, in what can only be described as a magical evening. Then, at the end of the evening, before returning to his hotel, Jack used Taylor's computer to make a post on the forum, telling those who couldn't attend what a special evening he had enjoyed with his Bogleheads in Miami. The *Miami Herald* covered the event and published a lovely story (with pictures) about our dinner with Jack in their Sunday business section. The following morning, the Bogleheads had reserved seating for Jack's keynote speech, which contained his usual sage advice (own the market, index, keep costs low, etc.).

Thus was born what has turned out to be an almost annual series of Bogleheads reunions.

Diehards II: Philadelphia, June 8–10, 2001

As a result of all the excitement created by the large number of posts on the forum about the Diehards I reunion with Jack Bogle, Mel received an e-mail from Dave Kirtland, a Boglehead who lived in New York. He offered to host Diehards II at his inherited family farm in Pennsylvania. The farm was near Philadelphia and near Vanguard's headquarters, both desirable features. On September 21, 2000, Dave and Mel posted a joint Diehards reunion invitation.

Sadly, on November 15, 2000, Dave Kirtland suffered a massive heart attack. Dave's widow, Anne, and her two sons, Ed and Steve, wanted to continue to host the Diehards II reunion in honor of Dave. The outpouring of support from the forum members was tremendous, and Diehards II went on as planned. The event included a guided tour of Vanguard (Jack Bogle was our guide), a Q&A session with Jack, a banquet followed by a speech by Jason Zweig (a senior writer at *Money* magazine at that time), and a barbecue picnic at the Kirtland family farm. In addition to Jack Bogle, Jason Zweig, and the Kirtland family, nearly 50 Bogleheads from throughout the United States and Canada attended.

After the Q&A with Jack Bogle, the late Rev. Bob Stowe presented Jack with a World War II British bugle, mounted on a plaque, with the inscription "*To Jack Bogle—The Conscience of the Industry—This token of our esteem, a 1942 British regimental bugle, symbolizes your clarion call to build an industry that protects and serves the average investor.—Your Bogleheads—Jun 9, 2001.*" And at the picnic, Mel presented the Kirtland family with a plaque on behalf of the Bogleheads that included the inscription "*You took Dave's dream and made it a reality.*"

The events of this enjoyable, yet very moving event were documented in the September 2001 issue of *Money* magazine, where Jason Zweig did a beautiful five-page story about the reunion titled "Here Come the Bogleheads." The *Philadelphia Inquirer* also did an article on our reunion, as did *Morningstar*.

Diehards III: Chicago, June 25–27, 2002

Carl Sibilski, the moderator of the Morningstar Vanguard Diehards forum at the time, approached Taylor and Mel with an invitation from *Morningstar*, offering to host the Diehards III reunion during their annual *Morningstar* conference. Since Jack Bogle was to be a speaker at the conference and *Morningstar* would handle all the arrangements (hotel, meeting rooms, reserved group seating for Jack's speech, etc.), all the necessary parts were in place, so Diehards III was scheduled.

Jack Bogle asked Mel to invite authors Bill Bernstein and Larry Swedroe to join him at the reunion for a discussion and question-and-answer session with the Bogleheads. As the moderator of the discussion, Mel noticed that Don Phillips, managing director of *Morningstar*, had slipped into the room, so Mel invited him to join the panel. Jack Bogle later commented that that was the smartest panel he had ever been a part of.

In addition to the conference activities, the reunion included a private tour of *Morningstar*'s offices, a wonderful luncheon on the roof deck overlooking downtown Chicago, and a meeting with some of *Morningstar*'s top executives, including Chairman and CEO Joe Mansueto.

Press coverage included interviews with CNN/Money and local TV stations.

Diehards IV: Denver, May 8–10, 2004

The Bogleheads moved west when Jack Bogle addressed the CFA Conference in Denver. The CFA folks agreed to handle the arrangements for a Diehards IV reunion as a supplement to their conference. Denver Boglehead Sherri Hender (forum name "Daisy Dog") served as the local reunion coordinator. Attendance continued to grow, as 71 Bogleheads from around the United States and Canada came to Denver. The agenda continued to evolve with the addition of a social reception, where Bogleheads could meet each other and chat. Other events included Jack's address to the CFA Conference, a Q&A with a panel of Jack Bogle, Bill Bernstein, and Rick Ferri, book signings, and an evening banquet with Jack Bogle.

The *Wall Street Journal* sent reporter Karen Damato and a photographer to cover our three-day event, and her story, along with several photos, appeared on the front page of the Money & Investing section of the May 14, 2004, issue of the *Wall Street Journal*. In addition, Denver's *Rocky Mountain News* provided local coverage of our event.

Diehards V: Las Vegas, May 15–16, 2006

Although Las Vegas might be the last place you'd expect to find a Bogle-heads reunion, it turned out to be ideal for Diehards V. The Las Vegas Money Show featured Jack Bogle as a speaker, and they invited the Bogle-heads to hold our reunion as part of their event. Las Vegas Boglehead Dale Bottoms served as the local coordinator, and attendance increased, with 83 Bogleheads attending.

The event continued to evolve with a welcome reception on day one followed by a Q&A with Jack Bogle, book signings by Jack Bogle and all the Bogleheads authors in attendance, and a Q&A with the Bogleheads authors (Rick Ferri, Taylor Larimore, Michael LeBoeuf, Mel Lindauer, and Bill Schultheis). The evening banquet was capped off when all those Bogleheads who had volunteered to help out with the reunion were personally presented with a Bogle bobblehead by Jack Bogle himself. (Who says it doesn't pay to volunteer?)

Diehards VI: Alexandria, Virginia, June 10–12, 2007

Following the successful reunions with links to various sponsoring organizations, the Bogleheads were ready to step out on their own. Ed and Patti Rager volunteered as local coordinators and headed up the small team hosting Diehards VI in Washington, D.C. They did an outstanding job, and the event went off flawlessly, with 117 Bogleheads in attendance.

Jack Bogle had previously named Taylor Larimore "King of the Bogleheads," and he called Mel Lindauer "The Prince of the Bogleheads." Realizing that the Bogleheads had no queen, Taylor and Mel decided to crown Laura, one of the premier posters on the Bogleheads forum, as "Queen of the Bogleheads" in a ceremony at the reunion. After she was crowned Queen Laura Dogu, she was then invited to participate in the Q&A with the experts as a panel member.

Sue Stevens and Ed Tower of Duke University's Economics Department joined the panel discussion, and Jack Bogle added a fireside chat with Bill Bernstein just prior to the evening banquet.

Diehards VII: San Diego, September 22–24, 2008

Following a return to the East Coast in 2007, it was time to head west again. Paul and Linda Globerson offered to act as local coordinators in San Diego for Diehards VII. The ability to spend time with Jack Bogle and the rest of the Bogleheads in an intimate setting makes these events special, so attendance was limited to 130 spots, which were quickly filled.

The San Diego reunion again featured a panel of experts including Bill Bernstein, Rick Ferri, Queen Laura, Michael LeBoeuf, Mel Lindauer, Bill Schultheis, Sue Stevens, and Ed Tower. Jack Bogle mentioned that he had enjoyed his impromptu fireside chat with Bill Bernstein prior to the last banquet and would like to continue that tradition, and what Jack wants, Jack gets!

The evening banquet was topped off when a group of attendees called the Boglettes performed a choreographed rendition of "Our Guy" for Jack Bogle. Jack obviously enjoyed it immensely, and after the performance, Jack posed for a picture with the Boglettes. That picture of Jack and his Boglettes appeared in a feature story that Art Carey did about Jack for the *Philadelphia Inquirer*.

Morningstar.com sent Christine Benz and a videographer to cover the event, and Christine taped a number of interviews with Jack Bogle, Bill Bernstein, Rick Ferri, Mel Lindauer, Queen Laura, and Michael LeBoeuf for viewing on Morningstar's web site.

Pearls of Wisdom

We asked all registered members of the Bogleheads forum to share some of their favorite pearls of wisdom about saving and investing for retirement. Some of the quotes here are original and others are familiar expressions worth repeating. The italics after each quote is the screen name of the Bogleheads' members who suggested it. The response to the request for pearls of Wisdom was overwhelming, and there was not enough room to include them all.

PEARLS ON SAVING AND PLANNING

"Save 10% of everything you earn." *J Daniels*

"Get your spending in check before worrying about how much you can save." *psu9932*

"Pay yourself first." *VictoriaF*

"When deciding when to retire, only two numbers are significant: how much money you have, and how long you will live. The rest is easy." *a2z*

"Plan your future first; then create a financial plan to support it." *Peter Foley*

"If your plan seems too simple, you've probably got a good plan." *deepdrive*

"If you have saved just enough to retire, you probably cannot afford to retire. The market may go down." *Jsl11*

"A younger investor should be focused on their savings rate rather than high investment returns." *haban01*

"Saving and investing wisely is your route to freedom." *nvboglehead*

"A happy financial retirement is the result of many years of staying the course, but more importantly, being too busy to mess up a well-designed investment plan." *Speedbump101*

"It's what you keep, not what you earn. Focus on net worth." *Bulldawg*

"Don't view it as saving. Think of it as buying independence." *Trebor*

"Minimize taxes as far as practicable." *Below The Radar*

"A proper withdrawal strategy in retirement is as important, or more so, than is an investment strategy in accumulation because time is no longer your ally." *Joe Bob*

"Early on, focus on your savings rate instead of your rate of return." *snoopdoug 1*

"Sew the seed of a miracle—start a retirement account for your baby for many decades of compounding returns." *Tonen*

"There is no such thing as a perfect plan." *Chaz*

PEARLS ON INVESTING

"To new investors: Your risk tolerance is probably much lower than you think." *Haberd*

"No one would ever have crossed the ocean if he could have gotten off the ship in the storm." *wilson08*

"Don't invest in things you don't understand." *cisco*

"If you think you are smarter than the market, just remember: 'A fool who considers himself wise is indeed a fool.'" *NYCPete*

"Live actively, invest passively." *Derek Tinnin*

"A new twist on an old favorite; KISS: Keep investing simple, stupid." *salem*

"Buying into active management is buying into a dream that probably will not occur." *DA*

"Beware of little expenses. A small leak can sink a great ship." *VictoriaF*

"Your life should be interesting; your investments should be boring." *VictoriaF*

"If you wouldn't feel comfortable underperforming the market for years at a time, the only investment for you is a total market index fund." *deepdrive*

"Do you want to put your kids, or your broker's kids, through college?" *speedbump101*

"Keep the money you will need in the next 3–5 years out of the stock market." *HueyLD*

"Costs are the one thing you can control when investing." *Index Fan*

"Keep it simple. Minimize the time spent on investments. Maximize the time spent on more important things." *ramsfan*

"View your risk tolerance through the darkest possible lens because you will probably experience it in that light at some point during your lifetime." *mikem*

"When it comes to investing, never underestimate the majesty of simplicity." *MarkNYC*

"Stock holders are the last to get paid in a long line of people." *gms*

"Dividend checks don't bounce." *unclemick*

"Investing doesn't require a PhD if you keep it simple and keep your expenses low." *Sally*

"The easiest way to double your money is to fold it in half." *cisco*

"Don't take any more risk than you need to meet your goals." *haberd*

"The only way to underperform the market after costs is to deviate from it." *drbagel*

"Investing ain't rocket science—they just make it look like it is." *jeff mc*

"A simple set of low cost mutual funds is your best defense for a healthy retirement!" *Russ Nelson*

"The more complicated the investment, the better it is for the person selling it, and the worse it is for the investor buying it." *Dale Maley*

"As Benjamin Graham said: Never have less than 25% or more than 75% of your portfolio in stocks." *Anonymous*

"As Ted Aronson said: It takes between 20 and 800 years of monitoring performance to statistically prove that a money manager is skillful rather than lucky." *Anonymous*

"Disciplined rebalancing is emotionally difficult. That is why one must have a written plan in advance, and stick to it!" *Below The Radar*

"Lifecyle funds—it really can be that easy." *RJW*

"You can't buy yesterday's returns—they're gone forever." *Compounding*

"Timing the market is like sticking your head into an angry hive of bees. You might get some honey, but you'll most likely get stung." *Xyrus*

"There are two types of financial experts; those that are lucky and those that aren't." *Xyrus*

"The pathway to the 'heaven' of investing is lined with the advice of our mentor, Jack Bogle." *normsie*

"Invest in the stock market as opposed to betting on the stock market." *Kathleen Ryan*

"Negative years WILL happen, perhaps several in a row. Expect it!" *Below The Radar*

"Never change your long-term investment plan based on short-term results." *petrico*

"Time and low costs are your friends; high expenses and taxes are your enemies." *Joe Bob*

"If it takes more than a few minutes to explain your investment plan to someone, it's probably too complicated." *Roverdog*

"Make sure your retirement portfolio can withstand a worst case scenario." *JaneDoe*

"Look at predictions based on historical returns with skepticism. Extrapolation beyond the range of a data set is risky." *vb*

"Don't try to time the market." *Kathleen Ryan*

"As John Kenneth Galbraith said: The only function of economic forecasting is to make astrology look respectable." *RadAudit*

"If your portfolio decline is 50 percent, you will need a 100 percent gain to get back to even." *krumw*

"The consistently superior performer is the market itself." *Derek Tinnin*

"Invest your time actively and your money passively." *Michael LeBoeuf*

"There is no crystal ball, and you don't need one." *Derek Tinnin*

"Your objective is to develop a diversified SWAN—Sleep Well At Night—portfolio through asset allocation that allows you to maximize your combined returns while minimizing risk." *RTR 2006*

"The best-kept secret in the investing world is the fact that almost nothing turns out as expected." *Wshang*

"Investing is a plow horse, not a race horse. Don't treat investing as a competitive event." *pkcrafter*

"If an investment sounds too good to be true, run as fast as you can in the other direction." *gotherelate*

"Do not mistake simple index fund portfolios as simplistic. They are actually quite sophisticated—standing on the shoulders of decades of peer-reviewed market research, a few Nobel prizes, and undeniable evidence of success." *Sunny*

"If you don't have time to read a good book or two on investing, you will be better served by simply putting your money in CDs." *Bulldog Bond*

"Until you've experienced the trauma of a large stock market decline, subtract 10 percent from the equity allocation you think you are comfortable with." *happy2*

PEARLS ON LIFE

"Be quick to listen and slow to speak." *Ron*

"Success is living your life the way you want." *robert birchell*

"If we don't learn from past mistakes, we are doomed to repeat them." *Sheepdog*

"Don't give investment advice to friends and family. Give ideas only." *Sheepdog*

"If you fail to plan, you plan to fail." *bilperk*

"Being charitable can result in some of the greatest returns during one's lifetime." *Random Musings*

"As Germaine Greer said: You're only young once, but you can be immature forever." *Imbogled*

"This time it may or may not be different." *CABob*

"Don't treat the highly likely as certain, and the highly unlikely as impossible." *Larry Swedroe*

"As Steven Wright said: Experience is something you don't get until just after you need it." *Imbogled*

"Live within your means, save for a rainy day, and enjoy life because it will end sooner than you want." *YDNAL*

"The simpler the explanation, the more likely it is to be true." *grandpajack*

"The best investment is in yourself through health and education." *Ziggy 75*

"The improbable is possible." *Indexer 88*

"As Albert Einstein said: Everything should be made as simple as possible, but not simpler." *LadyGeek*

"Live well within your means, and live well your entire life." *TenS2XS*

"You work all your life to earn stacks and stacks. But you never saw a hearse with luggage racks." *sunofpaul*

"What the large print giveth, the fine print taketh away." *Derek Tinnin*

"As Anne Herbert said: Libraries will get you through times of no money better than money will get you through times of no libraries." *Nisiprius*

"As John Bogle said: With most things in life, you get what you pay for. With investing, you get what you don't pay for." *Morse Code*

"If it seems too good to be true—it probably is." *deepdrive*

"Torture numbers long enough and they'll confess to anything." *wilson08*

"Money is freedom." *johnjtaylorus*

FINALLY, A FEW *REALLY* GREAT PEARLS

"Read a few good books recommended by the Bogleheads and you'll know more about investing than 99 percent of the population—including many advisors." *Roverdog*

"A fool and his money are soon parted, so get some sage advice at the Bogle heads.org web site." *KarlJ*

Recommended Reading

FOR NOVICE INVESTORS

The Bogleheads' Guide to Investing by Taylor Larimore, Mel Lindauer, and Michael LeBoeuf (Hoboken, NJ: John Wiley & Sons, 2007). A textbook for beginners that reflects the wisdom of John Bogle.

The Little Book of Common Sense Investing by John C. Bogle (Hoboken, NJ: John Wiley & Sons, 2007). This is a short, delightful-to-read book. The legendary founder of index funds explains the many reasons he recommends simple portfolios and broad market index funds for most investors.

All About Index Funds and *All About Asset Allocation* by Richard Ferri (New York: McGraw-Hill). Two easy-to-read guidebooks for sound Boglehead investing.

The New Coffeehouse Investor by Bill Shultheis (New York: Penguin Group, 2009). A little book with a big message: How to invest simply and successfully.

The Informed Investor by Frank Armstrong III (New York: American Management Association, 2003). An easy-to-understand explanation of how the market works.

Making the Most of Your Money Now by Jane Bryant Quinn (New York: Simon & Schuster, 2009). This is a recently updated classic of practical financial planning advice for every family.

The Millionaire in You by Michael LeBoeuf (New York: Crown Business, 2002). A primer on how to invest money and time intelligently to achieve financial freedom.

Straight Talk on Investing by Jack Brennan, Vanguard's chairman (Hoboken, NJ: John Wiley & Sons, 2002). A book that is elegantly simple, eminently sensible, and delightfully readable.

You've Lost It. Now What? by Jonathan Clements (Hoboken, NJ: Portfolio, 2003). An award-winning former *Wall Street Journal* columnist gives straightforward advice for ordinary people to invest successfully.

FOR INTERMEDIATE INVESTORS

Common Sense on Mutual Funds by John Bogle (Hoboken, NJ: John Wiley & Sons, 1999). Warren Buffett called this book "a must read for every investor."

The Four Pillars of Investing by Bill Bernstein (New York: McGraw-Hill, 2002). A brilliant, small-town doctor became fascinated with investing. The result is one of the best books on the subject.

A Random Walk Down Wall Street by Burton G. Malkiel (New York: Norton, 2007). This book is an investment classic, regularly updated. Burton Malkiel is a professor at Princeton and a former member of the Vanguard board of directors.

Unconventional Success by David Swensen (New York: Free Press, 2005). Yale's chief investment officer shares his insight of how Wall Street fails individual investors, and he tells us how to outperform the vast majority of investors.

ADVANCED READING ON SPECIFIC TOPICS

Asset Allocation by Roger C. Gibson (New York: McGraw Hill, 2000). The original handbook on asset allocation and still one of the best on the subject.

The ETF Book by Richard A Ferri (Hoboken, NJ: John Wiley & Sons, 2008). A complete guide to understanding exchange-traded funds (ETFs) and other exchange-traded products.

The Intelligent Investor by Benjamin Graham, with commentary by Jason Zweig (New York: HarperCollins, 2003). A stock valuation course in a book, beautifully written, with updated commentary by one of America's most respected financial writers.

Capital Ideas by Peter L. Bernstein (Hoboken, NJ: John Wiley & Sons, 2005). The founder of the *Journal of Portfolio Management* gives a fascinating history of the financial revolution of the past 35 years.

The Only Guide to a Winning Bond Strategy by Larry Swedroe (New York: St. Martin's Press, 2006). A good explanation of bonds and bond funds, and how to use them in a portfolio.

Your Money and Your Brain by Jason Zweig (New York: Simon & Schuster, 2007). How the new science of neuroeconomics can help us become more successful investors.

Glossary

active management: An investment strategy that seeks to outperform the average returns of the financial markets. Active managers rely on research, market forecasts, and their own judgment and experience in selecting securities to buy and sell.

adjusted gross income: A tax term for all your income, including salary, interest, dividends, and retirement income. It is adjusted for Social Security, IRA contributions, and other items.

alternative minimum tax (AMT): A separate tax system designed to assure that wealthy individuals and organizations pay at least a minimum amount of federal income taxes.

annualize: To make a period of less than a year apply to a full year, usually for purposes of comparison. For instance, a portfolio turnover rate of 36 percent over a six-month period could be converted to an annualized rate of 72 percent.

annuitant: A person who receives the payments made by an annuity contract.

annuity: Literally, a series of annual payments. In investing and insurance, a contract with an insurer that provides payments for the annuitant at regular intervals, often monthly. Often short for life annuity or for variable annuity.

assets under management (AUM): A fee structure where the adviser receives an annual fee based on a percentage of the client's assets being managed.

automatic reinvestment: An arrangement by which the dividends or other earnings from an investment are used to buy additional shares in the investment vehicle.

baby-boomer generation: The demographic group of 78 million people born between 1946 and 1964.

back-end load: A sales fee charged by some mutual funds when an investor sells fund shares. Also called a contingent deferred sales charge.

behavioral finance: The study of how humans behave with respect to financial matters. The key assumption is that humans do not always behave in a perfectly rational fashion.

benchmark index: A passive market index that is used to measure a fund manager's performance.

beneficiary: At the time of your death, the person who receives the life insurance settlement or the remaining portion of a retirement account, such as an IRA.

Best, A. M.: One of five agencies (A. M. Best Company, Fitch Ratings, Moody's Investors Service, Standard & Poor's, and Weiss Research) that issue letter-grade ratings of insurers' financial strength.

broker/broker-dealer: An individual or firm that buys or sells mutual funds or other securities for the public.

capital gain/loss: The difference between the sale price of an asset—such as a mutual fund, stock, or bond—and the original cost of the asset.

capital gains distributions: Payments to mutual fund shareholders of gains realized during the year on securities that the fund has sold at a profit, minus any realized losses.

cash investments: Short-term debt instruments—such as commercial paper, banker's acceptances, and Treasury bills—that mature in less than one year. Also known as money market instruments or cash reserves.

certified financial planner (CFP): An investment professional who has passed exams administered by the CFP Board of Standards on subjects such as taxes, securities, insurance, and estate planning.

certified public accountant (CPA): An investment professional who is state licensed to practice public accounting.

charitable gift annuity: A contract under which a charity, in return for a donation, agrees to pay one or two individuals specified lifetime payments.

chartered financial analyst (CFA): An investment professional who has met competency standards in economics, securities, portfolio management, and financial accounting as determined by the Institute of Chartered Financial Analysts.

closed-end fund: A mutual fund that has a fixed number of shares, usually listed on a major stock exchange.

commission-based financial planning: The salesperson receives a commission from the customer for selling financial products.

commodities: Unprocessed goods such as grains, metals, and minerals traded in large amounts on a commodities exchange.

consumer price index (CPI): A measure of prices for consumer goods and services at a given time. The percentage change in CPI is used to track the pace of inflation.

cost basis: The original cost of an investment. For tax purposes, the cost basis is subtracted from the sales price to determine any capital gain or loss.

cost-of-living adjustment (COLA): An annual increase in benefit payments from Social Security or from some defined benefit pension plans, based on a predetermined formula, usually the percentage increase in CPI.

CPI-indexed annuity: A fixed annuity whose payments are contractually linked to the consumer price index (CPI); not to be confused with an equity-indexed annuity.

custodian: Either (a) a bank, agent, trust company, or other organization responsible for safeguarding financial assets or (b) the individual who oversees the mutual fund assets of a minor's custodial account.

default: Failure to pay principal or interest on debt when due.

deferred annuity: An annuity in which the payments begin at a scheduled time in the future after the annuity is purchased; for example, an annuity purchased at age 65 that makes its first payment at age 80. Not to be confused with a tax-deferred annuity; almost all annuities are tax-deferred.

defined benefit pension plan: A retirement plan that pays employees a lifelong annuity each month after they retire. The annuity may or may not have a cost of living adjustment (COLA).

defined contribution pension plan: A retirement plan in which the employee is responsible for making contributions to the plan and managing the investments in the plan. A lump sum is available to the employee at retirement.

delayed retirement credit: The percentage increase in a worker's Social Security retirement benefit if payments begin after full retirement age (FRA) equal to 8 percent times the number of years and months that benefits are delayed beyond FRA but not past age 70.

depreciation: A decrease in the value of an investment.

derivative: A financial contract whose value is based on, or derived from, a traditional security (such as a stock or bond), an asset (such as a commodity), or a market index (such as the S&P 500 Index). Options and futures are two examples of derivatives.

discount broker: A brokerage that executes orders to buy and sell securities at commission rates lower than a full-service brokerage.

distributions: Either (a) withdrawals made by the owner from an individual retirement account (IRA) or (b) payments of dividends and/or capital gains by a mutual fund.

dividend yield: The annual rate of return on a share of stock, determined by dividing the annual dividend by its current share price. In a stock mutual fund, this figure represents the average dividend yield of the stocks held by the fund.

dollar-cost averaging: Investing equal amounts of money at regular intervals on an ongoing basis. This technique ensures that an investor buys fewer shares when prices are high and more shares when prices are low.

early retirement: Retirement prior to age 62, when a person is eligible for Social Security benefits.

efficient market: The theory that stock prices reflect all market information that is known by all investors. Also states that investors cannot beat the market because it is impossible to determine future stock prices.

Employee Retirement Income Security Act of 1974 (ERISA): A federal law that sets requirements for pension plans in private industry.

equity-indexed annuity: An annuity in which the payments vary in a way that is linked to a stock market index such as the S&P 500. Typically, they have complex structures, high commissions, high annual expenses, and steep surrender charges. Promoted as investments that achieve some of the higher return of stocks but limit your losses.

estate planning: The preparation of a plan of administration and disposition of one's estate using a will, trusts, gifts, power of attorney, and so forth.

exchange-traded fund (ETF): An investment product similar to a mutual fund only it trades on a stock market during the day rather than with the mutual fund company at the end of the day. New ETF shares are created and redeemed during the day by the fund company through a special trading relationship with authorized participants.

ex-dividend date: The date when a distribution of dividends and/or capital gains is deducted from a mutual fund's assets or set aside for payment to shareholders. On the ex-dividend date, the fund's share price drops by the amount of the distribution (plus or minus any market activity).

executor: The person responsible for settling your estate when you die.

expense ratio: The percentage of a portfolio's average net assets used to pay its annual expenses. It includes management fees, administrative fees, and any 12b-1 fees, and it directly reduces returns to investors.

Federal Reserve: The central bank that regulates the supply of money and credit throughout the United States. Its seven-member board of governors, appointed by the president, has significant influence on U.S. monetary and economic policy.

fee-only adviser: An arrangement in which a financial adviser charges a set hourly rate or an agreed-upon percentage of assets under management for a financial plan. The adviser can also charge a flat annual fee or charge a set amount for a specific financial planning task.

fiduciary relationship: The relationship between a financial adviser and the client in which the adviser is legally obligated to do what is best for the client.

Fitch Ratings: One of five agencies (A. M. Best Company, Fitch Ratings, Moody's Investors Service, Standard & Poor's, and Weiss Research) that issue letter-grade ratings of insurers' financial strength.

fixed-income annuity: See SPIA.

Form ADV: Forms financial advisers must file with the SEC or state securities department that include fee structure and background about the adviser.

front-end load: A sales commission charged at the time of purchase by some mutual funds and other investment vehicles.

full faith and credit: A pledge to pay interest and principal on a bond issued by the government.

full retirement age: The age when you can receive unreduced Social Security retirement benefits, between 65 and 67, based on your year of birth.

fund family: A group of mutual funds sponsored by the same organization, often offering exchange privileges between funds and combined account statements for multiple funds.

government pension offset: The Social Security provision for reducing or eliminating a person's benefit as a spouse if that individual also earned a government pension from work that was not covered by Social Security.

gross domestic product (GDP): The value of all goods and services provided by U.S. labor in a given year. One of the primary measures of the U.S. economy, the GDP is issued quarterly by the Department of Commerce.

guaranteed period (also period certain, term certain): A specified period of time, such as 10 years, during which an annuity is guaranteed to make payments, if not to the annuitant, then to the annuitant's beneficiary or estate.

guaranty association: See state guaranty association.

health savings account (HSA): An account in which contributions are tax-deductible and withdrawals are tax-free if used for qualifying medical expenses. Contributions can be made only when the contributor is enrolled in a high-deductible health plan that meets IRS limits.

hedge: A strategy in which one investment is used to offset the risk of another security.

immediate annuity (immediate income annuity): An annuity in which the payments begin as soon as the premium has been received and processed, for example, an annuity purchased in January 2010 that makes its first payment in February 2010.

income annuity: See SPIA.

index fund: An investment fund that attempts to match the performance of a market index such as the Standard & Poor's 500-Stock Index.

index provider: Companies that construct and maintain financial market indexes.

indexing: Indexing is an investment strategy to match the average performance of a market or group of stocks. Usually this is accomplished by buying a small amount of each stock in a market.

individual retirement account (IRA): A tax-advantaged account in which contributions are made with the intent of withdrawing funds upon retirement.

inflation-indexed annuity: A fixed annuity whose payments are contractually linked to the consumer price index (CPI); not to be confused with equity-indexed annuity.

inflation risk: The possibility that increases in the cost of living will reduce or eliminate the returns on a particular investment.

interest rate risk: The possibility that a security or mutual fund will decline in value because of an increase in interest rates.

investment adviser: A person or organization that makes the day-to-day decisions regarding a portfolio's investments. Also called an investment manager or portfolio manager.

investment policy statement (IPS): A written statement describing an investor's goals and preferences.

joint annuitant: A second person, usually the annuitant's life partner, who serves as one of the measuring lives in a joint annuity; payments continue for as long as either annuitant lives.

joint annuity: An annuity that pays out as long as either of two annuitants lives.

life annuity: An annuity in which the payments continue for the lifetime of the annuitant or for the lives of either of two joint annuitants.

life cycle fund: A fund that decreases its equity allocation over time based on a glide path, with a target date on which it will have become sufficiently conservative for an investor who starts withdrawals on or about that date. Also called a target date fund.

life expectancy: The average remaining years of life at a given age, based on a certain mortality table or experience study.

lifetime payout income annuity (LPIA): See SPIA.

limited partnership: An investment with a small number of general partners and a large number of limited partners. The maximum risk to a limited partner is the loss of the initial investment.

living trust: A living trust allows assets to pass directly to heirs without going through the probate process. Assets in a living trust are subject to estate tax.

load fund: A mutual fund that levies a sales charge when shares are either bought (a front-end load) or sold (a back-end load).

long-term capital gain: A profit on the sale of a security or mutual fund share that has been held for more than one year.

long-term care insurance: This type of health insurance picks up costs that traditional health insurance and Medicare do not, such as an extended stay in a nursing home and home care assistance.

management fee: The amount a mutual fund pays to its investment adviser for the work of overseeing the fund's holdings. Also called an advisory fee.

marginal tax rate: The rate at which each additional dollar of taxable income is taxed. Also referred to as the tax bracket.

market capitalization: A determination of a company's value, calculated by multiplying the total number of company stock shares outstanding by the price per share. Also called capitalization.

market risk: The possibility that an investment will decline in value because the entire investment market (usually the stock market) declines.

maturity/maturity date: The date when the issuer of a money market instrument or bond agrees to repay the principal, or face value, to the buyer.

Medicaid: Government health insurance that provides free coverage for low-income people of any age.

medical underwriting (of an annuity): A lower premium granted in exchange for evidence that the annuitant has a serious life-shortening medical condition.

Medicare: Government health insurance program for people age 65 and older at little to no cost. It does not include prescription drugs or routine doctor visits.

medigap insurance: This is a supplemental insurance policy that fills the gap between the health care that people need and the services not covered by Medicare.

Monte Carlo analysis (or simulation): A mathematical model that predicts the future based on the historical variation in past asset class returns.

Moody's Investors Service: One of five agencies (A. M. Best Company, Fitch Ratings, Moody's Investors Service, Standard & Poor's, and Weiss Research) that issue letter-grade ratings of insurers' financial strength.

mortality credit: The amount by which an annuity payout exceeds the prevailing interest rate, made possible by contributions of unspent premiums from shorter-lived annuitants.

net asset value (NAV): The market value of a mutual fund's total assets, minus liabilities, divided by the number of shares outstanding. The value of a single share is called its share value or share price.

no-load fund: A mutual fund that charges no sales commission or load.

nominal return: The return on an investment before adjustment for inflation.

nonqualified annuity: An annuity purchased by ordinary posttax dollars, whose payouts are treated partially as taxable investment earnings and partially as untaxed return of principal.

OASDI: The federal Old-Age, Survivors, and Disability insurance program, commonly called Social Security.

open-end fund: An investment entity that has the ability to issue or redeem the number of shares outstanding on a daily basis. Prices are quoted once a day, at the end of the day, at the net asset value of the fund (NAV).

operating expenses: The amount paid for asset maintenance or the cost of doing business. Earnings are distributed after operating expenses are deducted.

option: A contract in which a seller gives a buyer the right, but not the obligation, to buy or sell securities at a specified price on or before a given date.

period certain (also guaranteed period, term certain): A specified period of time, such as 10 years, during which an annuity is guaranteed to make payments, if not to the annuitant, then to the annuitant's beneficiary or estate.

portfolio transaction costs: The expenses associated with buying and selling securities, including commissions, purchase and redemption fees, exchange fees, and other miscellaneous costs. In a mutual fund prospectus, these expenses are listed separately from the fund's expense ratio. Does not include the bid/ask spread.

power of attorney: A written, legally binding document that gives another person the right to make financial or health-care-related decisions on your behalf.

premium: An amount that exceeds the face value or redemption value of a security or of a comparable security or group of investments. It may indicate that a security is favored highly by investors. Also refers to a fee for obtaining insurance coverage.

premium refund: A feature of an annuity that guarantees that the number of dollars paid in the premium will be paid out, if not to the annuitant, then to the annuitant's beneficiary or estate.

primary insurance amount (PIA): The monthly retirement benefit from Social Security for a worker whose benefit begins at full retirement age. The benefit for a worker in other circumstances or for a family member is a percentage of the worker's PIA.

prospectus: A legal document that gives prospective investors information about a mutual fund, including discussions of its investment objectives and policies, risks, costs, and past performance.

purchase fee: A fee charged by some mutual funds when an investor purchases shares in order to compensate current fund holders for the costs of purchasing illiquid securities. Unlike a front-end load, the fee is paid into the fund rather than to the fund company.

qualified annuity: An annuity purchased by direct transfer of qualified funds from an IRA, 401(k), or similar plan, and whose payouts are treated as taxable distributions.

real estate investment trust (REIT): A company that manages a group of real estate investments and distributes to its shareholders at least 90 percent of its net earnings annually.

real return: The actual return received on an investment after discounting inflation.

realized capital gain/loss: An increase (or decrease) in the value of a security that has become real because the security was sold. A realized gain is taxable to the shareholder during the tax year in which the security was sold; a realized loss is subtracted from realized gains in determining the taxable gains.

record date: The date used to determine who is eligible to receive a company's or fund's next distribution of dividends or capital gains.

redemption: The return of an investor's principal in a security. Bond redemption can occur at or before maturity; mutual fund shares are redeemed at net asset value when an investor's holdings are liquidated.

redemption fee: A fee charged by some mutual funds when an investor sells shares within a short period of time. Unlike a back-end load, it is paid to the fund itself.

registered investment advisor (RIA): An investment professional who is registered—but not endorsed—by the Securities and Exchange Commission (SEC).

reinvest date: See ex-dividend date.

reinvestment: Use of investment income to buy additional securities. Many mutual fund companies and investment services offer the automatic reinvestment of dividends and capital gains distributions as an option to investors.

required minimum distribution (RMD): The minimum amount the IRS mandates that you withdraw from IRA accounts and other tax-deferred retirement funds once you reach age 70½.

required rate of return: The minimum return needed on an investment portfolio to achieve a financial goal within a stated amount of time.

retirement earnings test: The Social Security formula for reducing or eliminating the benefit payable if the beneficiary is below full retirement age and is earning more than a certain amount from employment.

reverse mortgage: A contract with a lending institution that gives a homeowner retirement income by borrowing against the equity in the home, with no repayment needed while the individual is living in the home.

risk tolerance: An investor's ability or willingness to endure declines in the prices of investments while waiting for them to increase in value.

rollover: At retirement or end of service, an employee may roll his or her portion of a pension account into an IRA account without paying current income taxes or penalties.

Roth IRA: An individual retirement account that is funded with after-tax dollars and grows tax-free until money is withdrawn tax-free after age 59½.

safe withdrawal rate (SWR): The annual rate at which people can withdraw funds and not be expected to run out of money.

Securities and Exchange Commission (SEC): The agency of the federal government that regulates mutual funds, registered investment advisers, the stock and bond markets, and broker-dealers.

SEP-IRA: A retirement plan used by small businesses and sole proprietors to shelter income from taxes.

short-term capital gain: A profit on the sale of a security or mutual fund share that has been held for one year or less. A short-term capital gain is taxed as ordinary income.

SIMPLE IRA: A retirement plan used by some small companies but now rarely by sole proprietors.

single-premium immediate annuity (SPIA): See SPIA.

solo 401(k): A retirement plan used by sole proprietors. Also available as a Roth solo 401(k).

SPIA (single-premium immediate annuity): Customarily, a fixed annuity that pays out for the life of the annuitant or annuitants. Also known as an immediate income annuity, income annuity, fixed annuity, and lifetime payout immediate annuity.

spread: For stocks and bonds, the difference between the bid price and the asked price.

Standard and Poor's (S&P): One of five agencies (A. M. Best Company, Fitch Ratings, Moody's Investors Service, Standard & Poor's, and Weiss Research) that issue letter-grade ratings of insurers' financial strength.

standard deviation (σ): A measure of the degree to which a fund's return varies from its previous returns or from the average of all similar funds. The larger the standard deviation, the greater the likelihood (and risk) that a security's performance will fluctuate from the average return.

state guaranty association: A consortium of insurance companies, organized and regulated by state law, that protects policyholders if their insurance company becomes insolvent.

substantially equal periodic payments (SEPP): An IRS-established program that allows withdrawals from IRAs penalty-free, starting at any age.

survivor rights: When you die, your spouse continues to receive a portion of your pension. This right can be waived if both parties agree.

target date fund: See life cycle fund.

taxable account: An account subject to ordinary income tax each year. Includes personal, joint, trust, and custodial accounts.

taxable equivalent yield: The return from a higher-paying but taxable investment that would equal the return from a tax-free investment. It depends on the investor's tax bracket.

tax-advantaged account: Investment accounts that are either deferred from taxes until assets are withdrawn or free from any taxation upon normal withdrawal.

tax bracket: IRS tax tables that state the level of tax you must pay on the next dollar earned based on your total taxable income.

tax credit: A tax benefit that reduces your taxes by a fixed amount.

tax-deferred account: An account that delays the payment of income taxes on investment gains until the money is withdrawn.

tax-exempt bond: A bond issued by municipal, county, or state governments, whose interest payments are not subject to federal and, in some cases, state and local income tax.

tax-free account: All interest, dividends, and capital gains earned in a tax-free account are not subject to income tax now or in the future. An example is a Roth IRA.

tax-loss harvesting: Selling a security that has declined in value in order to deduct the capital loss from taxable income, but with the intention of remaining invested. The investor could either buy back the same security after 31 days to avoid a wash sale or buy a similar security immediately.

tax swapping: Creating a tax loss by the simultaneous sale of one fund and purchase of a similar fund; one method of tax-loss harvesting.

term certain (also guaranteed period, period certain): A specified period of time, such as 10 years, during which an annuity is guaranteed to make payments, if not to the annuitant, then to the annuitant's beneficiary or estate.

thrift savings plan (TSP): The defined-contribution plan offered to employees of the U.S. government, both civilian and military.

total return: A percentage change, over a specified period, in a mutual fund's net asset value, with the ending net asset value adjusted to account for the reinvestment of all distributions of dividends and capital gains.

traditional IRA: An individual retirement account (IRA) in which the earnings and pretax contributions are taxable when withdrawn after age 59½. Contributions can be deductible (pretax) or nondeductible (after-tax).

transaction fee (also known as a commission): A charge assessed by an intermediary, such as a broker-dealer or bank, for assisting in the sale or purchase of a security.

Treasury inflation-protected security (TIPS): A U.S. government debt obligation whose payments of principal and interest increase over time in proportion to the rate of inflation, based on the consumer price index.

Treasury security: A negotiable debt obligation issued by the U.S. government for a specific amount and maturity. Treasury securities include bills (one year or less), notes (1 to 10 years), and bonds (more than 10 years).

trust: Special term used to describe a wide range of vehicles used to own property. They are used when a person wants to put restrictions or controls on property during and after death. Trusts do not save you money on income taxes but can reduce estate taxes.

turnover rate: The amount of trading activity in a portfolio or mutual fund expressed as a percentage.

unit investment trust (UIT): An SEC-registered investment company that purchases a fixed, unmanaged portfolio of income-producing securities and then sells shares in the trust to investors, usually in units of at least $1,000. Usually sold by an intermediary such as a broker.

unrealized capital gain/loss: An increase (or decrease) in the value of a security that is not real because the security has not been sold. Once a security is sold by the portfolio manager, the capital gains/losses are realized by the fund, and any payment to the shareholder is taxable during the tax year in which the security was sold.

variable annuity (VA): An annuity whose payment is not a dollar value set in advance by contract but is linked to the performance of an underlying investment, often a stock portfolio.

volatility: The degree of fluctuation in the value of a security, mutual fund, or index, often expressed as a mathematical measure such as a standard deviation or beta. The greater the volatility, the wider the fluctuation between high and low prices.

wash sale rule: The IRS regulation that prohibits a taxpayer from claiming a loss on the sale of an investment if that investment, or a substantially identical investment, is purchased within 30 days before or after the sale.

Weiss Research: One of five agencies (A. M. Best Company, Fitch Ratings, Moody's Investors Service, Standard & Poor's, and Weiss Research) that issue letter-grade ratings of insurers' financial strength.

will: Basic estate planning document that controls the distribution of assets when you die and names an executor of your estate.

windfall elimination provision: The Social Security provision for reducing a person's benefit as a retired worker if that individual also earned a government pension from work that was not covered by Social Security.

yield to maturity: The rate of return an investor would receive if the securities held by a portfolio were held to their maturity dates.

About the Editors

Taylor Larimore (Miami, FL), CCL, has been dubbed by *Money* magazine as "the Dean of the Vanguard Diehards," and John (Jack) Bogle himself calls Taylor "The King of the Bogleheads." Now 86 and retired, he is a Boglehead to the core. He regularly spends hours per day answering questions for free on the bogleheads.org forum and, in doing so, regularly preaches the investment religion of Saint Jack. In his mind, his wealth is a direct result of following the time-tested investment wisdom of Bogle, the founder and retired chairman of the Vanguard Group. A graduate of the University of Miami's School of Business Administration, Taylor served as a World War II paratrooper in the 101st Airborne Division during the Battle of the Bulge, earning five combat decorations. An avid sailing enthusiast, Taylor was named the American Sailing Association's Instructor of the Year. Throughout his career, Taylor worked as a life insurance underwriter, revenue officer for the Internal Revenue Service, chief of the financial division for the Small Business Administration in South Florida, and a director of the Dade County Housing Authority. In 1986 Taylor became inspired when reading about the life and teachings of Jack Bogle. Combining his financial experience with Mr. Bogle's research and advice,

Taylor and his wife, Pat, saw their portfolio improve dramatically. Taylor now spends his time sailing and helping others discover the Boglehead way on the Bogleheads forum.

Mel Lindauer, CFS, WMS (Daytona Beach Shores, FL) was dubbed "The Prince of the Bogleheads" by Jack Bogle. An author and Forbes columnist, he's one of the leaders of the bogleheads.org forums where he has contributed nearly 27,000 posts, helping investors learn the Boglehead way to invest. A former Marine, he started investing in the late 1960s and has firsthand experience with both bull and bear markets. Together with Taylor, he initiated and continues to organize the grassroots Diehards' annual meetings. He's been quoted in a number of newspapers and magazines and has appeared on CNN-fn. Retired since 1997, he was founder and former CEO of a successful graphic arts company in the Philadelphia area for 30 years. Since retirement, he has earned credentials as a Certified Fund Specialist from the Institute of Business and Finance and as a Wealth Management Specialist from Kaplan College. He also holds commercial pilot and flight instructor licenses, and was commissioned a Kentucky Colonel by the Governor of his former home state of Kentucky.

Richard Ferri, CFA (Troy, MI) is a key member of the growing Bogleheads braintrust and the founder and CEO of the investment firm Portfolio Solutions, LLC. Rick, as he likes to be called, is a frequent writer for Forbes magazine. He worked at two major Wall Street firms for 10 years before starting Portfolio Solutions in 1999. His company manages close to $1 billion in separate accounts for individual investors utilizing low-cost ETFs and index funds in prudent asset allocation strategies. Rick earned a bachelor of science degree in business administration from the University of Rhode Island and a master of science degree in finance from Walsh College. He also holds the designation of Chartered Financial Analyst (CFA) from the CFA Institute in Charlottesville, Virginia. Rick is the author of five books on low-fee investing, including *The ETF Book: All You Need to Know about Exchange-Traded Funds, All About Index Funds*, and *All About Asset Allocation*. Rick was a fighter pilot in the United States Marine Corps prior to joining the investment industry in 1988, and is retired from the Marine Corps Reserves.

Laura F. Dogu is a Forbes columnist and a longtime poster on the Bogleheads forum. She participated as an investment panelist during the last three Diehard national meetings. With more than 54,000 posts, she was named "The Queen of the Bogleheads" in recognition of her efforts researching topics for the many Diehards who need assistance. Focusing on helping new investors develop a low-cost, tax-efficient, broadly diversified portfolio, she wrote the main investment planning post for new members and also developed the structure used by new posters requesting a portfolio review. In addition to her many contributions to the Bogleheads community, Laura is a career Foreign Service Officer with the Department of State, which she joined in 1991. Prior to joining the Department of State she worked for IBM for five years. Dogu earned a bachelor of business administration, a bachelor of arts, and a masters of business administration from Southern Methodist University. She also earned a Masters of Science in National Resource Strategy from the Industrial College of the Armed Forces, National Defense University.

Index

AARP, 4, 14, 16, 175
AB Disclaimer trust, 36
Account management, 86–88
Account ownership designations, 262
Account statements, 127
Actively traded funds, 40, 87
Activities of daily living (ADLs), 249, 251
Actuaries, 70
Adjusted basis, 26–27
Adjusted gross income (AGI), 56, 60, 156–157, 160, 251
Administrators, selection process, 264–265
Adult daycare, 248, 251
ADV Part II, 298
Advance directives/living wills (AD/LW), 270, 272
Advisers, listing of, 266. *See also* Professional advice
After-tax savings, 35, 162
Age-based profit-sharing plan, 85
Aggressive investments, 139, 145
Aging process, 240
AIG Life Insurance, 110

Air traffic controllers, government retirement plans, 71–72
Alaska Natives, health care programs, 246
Alimony, 24
Alternative minimum tax (AMT), 28
A.M. Best Company, 110–112, 235
American Council on Gift Annuities (ACGA), 103, 114
American Dream Savings Accounts, 51. *See also* Roth IRAs
American Indians, health care programs, 246
American International Group (AIG), 98, 108, 110
Annual gift tax exclusion, 280
Annual income, shortfall in, 11–12, 195–196
Annual reports, 127
Annual reviews, 15
Annuitants, 92, 94, 101, 104
Annuities, 66–69, 82–83, 92, 94–102, 106, 108–112, 163–164, 206, 209, 228, 260, 309
Annuitization, 96–97, 105–108, 209, 212, 217
Annulments, 262–263
Antenuptial agreements, 307–309
Art collections, 25, 256

Asset allocation, 8–9, 15, 143–146, 149, 205
Asset classes, 120–122, 124–126, 148
Asset list, estate planning, 265–266
Asset protection strategies
  estate planning, 255–280
  gift taxes, 280–282
  health insurance, 239–254
  importance of, 221
  income replacement, insurance, 221–237
Assets, generally
  noninvestment, 148–149
  under management (AUM) fee model,
    293–295
Assets subject to probate, 260–261
Assisted living, 208, 248–249, 251
Association group term life insurance, 223
Attorney, advice from, 36, 113, 261, 273, 277,
    279
Automatic investing, 138–140, 149
Automobiles, 10, 12, 14, 30, 312
Auton, Larry, 319–320
Average life expectancy, 92, 95
Average returns, 12
Averson, Ralph, 321

Baby boomer generation, 4–5, 178, 225, 289
Back-end loads, 128
Bait and switch, 298
Balanced portfolio, 131
Bank accounts, interest from, 24. *See also* Savings
    account
Bankruptcy, 12, 16, 79, 86, 309–311, 313–314
Banks/banking industry, 43, 233
Barclays Capital Aggregate Bond Index, 87
Barnitz, Barry, 320
Basis, 26, 36, 40, 276, 279–280
Bear markets, 124, 133, 141–143, 294
Behavioral finance, 288
Beneficiary/beneficiaries, 100, 194–195, 226,
    228–229, 258, 260, 263–264, 269,
    279–280, 305
Benz, Christine, 326
Bequests, 106, 278
Berkshire Hathaway, BRK Direct, 97
Bernstein, Bill, 321, 324–326
Bid/ask spreads, 39
Blend stocks, 121
Blue chip stocks, 121
Blue-collar workers, disability insurance, 233
Bogle, John Clifton
  awards and recognitions, 317–318, 323
  Boglehead reunions, 321–326
  books written by, 318
  childhood, 315
  educational background, 315
  family, 318

  as philanthropist, 326
  professional development, 143, 295, 315–316
  speaking engagements, 322–324
  Vanguard funds, 317
Bogle Financial Markets Research Center, 317
Bogleheads
  books, 320–321
  characterized, 318–319
  Guide series, 315
  local chapters of, 321
  mission, 326
  online forums, 319–320
  reunions, 321–327
  Wiki, 60, 88, 185, 315, 320
Bogleheads' Guide to Investing, The (Larimore
    et al.), 222, 287, 318–322
Bogleheads Internet forum, 299
Bogleheads Wiki, 60, 88, 185, 315, 320
Bogleheads.org, 318–319, 321, 326
"Bogle's Folly," 317
Bond allocation, 42
Bond funds, 41, 87, 121, 130, 139, 141,
    146–148, 194, 197
Bonds/bond investments, 8–9, 14, 23, 25,
    41–42, 48, 121, 123
Bottoms, Dale, 325
Bridging income, strategies for, 209–212, 216
Brokerage accounts, 129–130, 266
Brokerage firms, 4, 36, 129–130, 291, 299
Brokers, fee structure, 290. *See also*
    Commission sales
Budgeting, 6, 12–14, 19, 92, 188–190, 195,
    198–199, 208
Bull markets, 124, 133
Bush, George W., 274
Business, generally
  buy-sell agreements, 230, 270–271
  income/loss, 24, 52
  insurance, 230
  succession plan, 271
  transition of ownership, 271
Buying high, selling low, 133
Buying the distribution, avoidance
    of, 25
Buy-sell agreements, 230, 270–271

Calculators, types of, 12–16, 184–185, 195,
    207, 216
California Public Employees' Retirement System
    (CalPERS), 72–73
Canada, 41
Capital gains, 26–27, 35–36, 128, 130, 147,
    194, 280. *See also* Capital gains tax
Capital gains tax, 18, 21, 25–27, 36, 49, 162,
    211, 279
Capital improvements, 27

Capital loss, 25–26, 36
Carey, Art, 326
Carlson, Peter, 184
Carryforwards, 26, 36
Carryover, 26
Cash, 38, 42, 121, 123, 132, 224–225
Cash balance plan, 64–65, 69
Cash-equivalent securities, 42
Cash flow, 154, 207
Casualty, 27
Catch-up contributions, 49–50, 59, 247
Certificates of deposit (CDs), 8, 24, 42, 44–45,
    48, 121, 157
Certified financial planner (CFP), 288,
    296–297, 300
Certified public accountants (CPAs), 230
Cestui que trust, 268
ChampVa, 246
Charitable donations, 30
Charitable gift annuities (CGAs), 102–105, 114
Charitable remainder trusts, 269, 310
Chartered Financial Analyst (CFA), 297
Chartered Life Underwriter (CLU), 230, 236
Chatzky, Jean, 13
Checking accounts, 43
Child-care expenses, 226
Children
    custodial Roth IRAs, 6
    early retirement and, 207–208
    education expenses, 14, 208
    financial aid for, 209
    life insurance needs for, 223, 226–227
    Medicaid coverage, 246
    personal exemption for, 29
    Social Security benefits for, 170
Child support, 308, 311
Child tax credit, 157–158
Churning, 40
Civil Service Retirement System (CSRS), 71, 83
Cliff vesting schedule, 66
Closely held corporations, 229
Closing costs, 27
COBRA, 243–244
Coin collections, 25
Co-insurance, 240
Collectibles, tax treatment of, 25, 27
College tuition, 14, 156, 208–209, 280
Colleges and universities, gifts to, 102
Commission/commission sales, 39, 45, 60,
    128–130, 289–290
Commissioner's Standard Ordinary 2001
    Mortality Table, 96
Commission-free transactions, 130
Common law marriage, 171
Common Sense on Mutual Funds (Bogle), 321
Community property, 257–258

Community service, 5
Compensation, 50, 74
Complex products, 298–299
Compounding, 6–7, 12–13, 139, 141, 160, 192,
    212, 292
Computer software applications, 104, 176,
    198–199, 227
Condominums, 257
Conflicts of interest, 297, 299
Conservative investing/investors, 9, 16, 124,
    132, 139
Consumer Price Index (CPI), 67, 100, 172, 234
Contingencies, defined benefit plans, 68
Contingency planning, 16
Continuing care retirement communities
    (CCRCs), 249
Conversation Tracker, 319
Cooley, Philip L., 131
Coordinated care, 249
Coordination of benefits, 240–241
Copayments, 240, 245
Corporate bonds, 121, 147
Cost basis, 39
Cost control, 127–130, 134
Cost-of-living adjustment (COLA), 67, 71–72,
    80, 148, 171, 234
Cost reduction strategies, 14–15
Cox, Gail, 326
CPI-indexed annuities, 100–101
Credit, avoidance of, 6
Credit card debt, 13–14, 152, 154, 312–313
Credit counselors, 314
Creditors, 261, 264, 311–313
Custodial care, 249

Daily expenses, 14, 162
Damato, Karen, 324
Day-to-day operations, 127, 136, 178
Death
    of annuitant, 98–99
    of beneficiary, 305
    defined benefit plans, 74
    estate planning (see Estate planning)
    of family member, 16
    IRA withdrawals, 50
    joint tenancy with right of survivorship, 36
    managed payout funds, 114
Debt
    credit cards, 13–14, 152, 154, 312–313
    gross estate and, 278
    paying off, 152, 154
    prioritizing, 311, 313
Declining markets, 140, 142–143, 193
Deductibles, medical insurance, 241
Deferred compensation plans, 12
Deferred taxes, 36

Defined benefit (DB) employer retirement
    account
  advantages of, 61, 93
  annual benefit statements, 74
  benefit determination, 63–64
  benefits handbook, 73–74
  components of, 62, 73–74, 309
  contingencies, 68
  contribution limitations, 89
  defined, 62
  distributions, 190
  funding, 64–65, 69
  information resources, 63, 69, 71, 74–75
  investment risks, 65
  management of, 65
  mechanics of, 62–69
  minimum required funding, 65
  pension guarantees, 68–69
  private-sector plans, 62, 69–70
  public-sector plans, 62, 70–73
  receiving benefits, 66–67
  regulation of, 62–63, 65, 70, 73
  target benefit plans, 85–86
  types of, 64
  valuation of, 305
  vesting, 65–66
Defined contribution (DC) plans
  account management, 86–88
  benefits of, 77, 89
  defined benefit plan compared with,
    85–86, 89
  distributions, 190
  features of, 52, 61–62, 228, 288, 309
  information resources, 88
  rollovers, 89
  self-funded, 6
  types of, 78–86
  valuation, 305
Dell Computer (DELL), 38
Dental expenses, 28
Dependents, early retirement plans and, 208.
    See also Children
Designation of health-care surrogate (DHCS), 270
Die-broke strategy, 95
Dining out expenses, 10, 13
Disability
  defined, 233
  in defined benefit plans, 68
  financial impact of, 50, 170, 213–214
  Social Security requirements, 213–214
Disability income (DI) insurance, 231–236
Disclaimers, in wills, 267
Discretionary expenses, 18
Distributions, 25, 93, 190, 224. See also
    Required minimum distribution (RMD);
    Withdrawal rate

Diversification, 6, 8–9, 41, 86, 119–124,
    145, 151
Dividends, 24–25, 39, 93, 128, 194,
    206–207, 224
Divorce, 16, 68, 74, 226, 262–263,
    304–309, 314
Documentation, in estate planning, 263,
    265–271
Dogu, Laura, 321, 325–326
Dollar-cost averaging (DCA), 6–8, 106,
    140–141
Donor, gift taxes, 276
Down markets, 8, 12, 16–18
Downsizing, benefits of, 12, 14, 192
Durable power of attorney, 264, 269–270, 272
Dynasty trusts, 281–282

Early retirement
  ages to consider, 203–204
  bridging income, 209–212, 216
  budgeting for, 208
  case illustrations, 203
  defined, 202
  delaying, benefits of, 204
  disability, 213–214
  education expenses, 208–209
  employment status, 201–202, 206, 214–216
  family relationships, 207–208
  first year of, 208
  flexibility and, 216
  health care costs, 204–205
  household expenses, 205, 215
  income needs, 204–205, 215–216
  information resources, 216
  involuntary, 213
  psychological aspects, 206, 212–213, 215–216
  safe withdrawal rate (SWR), 205–207
  success factors, 211–212
  travel, 205
  unemployment, 212
  unretiring, 214–216
  windfalls, 202, 212
Earned income, 6, 24, 210
Economies of scale, 43
Education expenses, 50, 209, 226, 280
Education loans, 14
Efficient frontier, 122–123
Elderly population, 208, 246, 250, 252
Elimination period, 233–234
Elm Annuity Group, 100
Emergency funds, 42, 44–45, 205, 226
Emergency health care, 246–247
Emergency savings, 16
Emerging markets, 121, 147
Emotional investments, 133, 139
Employee Benefit Research Institute, 17, 62, 75

Employee benefits, 28, 80–81, 88
Employee Retirement Income Security Act
   of 1974 (ERISA), 62–63, 65, 70, 73,
   309–310, 313
Employee stock ownership plan (ESOP), 86, 89
Employer-provided benefits, 6, 12, 28, 79–80,
   84–85, 98, 139, 152–153, 203, 223, 232,
   243–244
Employment status, 5, 12, 16, 171–174, 187,
   201–202, 206, 215
Enhanced life estate, 258
Enron, 86, 119
Entertainment costs/expenses, 10, 13, 215
Equities, tax-efficient, 42
Equity asset class, 120
Equity funds, 40, 45, 87
Equity-indexed annuities, 92, 290–291
Equity investing, 8–9, 140, 143, 225
Equity to maximum loss, 142
Estate life insurance, 229–230
Estate planning
   administrators, selection process, 264–265
   annuities, 92, 94–95, 100, 191
   beneficiary designation, 264
   defined, 255
   divorce and, 262–263
   documentation requirements, 265–271
   fiduciaries, selection process, 264–265
   goals of, 255
   importance of, 11–12, 57
   information resources, 271–272
   life estates, 258
   marriage, 262–263
   Medicaid and, 113
   ownership, types of, 257–258
   permanent life insurance, 224
   prenuptial/postnuptial agreements, 263
   probate, 260–262
   property titling, 256–257
   property transfer at death, 258–260
   remarriage, 263
   trustees, selection process, 264–265
Estate settlement costs, 229
Estate tax, 274–279, 282
Everson, Mark W., 21
Exchange-traded funds (ETFs), 39–40, 87–88,
   129, 148
Ex-dividend date, 24
Executor, 261, 266
Exemption, generally
   laws, 310
   state taxes, 29
Exercise price, 28
Expected returns, 124, 143
Expense ratio, 40, 81, 127, 129,
   132, 289

Expert witnesses, 305
EZ-Quote (Berkshire Hathaway), 114

Fair market value, 280
Fama, Eugene, 288
Family caregivers, 250
Family-owned businesses, 16
Family relationships, 207–208
FDIC, 43–45, 109
Federal deficit, 178
Federal Employees Retirement System (FERS),
   71–72, 83
Federal government defined benefit plans, 70–72
Federal taxes, 22–29, 229
Fee-only financial planners, 292
Ferri, Richard, 321, 324–326
Fidelity, 53–54, 87
Fiduciary/fiduciaries, 63, 65, 262, 264–265,
   289, 298
Financial advisers
   designations, 296–297
   ethics, 298
   fee structures, 289–296, 299
   functions of, 67, 132, 285–286
   hourly bills, 294
   money manager distinguished from, 287, 300
   qualifications, 298
   on risk, 299
   selection factors, 297–300
   types of, 285, 301
Financial disaster
   bankruptcy, 313
   creditor's rights, 309–310
   financial advice, sources of, 313–314
   information resources, 314
   IRA plans, 309–310, 314
   prioritizing debt, 311, 313
   savings accounts, 310
   trust accounts, 310
   withdrawals from retirement plans, 310–311
Financial goals, 5
Financial habits, 6
Financial Industry Regulatory Authority
   (FINRA), 291
Financial markets, impact of, 8, 16–18
Financial plan, 9, 19
Financial planners, functions of, 11–12, 230
Financial planning, 11–12, 287–289
FIRECalc, 207, 216
Firefighters, government retirement plans, 71–72
First Investors Trust, 317
Fitch Ratings, 110–111, 235
Fixed immediate annuities, 92
Fixed-income investments, 8, 207
Flat-fee advisers, 295
Flat tax philosophy, 29

Flexible spending account (FSA), 56
Forbes, Malcolm, 274
Forecasting, 198
Foreclosure, 312
Foreign estate taxes, 278
Foreign tax credit, 40
Fortman, Joe, 326
Four-in-One fund, 87
401(k) plans
    annuities in, 164
    automatic, 80–82
    borrowing from, 52–53
    bridging income, 211
    characterized, 64–65, 217, 288
    conservative investments, 132
    contribution limits, 78–79, 82
    contributions to, 89, 139–140, 152
    employer matched contributions, 89, 152
    features of, 6, 8, 15, 42, 48, 80–81, 98
    fees, 81–84, 88, 162
    fiduciary responsibility, 79
    information resources, 82
    international funds in, 40
    life cycle funds in, 145–146
    limitations of, 81, 162
    loans from, 81
    management of, 78–79, 86
    matched contributions, 79–80, 139
    opting out, 81
    rebalancing considerations, 126–127
    rollovers, 80, 161, 210
    self-direct accounts, 86
    size of, 78–79
    solo, (see Solo 401(k) plans)
    tax-advantaged, 146
    thrift savings plan (TSP) compared with, 83
    unsuccessful investments, 88
    withdrawals from, 78, 81, 211, 217
403(b) plans
    annuities in, 164, 309
    contribution limits, 78–79
    contributions to, 160
    features of, 6, 8, 15, 54, 64–65,
        80–81
    fees, 82–83
    fiduciary responsibility, 79
    information resources, 82
    international funds in, 40
    limitations of, 82
    loans from, 81
    management of, 78, 86
    matched contributions, 79
    opting out, 81
    rollovers, 80
    self-directed accounts, 86
    size of, 78–79
    withdrawals from, 78, 81

457 plans
    contribution limits, 82
    features of, 8, 15, 54, 80–81, 217
    fees, 83
    fiduciary responsibility, 79
    limitations of, 83
    loans from, 82
    management of, 78, 86
    matched contributions, 79
    opting out, 81
    rollovers, 80
    self-directed accounts, 86
    size of, 78–79
    withdrawals from, 78, 82, 211, 217
Frakt, Alex, 319–320
Franklin, Benjamin, 21, 255
Fraud, 104
Free Application for Federal Student Aid
    (FAFSA), 209
French, Ken, 288
Front-end loads, 128
Full retirement age (FRA), 172–174, 179, 183
Full-time employment, 187, 215–216
Funding
    importance of, 64–65, 69
    information resources, 165
    priority of sources, 152–165
Funeral expenses, 222, 226
Future value, 305

Gains and losses, short- and long-term, 25–26
Garrett, Sheryl, 294
Garrett Planning Network, 294, 300
General investing, 36
Generational planning, 200. See also Estate planning
Generation-skipping transfer tax (GSTT), 276,
    278, 281–282
Genworth Financial, Cost of Care Survey, 248
Gift annuity. See Charitable gift annuities (CGAs)
Gift taxes
    annual exclusion, 280
    basis of property acquired by gift, 280
    filing requirements, 279, 281
    historical, 278–279
    information resources, 282
    law, 274–275
    property gifting, 281
    tax rates, 275–276
    types of, 253, 276, 278–279
Globerson, Paul and Linda, 325
Goal-setting, 5, 12, 136, 198
Gold investments, 25, 27
"Good life," defined, 5
Government bonds, 28, 121, 147
Government defined benefit plans, 71–72
Government employees, 170, 211, 232
Government health insurance programs, 18

Government pension offset (GPO), 71
Graduated vesting schedule, 66
Grantor retained annuity trust (GRAT), 269
Grantor retained unitrust (GRUT), 269
Grocery bills, 13
Gross estate, 229, 277–278, 281
Gross income, 6, 15, 30
Group term insurance, 223
Growth funds, 147
Growth investing, 121, 124, 153
Guarantees, pension, 68–69
Guaranty associations, 108–109. *See also* State
    guaranty associations
Guaranty Corporation, 110
Guru Guide to Money Management (Boyett/
    Boyett), 112

Half-retirement, 208
Happiness, sources of, 5, 19
Health-care aides, 249
Health-care costs/expenses, 18, 50, 204–205
Health insurance
    brokers, 244
    deductibles, 14
    development of, 239
    importance of, 239, 254
    information resources, 244, 248, 253
    long-term care insurance, 248–253
    medical insurance, 240–247
    postretirement, 9
    premiums, 50
    supplemental policies for retirees (Medigap),
        245, 247
Health maintenance organizations (HMOs),
    242, 248
Health savings account (HSA), 55–56, 59,
    161–162, 247–248
Healthy practices, 4, 14
Hedge funds, 298
Hender, Sherri, 324
Hewlett-Packard (HP), 38
High-deductible health plan (HDHP), 248
High-net-worth individuals, 28, 35, 58–59, 179
HIPAA (Health Insurance Portability and
    Accountability Act of 1996), 241
Historical returns, 196
Hobbies, 5, 208–209, 215
Holding period, 24–25, 280
Home
    downsizing, 14
    equity in, 149, 211, 217
    income from, 192–193
    sale of, 14–15, 25–27, 157
Home equity line of credit (HELOC), 211
Home equity loans, 14, 149, 192
Home health care, 248, 250–251
Homestead statute, 259–261

Hospice care, 248, 250–251
Hospital insurance, 245
Hot funds, 132
Household expenses, 205, 215
Household furnishings, 256
Household workers, 170
Housing market, 9, 12, 18. *See also* Home
Hubbard, Carl M., 131
Hybrid advisers, 297

Illiquidity, 127, 229
Immediate income annuities, 92
Immunizations, 241
Income, generally
    deferred, 158–159
    gap, 11–12, 14–15
    generation, 5, 131
    portfolio, 130
    tax (*see* Income tax)
Income tax, 10, 18, 21, 23–27, 29, 35–36,
    48–49, 154–155, 159–160, 163, 181
Indemnity plans, 242, 248
Index funds, 38, 81, 83, 87, 128–129, 147
Indian Health Service (IHS), 244, 246
Individual ownership, 257
Individual retirement accounts. *See* IRAs
Inefficent mutual funds, 147–148
Inflation, 11–12, 18, 43, 100–102, 132, 148,
    196, 206–207, 305
Inflation-adjusted returns, 143
Inheritance, 36, 51–52, 55, 57, 92, 100, 191,
    193–194, 196, 200, 212
In-network providers, 241
Insolvency, 108–109
Insurance. *see specific types of insurance*
    adjustments to, 14
    deductibles, 13–14
    importance of, 16
    planning for (*see* Insurance planning)
Insurance agents
    functions of, 227–228, 230, 235
    selection factors, 230, 236
Insurance company, annuities, 108
Insurance planning
    for business needs, 230
    disability income, 230–236
    estate settlement costs, 229–230
    importance of, 221–222, 225–226
    information resources, 227, 235–236
    life, 222–227, 234–236
    needs analysis, 226–227, 237
    pension maximization, 228–229
    shopping process, 234–236
    wealth accumulation, 227–228
Interest-free loans, 36
Interest income, 7, 24, 206. *See also*
    Interest rates

Interest rates, 14, 81, 94, 106, 108, 148, 152, 211, 224
Internal Revenue Code, 267, 274, 277
Internal Revenue Service (IRS)
    functions of, 22, 50, 55, 147, 159, 169, 175, 247, 262, 275, 313
    72(t) exemption, 209
    tax tables, 104
    wash sale rule, 38
    web site, 165, 176
International Board of Standards and Practices for Certified Financial Planners (IBCFP), 296
International funds, 40, 42
Internet savings accounts, 43
Intestate succession statute, 261–262
Investing mistakes
    information resources, 133–134
    types of, 131–133
Investing principles
    cost control, 127–130, 134
    diversification, 119–123
    income portfolio, 130
    information resources, 133–134
    rebalancing, 123–127
    success factors, 133
    total return portfolio, 131
Investment costs, 132. See also Commission; Expense ratio; Transaction costs
Investment expenses, 28, 45
Investment firms, functions of, 6. See also Brokerage firms
Investment-grade bonds, 121, 130, 148
Investment income, 10
Investment manager, financial adviser vs., 301
Investment philosophy, sample, 137–138
Investment plan, 134, 287
Investment policy statement (IPS), 131–132, 135–139, 141, 149, 151
IRAs. See Roth IRA; Traditional IRA
    after-tax, 153
    beneficiaries, 309
    benefits of, 45
    borrowing from, 51
    catch-up contributions, 49–50, 59
    contribution limits, 48–49, 50, 52, 58–59, 162
    conversions, 55, 59–60
    defined, 46
    distributions, 197–198
    evolution of, 49
    fees, 45, 47, 53
    flexibility in, 87
    income limits, 59–60
    information resources, 60
    legislation, 48–49

life cycle funds in, 145–146
    nondeductible, 50, 56, 58–59, 163–165
    penalties for withdrawal, 48, 50–51, 195, 209
    rebalancing considerations, 126–127
    required minimum distributions, 51, 98, 159
    rollovers, 53–54, 67, 84, 98, 152, 164, 190, 195, 197, 247
    self-employed, 52–54, 59
    SEPP program, 209–210
    spousal, 49, 54
    stretch, 55
    target retirement funds, 41–42
    tax-advantaged, 146
    tax-deferred, 40
    transfers, 60
    valuation of, 304–305
    withdrawals from, 48, 50–52, 56, 98, 197
Irrevocable life insurance trusts (ILITs), 268–269
Irrevocable trusts, 230, 268–269
IRS publications, information resources, 21–22, 24–27, 30, 60, 176, 182, 195
IRS tax forms
    Form 56, 262
    Form 706, 277
    Form 1040, 23–24, 50
    Form 1040, Schedule D, 25
    Form 1099-DIV, 25, 27
    Form 1099-INT, 24
    Form 1099-R, 104
    Form 6251, 28
    Form SS-4, 261
    Form W-2, 24, 74
iShares Dow Jones U.S. Index (IYY), 38

Jewelry, 25, 256
Job changes, insurance considerations, 232–233
Joint accounts, 36
Joint and survivor annuity, 66–69, 228
Joint annuities, 94, 97–99, 101
Joint life expectancy, 195
Jointly owned property, 260
Joint ownership, 257, 259
Joint tax returns, 23, 27, 50–51
Joint tenancy with right of survivorship, 36
Junk bonds, 121

Kahneman, Daniel, 288
Key-person insurance, 230
Kickbacks, 88, 299
Kirtland, Dave, 323

Labor unions, 62
Large-cap funds, 147
Large cap stocks, 121
Larimore, Taylor, 319, 321–322, 324–326
Law enforcement, government retirement plans, 71–72

Lawsuit settlements, 212
Layoffs, 86, 213
Lead trusts, 269
LeBoeuf, Michael, 322, 325
Lee, Don, 326
Legal fees, 226
Legal issues, 36, 113, 273, 277, 279
Legislation
    American Recovery and Reinvestment Tax Act
        of 2009, 243
    COBRA, 243–244
    Economic Growth and Tax Relief Reconcilia-
        tion Act of 2001 (2001 Tax Act), 274–275
    Employee Retirement Income Security Act
        of 1974 (ERISA), 62–63, 65, 70, 73,
        309–310, 313
    HIPAA (Health Insurance Portability and
        Accountability Act of 1996), 241, 243
    Investment Advisor Act of 1940, 293
    Pension Protection Act of 2006, 80
    tax laws, generally, 78, 198–199
    Taxpayer Relief Act of 1997, 51
    Tax Reform Act of 1986, 290
    transfer of property at death, 258–260
    Uniformed Services Former Spouses
        Protection Act, 306
    Uniform Gifts to Minors Act, 266
Lehman Aggregate Index, 87
Lehman Brothers, 86, 119
Leisure activities, 4
Liar's Poker (Lewis), 290
Lies Your Broker Tells You (Saler), 290
Life annuity, 92. See also Annuities
Life cycle funds, 136–137, 143–146, 149
Life estates, 258
Life expectancy, 92, 98, 101, 182, 195–196,
    209, 224
Life insurance
    beneficiaries, 309
    cash value, 227
    death benefits, 224–225, 228
    estate settlement costs, 229–230
    family and dependents, 225–226
    importance of, 14, 110
    income needs, 223
    irrevocable trusts, 268
    needs analysis, 226–227
    permanent, 224–225, 227–228
    policy termination, 227
    premiums, 223–225, 227–228, 279
    probate process, 260
    purpose of, 222, 225–226
    settlement options, 222
    shopping for, 234–236
    term, 223–224, 227–228
    types of, 222–225
Life plan, 1

Life span, 4
Lifestyle, 5, 9–10, 12, 14, 16, 92, 187, 196
Life tenant, 258
Limited partnerships, 290
Lindauer, Mel, 319, 321–326
Liquidation, 60, 229
Liquidity, 42–43, 197, 279
Living expenses, 107, 196–197
Living will, 264, 270, 272
Load funds, 128, 290
Loans, types of, 14, 36, 149, 192–193, 211
Local government, defined benefit plans, 72–73
Local taxes, 30, 175
Longevity, 70, 93, 100, 102, 178–179, 181,
    183, 240
Long-term bonds, 121, 224
Long-term capital gains, 27, 39
Long-term care, 228
Long-term care (LTC) insurance
    cost of, 248–250
    coverage, 248, 250–252
    elimination period, 251
    employer-provided, 250
    exclusions, 252
    importance of, 110, 240
    individual policies, 250–251
    inflation protection provision, 250–251
    information resources, 253
    limitations, 252
    long-term care defined, 249–250
    Medicaid, 250, 252–253
    Medicare, 252–253
    nonforfeiture benefits, 251–252
    partnership policies, 250
    premiums, 251–252
    purchase process, 250–252
    renewability, 252
    restoration of benefits, 251
    shared benefit coverage, 252
Long-term disability (LTD), 231–232
Losses, portfolio diversification and, 120
Lottery winnings, 13, 212–213
Low-income earners/taxpayers, 49, 57, 60
Low-risk investors, 132
Lump sum payments/distributions, 11, 62, 67,
    190–191

Madoff, Bernie, 299
Mahaney, Jim, 184
Managed payout funds, 113–114
Management fees, 45, 82
Mansueto, Joe, 324
Marginal tax bracket, 51, 57, 159, 161
Marginal tax rate, 23–24, 36, 40–41, 56, 58, 84,
    165, 175
Marital status, significance of, 16, 23, 36, 171,
    225–226

Market conditions, impact of, 8, 12, 16–18, 196
Market downturns, 124–125, 216. *See also*
    Declining markets
Market moves, reaction to, 133, 136, 139
Market price, 28
Market rallies, 38
Market risk, 120
Market value, 30
Marriage, defined by Social Security, 171
Married couples, 69, 208, 262–263, 274,
    277–278. *See also* Married couples, filing
    jointly; Married couples, filing separate
    returns
Married couples, filing jointly, 23, 27, 50–51,
    175, 177, 198
Married couples, filing separate returns, 26, 50
Matched contributions, 6, 79–80, 139, 152, 161
Medicaid, 113, 244, 246, 250, 252–253, 270
Medical expenses, 28, 204, 208, 280
Medical Information Bureau (MIB), 235
Medical insurance
    access to, 240
    employer-provided, 243–244
    government health plans and accounts,
      244–247
    health savings accounts (HSAs), 247–248
    high-deductible health plan (HDHP), 248
    indemnity plans, 242, 248
    for individuals, 244
    information resources, 240
    managed care plans, 242–243, 248
    maximum plan limits, 241
    medical care providers, 243
    Medigap, 245, 247
    for self–employed, 244
    terminology, 240–241
    types of, 242–243
Medicare, 4, 9–10, 77, 155, 179, 205, 216, 232,
    241, 244–245, 247, 252–254
Medigap, 245, 247
MetLife, 107
Mid-America Foundation, 104
Mid-cap stocks, 121
Mid-career investors, 143
Military personnel
    disability benefits, 232
    divorce issues, 306–307
    early retirement, 212
    health care programs, 246
    pensions, 72
    retirement plans, 83
    Social Security benefits for, 170
Moderately inefficient mutual funds, 147
Modern economics, 10
Modern portfolio theory (MPT), 122–123
Modified adjusted gross income (MAGI),
    50–51, 59, 210

Money management, 287, 300
Money market accounts, 157
Money market funds, 8, 24, 38, 42–45, 121,
    139, 197
Money purchase pension plans, 85–86, 89
Monte Carlo simulation analysis, 12, 207, 288
Moody's, 110–111, 235
Moral hazard, 109
Morgan, Walter, 316
Morningstar Vanguard Diehards Forum, 315,
    319
Morris, Charles, 5
Mortality charges, 227
Mortality credits, 105–106
Mortgage-backed bonds, 121, 147
Mortgage loans, 14, 156, 192–193,
    211, 311
Moving average, 113
MSNMoney.com, 14
Multiple-asset allocation, 123
Multiple sclerosis, 98
Municipal bonds/municipal bond funds, 24,
    41–42, 45, 147, 194
Mutual Benefit Life, 108
Mutual funds
    bonds, 194
    broad-based low-expense, 6
    capital gains, 25, 49
    characterized, 113–114
    CREF, 82
    dollar cost averaging, 7
    expense ratio, 127
    fees, 128–129, 295–296
    health savings account, 52
    low-cost, 88
    overpriced, 81
    risk management strategies, 8
    selection factors, 132
    stock, 8
    tax efficiency of, 39–40, 147–148
    tax loss harvesting, 36
    tax treatment of, 24
    top-performing, 136
    trading costs, 127–128
    12b-1 fees, 128–129

National Association of Consumer Bankruptcy
    Attorneys, 314
National Association of Personal Finance
    Advisers (NAPFA), 288, 300
National Association of State Comprehensive
    Health Insurance Plans, 246
National Association of State Retirement
    Administrators, 74–75
National Bureau of Economic Research, 70
National Federation of Credit
    Counselors, 314

National Organization of Life and Health Insurance Guaranty Associations (NOLHGA), 108–109, 114
Natural disasters, 16
Near retirement investors, 142, 144
Needs, wants distinguished from, 6, 9–10
Net worth, 9
Net worth statement, 199
New Money Dynamics (VanCaspel), 288
No-commission/no-cost trading, 130
No-load funds, 128–129
Nondeductible IRAs, 50, 56, 59, 163–165
Non-life cycle funds, 146
Nonprofit organizations, charitable gift annuities (CGAs), 102–105
Non-qualified annuity, features of, 153
Nonretirement assets, 217
Nonretirement taxable accounts, 42–44
Normal retirement age, 63–64, 68, 71–72, 216
Notice to creditors, 261
Number, savings, calculation of, 9–11
Number, The (Eisenberg), 9, 19
Nursing homes, 208, 248, 250–251

Office of General Counsel of the New York State Insurance Department, 110
Old-Age, Survivors, and Disability Insurance (OASDI), 169
Older investors, strategies for, 13–14, 141–142
Online banking, 43
Opportunity cost, 10, 108
Ordinary income, 24–25, 27, 36, 40, 104
Ordinary life estate, 258
Out-of-pocket expenses, 241, 250
Overpriced funds, 81, 87
Ownership, 27, 257–258

Partial disability, 232
Partnerships, 24, 195
Part-time employment, 171, 181, 202, 206, 214
Payable on death (POD) accounts, 44, 259, 267
Payroll taxes, 155–156, 169, 171
Penalties, IRA withdrawals, 48, 50–51, 209
Pension Benefit Guaranty Corporation (PBGC), 69–70
Pension/pension plans, 9, 11–13, 24, 68–69, 74, 85, 89, 107, 195, 203, 206, 216, 228
Performance of funds, chasing, 132–133
Period certain, 100
Permanent insurance, 224–225, 228, 230
Permitted disparity, 63
Personal accounts, 36
Personal care expenses, 13
Personal property, 30, 256–259
Phillips, Don, 324
PIMCO Total Return, 87

Point of service (POS) health plans, 242–243, 248
Political activities, 4
Ponzi scheme, 104
Portfolio, generally
    annual checkup, 15
    annual review of, 141
    diversification, 145, 151
    rebalancing, 9
    tax management, 148
    turnover in, 40
Powers of attorney, 269–270
Preferred provider organizations (PPOs), 242, 248
Premarital agreements, 263, 307–309
Premiums, 69, 92, 94, 97–98, 223–224, 233–234
Prenuptial/postnuptial agreements, 263, 307–309
Prescription drug insurance, 14, 245
Present value, 305
Preventive care, 241
Primary residence, defined, 26
Principal Financial Group, 100
Private-activity bonds, 28
Private-sector defined benefit plans, 62, 69–70
Probate, 36, 259–262, 264, 267
Professional advice
    financial advisers, 285–286, 297–300
    information resources, 300–301
    money managers, 287, 300
    need for, 286–287
    second opinions, 299
Profit-sharing plan, 84–85, 89, 98, 309
Property
    basis of, 26–27, 279–280
    gifting, 281
    rights, 262
    sale of, 25
    taxes, 29, 266
    titling, 256–257
    transfer at death, 258–260
    types of, 256–257
Proprietary funds, 82
Prospectuses, 127–128, 144
Providers, medical care, defined, 241, 243
Psychological factors, 140, 206, 212–213, 215–216
Public education employees, 78
Public housing assistance, 113
Public-sector defined benefit plans, 62, 69–70

Qualified annuity, features of, 153
Qualified corporate dividends, 24
Qualified domestic relations order (QDRO), 68, 306

Qualifying terminable interest property, 278
Quality of life, 240

Railroad retirement benefits, 176
Railroad workers, 170, 232
Rating agencies, 110–112, 235
Rational Decumulation (Babbel/Merrill), 112
Real estate, 12, 18, 29–30, 147. *See also* Home;
    Personal property
Real property, 257–258
Rebalancing, 123–127, 134, 141, 146, 199
Recreational activities, 5
Redemptions, 27
REDUX system, 72
Refinancing, 14
Registered investment adviser (RIA), 293,
    297–298
Reinvestment, 7, 39, 126
REITs, 56, 147–148, 164
Relative value, 161
Relocation, 12, 14–15, 192
Remainderman, 258
Remarriage, 226, 263
Renewability, disability insurance (DI), 233
Rental property, 15, 24, 27, 195, 206
Replacement income, 234
Required minimum distribution (RMD), 51, 55,
    58, 98, 159, 195, 197–199
Respite care, 248, 251
Retail index mutual funds, 317
Retirement, generally
    duration of, 4
    evolution of, 4
    goals for, 5
    reasons for, 16
Retirement age, 9, 16–17, 58, 172–173,
    179–180, 202. *See also* Normal retirement
    age
Retirement date, 9–10, 145
Retirement Living Information Center,
    29–30
Retirement plans/planning
    asset allocation, 143–146
    components of, 1, 5–7, 9, 18–19
    divorce, impact on, 304–305
    goals, 198
    information resources, 149
    investment policy statement (IPS), 135–136,
        149
    life expectancy and (*see* Life expectancy)
    noninvestment assets, 148–149
    plan development, 135–136
    plan implementation, 138–141
    risk management, 141–143
    success factors, 149
    taxation considerations, 146–149
    withdrawals from, 310–311

Revenue sharing, 88
Reverse mortgages, 192–193, 211
Reversionary interest, 278
Revocable trusts, 268
Riders, disability insurance (DI), 234
Risk assessment tools, 143
Risk-averse investors, 93, 106
Risk-free funds, 87
Risk-free rate of return, 193
Risk management, 120, 132, 141–143
Risk minimization strategies, 6
Risk profile, 120
Risk-return analysis, 141
Risk-reward analysis, 122–123, 134
Risk tolerance, 8, 91, 106, 141–142, 288, 299
Roth, William, 51
Roth 401(k), 84
Roth IRA
    catch-up contributions, 59
    contributions to, 51, 53, 57, 59, 158, 160, 165
    conversion to, 53, 58–60, 158, 198
    cost comparison, 160–162
    custodial, 6
    defined, 48
    establishment of, 49
    features of, 10, 14–15, 153, 159–160, 210
    income limits, 59
    limitations of, 84
    relative value of, 161
    rules, 51–52
    solo, 52, 53
    stretch, 52
    tax benefits from, 160
    traditional IRA compared with, 56–58, 84
    withdrawals from, 51–53, 56, 157, 197, 210, 217
Royalties, 24
Rule of 72, 7

Sabbaticals, 202, 212
Safe withdrawal rate (SWR), 205–207, 215
Sales loads, 128
Sales taxes, 29–30
Same-sex marriage, 171
S&P 500, 38, 83, 87, 317
Savings account, individual taxable
    capital gains, 35
    characterized, 121, 157, 310
    high-interest, 42
    income tax, 35
    information resources, 44–45
    nature of, 45
    nonretirement taxable accounts, 42–44
    tax loss harvesting, 36–39
    tax minimization strategies, 39–42
    types of accounts, 36
Savings bank life insurance (SBLI), 223
Savings bonds, 30

Savings habits, 12, 15–16
Savings plan, 6, 8, 11, 13–14
Scams, 104
Schultheis, Bill, 321, 325
Scientific formulas, avoidance of, 11–12
Second homes, 12
Second marriages, 36, 263. *See also* Remarriage
Securities and Exchange Commission (SEC), 291, 297–298
Self-directed accounts, 86–88
Self-employed IRAs, 52–54, 59
Self-employment, 52–54, 59, 156, 202, 244
Self-insurance, 251
Self-settled trusts, 268
Sell high, buy low strategy, 9
SEP, 8, 15
SEP-IRA, 52–54, 59
Settlement fees, 27
72(t) exemption, 209
Short-term disability (STD), 231–233
Sibilski, Carl, 324
SIMPLE (Savings Incentive Match Plan for Employees) IRA, 8, 15, 52–54, 59
Single-life annuity, 98–99
Single-parent families, 226
Single-premium immediate annuity (SPIA)
    charitable gift annuities (CGAs), 102–105
    compared with other investments, 93–94, 163
    contract terms, 92
    defined, 91, 114
    features of, 92–94, 114
    fees, 112
    gender differences, 97
    guaranteed periods, 99–100
    income from, 113–114
    inflation effects, 100–102
    information resources, 114
    mechanics of, 94–97
    medical underwriting, 97–98
    payouts, 91–94, 100–101
    premium refunds, 92, 94, 99–100
    purchase of, 92, 112
    qualified *vs.* unqualified investments, 98
    ratings of, 113–114
    risk tolerance and, 91, 114
    safety of, 92, 108–110, 115
    single *vs.* joint annuities, 98–99
Single retirees, early retirement issues, 207–208
Single taxpayer, tax on Social Security benefits, 175
Skilled nursing facilities, 245, 248, 250
Small businesses, 153, 230
Small-cap funds/stocks, 121, 147
Smith, Adam, 10
Social Security
    amount of benefit, 172–173, 191–192
    annual statement, 171–173, 226
    application for benefits, 171, 180, 182
    benefit calculators, 184–185
    bridging income with, 206
    collecting benefits, 180–184
    cost-of-living adjustment (COLA), 171, 214
    coverage, 170
    defined benefit plans and, 63–64
    delayed retirement credit, 180
    disability insurance and, 234
    divorce and, 307
    early retirement and, 215
    eligibility for benefits, 171
    financial outlook, 178–179, 185
    full retirement age (FRA), 172–174, 179, 183
    historical perspectives, 169
    importance of, 4, 9, 10–11, 15, 18, 107, 133, 142, 185
    income from, 195
    income to, 176, 178
    inflation-adjusted benefits, 179
    information resources, 172, 185
    mandatory payment at age 70, 180
    outflow of, 176, 178
    payroll taxes, 77, 155, 169, 171
    pension from noncovered employment, 174
    preretirement earnings, significance of, 172, 215
    reform, 179
    retirement ages, minimum/maximum, 179–180
    retirement benefits, 171–173
    spousal benefits, 180–184
    survivor benefits, 171–173, 183, 226
    taxation of benefits, 27–28, 170, 174–177, 179, 182, 191
    trust funds, 178
    types of benefits, 10, 71, 142
    windfall elimination provision, 174
    working while receiving benefits, 173–174
Social Security Administration (SSA)
    application rules, 182
    benefits calculation, 174
    disability benefits, 213
    functions of, 10, 63, 171, 184
    information resources, 226, 234
    Publication 05-10007, 71
    Publication 05-10045, 71
    regulation by, 169
    retirement age, defined, 202
    starting/stopping benefits, 181
    web site, 172, 179
Social Security Handbook, 226, 232
Soft retirement, 202, 214
Sole proprietorships, 54
Solo 401(k) plans, 52–54, 59
Spartan, bond funds, 87

SPDR
    Barclays Capital TIPS (IPE), 88
    MSCI ACWI ex-US (CWI), 38
Special needs trusts, 269
Specific risk, 120–121
Spend-down, defined, 250
Spending calculations, affordable, 15
Spending habits, 6, 10, 12, 15, 188–189, 200,
    208
Spousal benefits, Social Security, 171–173,
    183–184
Spousal IRA, 49, 54
Spousal share law, 263
Spousal support, 308, 311
    Standard & Poor's, 110–112, 235
Standard of living, 18
State Children's Health Insurance Program
    (SCHIP), 244
State government defined benefit plans, 72–73
State guaranty associations, 92, 99, 108–109,
    115
State guaranty fund, 103
State pension plans, 70
State taxes, 22, 29–30, 156, 161, 175
Stern, Hersh, 114
Stevens, Sue, 325–326
Stock investments, 8, 24–26, 40–41, 48, 56,
    120–121, 123, 147
Stock options, 28, 38
Stowe, Bob, 323
Straight-life annuity, 69, 228
Stress management, 240
Stretch IRAs, 52, 55
Substantially equal periodic payments (SEPP),
    51, 209, 212, 216
Succession planning, 271
Summary of material modifications (SMM), 73
Summary plan description (SPD), 73
Sunset provision, 277
Surrender fee/charges, 163–164
Surviving child, 170
Surviving spouse, 26, 67–68, 170–172,
    179–181, 183, 228, 260
Survivor expectancy, 195
Survivor's benefits, 307
Survivorship, 96, 225
Swedroe, Larry, 321, 324
Systematic risk, 120–121

Target allocations, 199
Target benefit plan, 85–86, 89
Target retirement funds, 41
Taxable account, 153, 162–163, 194, 197
Taxable estate, defined, 277
Tax-advantaged accounts, tax consequences of,
    194–195

Tax adviser, functions of, 78, 98
Tax analysis, annual, 30
Taxation
    deferred taxes, 80
    federal, 22–28, 30
    income (see Income tax)
    information resources, 30–31
    local, 30
    purpose of, 21
    state, 28–30
    tax code/law, 22, 24
Tax basis, 56
Tax brackets, 28, 35–36, 41, 43–44, 58, 60, 84,
    137, 147, 159, 193, 198
Tax code, 12, 18, 22, 24, 52, 56, 181
Tax credit, 49, 57, 157–158
TaxCut, 176, 199
Tax-deductible retirement accounts, 154–159
Tax deductions, qualification for, 157–158
Tax-deferred accounts, 8, 40, 197, 199
Tax-deferred funds, 148
Tax-deferred plans, relative value of, 161
Tax-deferred portfolio, rebalancing, 126–127
Tax-deferred savings, 13, 15
Tax diversification, 57–58
Tax-efficient investments, 146–147, 149, 151
Tax-exempt bonds, 24, 28, 147
Tax Foundation, 29
Tax-free accounts, 8
Tax-free bonds, 23
Tax-free growth. See IRAs; Roth IRA
Tax laws, 78, 146
Tax levies, 50, 313
Tax liability, 48, 127–128, 130, 147, 152, 194
Tax loss harvesting, 36–40, 45
Tax minimization strategies, 39–42, 146
Taxpayer identification number, 261–262
Tax rates, 8, 23–24, 27, 29, 39–40. See also
    Marginal tax rate
Tax Reform Act of 1986, 290
Tax returns, 23, 277, 279, 281
Tax shelters. See IRAs
Tax swap, 38
Teachers, 403(b) plans, 82
Tenancy by the entireties property, 257,
    260, 262
Tenancy in common, 257, 262
Term certain, 100
Term insurance
    importance of, 14, 228, 277
    key-person, 230
    life, 223–224, 226
Three-factor model of investing, 288
Thrift savings plan (TSP), 83–84, 146, 161,
    164–165
TIAA-CREF, 82, 164

Time value of money, 6–9, 95
Total costs, 132
Total-market stock fund, 120, 146
Total-return portfolio, 131
Totten trust, 259
Tower, Ed, 325–326
Trading agreements, 130
Trading costs, 127–130
Traditional IRA
    catch-up contributions, 59
    contribution limits, 49–50, 59
    conversion to Roth IRA, 58–59, 210
    deductible contributions, 55–56
    defined, 48
    features of, 98, 153
    income limits, 59
    required minimum distribution (RMD), 198
    rollovers, 197
    Roth 401(k) distinguished from, 84
    Roth IRA distinguished from, 51–52
    rules, 49–51
    stretch, 55
    withdrawals from, 52, 57–58, 195, 197
Transaction costs/fees, 87, 125, 134, 163
Transfer of property, 277–278
Transfer on death accounts, 259
Transparency, 298
Transportation costs, 10
Travel expenses, 12, 205, 215
Treasury bills, 178
Treasury bonds/Treasury bond funds, 87, 106, 139, 178
Treasury inflation-protected securities (TIPS), 56, 87, 148
Treasury notes, 107, 178
Tricare/Champus, 246
Trust(s)
    accounts, 36, 310
    as beneficiary, 264
    charitable, 269
    defined benefit plan, 64–65, 69
    estate planning, 272
    estate taxes, 281–282
    funds, 178
    objectives of, 267–268
    people involved in, 268
    probate process, 261
    revocable *vs.* irrevocable, 268
    special needs, 269
    tax treatment of, 24
    types of, 267–268
Trustee, 88, 194, 258, 260, 264–265, 312
TurboTax, 176, 199
Turnover ratio, 40
12b-1 fees, 128–129

Unconscious consumption, 13
Underfunded retirement plans, 69–70
Underwriters, functions of, 235–236
Underwriting, 94, 97–98, 225, 229, 235–236
Unemployment, 212
Unemployment compensation, tax treatment of, 24
Unified credit, 274–275
Uniform Gifts to Minors Act, 266
Uninsured population, 239–240
United Airlines, 79
U.S. Census Bureau, 72, 231
U.S. Department of Defense Military Health System, 246
U.S. Department of Health and Human Services, 246, 248
U.S. Department of Housing and Urban Development, 314
U.S. Department of Justice, 314
U.S. Department of Labor, 12, 74, 243
U.S. Department of the Treasury, 248
U.S. Office of Personnel Management, 71–72, 74
U.S. stock index returns, worst cases, 144
U.S. Treasuries, 30, 64, 87, 94, 106–107
Universal life (UL) insurance policies, 224–225
Unretiring, reasons for, 214–216
Updegrave, Walter, 110
Use test, 27
Usual, customary, and reasonable charges, 241

Vacation home, 27
Vacations, 208. *See also* Travel expenses
Valuation, 277, 279, 304–305
Value funds, 87
Value stocks, 121
Vanguard Diehards reunions, 321
Vanguard Group
    annuities, 97
    characteristics of, 40, 54, 60, 88, 140, 164, 295, 315
    500 Index Fund, 317
    Flagship clients, 295–296
    FTSE All-World ex-US (VFWIUX) fund, 38, 41
    FTSE All-World ex-US ETF (VEU), 38, 88
    inflation-adjusted annuities, 100
    IRA fees, 53
    Large Cap Index, 38
    managed payout funds, 113–114
    money markets, 43–44
    New York Tax Exempt Money Market, 44
    Prime Money Market, 43–44
    STAR fund, 140
    Target Retirement funds, 143, 146
    Tax Equivalent calculator, 41, 44
    Total Bond Market (BND), 88

Vanguard Group *(Continued)*
  Total Bond Market Index Fund (VBTLX),
    292
  Total International Stock Market (VGTSX)
    fund, 38, 41
  Total Stock Market ETF (VTI), 38, 88
  Total Stock Market Index Fund (VTSAX),
    80, 292
  Voyager Select customers, 296
  web site, 44, 143
Variable annuities, 92, 163–165, 290–291
Variable universal life (VUL) insurance, 225
Vesting, 65–66, 203
Veterans Administration (VA), 246
Vision, importance of, 5, 19
Volatility, 8, 40, 121, 130
Volunteerism, 5, 215–216

Waiting period, disability insurance (DI), 233
Walz, Daniel T., 131
Wants *vs.* needs, 6, 9–10
Wash sale, 26, 38
Washington (state), tax provisions, 29, 103, 258
"Ways of life" concept, 5
Wealth accumulation, 11, 227–228
Wealth of Nations, The (Smith), 10
Weiss, Martin D., 112
Weiss Research, 112, 235
Well-being, 4–5, 22
Wellington Fund, 316
What Color Is Your Parachute? In Retirement
  (Bolles/Nelson), 5, 18
Where Are the Customers' Yachts? (Schwed), 290
Whole life (WL) insurance, 110, 224–225

Wills, 261–263, 266–267, 272. *See also* Living
  will
Windfall elimination provision (WEP), 71
Windfalls, 174, 202, 212
Withdrawal rate
  account selection, 197–198
  amount of, 195–197
  budgeting worksheets, 198–199
  calculation of, 207
  determination of, 11–12, 16, 142
  4 percent, 195–196, 206
  hardship cases, 210–212
  information resources, 199
  reasons for, 194
  safe withdrawal rate (SWR), 205–207
  strategy development, 18
  tax consequences of, 153–156,
    194–195
  total-return portfolio, 131
Work-related expenses, 156
Worksheets, budgeting process, 198–199
Worthless investments, 290
Written retirement plan, importance of,
  19, 131

Yield, 107, 121, 130
*You Don't Have to Be Rich: Comfort, Happiness,
  and Financial Security on Your Own Terms*
  (Chatzky), 5, 18
Young investors, 13, 19, 141–143
Your Federal Income Tax for Individuals
  (IRS Publication 17), 21–22, 27, 30

Zweig, Jason, 323